New York from A to Z

NEW YORK
FROM A to Z

The Traveler's Look-up Source
for the Big Apple

Paul Wasserman

CAPITAL
BOOKS, INC.
Sterling, Virginia

Capital Books, Inc.
P.O. Box 605
Herndon, Virginia 20172-0605

ISBN 1-892123-78-9 (alk.paper)

Library of Congress Cataloging-in-Publication Data
Wasserman, Paul.
New York from A to Z : the traveler's look-up source for the Big Apple / Paul Wasserman.—1st ed.
p. cm.
ISBN 1-892123-78-9 (acid-free paper)
I. New York (N.Y.)—Guidebooks. 2. New York (N.Y.)—Directories.
I. Title.

F128.18 .W34 2002
917.47'10444—dc21   2001052995

Printed in the United States of America on acid-free paper that meets the American National Standards Institute Z39-48 Standard.

First Edition

10 9 8 7 6 5 4 3 2 1

This book is respectfully dedicated
to those who lost their lives
in the tragic events of September 11, 2001.

Contents

Acknowledgments

No work of such an enormous scope could have been prepared without cooperation and assistance from countless individuals in the organizations represented in this volume's content. The author extends his deepest gratitude to them for their generous response to his inquiries and requests for details about their functions and operations. In the preparation of the manuscript valuable editorial assistance was received from Jeanne O'Connell. Yu Hsiu Wang and Karen Patterson of the library of the College of Information Studies at the University of Maryland were invaluable in their support and assistance during the research process. Phyllis Levy aided in early stages of Web site verifications. Peggy Barrett performed with infinite patience, good spirit, and diligent application in carrying out the arduous task of word processing a difficult manuscript in its entirety while also aiding invaluably in Web site verifications. And Paula Berard contributed excellently and painstakingly in thoroughly checking the integrity of the cross-reference structure while also working to ensure editorial consistency throughout the volume.

Foreword

Just at the very time when this book was in its final stages of preparation, the horrible events at the World Trade Center took place. In the immediate aftermath, concern about so infinitely less important a matter as the content of this work was dwarfed by the staggering human toll and the wanton destruction of such a vital and vibrant section of the city. In time, New Yorkers overcame their sorrow and grief and moved heroically to restore their city, to doggedly revitalize its spirit, and to go forward indomitably with optimism toward the future. In similar spirit, we have sought to forge ahead in completing this book because we had no doubt whatever that the city would gradually recapture the place it has so long held in hearts and minds as the principal destination of visitors from the United States and everywhere else in the world, and that they would return in record numbers.

We have revised the content to reflect changes in the features of lower Manhattan that the terrorist acts wrought. Therefore, the entries that had been prepared to describe the World Trade Center and its characteristics and features, as well as elements of the immediate surrounding area of Manhattan, which no longer exist or operate, have been eliminated. And we have monitored developments to reflect in the book's entries the state of affairs in the lower portions of Manhattan up to late October 2001.

Introduction: How to Use This Book

The idea underlying this book's content is to offer its users an arrangement and specific descriptive details in the simplest and most accessible form with precise information on what they seek rather than lengthy descriptive accounts. It is an easy-to-use tool arranged alphabetically. To find information, turn directly to the entry where the basic details are provided.

Example: To learn about the Frick Collection turn to the entry under F:

The Frick Collection 1 E 70th St. at Fifth Ave. (202) 288-0700 www.frick.org

Located at one of New York's most exquisite Beaux Arts mansions, the former home of tycoon Henry Clay Frick contains a world-class collection of European masterpieces, including paintings, furnishings, sculptures, and decorative arts. The experience of visiting is akin to entering an extraordinarily beautiful private home arranged with the utmost taste, where expense was no obstacle. The indoor garden court with reflecting pool is a particularly delightful feature. Subway: 6 to 68th St. Open Tues–Sun, hours vary. Admission charge. No credit cards.

For information by category, look for it in the alphabetical listing under the subject sought.

Example: To learn about WALKING TOURS, simply turn to that entry under W for a listing of all the specific entries offering such tours. Then turn to the specific WALKING TOUR, for example, Big Onion Walking Tours, for the details on that particular tour:

Big Onion Walking Tours P.O. Box 20561 Cherokee Station NY 10021 (212) 439-1090, fax (212) 794-0064 www.bigonion.com

This company schedules a wide array of sightseeing tours by knowledgeable and well-prepared guides. Excursions focus on ethnic neighborhoods and historic districts all over the city and last 2 to 2½ hours and are moderately priced.

Note also that the alphabetical listings offer innumerable cross-references to redirect the user: Example: Bronx Zoo, *see* International Wildlife Conservation Park; Brooklyn Heights Promenade, *see* The Promenade. Similarly, cross-references will lead the user from an entry where the information is not given, to the precise designation under which it can be found. For example: Billiards, *see* Pool.

What Is Included and Not Included

New York City From A to Z contains some 2,000 entries across the entire range of features and attractions of all five of the city's boroughs. Some categories, such as hotels, restaurants, retail stores, night clubs, and bars, because they literally number in the thousands, have been screened to incorporate a selective listing. Hotel accommodations included in the book have been carefully chosen to offer the user descriptive details of establishments across a wide range of locations and price levels. Restaurants have been selected to offer the reader citywide choices reflecting the widest possible range of culinary and ethnic specialties with varying cost categories. Bars and night clubs listed offer a broad sweep of types of ambiance, entertainment forms, and price variations. Retail stores are for the most part limited to the city's principal department stores plus the most outstanding, unusual, or popular retail outlets.

For every other category we have been extremely inclusive, providing entries for the city's attractions and places of interest. This is especially true for museums, entertainment centers, public attractions, theatres, parks, tourist services, important buildings, monuments, and many other types of visitor destinations.

Particularly unique features that should be of special appeal to tourists are the entries: Events in New York and Events in New York by Month. These contain an extensive listing of festivals, parades, celebrations, and other activities that draw thousands of onlookers each year.

Abbreviations Used in This Book

ATM = automated teller machine
Ave. = Avenue
Blvd. = Boulevard
btw = between
DJ = Disk Jockey
Dr. = Drive
E = East
ext. = extension
Fri = Friday
Hwy. = Highway
Jr. = Junior
Mon = Monday
Mt. = Mount
NYC = New York City
NYU = New York University
Pkwy. = Parkway
Pl. = Place
P.S. = Public School
Pt. = Point
Rd. = Road
S = South
Sat = Saturday
Sr. = Senior
St. = Street
St. = Saint
Sun = Sunday
Tues = Tuesday
Thurs = Thursday
UN = United Nation
U.S. = United States
W = West
Wed = Wednesday

A. Philip Randolph Square *see* Randolph Square.

AT&T Building *see* Sony Building.

Abigail Adams Smith Museum *see* Mount Vernon Hotel Museum and Garden.

Abyssinian Baptist Church 132 Odell Clark Pl. W, at 138th St. btw Lenox and Seventh Aves. (212) 862-7474 www.abyssinianbaptist church.org

    This church was founded in 1808 to serve the African-American community. Well-attended Sunday services feature the celebrated gospel choir and organ music. Under early leadership by Adam Clayton Powell Sr., Congressman Adam Clayton Powell Jr., and successive pastors, the congregation has received national attention for social and political activism. Subway: 2, 3 to 135th St.

Academy of American Poets 584 Broadway btw Houston and Prince Sts. (212) 274-0343 www.poets.org

    The academy sponsors various poetry-related events at different venues, including the Morgan Library, some with admission and some free. It offers numerous awards and promotes poetry reading by making poems accessible on the Web. Subway: B, D, F to Broadway-Lafayette St.

Access for All published by Hospital Audiences Inc., 220 W 42nd St., NY 10036 (212) 284-4100

    This booklet, available for $5, describes access for the disabled to city theatres, museums, and other cultural institutions. It provides specific information for each site, including parking, entrance, restroom, and telephone locations, visual and hearing aid services, and height and width dimensions where applicable.

Access Guide to New York City published by the Junior League of the City of New York, 130 E 80th St., NY 10028

This free list identifies city buildings providing access for the disabled.

Accommodations Express (800) 444-7666, fax (609) 525-0111 www. accommodationsexpress.com

This company offers hotel rooms across a broad range of prices at discounted rates.

Accommodations in New York *see* Bed-and-Breakfast Rental Agencies, Bed-and-Breakfasts, Hostels, Hotel Accommodations, Hotel Reservation Agencies, YMCA/YWCAs.

Acquavella 18 E 79th St. btw Fifth and Madison Aves. (212) 734-6300

Spacious gallery areas feature exhibitions of major late-nineteenth- and early-twentieth-century painters and sculptors. Subway: 6 to 77th St. Mon–Fri 10 a.m.–5 p.m.

Active Sports Activity *see* Participatory Sports Activity.

Adam Clayton Powell Jr. State Office Building 163 W 125th St. at Adam Clayton Powell Blvd. (212) 749-5298

Exhibits in the 2nd-floor gallery celebrate films by and about African-Americans. Note work of Black film makers from Africa, the Caribbean, and South America. It also features special and unique film showings on African-American themes. Subway: A, B, C, D, 2, 3 to 125th St. Admission charge.

Admiral George Dewey Promenade Battery Park

Named for the Spanish-American War hero, the promenade edges sculpture- and statuary-filled Battery Park at the scenic tip of lower Manhattan. Benches along the path encourage harbor viewing. Subway: 1, 9 to South Ferry.

Adventure on a Shoestring (212) 265-2663

This organization, founded in 1963, provides neighborhood weekend walking excursions, rain or shine, in Manhattan and other boroughs.

Afghan Kebab House 764 Ninth Ave. btw 51st and 52nd Sts. (212) 307-1612

This restaurant chain serves Afghan cuisine, varying slightly at its three locations. Selections include traditional well-spiced kebabs, vegetarian boiled dumplings, and combination platters. No alcohol is served, but patrons may bring their own. Other locations are at 1345 Second Ave. between 70th and 71st Sts. (212) 517-2776, and 74-16 Thirty-Seventh Ave. between 74th and 75th Sts. in Jackson Heights, Queens. Hours vary slightly at each venue, but they are open from about midday to 10 p.m., and major credit cards are accepted at these moderately priced places. Subway: C, E to 50th St.; 6 to 68th St.-Hunter College; E, F, G, R to Jackson Heights-Roosevelt Ave.

Afghan Restaurants *see* Afghan Kebab House, Pamir.

African-American Day Parade (212) 348-3080
The route for this annual parade held on a Sunday in September through Harlem is along Adam Clayton Powell Jr. Blvd., starting at 111th St. Marchers and spectators of all ages and occupations celebrate the occasion. Music by hundreds of bands is loud and lively. Subway: B, C to Cathedral Pkwy.-110th St.

African American Wax Museum 316 W 115th St. btw Frederick Douglass Blvd. and Manhattan Ave. (212) 678-7818
This growing museum was founded by sculptor/painter Raven Chanticleer, who creates wax figures of notable African-Americans from many fields, including Nelson Mandela, Harriet Tubman, Josephine Baker, Malcolm X, and Magic Johnson. Subway: B, C to 116th St. Tues–Sun 1 p.m.–6 p.m. Closed Mon. Admission charge.

African Arts Festival Boys and Girls High School, 1700 Fulton St., Brooklyn (718) 638-6700
This five-day-long celebration held at the end of June and early July has been running for 30 years and is a family event featuring live music, a talent contest, children's activities, and much, much more, offering entertainment from morning to late night each day. Subway: A, C to Utica Ave. Admission charge.

Africans in New York *see* Washington Heights.

Airport Transportation *see* John F. Kennedy International Airport, LaGuardia Airport, Newark International Airport.

Aladdin 317 W 45th St., NY 10036 btw Eighth and Ninth Aves. (212) 246-8580, fax (212) 246-6033 www.aladdinhotel.com
These are basic accommodations for the very budget-conscious. Dorm

and private rooms are available at inexpensive rates. Major credit cards. Subway: A, C, E to 42nd St.-Port Authority.

Alamo 304 E 48th St. btw First and Second Aves. (212) 759-0590

Comfortable main- and 2nd-floor dining areas provide innovative and more typical Mexican and Tex-Mex fare. Order the house guacamole and enjoy watching it created table-side. Subway: 6 to 51st St. Lunch Mon–Fri, dinner Mon–Sat. Major credit cards.

Aleppo in Flatbush

This pleasant suburban area in Brooklyn's Midwood section derives its name from Aleppo, the ancestral city of Abraham, and is home to long-time Syrian Jewish residents and more recent Israeli arrivals. One- and two-family houses, tree-lined streets, and many houses of worship characterize the neighborhood. Subway: F to Kings Hwy.

Alfred Pommer (212) 979-2388

Scheduled as well as private walking tours of a number of the city's unique neighborhoods, treating architectural and historical features, are conducted by this well-qualified licensed specialist on weekends as well as during the week.

Algonquin Hotel 59 W 44th St. btw Fifth and Sixth Aves., NY 10036 (212) 840-6800 or (800) 555-8000, fax (212) 944-1419 www.cam berlyhotels.com

This recently refurbished hotel, designated a NYC historic landmark in 1996, earned fame during the 1920s as a regular haunt of the Round Table group of *New Yorker* magazine wits and other literary luminaries. After-noon tea is still served in the Oak Room. The comfortable bar displays Al Hirschfeld drawings. Room rates are moderately high at this convenient midtown location. Subway: S, 4, 5, 6, 7 to Grand Central-42nd St.

Alice Austen House 2 Hylan Blvd., Staten Island (718) 816-4506

This restored seventeenth-century cottage was once the home of Alice Austen (1866–1930), an amateur photographer of turn-of-the-century Staten Island life, whose pioneering work was recognized only late in life. The home and museum shows a documentary film on Austen and rotating photo exhibits. There are spectacular harbor views from the surrounding grounds. Subway: 1, 9 to South Ferry; N, R to Whitehall St., then ferry to Staten Island. From Staten Island St. George Ferry Terminal, take Bus S51 to Bay St. and Hylan Blvd. Open Thurs–Sat noon–5 p.m. Modest admission charge.

Alice Tully Hall 70 Lincoln Plaza btw 62nd and 66th Sts., Amster-dam and Columbus Aves. (212) 875-5000

The resident chamber music society offers a full program each season. The hall is home to additional music, dance, and performance art events. It has comfortable seating and excellent acoustics. Subway: 1, 9 to 66th St.-Lincoln Center.

Alison on Dominick 38 Dominick St. btw Hudson and Varick Sts. (212) 727-1188 www.alisonondominick.com

This west SoHo hideaway features imaginative contemporary French cuisine and romantic ambiance. Prices are fairly expensive, and reservations are advisable. Subway: C, E to Spring St. Dinner Tues–Sun. Major credit cards.

All Star Café 1540 Broadway at 45th St. (212) 840-TEAM

This sports-theme restaurant is notable in its class for the large mounted collection of memorabilia from sports celebrities. Subway: N, R, S, 1, 2, 3, 7, 9 to Times Square-42nd St. Open daily 10 a.m.–midnight.

Alley Pond Environmental Center 228-06 Northern Blvd. off Cross Island Pkwy., Queens (718) 229-4000 www.alleypond.com

Located at the northern end of 635-acre Alley Pond Park, the center includes a zoo for small animals, a little aquarium, and some interactive exhibits. There are special events as well as nature walks provided through park marshes and woodlands. Subway: 7 to Main St., then Bus Q12 east to Northern Blvd. Open Mon–Sat 9 a.m.–4:30 p.m.; Sun 9:30 a.m.–3:30 p.m. Closed July and August. Admission free, but special programs and events are priced.

Alliance Française 22 E 60th St. btw Park and Madison Aves. (212) 355-6100

This central facility for all things French offers language classes, film screenings, a fine library collection, and many cultural events for both members and non-members. Subway: N, R to Fifth Ave.; 4, 5, 6, to 59th St. Open Mon–Thurs 9 a.m.–8 p.m.; Fri 9 a.m.–5 p.m.

Alphabet City east of First Ave. btw Hudson and 14th Sts.

This area, named for lettered rather than numbered streets, reflects recent and strenuous community and city revitalization efforts. Once considered unsafe, this neighborhood now offers a selection of livable quarters, off-beat bars, cafés, and artist hangouts, but retains a pervasive bohemian flavor. Subway: L to First Ave.

Alternative Museum 594 Broadway btw Houston and Prince Sts. (212) 966-4444 www.alternativemuseum.org

Founded and operated by artists, this museum no longer exhibits works deemed unrecognized due to race, gender, and political or economic factors in physical form in a public space. It has been transformed completely into an Internet site, where it mounts its varied multimedia and digital exhibits for viewing at its Web location.

Alternative Music *see* Rock, Alternative, and Ethnic Music.

Altman Building *see* B. Altman Building/New York Public Library Science, Industry, and Business Library.

Alvin Ailey American Dance Theater 211 W 61st St. btw Seventh and Eighth Aves. (212) 767-0590 www.alvinailey.org

This theatre is the home of the modern dance and ballet repertory company of renowned choreographer and dancer Alvin Ailey. It also presents the work of other choreographers, focusing on the celebration of Black culture and music, at this and other locations. Plans are intensively under way to develop a new, much larger site for this company to replace its present crowded quarters. Subway: A, B, C, D, 1, 9 to 59th St.-Columbus Circle.

Alwyn Court Apartments 180 W 58th St. at Seventh Ave.

The apartment house interior is open to residents and guests only, but the spectacular French Renaissance-style exterior, dating from 1909, merits careful inspection. Intricate terra-cotta carvings depict dragons, crowns, and fanciful flora and fauna. Subway: A, B, C, D, 1, 9 to 59th St.-Columbus Circle.

Amato Opera Theatre 319 Bowery at E 2nd St. (212) 228-8200

This small 107-seat theatre presents impressive weekend performances of Italian and other classic operas at reasonable prices. The theatre also creates operatic productions specifically designed for children, called Opera in Brief. The 2001–2002 season marks the fifty-fourth consecutive season. Subway: 6 to Bleecker St.

Ambassador Grill Regal UN Plaza Hotel, One UN Plaza at E 44th St., off First Ave. (212) 702-5014

This well-named, elegant restaurant provides excellent traditional food and service at fairly expensive prices. Dinner reservations suggested. Subway: S, 4, 5, 6, 7 to Grand Central-42nd St. Open daily from breakfast through dinner. Major credit cards.

Ambassador Theatre 215 W 49th St. btw Broadway and Eighth Ave. (212) 239-6200

Dating from the 1930s, this performance center has been the venue for many award-winning theatrical productions. Subway: 1, 9 to 50th St.

American Academy of Arts and Letters Audubon Terrace, Broadway btw 155th and 156th Sts. (212) 368-5900

Merged with the National Institute of Arts and Letters in 1976, this organization elects to membership notable representatives of American literary and arts communities. Temporary exhibits include a display of original manuscripts from the research library collection. Subway: 1 to 157th St. Open Thurs–Sun 1 p.m.–4 p.m. Admission free.

American Airlines Theatre 229 W 42nd St. btw Broadway and Eighth Ave. (212) 281-9800

The refurbished and renamed Selwyn Theater is a new venue for non-profit Roundabout Theatre Company's productions of dramatic and musical performances. *See also* Roundabout Theatre Company.

American Ballet Theatre at Metropolitan Opera House, W 64th St. and Columbus Ave. at Lincoln Center (212) 362-6000, and at City Center, 130 W 56th St. btw Sixth and Seventh Aves. (212) 581-1212 www.abt.org

This renowned company stages classic and contemporary dance at each location during different seasons. Subway: (Metropolitan Opera House) 1, 9 to 66th St.-Lincoln Center; (City Center) N, R to 57th St.

American Bible Society 1865 Broadway at 61st St., NY 10023 (212) 408-1200 www.americanbible.org

This interdenominational society continues its long-time mission distributing the Bible and, more recently, Scripture excerpts. Exhibitions, educational programs, and an extensive research library collection provide unique access to biblical and related information. Subway: A, B, C, D, 1, 9 to 59th St.-Columbus Circle. Open Mon–Wed and Fri 10 a.m.–6 p.m.; Thurs 10 a.m.–7 p.m.; Sat 10 a.m.–5 p.m. Admission free.

American Craft Museum 40 W 53rd St. btw Fifth and Sixth Aves. (212) 956-3535 www.americancraftmuseum.org

Spacious galleries and library resources focus on twentieth-century and contemporary American crafts in a range of media and materials, including textiles, jewelry, wood, ceramic, and metal. The museum mounts special exhibits and programs for children. Subway: E, F to Fifth Ave. Open Tues–Sat 10 a.m.–6 p.m. Closed Mon and holidays. Admission charge.

American Crafts Festival at Lincoln Center btw 62nd and 66th Sts., Amsterdam and Columbus Aves. (212) 875-5500

This annual festival on two successive weekends in June each year displays a wide variety of crafts and includes demonstrations. Subway: 1, 9 to 66th St.-Lincoln Center.

American Ethnic Parade *see* International Cultures Parade.

American Financial History Tours *see* World of Finance Tours.

American International Building 70 Pine St. near the New York Stock Exchange

The classic Art Deco exterior and lobby distinguish one of the first skyscrapers set back from the street in response to 1916 city requirements regarding spatial relationships between building and site. Subway: 2, 3 to Wall St.

American Irish Historical Society 991 Fifth Ave. btw 80th and 81st Sts. (212) 288-2263

Maintained by the society since 1940, this Beaux Arts decorative townhouse was once the home of U.S. Steel President William Ellis Corey. The library collection and occasional exhibits focus on Irish immigration and the U.S. experience. The reference library is open by appointment only. Subway: 6 to 77th St.

American Jewish Historical Society *see* Center for Jewish History.

American Merchant Marines Memorial Battery Park btw State St., the Hudson River, and Battery Pl.

Located at the north end of Battery Park is this arresting sculpture depicting a half-submerged man stretching out his arms for help. Subway: 1, 9 to South Ferry; 4, 5 to Bowling Green.

American Museum of Natural History Central Park W at W 79th St. (212) 769-5100 www.amnh.org

This is perhaps the largest museum of its kind in the world, with a collection of millions of artifacts and forty exhibition halls on four floors, featuring the history of cultures and peoples, mammals of Asia and Africa, amazing gemstones, and the enormous dinosaur fossils that so enthrall youngsters. Subway: 1, 9 to 79th St.; C to 81st St. Open daily with evening hours Fri and Sat. Suggested donation. *See also* City Pass.

American Museum of the Moving Image Thirty-Fifth Ave. at 36th St., Astoria, Queens (718) 784-0077 www.ammi.org

This museum, in an old Paramount Pictures facility, explores the history, technology, impact, and future of movie, TV, and video arts. Interactive exhibits, demonstrations, memorabilia, and screenings cover all aspects of visual media. Subway: G, R to Steinway St. Bus: Q66, Q101. Open Tues–Sat. Admission charge.

American Numismatic Society Audubon Terrace, Broadway btw 155th and 156th Sts. (212) 234-3130 www.amnumsoc.org

This society, founded in 1858, maintains a fascinating collection of coins, medals, and paper money. The reference library, open to the public, documents the history of money from earliest times. The society was planning to move in 2002 to a new site in downtown Manhattan at 140 William St. at Fulton St. Subway: 1 to 157th St. Closed Mon. Admission free.

An American Place 565 Lexington Ave. (212) 888-5650

Highly respected for inventive new American cuisine by a celebrated chef, this is a very popular, moderately expensive restaurant where reservations are needed. It is located in The Benjamin Hotel. Subway: 6 to 51st St.; E, F to Lexington Ave. Open daily for lunch and dinner, brunch on weekends. Major credit cards.

American Place Theatre 111 W 46th St. btw Sixth and Seventh Aves. (212) 840-3074

Contemporary drama is the usual fare at this theatre. Subway: N, R, S, 1, 3, 7, 9 to 42nd St.-Times Square.

American Restaurants *see* Ambassador Grill, An American Place, Aureole, Blue Water Grill, Bridge Café, Bubby's Restaurant Bar and Bakery, Cornelia Street Café, Four Seasons Restaurant, Gramercy Tavern, Hard Rock Café, Hudson River Club, Joe Allen, Judson Grill, Lucky Strike, Main Street, New World Grill, Popover Café, River Café, Sardi's, Savanna, Supper Club, Tavern on the Green, TriBeCa Grill, The "21" Club, Union Square Café, Verbena, Water Club, Water's Edge, Zoë. *See also* Contemporary Restaurants.

American Standard Building 40 W 40th St. btw Fifth and Sixth Aves.

This striking 1924 Gothic-style building by Raymond Hood is notable for its black brick- and gold-trimmed façade and gold tower. Subway: S, 4, 5, 6, 7 to Grand Central-42nd St.

American Telephone and Telegraph Building *see* Sony Building.

Americas Society 680 Park Ave. at 68th St. (212) 249-8950 www.americas-society.org

Devoted to expanding U.S. awareness of Canadian and South and Central American art and cultures, the society presents temporary exhibits in a handsome townhouse designed by McKim, Mead & White around 1910. Subway: 6 to 68th St.-Hunter College. Closed Mon. Admission free.

Amsterdam Billiard Club 344 Amsterdam Ave. btw 76th and 77th Sts. (212) 496-8180

This upscale club provides many pool tables in a comfortable environment. A bar and light refreshments are in a separate room. A second location is at 210 E 86th St. between Second and Third Aves. (212) 570-4545. Subway: (Amsterdam Ave.) 1, 9 to 79th St.; (E 86th St.) 4, 5, 6 to 86th St. Open daily 11 a.m.–3 or 4 a.m. Major credit cards.

Amusement Parks *see* Astroland, Deno's Wonderwheel Park, Nellie Bly Amusement Park.

Angelica Kitchen 300 E 12th St. btw First and Second Aves. (212) 228-2909

Carefully prepared organic vegan cuisine, fresh bakery goods, and moderate prices attract vegetarian and health food patrons and make this one of the city's finest vegetarian restaurants. Subway: N, R, 4, 5, 6 to 14th St.-Union Square; L to First Ave. Open daily for lunch and dinner. No credit cards.

Angelika Film Center 18 W Houston St. at Mercer St. (212) 777-FILM www.angelikafilmcenter.com

Multi-screen cinema features independent and off-beat American and foreign films. Upstairs café provides light fare. Subway: B, D, F, Q to Broadway-Lafayette St.; N, R to Prince St.; 6 to Bleecker St. Open daily. No credit cards.

Annex Antiques Fair and Flea Market Sixth Ave. from 24th to 27th Sts. (212) 243-5343

Open weekends year-round, this area is a well-known central neighborhood for parking lot markets and antique shop browsing for every imaginable and some unimaginable types of stuff. Subway: F to 23rd St. Open Sat and Sun.

Ansonia Hotel 2109 Broadway btw 73rd and 74th Sts.

This highly ornate 1904 Beaux Arts apartment house attracted celebrated musicians early in its history due to exceptional soundproofing. Babe Ruth was a later occupant. A public display in the lobby documents an unusual history. Subway: 1, 2, 3, 9 to 72nd St.

Anthology Film Archives 32 Second Ave. at 2nd St. (212) 505-5181

These archives have a large collection and research library holdings devoted to history, preservation, and screening of U.S. and foreign independent films. It is also a center for screenings, lectures, and other film-related special events; some are priced and some are free. Subway: F to Second Ave. Open Mon–Fri 10 a.m.–6 p.m. No credit cards.

Antiquarian Book Fair Seventh Regiment Armory, Park Ave. btw 66th and 67th Sts. (212) 777-5218

This is a dependable annual venue for the sale of rare books, manuscripts, maps, and related collector items. Free appraisals are available to Sunday patrons. Program runs Thurs–Sun, normally in mid-April. Subway: 6 to 68th St.-Hunter College.

Antique Flea and Farmers Market P.S. 183, E 67th St. btw First and York Aves.

This is an indoor and outdoor all-day Saturday sale of fresh produce and antiques by many vendors. Subway: 6 to 68th St.-Hunter College.

Antiques *see* Flea Markets.

Antiques Fair and Collectibles Market corner of Broadway and Grand St. (212) 682-2000

Outdoor flea market open weekends year-round selling all kinds of different items. Subway: J, M, N, R, Z, 6 to Canal St.

Antiques Show in Winter *see* Winter Antiques Show.

Anushka Day Spa 241 E 60th St. btw Second and Third Aves. (212) 355-6404

This spa offers regular intensive body contouring and skin revitalization sessions and consultation. Subway: N, R to Lexington Ave.; 4, 5 6 to 59th St. Open Mon–Sat. Major credit cards.

Apartment Buildings *see* Alwyn Court Apartments, Ansonia Hotel, Apthorp Apartments, The Dakota, Eagle Warehouse, El Dorado Apartments, Majestic Apartments, Manhattan Park, Peter Cooper Village, San Remo Apartments, Stuyvesant Town, Washington Square Village Apartments.

The Apollo Theater 253 W 125th St. btw Adam Clayton Powell Jr. and Frederick Douglass Blvds. (212) 531-5305 or (212) 749-5838 www.apolloshowtime.com

This legendary venue for established and emerging Black musicians and entertainers has been around since the 1930s. It presents live jazz, blues, and contemporary music each night, with aspiring talent showcased at the weekly amateur night. Subway: A, B, C, D, 2, 3 to 125th St. Major credit cards.

Appetizing Stores *see* Specialty Food Stores and Bakeries.

Apthorp Apartments 2207 Broadway at 79th St.

This Italian Renaissance-style 1908 building commissioned by William Waldorf Astor continues to provide luxury apartments. It has a spectacular inside courtyard. Subway: 1, 9 to 79th St.

Aqua Grill 210 Spring St. at Sixth Ave. (212) 274-0505

A SoHo location and a well-deserved reputation for fresh seafood make this a popular, if somewhat expensive, restaurant choice. Subway: C, E to Spring St. Lunch and dinner Mon–Fri, brunch and dinner Sat–Sun. Major credit cards.

Aquarium for Wildlife Conservation Surf Ave. and W 8th St., Coney Island, Brooklyn (718) 265-FISH www.nyaquarium.com

Located ocean-side near the boardwalk, this venerable aquarium provides up-to-date demonstrations and exhibits. Children can have near-hands-on experiences with aquatic inhabitants and habitats of great appeal. Subway: D, E to W 8th St. Open daily. Admission charge. Major credit cards.

Aquavit 13 W 54th St. btw Fifth and Sixth Aves. (212) 307-7311

This decorative 8-story atrium restaurant is in the city home of the late New York Governor Nelson Rockefeller. The main dining room features traditional and contemporary Scandinavian cuisine, a wide selection of aquavits and wine, and a smorgasbord appetizer sampler at fairly expensive prices. Less expensive selections are available in the upstairs café. Subway: E, F to Fifth Ave.; Q to 57th St. Lunch Mon–Fri, dinner Mon–Sat, brunch Sun. Major credit cards.

Aqueduct Racetrack 110th St. and Rockaway Blvd., Queens (718) 641-4700

Thoroughbred racing weekdays October–May. Subway: A to Aqueduct Racetrack. No credit cards.

Arabs in New York *see* Atlantic Avenue.

Archives of American Art 1285 Sixth Ave. btw 51st and 52nd Sts. (212) 399-5015

This Smithsonian Institution regional research facility maintains and acquires documents and memorabilia relating to visual art and artists. Subway: E, F to Fifth Ave.; B, D, F, Q to Rockefeller Center. Open Mon–Fri. Admission free.

Argentineans in New York *see* Jackson Heights.

Argosy Bookstore 116 E 59th St. btw Park and Lexington Aves. (212) 753-4455 www.argosybooks.com

This store is well known for its vast stock of hard-to-find and used books, posters, and prints. It also houses a unique map collection. Subway: 4, 5, 6 to 59th St. Open Mon–Sat 10 a.m.–6 p.m. Closed Saturdays May–September. Major credit cards.

Arizona 206 206 E 60th St. btw Second and Third Aves. (212) 838-0440

This cozy venue is for patrons seeking creative twists on Southwest cuisine at moderately expensive prices. The attached café features a less expensive selection of delicious house appetizers. Subway: 4, 5, 6 to 59th St. Lunch and dinner daily. Major credit cards.

Arlene Grocery 95 Stanton St. btw Ludlow and Orchard Sts. (212) 358-1633 www.arlenegrocery.com

This intimate and informal club welcomes aspiring rock bands of all types. Subway: F to Second Ave.; J, M, Z to Essex St. Admission free except Fri and Sat nights. No credit cards. Open daily.

Art and Design Museums *see* Alternative Museum, American Craft Museum, Cooper-Hewitt Design Museum, Dahesh Museum, Fashion Institute of Technology, Forbes Magazine Galleries, Grey Art Gallery and Study Center at New York University, Metropolitan Museum of Art, Municipal Art Society, El Museo del Barrio, Museum of American Folk Art, Museum of American Illustration, Museum of Modern Art, National Academy of Design, Neue Galerie, Newhouse Center for Contemporary Art, Nicholas Roerich Museum, Noguchi Museum, P.S. 1 The Institute for Contemporary Art, Pierpont Morgan Library, Studio Museum in Harlem, Whitney Museum of American Art, Whitney Museum of American Art at Philip Morris Building. *See also* Ethnic and Community Museums, Historical Museums, Major New York City Museums, Media Museums, Military Museums, Museums of Particular Interest to Children and Teens, Science and Technology Museums, Specialized City Museums.

Art Films *see* Foreign and Independent Films.

Art Galleries *see* Acquavella, Drawing Center, Grey Art Gallery and Study Center at New York University, Henry Street Settlement Abrons Art Center, Hirschl and Adler Galleries, Holly Solomon Gallery, Leo Castelli, M. Knoedler and Co., Marlborough Gallery, Mary Boone Gallery, Municipal Art Society, Pace Wildenstein Gallery, Paula Cooper Gallery, Schomburg Center for Research in Black Culture, Snug Harbor Cultural Center, Ukrainian Institute of America, White Columns. *See also Art Now Gallery Guide.*

Art Now Gallery Guide

This monthly listing of current gallery exhibitions is available free at many bookstores and galleries and is also sold at newsstands.

The Art Show Seventh Regiment Armory, Park Ave. btw 66th and 67th Sts. (212) 766-9200

This late-February event is sponsored by the Art Dealers Association of America and shows sculpture, paintings, and prints during the city's largest annual activity of its kind. Subway: 6 to 68th St.

Art Tours of Manhattan (212) 772-3888

Walking tours aim to meet specific customer interests in museum and gallery exhibits, local artist studios, and other facets of the current art scene.

Arthur's Tavern 57 Grove St. btw Bleecker St. and Seventh Ave. (212) 675-6879 www.arthurstavernnyc.com

This pleasant Village bar showcases pianists and combos designed to enthrall the jazz buff clientele. Subway: 1, 9 to Christopher St.-Sheridan Square. No cover charge. No credit cards.

ARTime (718) 797-1573

Art historians design 90-minute Saturday tours of SoHo and Chelsea galleries to interest children and families.

Arturo's 106 W Houston St. at Thompson St. (212) 677-3820

Arturo's features a winning combination of live jazz and standout pizza at moderate prices. Subway: 1, 9 to Houston St.; A, B, C, D, E, F to W 4th St. Open daily mid-afternoon until late. Major credit cards.

Asia Society 725 Park Ave. at 70th St. (212) 288-6400 www.asia society.com

Following extensive renovations, this institution, begun in 1956, reopened to the public in October 2001. It promotes cultural ties between the United States and Asia, while its exhibitions showcase artistic works from important public and private collections. It also offers many educational conferences and public performances bearing upon Asian culture, history, and art. Subway: 6 to 68th St.-Hunter College. Closed Mon. Admission charge. No credit cards.

Asian Restaurants *see* Cendrillon Asian Grill, Penang. *See also* Chinese Restaurants, Indian Restaurants, Japanese Restaurants, Korean Restaurants, Thai Restaurants, Vietnamese Restaurants.

Asians in New York *see* Flushing, Lower East Side, Woodside.

Asphalt Green 1750 York Ave. at 91st St. (212) 369-8890
Well-run fitness and community center with Olympic-size pool now occupies the site of an old asphalt plant. Subway: 4, 5, 6 to 86th St. Open daily from early morning to evening for members or for a daily admission charge.

Asser Levy Playground E 23rd St. and Asser Levy Pl. near the East River (212) 447-2020
This city-run public athletic center and indoor swimming pool was named for the first Jewish immigrant citizen. Located at the northeast corner of Peter Cooper Village, the playground is specifically designed to accommodate children with disabilities. Subway: 6 to 23rd St., then Bus M23 to Peter Cooper Village.

Astor Place Lafayette St., Fourth Ave., and 8th St.
The plaza named for mid-nineteenth-century real estate mogul John Jacob Astor is notable for the handsome reconstruction of an early subway kiosk, Bernard Rosenthal's imposing black square sculpture, and daily skateboard activity. Subway: 6 to Astor Pl.; N, R to 8th St.-NYU.

Astor Place Theatre 434 Lafayette St. btw E 4th St. and Astor Pl. (212) 254-4370
This has been a venue since the early 1990s for comedy performance artists. Subway: 6 to Astor Pl.

Astoria Queens
The center for the city's large Greek community, this stable neighborhood increasingly attracts other ethnic concentrations. Heavily used for film making through the 1960s, area motion picture studios have been restored for active movie and TV production. Three bridges—the Queensboro, the Triborough, and Hell's Gate—connect this corner of Queens to

Manhattan. Astoria Park is one of the city's prettiest stretches of greenery, with choice views of Manhattan. Subway: N to Ditmars Blvd.

Astroland 1000 Surf Ave. and W 8th St., Coney Island, Brooklyn (718) 372-0275

The boardwalk and this 1920s-era amusement park remain treats for children of all ages. The properly terrifying roller coaster was declared a NYC landmark in 1988. Subway: D, F to W 8th St.-NY Aquarium. Open daily from midday in summer season, weather permitting. No credit cards.

At Home in New York (212) 956-3125 or (800) 692-4262

This company lists selected, modestly priced hosted and unhosted accommodations in private properties throughout the city.

Athletics *see* Fitness Centers, Participatory Sports Activity, Spectator Sports.

Atkinson Theatre *see* Brooks Atkinson Theatre.

Atlantic Antic Street Festival (718) 875-8993

On the last Sunday in September this celebration in Brooklyn of all things Arab features music, belly dancing, enthusiastic spectator participation, and enticing Middle Eastern fare. It takes place along Atlantic Ave. from Flatbush Ave. to Furman St. Subway: N, R to Court St.; 2, 3, 4, 5 to Borough Hall.

Atlantic Avenue btw Henry and Clinton Sts., Brooklyn

Located between Brooklyn Heights and Cobble Hill, this is the heartland for the Arab-American community. It bustles with wonderful restaurants, retail shops, and sidewalk vendors featuring Middle Eastern flavors and products. Subway: N, R to Court St.; 2, 3, 4, 5 to Borough Hall.

Atlantic Kayak Tours (914) 246-2187

This organization offers kayak rentals, lessons, and tours of NYC harbor and around Manhattan island.

Atlantic Theatre Company 336 W 20th St. btw Eighth and Ninth Aves. (212) 645-8015

This company had its beginnings in workshops taught by David Mamet and William H. Macy. Current productions emphasize the new and provocative. Subway: 1, 9, C, E to 23rd St.

Auction Houses *see* Christie's, Sotheby's, Swann Galleries, Tepper Gallery, William Doyle.

Audubon Terrace btw Riverside Dr. and Broadway and 155th and 156th Sts.

Sited on former property of naturalist John James Audubon, this building complex of Beaux Arts buildings and a vast adjoining marble plaza was designed to accommodate special museums and society headquarters. Here can be found the American Academy of Arts and Letters, the American Numismatic Society, and the Hispanic Society of America. Subway: 1 to 157th St.

Aureole 34 E 61st St. btw Madison and Park Aves. (212) 319-1660

Contemporary French-influenced American cuisine and impressive wines at some of the higher prices in town. Look for sophisticated game and beef selections, creative seafood appetizers, and signature sculpted desserts. Reservations required. Subway: 4, 5, 6 to 59th St.; N, R to Lexington Ave. Lunch Mon–Fri, dinner Mon–Sat. Closed Sun. Major credit cards.

Avalon Registry P.O. Box 1362, Radio City Station, NY 10101 (212) 245-0250

Reasonable hourly rates and transportation charges make this professional baby-sitting agency a welcome service. Make telephone arrangements during business hours or leave messages at other times for call back. Credit cards are accepted for this service provided in hotels as well as residences.

Aveda Institute 233 Spring St. btw Sixth Ave. and Varick St. (212) 807-1492 www.aveda.com

Skin and body treatment facility, hairdressing salon, and retail shop feature the company's botanical products. Subway: C, E to Spring St.; 1, 9 to Houston St. Open Mon–Sat, hours vary. Major credit cards.

Avenue of the Americas

This wide, busy north–south thoroughfare is still called Sixth Ave. by most New Yorkers. It's something of a dividing line between the more luxurious and genteel Fifth, Madison, and Park Aves. on the east and the more earthy streets on the west.

Avery Fisher Hall at Lincoln Center btw 62nd and 66th Sts., Amsterdam and Columbus Aves. (212) 875-5030 www.lincolncenter.org

Now renowned for acoustics as well as performance, this venue is home to New York Philharmonic concerts and Lincoln Center classical music and jazz series. Subway: 1, 9 to 66th St.-Lincoln Center.

Avon Center Spa and Salon Trump Tower, 725 Fifth Ave. btw 56th and 57th Sts., 6th Floor (212) 755-2866 www.avon.com

The history of this present, well-equipped modern spa traces product development and marketing to a late nineteenth-century door-to-door Bible salesman. Subway: E, F to Fifth Ave.; 4, 5, 6 to 59th St. Open Mon–Sat, hours vary. Major credit cards.

Away Spa and Gym at W Hotel 541 Lexington Ave. at 50th St., 4th Floor (212) 407-2970 www.theawayspa.com

This establishment offers a wide range of regular and specialized services in very attractive quarters. Subway: 6 to 51st St.; E, F to Lexington Ave. Open daily, hours vary. Major credit cards.

B. Altman Building/New York Public Library Science, Industry and Business Library (SIBL) 188 Madison Ave. at 34th St. (212) 930-0747 www.nypl.org/research/sibl

Housed in a fine old department store building, SIBL provides free public access to extensive library and electronic resources and leading-edge technology in science and business fields. Subway: 6 to 33rd St. Open Mon–Sat. Hours vary.

B. Smith's 320 W 46th St. btw Eighth and Ninth Aves. (212) 315-1100

The location and eclectic menu appeal to theatre personalities and pre-theatre diners. Moderate prices with music after 9 p.m. on Fri and Sat. Subway: C, E to 50th St.; A, C, E to 42nd St.-Port Authority. Lunch and dinner Mon–Sat, Sun brunch. Credit cards except Diners and Discover.

BAM Next Wave Festival *see* Next Wave Festival.

BAM Rose Cinemas 30 Lafayette Ave. btw Flatbush Ave. and Fulton St., Brooklyn (718) 623-2770

This attractive multi-screen theatre affiliated with the Brooklyn Academy of Music shows first-run art films. Subway: B, M, N, R to Pacific St.; G to Fulton St. No credit cards.

BB King Blues Club and Grill 237 W 42nd St. btw Seventh and Eighth Aves. (212) 997-4144 www.bbkingblues.com

This spacious supper club with adjacent restaurant, Lucille's Grill, is oriented to those who prefer to sway while sitting and listening to the music that runs the spectrum of jazz forms. Subway: N, R, S, 1, 2, 3, 7, 9 to 42nd

St.-Times Square. Open from 11 a.m. daily. Usually two shows nightly. Admission price varies. Major credit cards.

Babbo 110 Waverly Pl. btw Sixth Ave. and MacDougal St. (212) 777-0303

Persistently inventive and delicious Northern Italian selections encourage experimentation and a return visit to this popular Village spot where the prices are moderately expensive. Subway: A, B, C, D, E, F, Q to W 4th St.-Washington Square. Open daily for dinner. Major credit cards.

The Baby Sitters' Guild 60 E 42nd St., Suite 912 (212) 682-0227 www.babysittersguild.com

The guild has offered dependable baby-sitting services since 1940 at competitive hourly rates plus transportation. Multi-lingual licensed staff accommodates requests for sixteen languages. Cash only. Call daily 9 a.m.–9 p.m.

Baby-sitting *see* Avalon Registry, Baby Sitters' Guild.

Bainbridge bounded by Bainbridge, Jerome, and Webster Aves. and E Mosholu Pkwy., Bronx

Still largely Irish and Democratic, this neighborhood borders both fine parkland and devastated areas. The local Irish Immigration Reform Movement continues a tradition of political involvement. Subway: D to Norwood-205th St.; 4 to Mosholu Pkwy.

Bakeries *see* Specialty Food Stores and Bakeries.

Baktun 418 W 14th St. btw Ninth Ave. and Washington St. (212) 206-1590 www.baktun.com

This modest but distinctly entertaining night club has changing bands and shows. Subway: A, C, E, L to 14th St. Open on certain nights. Admission charge varies. Major credit cards.

Balducci's 424 Sixth Ave. at 9th St. (212) 673-2600

This prestigious grocery store has long been known for singular meat, produce, cheese, and prepared food. Balducci's specializes in gourmet fare of every kind, with many products bearing its own brand name. Subway: A, B, C, D, E, F, Q to W 4th St.-Washington Square. Daily 7 a.m.–8:30 p.m. Major credit cards.

Ballet *see* Dance.

Balthazar 80 Spring St. btw Broadway and Crosby St. (212) 965-1414

This is probably as close to Parisian ambiance and bistro fare as you'll find in New York City. Bring money and a taste for celebrity watching. The raw bar and wonderful bread are special treats. Subway: C, E, 6 to Spring St. Open daily from lunch to very late dinner. Major credit cards.

Bambou 243 E 14th St. btw Second and Third Aves. (212) 358-0012

This upscale, lively Caribbean restaurant has a French flavor that suggests a Haitian ambiance of one's dreams, featuring tasty island dishes at moderately expensive prices. Reservations suggested. Subway: L to Third Ave. Open for dinner daily except Sun. Major credit cards.

Banco Stabile corner Mulberrry and Grand Sts.

The bank of choice on the Lower East Side for Italian immigrants during the early 1900s, this historic structure dates from the middle of the nineteenth century. Subway: J, M to Bowery; B, D, Q to Grand St.

Bang On a Can Festival (212) 777-8442 www.bangonacan.org

Annual international gathering of composers and performers involved in serious experimental and innovative music. Various locations around town, but recently it has been held in October in collaboration with the Brooklyn Academy of Music during the Next Wave Festival.

Bar Code/Galactic Circus 1540 Broadway btw 45th and 46th Sts. (212) 869-9397

This is a 2-story conglomeration of video games and other forms of electronic amusements and games plus food that delights kids at parents' expense every day until 4 p.m. Then it becomes an adults-only night club with a cover charge on Fri and Sat nights. Subway: N, R, S, 1, 2, 3, 7, 9 to 42nd St.-Times Square. Open daily 11 a.m.–2 a.m.

Barbecue and Ribs Restaurants *see* Brother Jimmy's Carolina Kitchen BBQ, Cowgirl Hall of Fame, Dallas BBQ, Emily's Restaurant, The Hog Pit, Sylvia's, Virgil's Real BBQ. *See also* Southern Restaurants.

Barbetta 321 W 46th St. btw Eighth and Ninth Aves. (212) 246-9171

Open since 1906, this restaurant provides elegant Old World charm and impeccable Northern Italian food in two antique-filled townhouses. The outdoor garden is delightful for summer dining. Fairly expensive, with reservations advisable. Subway: A, C, E to 42nd St.-Port Authority; C, E to 50th St. Lunch and dinner Tues–Sat. Closed Sun and Mon. Major credit cards.

Barbizon Hotel 140 E 63rd St. at Lexington Ave., NY 10021 (212) 838-5700 or (800) 223-1020, fax (212) 888-4271

Once a popular residence for women only, renovated and fully modern facilities are open to all and include a health and fitness club with Olympic-size pool. Room rates are moderately expensive. Subway: 4, 5, 6 to 59th St.; N, R to Lexington Ave.

Bard Graduate Center for Studies in the Decorative Arts 18 W 86th St. btw Central Park W and Columbus Ave. (212) 501-3000 www.bgc.bard.edu

This handsome townhouse center fosters study and exhibit of home furnishings and the decorative arts with rotating exhibitions. Subway: B, C to 86th St. Open Tues–Sun 11 a.m.–5 p.m. Closed Mon. Modest admission charge.

Bargemusic Fulton Ferry Landing at Water St., Brooklyn (718) 624-4061 www.bargemusic.org

An intimate chamber-music hall seating 130 inside a barge moored under the Brooklyn Bridge. World-class musicians and spectacular vistas promise a unique experience. Performances are held on weekend evenings and Sun matinees. Subway: 2, 3 to Clark St.; A, C to High St. Varying admission charges.

Barnard College Broadway and 117th St. (212) 854-5262 www. barnard.columbia.edu

Established within Columbia University in 1889 for the higher education of women, Barnard retains its single-sex status, independence, and distinguished reputation. The entrance is on Broadway just north of 116th St. Subway: 1, 9 to 116th St.

Barnes & Noble Main store at 105 Fifth Ave. at 18th St. (212) 807-0099

This familiar bookstore chain operates multiple well-stocked branches with books, videos, and music throughout the city, including Barnes & Noble Jr. stores for children. The biggest of its New York stores carries a large range of periodicals and newspapers at 2289 Broadway and 82nd St. (212) 362-8835. Call (212) 727-4810 for details of individual store events and programs. Subway: L, N, R, 4, 5, 6 to 14th St.-Union Square. Open daily, hours vary. Major credit cards.

Barney Greengrass 541 Amsterdam Ave. btw 86th and 87th Sts. (212) 724-4707

With takeout and cafeteria-type sit-down, few establishments rival Barney the Sturgeon King for sturgeon, lox, and whitefish, all at moderate prices. Subway: 1, 9 to 86th St. Breakfast and lunch Tues–Sun. Takeout until 6 p.m. Closed Mon. Cash preferred to credit cards.

Barney's New York 660 Madison Ave. at 61st St. (212) 826-8900 www.barneys.com

This elegant, high-priced department store has come a long way from its 1923 start as a men's resale clothier. The store is well known for its stylish selection of men's and women's designer fashions, smart home furnishings, and attractive children's clothing. Subway: 4, 5, 6 to 59th St.; N, R to Fifth Ave. Open daily, hours vary. Major credit cards.

El Barrio

The center of the city's Latin population, called Spanish Harlem or El Barrio, runs from the northeast corner of Central Park to the 140s and the Harlem River. It has been predominantly Puerto Rican, but East Harlem also includes a strong Haitian presence and the small remainder of an older Italian working-class section around 116th St. and First Ave. The main drag on 116th St. is the bustling scene of sales of every type of food, fruits, and clothing. Subway: 6 to 116th St.

Barrio Museum *see* El Museo del Barrio (under M).

Barrymore Theatre *see* Ethel Barrymore Theatre.

Bars *see* Carlyle Hotel, Keen's Steak House, King Cole Bar, McSorley's Old Ale House, Minetta Tavern, Old Town, Oyster Bar at Grand Central, Pete's Tavern, Walker's.

Bartow-Pell Mansion Museum and Garden 895 Shore Rd. at Pelham Bay Park, Bronx (718) 885-1461

This handsome nineteenth-century private residence was acquired and restored by the city. Greek Revival furnishings and extensive formal gardens are well maintained by the International Garden Club. Subway: 6 to Pelham Bay Park, then walk about a mile or continue by taking Bus BX45. Open Wed, Sat, Sun, noon–4 p.m. Modest admission charge.

Baruch College of the City University of New York 17 Lexington Ave. at 23rd St. (212) 802-2000 www.baruch.cuny.edu

Named for the celebrated financier Barnard Baruch, this college began as the business school branch of City College. Today it operates schools of business, liberal arts and sciences, and public affairs as well as a number of specialized institutes, such as the Weissman Center for International Business. Subway: 6 to 23rd St.

Baseball *see* Brooklyn Cyclones Baseball Team, New York Mets, New York Yankees.

Baseball Season (April–September)

Major League home teams are based at Shea Stadium (Mets) and Yankee Stadium (Yankees).

Basketball (participatory sport) *see* Chelsea Piers Sports Center, Jacob Riis Park, North River Park, Riverbank State Park.

Basketball (spectator sport) *see* New York Knicks, St. John's University Red Storm.

Basketball Season (October–April)

Local New York Knickerbockers (Knicks) play home games at Madison Square Garden.

Bastille Day

Alliance Française celebrates this French national event on the closest Sunday to July 14. Call (212) 355-6100 for details of holiday celebrations.

Bateaux New York Suite 200A Chelsea Piers, Pier 62, 23rd St. at West Side Hwy., NY 10011-1015 (212) 352-2022 www.bateauxnew york.com

This company offers scheduled brunch and dinner cruises around New York harbor, featuring music, dancing, entertainment, and skyline views in a luxurious, glass-enclosed vessel. Reservations are required. Subway: C, E to 23rd St.

Battery Park Broadway at Battery Pl.

This extensive public park at Manhattan's southern tip is named for a shoreline gun battery built during the War of 1812. The area contains a wealth of historic sites, monuments, statuary, and opportunities for stunning harbor views. Subway: 1, 9 to South Ferry; 4, 5 to Bowling Green.

Battery Park City bounded by Chambers and West Sts. and Battery Park

This mini-city, developed on 92 acres of reclaimed landfill along the Hudson River, is a mix of residential, commercial, and open space and is the site of the World Financial Center. It is also the site of the popular esplanade walkway and park that runs along the Hudson River north and south from the World Financial Center. Subway: N, R, 1, 9 to Cortlandt St.

Bay Ridge Brooklyn bounded by 61st and 86th Sts. and Gowanus Expressway and Upper New York Bay

This land, purchased from Native Americans by the Dutch West India Company in 1652, eventually became a favored neighborhood for Scandinavian and Italian populations. Following a post–World War II influx of Chinese and other nationalities, the area retains a comfortable, largely suburban character. Subway: R to 77th St.

Bayard-Condict Building 65 Bleecker St. btw Broadway and Lafayette St. at Crosby St.

This graceful 1898 office building is the only NYC work designed by the famous architect Louis Sullivan. Subway: B, D, F, Q to Broadway-Lafayette St.

Beaches *see* Brighton Beach, Coney Island, Jacob Riis Park, Manhattan Beach, Orchard Beach, The Rockaways.

Beacon Theatre 2124 Broadway btw 74th and 75th Sts. (212) 496-7070

Former Art Deco movie palace with fine acoustics is a favorite venue for concerts and is also used for occasional theatrical performances. Subway: 1, 2, 3, 9 to 72nd St.

Beaumont Theatre *see* Lincoln Center Theatre.

Becco 355 W 46th St. btw Eighth and Ninth Aves. (212) 397-7597

This busy and very popular family-style Italian restaurant serves antipasto, salad, and pasta selections at highly affordable prices. Reservations are a good idea. Subway: A, C, E to 42nd St.-Port Authority. Open for lunch and dinner. Major credit cards.

Beck Theatre *see* Martin Beck Theatre.

Bed and Breakfast Network of New York Suite 602, 134 W 32nd St., NY 10001 (212) 645-8134

This company arranges daily, weekly, and monthly hosted and unhosted accommodations, including multi-occupancy apartment suites.

Bed and Breakfast on the Park 113 Prospect Park W btw Sixth and Seventh Aves., Park Slope, Brooklyn 11215 (718) 499-6115, fax (718) 499-1385 www.bbnyc.com

This townhouse in the Park Slope area overlooks Prospect Park and offers eight double-occupancy rooms for rent, usually for a two-night minimum stay. Full breakfast is included in rates, which vary according to the specific accommodation. Subway: F to Seventh Ave. Major credit cards.

Bed-and-Breakfast Rental Agencies *see* At Home in New York, Bed and Breakfast Network of New York, City Lights Bed and Breakfast,

City Sonnet, Gamut Realty Group, New World Bed and Breakfast, Urban Ventures.

Bed-and-Breakfasts *see* Bed and Breakfast on the Park, Chelsea Brownstone, Foy House, Inn at Irving Place.

Bedford Street south of Christopher St.

This charming, quiet, well-kept, high-rent area is one of Greenwich Village's oldest. Subway: 1, 9 to Christopher St.-Sheridan Square.

Bedford-Stuyvesant Brooklyn bounded by Broadway and Saratoga, Flushing, Atlantic, and Classon Aves.

This area east of Fort Greene survives long-standing inner-city problems and racial conflict. Public and private economic development enterprises and an active African-American community are making determined efforts to reverse decades of urban neglect. Subway: G to Bedford-Nostrand Aves.

Bedloe's Island *see* Liberty Island.

Beekman Place bounded by East River and First Ave., 49th and 51st Sts.

Elegance and understatement characterize this small luxurious residence area for the rich and famous. Subway: 6 to 51st St.

Belasco Theatre 111 W 44th St. btw Sixth and Seventh Aves. (212) 239-6200

Built in 1908 by innovative playwright and all-round impresario David Belasco, this performance venue theatre retains a reputation for arresting productions. Subway: N, R, S, 1, 2, 3, 7, 9 to 42nd St.-Times Square.

Belmont Arthur Ave. and Fordham Rd., Bronx

Belmont was largely farmland until the late nineteenth century, when housing and commercial development were spurred by the extension of the Third Ave. elevated and construction of the Bronx Zoo. A population influx in the twentieth century led to neighborhood characterization as the Little Italy of the Bronx. Arthur Ave. is a busy street, with many shops offering tempting Italian food choices. Subway: B, D to Fordham Rd. followed by a 15-minute walk east to Arthur Ave.

Belmont Park and Race Track Hempstead Pkwy. and Plainfield Ave., Elmont, Long Island (718) 641-4700

This is a popular thoroughbred all-season race track. The park also offers Breakfast at Belmont family programs on weekends and holidays. Children will enjoy tram and pony rides and general horse-watching opportunities. Races take place Wed–Sun from May to October. Take Belmont Special Bus from Penn Station to Belmont Park or Long Island Station to Belmont Race Track stop. No credit cards.

Belmont Stakes Hempstead Pkwy. and Plainfield Ave., Elmont, Long Island (718) 641-4700
Belmont Park and Race Track is home to the Triple Crown's Belmont Stakes in June.

Belvedere Castle *see* Central Park Belvedere Castle, Central Park Conservancy.

Bemelman's Bar *see* Carlyle Hotel.

Ben Benson's Steak House 123 W 52nd St. btw Sixth and Seventh Aves. (212) 581-8888
Quintessential steakhouse atmosphere and fare make this a reliable choice for prime ribs, steak, chops, seafood, and well-prepared accompaniments at fairly expensive prices. Reservations suggested. Subway: N, R to 49th St. Lunch Mon–Fri, dinner daily. Major credit cards.

The Benjamin 125 E 50th St. at Lexington Ave., NY 10022 (212) 715-2500, fax (212) 715-7525 www.thebenjamin.com
Major refurbishment of the historic Hotel Beverly has created an up-to-date executive suite establishment. Offers full conference and high-tech communication facilities. Everything is first-rate, including An American Place restaurant located in the hotel. Prices are very steep, and services and facilities are outstanding. Subway: 6 to 51st St.; E, F to Lexington Ave.

Bensonhurst Brooklyn bounded by 61st St., McDonald Ave., Gravesend Bay, and Fourteenth Ave.
Once a largely homogeneous Italian enclave, Bensonhurst grew exponentially in neighborhood diversity in the twentieth century but retains much of its pleasant family, home, and church flavor. Several well-known Italian restaurants are located within the area. Subway: B, M to Eighteenth Ave.

Bergdorf Goodman 754 and 745 Fifth Ave. btw 57th and 58th Sts. (212) 753-7300
Long the ultimate in department store elegance for women's clothing and accessories, Bergdorf's maintains a similarly stylish and high-priced men's store across the street. Subway: E, F, N, R to Fifth Ave. Open Mon–Sat. Hours vary. Major credit cards.

Le Bernardin 155 W 51st St. btw Sixth and Seventh Aves. (212) 489-1515

Acclaimed as the best seafood restaurant in town, the menu features the freshest fish creatively prepared and beautifully served. The atmosphere and decor contribute to an exemplary and highly pleasurable dining experience, and this, of course, is reflected in the very high prices. Reservations well in advance are advisable. Subway: B, D, F, Q to 47th-50th Sts.-Rockefeller Center. Lunch Mon–Fri, dinner daily. Major credit cards.

Bessie Schonberg Theatre *see* Dance Theatre Workshop.

Best Western Manhattan 17 W 32nd St., NY 10001 (212) 736-1600 or (800) 567-7720, fax (212) 563-4007

This redecorated and modernized hotel offers reasonable rates and easy access to a busy city shopping area. Subway: B, D, F, N, Q, R to 34th St.-Herald Square.

Beth Hamedrash Hagodol Synagogue 50-64 Norfolk St. btw Grand and Broome Sts.

Well-preserved synagogue, once a Baptist Church, houses the oldest Orthodox congregation in the city to worship in one location. Subway: F, J, M, Z to Delancey St.

Bethesda Terrace *see* Central Park Bethesda Fountain and Terrace.

Bialystoker Synagogue 7-11 Willett St. off Grand St. (212) 475-0165

This former Methodist church was purchased in 1905 by Orthodox Jewish immigrants from Poland. Restoration work has resulted in a jewel-like interior. To see it, phone ahead to arrange for someone to show it before 10 a.m. Subway: F, J, M, Z to Delancey St.-Essex St.

Bice 7 E 54th St. btw Fifth and Madison Aves. (212) 688-1999

This stylish Art Deco restaurant has served fine Northern Italian cuisine for more than a decade. It continues to receive high marks from its well-heeled and satisfied patrons. Reservations suggested. Subway: 6 to 51st St.; E, F to Fifth Ave. Lunch and dinner daily. Major credit cards.

Bicycle Rentals *see* Central Park Loeb Boathouse.

Bicycle Tours *see* Central Park Bicycle Tours.

Bicycling

Central Park is a favorite place for cyclists, with its 7-mile circular drive that is closed to traffic on weekends and during certain hours on weekdays.

Bike rentals can be arranged at Central Park Loeb Boathouse on the Central Park Lake, mid-park near Fifth Ave. at E. 74th St. (212) 246-0520. Subway: 6 to 77th St. *See also* Cunningham Park, Dyckman Fields, Riverbank State Park, Riverside Park.

Big Apple Circus Damrosch Park at Lincoln Center btw 62nd and 66th Sts., Amsterdam and Columbus Aves. (212) 268-2500 www. bigapplecircus.org

This NYC-developed small circus follows a particular theme each year November–May and is geared to provide maximum enjoyment for children of all ages. Subway: 1, 9 to 66th St.-Lincoln Center. Ticket prices vary.

Big Apple Greeter 1 Centre St. at Chambers St., NY 10007 (212) 669-2896, fax (212) 669-3685 www.bigapplegreeter.com

This welcoming public service responds to out-of-towner requests for tours of NYC neighborhoods and attractions. Well-trained volunteer greeters are matched to visitor interests and language and accessibility requirements, and it is available without charge. The office is open Mon–Fri during usual business hours. Calling or writing ahead of time is very much encouraged. Subway: 4, 5, 6 to Brooklyn Bridge-City Hall.

Big Apple Parents' Paper 9 E 38th St., NY 10016 (212) 889-6400

This paper is available at children's museums, toy stores, and other likely spots around the city. It lists happenings and activities of interest to parents and is issued monthly and distributed free at many locations and also sold on a regular subscription basis.

Big City Kites 1210 Lexington Ave. at 82nd St. (212) 472-2623

This company's definition of kites extends to indoor mobiles and wall hangings as well as traditional versions. They also offer marvelous specialty kites, darts and accessories, and kite-repair services. Subway: 4, 5, 6 to 86th St. Open Mon–Sat, hours vary. Major credit cards.

Big Onion Walking Tours P.O. Box 20561, Cherokee Station, NY 10021 (212) 439-1090, fax (212) 794-0064 www.bigonion.com

This company schedules a wide array of sightseeing tours by knowledgeable and well-prepared guides. Excursions focus on ethnic neighborhoods and historic districts all over the city and last 2 to 2½ hours and are moderately priced.

Bike New York: The Great Five Boro Bike Tour (212) 932-2453 www.bikenewyork.com

Annual early-May 42-mile ride from Battery Park to Staten Island is the largest cycling event in the United States. The streets are cleared of cars all through the city for this tour, which goes to every borough before ending in a celebratory party in Staten Island before the free ferry return.

Bike Rentals *see* Central Park Loeb Boathouse.

Billiard Club 220 W 19th St. btw Seventh and Eighth Aves. (212) 206-7665

Upscale pool club with thirty-six tables offers alcoholic and non-alcoholic drinks in a small bar. Subway: C, E to 23rd St. Open daily from 11 a.m. Rates vary with time and day. Major credit cards.

Billiards *see* Pool.

Biography Bookshop 400 Bleecker St. at 11th St. (212) 807-8655

This entire store is devoted to recent titles on a wide range of personalities. It includes a section on gay and lesbian biography. Subway: L to Eighth Ave.; A, C, E to 14th St. Open daily, hours vary. Major credit cards.

Birdland 315 W 44th St. btw Eighth and Ninth Aves. (212) 581-3080 www.birdlandjazz.com

This supper club offers good food, well-located seating, and fine sound for first-rate jazz performed by well-known performers. Subway: A, C, E, to 42nd St.-Port Authority. Nightly dinner service and music performances. Charges for music. Major credit cards.

Bite of the Apple Central Park Bicycle Tour *see* Central Park Bicycle Tours.

Bitter End 149 Bleecker St. btw La Guardia Pl. and Thompson St. (212) 673-7030 www.bitterend.com

A folk music showcase since the 1960s, this small Village club also features blues, rock, and jazz talent. Subway: A, B, C, D, E, F, Q to W 4th St. Admission charge. Major credit cards.

Black Film Festival (212) 749-5298

Held annually in August during Harlem Week at the Adam Clayton Powell Jr. State Office Building Gallery, 163 W 125th St. at Adam Clayton Powell Blvd. Subway: A, B, C, D, 2, 3 to 125th St. Admission charge.

Black History Month

The Black experience is a major focus of NYC educational and cultural organizations throughout February, with many special events scheduled at various venues around town.

Black World Championship Rodeo (212) 860-2986

This rodeo is held every spring to highlight African-American involvement in the history of the American West. It takes place on Randall's Island in May.

Bleecker Street

Bleecker Street in Greenwich Village on both sides of Sixth Ave. has a long history of cafés and bars (east) and small, often unique shops (west). The area to the east allows for concentrated sampling of contemporary music. Subway: A, B, C, D, E, F, Q to W 4th St.

Blessing of the Animals Cathedral of St. John the Divine, 1047 Amsterdam Ave. at 112th St. (212) 316-7540

The October feast of St. Francis of Assisi is celebrated by a well-patronized ceremonial blessing of New Yorkers' pets. There follows a celebration and musical program, which is very popular, for which there is an admission charge, and with tickets sold out well in advance. Subway: 1, 9 to Cathedral Pkwy.-110th St.

Bliss Spa 568 Broadway at Prince St., 2nd Floor (212) 219-8970 www.blissworld.com

Relaxing spa treatments are enhanced by access to a buffet of attractively presented healthy snacks. Subway: N, R to Prince St. Open Mon–Sat, hours vary. Major credit cards.

The Block Beautiful E 19th St. btw Third and Park Aves.

The agreeably harmonious appearance of the restored 1920s houses on this serene, tree-lined street with decorative details on and in front of the buildings justify the name and a visit to this area, which was home to a number of theatrical stars of the early twentieth century. Subway: L to Third Ave.; 6 to 23rd St.

Bloomingdale's 1000 Third Ave. at 59th St. (212) 807-2000 www.bloomingdales.com

Enormous 9-story, block-long department store has a well-earned reputation for stylish and variegated merchandise ranging from cosmetics and clothing to furniture and food. It maintains many specialty boutiques and concessions and a number of in-house restaurants. Subway: N, R to Lexington Ave.; 4, 5, 6 to 59th St. Open daily, hours vary. Major credit cards.

The Blue Note 131 W 3rd St. btw MacDougal St. and Sixth Ave. (212) 475-8592 www.bluenote.net

Long-time premier jazz supper club offers a nightly schedule of big-name performers and less pricey post-show jam sessions on weekends. Subway: A, B, C, E, F, Q to W 4th St.-Washington Square.

Blue Rabbit International House 730 St. Nicholas Ave. near 145th St., NY 10031 (212) 491-3892 or (800) 6HOSTEL

This hostel provides dormitory lodging, a few double rooms, and kitchen access at very low prices and is located in a safe neighborhood close to a subway station. Reserve well in advance for busy seasons. Subway: A, B, C, D to 145th St. Cash or traveler's checks only.

Blue Water Grill 31 Union Square W at 16th St. (212) 675-9500

This restaurant's busy atmosphere and moderate prices attract an enthusiastic clientele. Raw bar and seafood specialties are featured, but many non-oceanic entrées and enticing desserts are available. Subway: L, N, R, 4, 5, 6 to 14th St.-Union Square. Lunch, dinner daily. Major credit cards.

Blues *see* Jazz Spots.

Bo Ky 80 Bayard St. btw Mott and Mulberry Sts. (212) 406-2292

This small informal Chinese-Vietnamese restaurant specializes in fragrant and filling noodle and fish soups at bargain prices. Subway: J, M, N, R, Z, 6 to Canal St. Lunch and dinner daily. Cash only.

Boat Tours *see* Atlantic Kayak Tours, Bateaux New York, Circle Line Cruises, New York Waterway, The Peking, Royal Princess and Excalibur, Spirit of New York Cruises, Staten Island Ferry, Statue of Liberty/Ellis Island Museum Ferry, World Yacht Cruises. *See also* Bus Tours, Helicopter Tours, Limousine Tours, Special Interest Tours, Walking Tours.

Boating

Rowboats can be rented at the Loeb Boathouse located on the 18-acre Central Park Lake near Fifth Ave. at E 74th St. (212) 517-4723. The 60-acre lake in Prospect Park in Brooklyn is where pedal boats are for rent at the Wollman Memorial Rink on weekends and holidays from April until Memorial Day (718) 282-7789. Subway: (Loeb Boathouse) 6 to 77th St.; (Wollman Memorial Rink) D to Parkside Ave.

Boca Chica 13 First Ave. at 1st St. (212) 473-0108

Lively, inexpensive spot to enjoy bountiful portions of spicy Brazilian and other Latin American dishes with music and dancing on weekends. Subway: F to Second Ave. Dinner Mon–Sat, Sun brunch. Major credit cards.

Bohemian Hall *see* Czechoslovak Festival.

Bond Street 6 Bond St. btw Broadway and Lafayette St. (212) 777-2500

This restaurant is notable for its stunning Japanese decor and beautifully presented cuisine. Choose from a wide array of sake and sushi in the cocktail lounge. Subway: 6 to Bleecker St. Dinner daily. Major credit cards.

Book and Poetry Readings *see* Academy of American Poets, Dia Center for the Arts, Drawing Center, Knitting Factory, Lincoln Center Library for the Performing Arts, Metropolitan Museum of Art, New School University, New York Public Library, New York Society of Ethical Culture, Nicholas Roerich Museum, 92nd Street Y, Nuyorican Poets Café, Performing Garage, *Poetry Calendar*, Poetry Project, Poetry Society of America, Poets' House, Rizzoli, St. Mark's Poetry Project, Strictly Roots, Symphony Space, Writers in Performance/Manhattan Theatre Club, Writer's Voice/West Side YMCA. *See also* Public Lectures.

Books of Wonder 16 W 18th St. btw Fifth and Sixth Aves. (212) 989-3270 www.booksofwonder.com

This delightful children's bookstore schedules story hours and author talks. Subway: L, N, R, 4, 5, 6 to Union Square. Open daily, hours vary. Major credit cards.

Bookstores *see* Argosy Bookstore, Barnes & Noble, Biography Bookshop, Books of Wonder, Borders Books and Music, Coliseum Books, Complete Traveller Bookstore, Drama Bookshop, Forbidden Planet, Gotham Book Mart, Gryphon Book Shop, Hacker Art Books, Liberation Book Shop, Murder Ink, Mysterious Bookshop, New York Palace Hotel, Rizzoli, St. Marks Bookshop, Shakespeare & Company, Strand Book Store, Strictly Roots, Three Lives and Company, Tompkins Square Books and Records, Tower Books Records and Video, Unoppressive Bargain Books.

Boone Gallery *see* Mary Boone Gallery.

Booth Theatre 222 W 45th St. btw Broadway and Eighth Ave. (212) 239-6200

This well-maintained theatre, named for the celebrated nineteenth-century actor Edwin Booth, has a long history of successful productions. Subway: N, R, S, 1, 2, 3, 7, 9 to Times Square-42nd St.

Borders Books and Music 461 Park Ave. at 57th St. (212) 980-6785
www.borders.com

This major chain offers an impressive inventory, helpful staff, and a coffee bar. Other location at 550 Second Ave. between 31st and 32nd Sts. (212) 685-3938. Subway: (Park Ave. store) 4, 5, 6 to 59th St.; (Second Ave. store) 6 to 33rd St. Open daily, hours vary. Major credit cards.

Borough Park Brooklyn

Bounded by 37th St., McDonald Ave., 64th St., and Eighth Ave., this is home to a large community of Hasidic Jews. The neighborhood is largely middle class and self-contained, featuring many Orthodox synagogues, religious schools, and celebrations of ritual feast days. Its main shopping area is along Thirteenth Ave. Subway: B, M to 55th St.

Boroughs of New York

The five boroughs of the Bronx, Brooklyn, Manhattan, Queens, and Staten Island are distinct administrative divisions of NYC covering 301 square miles on the mainland (the Bronx), islands in the New York Bay (Manhattan and Staten Island), and Long Island (Brooklyn and Queens). *See also* entries for individual boroughs.

Boston Comedy Club 82 W 3rd St. btw Thompson and Sullivan Sts. (212) 477-1000

This club is named after the owner's hometown. The club's exuberant audience appraises established and aspiring comedy acts from all over. Subway: A, B, C, D, E, F, Q to W 4th St.-Washington Square. Open nightly. Cover charge and two-drink minimum on weekends. Major credit cards.

The Bottom Line 15 W 4th St. at Mercer St. (212) 228-6300 www.
bottomlinecabaret.com

This large cabaret has long been a popular place to check out the old and new in rock, jazz, folk, and country music performers. Subway: N, R to 8th St.-NYU; A, B, C, D, E, F, Q to W 4th St. Open nightly, usually with two shows. Cover charge. No credit cards.

Bouley Bakery 120 W Broadway btw Duane and Reade Sts. (212) 964-2525

Expect premium French-American food, bread, and prices in enterprising master chef David Bouley's intimate restaurant. Innovative culinary combinations and the freshest ingredients characterize his menus. Subway: 1, 9 to Franklin St. Lunch and dinner daily. Major credit cards.

Bouterin 420 E 59th St. near First Ave. (212) 758-0323

Charming decoration and satisfying fare shout *provençal* in this French country dining room. Lamb stew and bouillabaisse are typical menu items; vegetarian selections are also available at this moderately expensive, beautifully appointed restaurant where reservations are suggested. Subway: 4, 5, 6 to 59th St.; N, R to Lexington Ave. Dinner served daily. Major credit cards.

Bouwerie Lane Theatre 330 Bowery at Bond St. (212) 677-0060

This late-nineteenth-century, cast-iron bank building now houses Jean Cocteau Repertory Company presentations of dramatic performances. Subway: A, F to Second Ave.; 6 to Bleecker St.

The Bowery

This mile-long thoroughfare in Lower Manhattan running from Chatham Square to Cooper Square has gone through many identity changes, from colonial farmland, to nineteenth-century elegance, to early-twentieth-century squalor. Stretching through Chinatown with a middle concentration of commercial shops and cafés and clubs at the north end, areas along the Bowery are currently the focus of renovation and gentrification efforts. Subway: J, M to Bowery.

Bowery Ballroom 6 Delancey St. at Bowery (212) 533-2111 www. boweryballroom.com

This roomy venue for an impressive variety of rock acts is notable for fine acoustics and staging, sensible seating arrangements, and conveniently located bars. Subway: J, M to Bowery; 6 to Spring St. Open on nights bands perform. Admission charge. Cash only. Minimum drinks charge.

Bowery Savings Bank Building 130 Bowery at Grand St. and 110 E 42nd St. btw Park and Third Aves.

Monumental sister buildings are characterized by handsome façades and vast domed interiors featuring marble columns. Bank and branches were purchased by Home Savings Bank in 1992. Subway: (Bowery building) B, D, Q to Grand St.; (42nd St. building) B, D, F, Q to 42nd St.

Bowling *see* Bowlmor Lanes, Leisure Time Bowling and Recreation Center.

Bowling Green

This small oval green space at the foot of Broadway and north of Battery Park is NYC's oldest public park, dating from colonial times. Fully restored by the city in the twentieth century, the area retains indications of its historic past. Subway: 1, 9 to South Ferry; N, R to Whitehall St.

Bowlmor Lanes 110 University Pl. btw 12th and 13th Sts. (212) 255-8188 www.bowlmor.com

In addition to forty-two lanes, this historic bowling alley has been put to post-modern use and also offers food and drink, a sports bar, party rooms, a dance floor, and upper-level tennis courts. Subway: L, N, R, 4, 5, 6 to 14th St.-Union Square. Open daily, hours vary. Major credit cards.

Bowne House 3701 Bowne St. at Thirty-Seventh Ave., Flushing, Queens (718) 359-0528

This saltbox structure was built in 1661 by religious dissenter John Bowne, who held then-illegal Quaker meetings in the kitchen. Subsequently occupied by nine generations of Bownes, the house has become an emblem for religious tolerance. It is both a national and a city landmark. Periodic exhibitions and lectures are held in the gallery. Subway: 7 to Main St., then Bus Q12 or Q28. Open afternoons Tues–Sun. Modest admission charge.

Boxing *see* Golden Gloves Boxing Championships, Madison Square Garden.

Brandy's Piano Bar 235 E 84th St. btw Second and Third Aves. (212) 650-1944 www.brandyspianobarnyc.com

A big attraction here is nightly staff renditions of Broadway show music and other popular tunes. Subway: 4, 5, 6 to 86th St. Open nightly 4 p.m.–4 a.m. Music starts at 9:30 p.m. Two-drink minimum. No credit cards.

Brazilian Carnival W 46th St.

This annual all-day music and dancing fiesta celebrates Brazil's Independence Day on the first Saturday in September from early morning to 9 at night. The liveliest spot is at the corner of Sixth Ave. and 46th St. Subway: B, D, F, Q to 47th-50th Sts.-Rockefeller Center.

Brazilian Restaurants *see* Boca Chica, Cabana Carioca, Churrascaria Plataforma, Ipanema.

Brecht Forum 122 W 27th St. btw Sixth and Seventh Aves., 10th Floor (212) 242-4201

This group offers educational programs and discussions centered on liberal themes, plus lectures and literature readings. Subway: 1, 9 to 28th St.

Bridge Café 279 Water St. at Dover St. (212) 227-3344

This cheerful old restaurant features homey food at affordable prices and a great variety of beers and domestic wines. It is located just north of the South Street Seaport. Subway: A, C, J, M, Z, 2, 3, 4, 5 to Fulton St.-Broadway Nassau.

Bridges *see* Brooklyn Bridge, George Washington Bridge, Queensboro Bridge, Verrazano-Narrows Bridge, Williamsburg Bridge.

Brighton Beach Brooklyn

Long a Russian Jewish enclave, this neighborhood is bounded by Neptune Ave., Corbin Pl., the Atlantic Ocean, and Ocean Pkwy. This seaside area and its boardwalk along the sea have been revitalized by the post-1970s influx of Russian émigrés. Designated "Little Odessa," this part of New York is the destination for Russian shopping, foods, restaurants, and boisterous and lively entertainment. Subway: D, Q to Brighton Beach.

Broadhurst Theatre 235 W 44th St. btw Broadway and Eighth Ave. (212) 239-6200

This is one of several early-twentieth-century theatres maintaining a record of well-reviewed productions. Subway: N, R, S, 1, 2, 3, 7, 9 to Times Square-42nd St.

Broadway

This wide thoroughfare runs the length of Manhattan, but the name Broadway is used synonymously with the world-famous term "Great White Way" for the theatrical district in and around Broadway from 42nd to around 50th Sts. This appellation stems from the thousands of bright lights illuminating the area. Central Times Square has seen enhanced security and cleaning activity in recent years, making it an exceedingly busy and family-friendly place from early morning to late at night. Subway: N, R, S, 1, 2, 3, 7, 9 to Times Square-42nd St.

Broadway Diner 590 Lexington Ave. at E 52nd St. (212) 486-8838

Re-creating the flavor and fare of the 1950s, this upscale coffee and hamburger destination is a particularly good breakfast choice. A second location is at 1726 Broadway at W 55th St. (212) 765-0909. Subway: (Lexington Ave.) 6 to 51st St.; (Broadway) B, D, E to Seventh Ave. Open daily, hours vary. No credit cards.

Broadway Inn 264 W 46th St. btw Broadway and Eighth Ave., NY 10036 (212) 997-9200 or (800) 826-6300, fax (212) 768-2807 www.broadwayinn.com.

This homey and hospitable little hotel in the theatre district provides nicely decorated, clean, small rooms and includes continental breakfast at modest room rates. Subway: A, C, E to 42nd St.-Port Authority. Major credit cards.

Broadway on Broadway Times Square (212) 768-1560

One Sunday in early September cast members from current Broadway musicals give a free public outdoor show at midday. Subway: N, R, S, 1, 3, 7, 9 to 42nd St.-Times Square.

Broadway Theatre 1681 Broadway btw 52nd and 53rd Sts. (212) 239-6200

Built to show movies in the 1920s, this converted theatre is notable for staging long-running musicals. Subway: 1, 9 to 50th St.

Broadway Theatres *see* Ambassador Theatre, American Airlines Theatre, Belasco Theatre, Booth Theatre, Broadhurst Theatre, Broadway Theatre, Brooks Atkinson Theatre, Cort Theatre, Ethel Barrymore Theatre, Eugene O'Neill Theatre, Gershwin Theatre, Golden Theatre, Helen Hayes Performing Arts Center, Imperial Theatre, Lunt-Fontanne Theatre, Lyceum Theatre, Majestic Theatre, Marquis Theatre, Martin Beck Theatre, Minskoff Theatre, Music Box Theatre, Nederlander Theatre, Neil Simon Theatre, New Victory Theatre, Palace Theatre, Plymouth Theatre, Richard Rodgers Theatre, Royale Theatre, St. James Theatre, Shubert Theatre, Studio 54, Virginia Theatre, Walter Kerr Theatre, Winter Garden Theatre. *See also New York* magazine, *The New Yorker, Time Out New York, Village Voice.*

The Bronx

At one time the city's northernmost borough was known best for its well-to-do suburban enclave with its Grand Concourse lined by handsome apartment buildings. Later it became infamous for its violence and urban decay, which were quite pronounced in the South Bronx section. But the attractions of the only borough of the city attached to the mainland of North America remain appealing, and much of the disintegration of the 1960s to the 1990s is gradually being remedied. The Bronx remains home to some of the city's most attractive visitor destinations, including its celebrated botanic garden and the largest and oldest zoo in New York. Pelham Bay Park in the northeastern part of the borough is the city's largest park, and among its other notable tourist enticements are the Belmont neighborhood Little Italy and the New England-like City Island, with its distinctive small-town and maritime flavor.

Bronx Botanical Garden *see* New York Botanical Garden.

Bronx Community College *see* Hall of Fame for Great Americans.

Bronx County Historical Society Museum 3266 Bainbridge Ave. btw Van Cortlandt Ave. and 208th St., Bronx (718) 881-8900 www. bronxhistoricalsociety.org

This museum is located in an eighteenth-century farmhouse known as the Valentine Varian House. The society also sponsors tours exploring various neighborhoods and aspects of the Bronx. Subway: D to Norwood-205th St. Open Sat and Sun afternoons. Modest admission charge.

Bronx Museum of the Arts 1040 Grand Concourse at 165th St., Bronx (718) 681-6000

Museum collections and exhibits concentrate on contemporary works by minority and women artists, local talent, and distinctly urban art forms, including graffiti. Subway: 4, B, D to 161st St.-Yankee Stadium. Open Wed–Sun, hours vary. Modest admission charge.

Bronx Zoo *see* International Wildlife Conservation Park.

Brooklyn

This is the city's most populous borough, with some 2.5 million residents. If it were a separate city, it would be the fourth largest in the United States. Second only to Manhattan, this 70-square-mile area on the southeast tip of Long Island is the city's most popular place to visit. Its ethnically diverse neighborhoods are almost as innumerable as its celebrated attractions, such as Brooklyn Heights, Coney Island, and Prospect Park. What Brooklyn holds in store for the visitor is a fascinating mélange of strikingly different and interesting cultures, reflecting the lives of the many inhabitants who make their homes in this vibrant borough.

Brooklyn Academy of Music (BAM) 30 Lafayette Ave. btw Flatbush Ave. and Fulton St. (718) 636-4100 www.bam.org

The world-class and oldest U.S. performing arts center, BAM offers outstanding classical and avant-garde music, dance, and drama in a number of performance spaces. Brooklyn Philharmonic is the resident company, and an annual international Next Wave Festival each fall and winter showcases contemporary cutting-edge works and performers. BAM also sponsors during July and August its Concerts in the Park series, with performances at a number of Brooklyn parks. Information and park directions are available at (212) 360-8290 or www.cityparksfoundation.org. Subway: G to Fulton St.; D, Q, 2, 3, 4, 5 to Atlantic Ave.; B, N, R to Pacific St.

Brooklyn Academy of Music Next Wave Festival *see* Next Wave Festival.

Brooklyn Attitude Tours (718) 398-0939

This group offers two types of tours, usually on Saturday. One is a combination of bus and walking. The other is limited to walking, using public transportation while concentrating on only two or three interesting neighborhoods.

Brooklyn Beerfest N 11th St. btw Berry St. and Wythe Ave., Brooklyn (718) 486-7422

This annual September beer- and ale-tasting event is held outside the Brooklyn Brewery in Williamsburg and includes informal chats on beer-making and characteristics by industry representatives. Subway: L to Bedford Ave.

Brooklyn Borough Hall 209 Joralemon St. at Fulton and Court Sts. (718) 875-4047

This majestic restored Greek Revival building dates to the mid-nineteenth century and features a cast-iron and brass cupola and Tuckahoe marble inside and out. Subway: 2, 3, 4, 5 to Borough Hall.

Brooklyn Botanic Garden 1000 Washington Ave. btw Eastern Pkwy. and Empire Blvd. (718) 623-7200 www.bbg.org

Fifty acres of gardens, originally designed in 1910 by the famed Olmstead brothers, include a rose garden, children's garden, garden for the blind, and Shakespeare garden. Other major attractions are the authentic Japanese garden, bonsai collection, and annual cherry blossom festival. Subway: 2, 3 to Eastern Pkwy.-Brooklyn Museum. Closed Mon. Hours vary on other days. Modest admission charge. No credit cards.

Brooklyn Bridge over East River btw Manhattan and Brooklyn

Construction of the first steel suspension bridge took 14 years, finally opening in 1883 to world acclaim as an engineering and architectural wonder. The soaring span provides stunning views of the New York harbor and skyline and invites a 40-minute walk across its entire length. Subway: (in Manhattan) 4, 5, 6 to Brooklyn Bridge-City Hall; (in Brooklyn) A, C to High St.

Brooklyn Bridge Day

Celebration of this spectacular landmark occurs on its anniversary on May 24.

Brooklyn Center for the Performing Arts Brooklyn College campus, one block west of junction of Flatbush and Nostrand Aves. (718) 951-4530 www.brooklyncenter.com

The center hosts a series of musical and dance events during the academic year. Soloists of international acclaim and traveling opera companies are among the attractions. Subway: 2, 5 to Flatbush Ave.-Brooklyn College.

Brooklyn Center for the Urban Environment Tours Tennis House, Prospect Park, Brooklyn (718) 788-8500

Tours cover a variety of Brooklyn areas, focusing on natural and architectural aspects. Summertime programs offer eating and walking investigations of ethnic neighborhoods.

Brooklyn Children's Museum 145 Brooklyn Ave. at St. Mark's Ave., Brooklyn (718) 735-4400

Founded in 1899 as the first children's museum, the completely modernized spaces and imaginative programs appeal to teenagers as well as the very young. Changing exhibits and workshops on the way things work and on global cultures emphasize interactive hands-on learning. Subway: 3 to Kingston Ave.; C to Kingston-Throop. Closed Mon and Tues. Hours vary on other days. Modest admission charge.

Brooklyn Conservatory of Music Concert Hall 58 Seventh Ave. at Lincoln Plaza, Brooklyn (718) 622-3300 www.brooklynconservatory. com

In addition to first-rate music education programs, the conservatory presents concerts in a completely restored 5-story mansion in the heart of Brooklyn's Park Slope neighborhood. Subway: F to Seventh Ave.

Brooklyn Cyclones Baseball Team www.brooklyncyclones.com

In June 2001 baseball returned to Brooklyn for the first time since the borough was deserted by the Dodgers. The new minor-league New York Mets farm team plays its home games at the new Key Span Park in Coney Island, at Surf Ave. between W 16th and W 19th Sts. Ticket and schedule information is available at (718) 449-8497. Subway: B, D, F, N to Coney Island-Stillwell Ave.

Brooklyn Heights

The neighborhood is bounded by Columbia Heights and Brooklyn-Queens Expressway, Court St., Cadman Plaza W, and Atlantic Ave. It is one of the city's loveliest and most affluent areas. Well-preserved nineteenth-century brownstone houses and tree-lined streets characterize the pleasant hilltop neighborhood that was NYC's first suburb. A riverfront promenade offers panoramic views of Manhattan skyscrapers across the East River. Subway: N, R to Court St.; 2, 3, 4, 5 to Borough Hall.

Brooklyn Heights Promenade *see* The Promenade.

Brooklyn Historical Society Museum 128 Pierrepont St. at Clinton St., Brooklyn (718) 254-9830 www.brooklynhistory.org

After a considerable building renovation, the museum reopened at the end of 2001. Here one can find exhibitions on the borough's history and development, the role that the construction of the Brooklyn Bridge played, Coney Island's place in the history of Brooklyn, and material on baseball's early years and the old Brooklyn Dodgers. The museum also sponsors walking tours of Brooklyn neighborhoods. Subway: N, R to Court St.; 3, 4, 5 to Borough Hall. Open Tues–Sat afternoons. Modest admission charge. No credit cards.

Brooklyn Information and Culture (BRIC) 647 Fulton St., Brooklyn 11217 (718) 855-7882 www.brooklynny.org

This group offers information about activities and events in Brooklyn. BRIC also issues a free quarterly calendar of what's happening in the borough, *Meet Me in Brooklyn.*

Brooklyn Museum of Art (BMA) 200 Eastern Pkwy. at Washington Ave., Brooklyn (718) 638-5000

Housed in a monumental Beaux Arts building, BMA's impressive collections are particularly strong in ancient Egyptian, African, and American art and sculpture. Public programs are extensive, including lectures, concerts, films, tours, and children's shows. Recent exhibitions of controversial contemporary works have drawn wide attention and large crowds to the institution. Subway: 2, 3 to Eastern Pkwy.-Brooklyn Museum. Open Wed–Sun, hours vary. Modest admission charge. No credit cards.

Brooklyn Navy Yard East River at Wallabout Bay

At the southern end of Williamsburg at the East River at Wallabout Bay is the vast and now deserted construction site of some of the famous battleships of World War II. It continues to be considered as the site for prospective new ventures. Subway: F to York St.

Brooklyn Public Library Grand Army Plaza at Flatbush Ave. and Eastern Pkwy., Brooklyn (718) 730-2100 www.brooklynpublic library.org

The central library of the Brooklyn library system is located in a 1941 Art Deco structure built to resemble an open book. Bronze figures sculpted over the entrance represent characters drawn from American literature. The building's grandeur rivals the better known New York Public Library main building. The library sponsors a wide range of public lectures and readings. Subway: 2, 3 to Grand Army Plaza.

Brooks Atkinson Theatre 256 W 47th St. btw Broadway and Eighth Ave. (212) 719-4099

This fine old theatre, renamed in 1960 for the revered *New York Times* drama critic, continues to stage successful productions. Subway: 1, 9 to 50th St.

Brother Jimmy's Carolina Kitchen BBQ 1461 First Ave. at E 76th St. (212) 288-0999

This restaurant features good ol' down-home food at moderate prices and a late-night bar. A second location is at 428 Amsterdam Ave. at W 70th St. (212) 501-7515. Subway: (First Ave.) 6 to 77th St.; (Amsterdam Ave.) 1, 2, 3, 9 to 72nd St. Open Thurs–Sun for lunch. Dinner served every day. Major credit cards.

Brownie's 169 Ave. A btw 10th and 11th Sts. (212) 420-8392

Local bands and comfortable hangout flavor tend to pack in the college crowd. Subway: F to Second Ave. Open nightly from 8 p.m. Admission charge. Cash only. Minimum drink charge.

Bryant Park Sixth Ave. btw W 40th and 42nd Sts. www.bryant park.org

This city-renovated 7 acres of green space in mid-Manhattan is a beautiful place for year-round relaxation. Lively summertime programs feature free performances of music and dance, and old-time movie favorites are shown on Monday nights. The park also contains an attractive outdoor café. Subway: N, R, S, 1, 2, 3, 7, 9 to Times Square-42nd St.

Bryant Park Film Festival Sixth Ave. btw W 40th and 42nd Sts.

This festival provides movie classics on a giant outdoor screen free every Monday, early evening (rain date Tuesday), from mid-June to Labor Day. Details are available at (212) 512-5700. Subway: N, R, S, 1, 2, 3, 7, 9 to Times Square-42nd St.

Bubby's Restaurant Bar and Bakery 118 Hudson St. btw Franklin and N Monroe Sts. (212) 219-0666

This homey restaurant offers healthful traditional food in TriBeCa at unpretentious prices. Subway: 1, 9 to Franklin St. Lunch and dinner daily. Major credit cards.

Budget Accommodations *see* Hostels, YMCA/YWCAs.

Buggy Rides *see* Horse-Drawn Carriage Rides.

Burgers *see* Hamburgers.

Bus Maps *see* Maps of New York City.

Bus Tours *see* City Sightseeing, Discovery Tour, Gray Line Sightseeing, Harlem Spirituals, Harlem Your Way!, Kramer's Reality Tours,

92nd Street Y, Val Ginter Walking Tours. *See also* Boat Tours, Helicopter Tours, Limousine Tours, Special Interest Tours, Walking Tours.

Buses

New York City is served by more than 200 bus lines. In Manhattan buses run uptown on First, Third, Madison, Sixth, Eighth, and Tenth Aves. Going downtown they are on Second, Fifth, Seventh, and Ninth Aves. They also run crosstown at 14th, 23rd, 34th, 42nd, 57th, 65th, and 79th Sts. Free transfers are available to crosstown and vice versa. Fare in Manhattan and the Bronx is $1.50 in exact change (no bills) or a token. Seniors and disabled travel at half price. Small children ride free. Buses are often stuck in traffic, but they are less expensive than taxis and cleaner, quieter, and safer than subways, which are very much faster. Information on city buses is available at the New York City Transit Authority (718) 330-1234.

CBGB & OMFUG 315 Bowery at Bleecker St. (212) 982-4052
The acronym name of this widely known punk-rock club recalls its 1973 opening as a venue for country, bluegrass, blues, and other music for uplifting gourmandizers. They have somewhat less impressive bookings in recent times, but still loud and jumping. Subway: 6 to Bleecker St. Open nightly. Admission charge. No credit cards.

CBS Building 51 W 52nd St. at Sixth Ave.
This handsome 38-story building designed by Eero Saarinen and built in 1965 houses the Columbia Broadcasting System corporate headquarters. Subway: B, D, F, Q to 47th-50th Sts.-Rockefeller Center.

C.M. Tours *see* Discover NY City Walking Tours.

CRS (800) 555-7555 www.crshotels.com
Central Reservation Service offers discounted hotel rates in various cities, including NYC. Payment is made to the hotel upon arrival.

Cabana Carioca 123 W 45th St. btw Sixth Ave. and Broadway (212) 581-8088 www.cabanacarioca.citysearch.com
This lively decorative restaurant serves large portions of Brazilian and Portuguese specialties without stretching the pocketbook. For an authentic Brazilian experience, try the assertive indigenous drink *caipirinha*. Subway: N, R, S, 1, 2, 3, 7, 9 to Times Square-42nd St. Lunch and dinner daily. Major credit cards.

Cabarets *see* Comedy Clubs, Night Clubs, Supper Club.

Cabs *see* Taxis.

Café Boulud Surrey Hotel, 20 E 76th St. btw Fifth and Madison Aves. (212) 772-2600

Café offers consistently delicious selections in four basic categories—classic French, seasonal, vegetarian, and a variety of national cuisines—at prices reflecting chef Daniel Boulud's well-deserved reputation. Compares favorably with Boulud's even more upscale and expensive flagship restaurant, Daniel. Subway: 6 to 77th St. Lunch Tues–Sat, dinner daily. Reservations suggested. Major credit cards.

Café Carlyle *see* Carlyle Hotel.

Café des Artistes 1 W 67th St. btw Central Park W and Columbus Ave. (212) 877-3500 www.cafedesartistesnyc.com

Close to the Lincoln Center complex, this delightful restaurant is a perfect choice for pre- and post-dining and proof positive that an intimate, special-occasion ambiance can be created in a fairly large space. Although the tariff is high, so is enjoyment of the sprightly Howard Chandler Christy murals on the walls and delicious continental menu. Subway: 1, 9 to 66th St.-Lincoln Center. Lunch Mon–Fri, brunch Sat–Sun, dinner daily. Major credit cards.

Café Gitane 242 Mott St. btw Prince and Houston Sts. (212) 334-9552

Informal coffee- and teahouse offers inventive salads, sandwiches, and desserts, and very cheerful service. Subway: B, D, F, Q to Broadway-Lafayette St. Open daily from 9 a.m. No credit cards.

Café on Five Bergdorf Goodman, 754 Fifth Ave. btw 57th and 58th Sts. (212) 753-7300

This cozy inexpensive tea shop provides a welcome shopping break. Subway: E, F, N, R to Fifth Ave. Open daily from 11 a.m. Major credit cards.

Caffé Bianco 1486 Second Ave. btw 77th and 78th Sts. (212) 988-2655

Delightful uptown meeting spot is known for fine coffee, decadent desserts, and summertime seating in a backyard garden. Subway: 6 to 77th St. Daily 11 a.m.–11 p.m. Major credit cards.

Caffé Dante 79-81 MacDougal St. btw Hudson and Bleecker Sts. (212) 982-5275

Provider of excellent coffee variations and Italian sweets since 1915, the café is favored by local NYU students and faculty. Subway: A, B, C, D, E, F, Q to W 4th St. Open daily 10 a.m.–2 a.m. No credit cards.

Caffé Ferrara 195-201 Grand St. btw Mott and Mulberry Sts. (212) 226-6150

Flagship Grand St. operation has been serving espresso and variations inside and outside since 1892. Great sandwiches, pastries, and specialties at all locations reflect the Little Italy origins. Other locations: 1700 Broadway at 53rd St. (212) 581-3335 and 363 Madison Ave. at 45th St. (212) 599-7800. Subway: (Grand St.) N, R to Canal St.; 6 to Spring St.; (Broadway) 1, 9 to 50th St.; (Madison Ave.) S, 4, 5, 6, 7 to Grand Central-42nd St. Open daily 8 a.m.–midnight. No credit cards.

Caffé La Fortuna 69 W 71st St. btw Central Park W and Columbus Ave. (212) 724-5846

Comfortable West Side coffeehouse with garden is a fine choice for peace and quiet and spectacular Italian pastries. Subway: B, C to 72nd St. Open daily noon–midnight. Cash only.

Caffé Reggio 119 MacDougal St. btw Bleecker and W 3rd Sts. (212) 475-9557

Billed as the oldest Greenwich Village coffeehouse, Reggio's features an intimate ambiance, outside seating in pleasant weather, and typically good coffee and pastry choices. Subway: A, B, C, D, E, F, Q to W 4th St. Open Mon–Fri 9 a.m.–2 a.m., Sat–Sun 9 a.m.–4 a.m. No credit cards.

Caffé Roma 385 Broome St. btw Mulberry and Mott Sts. (212) 226-8413

Another contender for oldest coffeehouse honors, Roma's boasts authentic old-time furnishings and a display of homemade Italian goodies, as well as a wonderful *baba au rhum*. Subway: 6 to Spring St., J, M to Bowery. Open daily 8 a.m.–midnight. No credit cards.

Cafés *see* Café Gitane, Caffé Bianco, Caffé Dante, Caffé Ferrara, Caffé La Fortuna, Caffé Reggio, Caffé Roma, E.A.T., Elephant and Castle, Sarabeth's Kitchen. *See also* Coffee and Cakes.

Cajun 129 Eighth Ave. near 15th St. (212) 691-6174

You won't have to leave the city to get a low-cost trip to New Orleans. Cajun's creole fare and live jazz create a genuine Bourbon Street ambiance. Subway: A, C, E, L to 14th St. Open nightly from 4 p.m. for dinner. Music begins after 8 p.m. Major credit cards.

Cajun Restaurants *see* Cajun, Great Jones Café, Mardi Gras. *See also* Southern Restaurants.

Campbell Funeral Home *see* Frank E. Campbell Funeral Chapel.

Canaan Baptist Church of Christ 132 W 116th St. btw Adam Clayton Powell Jr. Blvd. and Lenox Ave. (212) 866-0301

Participation of a large, enthusiastic congregation and fervent and skilled gospel choirs make for a joyful Sunday morning service. Gospel music is also available at the church on some Sunday afternoons. Subway: 2, 3 to 116th St.

Canal Street

This broad street is at TriBeCa's northern end and runs across town and through Chinatown. Beginning at its western end it is filled with stores and outdoor displays of bargains in hardware, electronics, car accessories, clothing, and other assorted goods. In Chinatown, with its bazaars and banks, Canal Street offers a unique glimpse into stateside Chinese enterprise and is a great place to stroll and shop among the crowds. Here can be found a dizzying array of goods, from handsome and expensive Chinese imports, to routine street vendors selling their wares, to flea market miscellanea, to fresh seafood and produce. Subway: 1, 9 to Canal St. (on west); A, C, E to Canal St. (at Sixth Ave.); J, M, N, R, Z to Canal St. (at Chinatown).

Canton 45 Division St. near the Bowery (212) 226-4441

You will pay a little bit more for Chinese fare, but not to worry. The restaurant has been well known and patronized for decades due to its superior, individually prepared Cantonese dishes and extremely pleasant service. Seafood is a specialty. Subway: F to E Broadway. Open daily noon–10 p.m. Beer only served, but bring your own bottle. No credit cards.

Carapan 5 W 16th St. btw Fifth and Sixth Aves. (212) 633-6220

Tranquil spa-like facility aims to provide a boost for body and spirit. Subway: F to 14th St.; L to Sixth Ave. Open daily 10 a.m.–9:45 p.m. Major credit cards.

La Caravelle Shoreham Hotel, 33 W 55th St. btw Fifth and Sixth Aves. (212) 586-4252

For a generous taste of gracious living, head for La Caravelle, where fine French cuisine and impeccable service have been available for many years. The harmonious decor, featuring Jean Page's murals, contributes to an elegant and thoroughly delightful, if not inexpensive, experience. Subway: Q to 57th St. Lunch Mon–Fri, dinner Mon–Sat. Closed Sun. Reservations suggested. Major credit cards.

Caribbean Restaurants *see* Bambou, Island Spice, Lola, Negril, Patria, S.O.B.'s, Tropica.

Carl Schurz Park btw 84th and 90th Sts., East End Ave., and East River

Named for the nineteenth-century German-American military, government, and editorial notable, the park is an Upper–East Side haven of rec-reation areas, playgrounds, and urban greenery. A wide walkway along the East River offers great views of river activity, bridges, and islands. Subway: 4, 5, 6 to 86th St., then Bus M86 to the park.

Carlyle Hotel 35 E 76th St. btw Madison and Park Aves. (212) 744-1600

A bastion of gentility-cum-celebrity, this fine hotel has provided privi-lege and privacy to Astors, Kennedys, Princess Di, Elizabeth Taylor, and the like throughout its seventy-odd years. Luxurious appointments abound, and attendance by the loyal and discreet staff may be taken for granted. For the well-heeled resident and non-resident alike, there's the Café Carlyle (212) 570-7189, presenting regular engagements of Bobby Short's urbane piano music and other top cabaret performers. Murals by the famed *Madeleine* illustrator surround cocktailers in the swanky Bemel-man's Bar. Subway: 6 to 77th St.

Carmine's 2450 Broadway btw 90th and 91st Sts. (212) 362-2200 and 200 W 44th St. btw Broadway and Eighth Ave. (212) 221-3800 www.carminesnyc.com

Two locations of this Southern Italian restaurant provide the quintes-sential family-type experience, and the bigger the family the better the bar-gain. Absolutely enormous portions seem to vie with the size of the rooms, but informality rules and the hearty food is delicious. Prices are moderate and reservations are suggested. Subway: (Broadway) 1, 2, 3, 9 to 96th St.; (W 44th St.) N, R, S, 1, 2, 7, 9 to Times Square-42nd St. Lunch and dinner daily. Major credit cards.

Carnegie Delicatessen 854 Seventh Ave. btw 54th and 55th Sts. (212) 757-2245

Long considered a candidate for archetypal NYC deli honors, the Car-negie's late-night hours and midtown location are partial explanations for the customer stream. But clearly, legendary chicken soup, overstuffed sandwiches, New York cheesecake to die for, and similar selections are the main attraction. Expect crowded quarters and impatient service, but don't pass it up. Moderate prices for enormous portions. Subway: N, R to 57th St. Open daily 6:40 a.m.–4:00 a.m. Cash only.

Carnegie Hall 154 W 57th St. at Seventh Ave. (212) 247-7800 www.carnegiehall.org

Successive renovations of philanthropist Andrew Carnegie's storied concert hall have restored its excellent acoustics and original 1891 grandeur. Solo and orchestral performance at the hall remains a reliable indicator of musical arrival, and performers ranging from Arturo Toscanini to the Rolling Stones have appeared over the years. Hour-long guided tours of the building are available through the day, and the small Rose Museum on the 2nd floor provides fascinating historical records and memorabilia. Subway: N, R to 57th St.

Carnival on 46th Street *see* Brazilian Carnival.

Carolina 1409 Mermaid Ave. at W 15th St., Coney Island, Brooklyn (718) 714-1294

This long-familiar, inexpensive Italian restaurant continues to serve wonderful homey food at low prices. Subway: B, D, F, N to Coney Island-Stillwell Ave. Lunch and dinner daily. Major credit cards.

Caroline's Comedy Club 1626 Broadway btw 49th and 50th Sts. (212) 757-4100 www.carolines.com

A reliable venue to enjoy well-established big-name comedians and some really hot up-and-coming ones. Caroline's also houses an upscale Italian restaurant. On weekend afternoons, Caroline's Kid's Klub aims to catch the family crowd. Subway: 1, 9 to 50th St.; N, R to 49th St. Open nightly. Cover charge, Fri and Sat drink minimum. Major credit cards.

Carousel in Central Park *see* Central Park Carousel.

Carriage Rides *see* Horse-Drawn Carriage Rides.

Carroll Gardens

This small, friendly Brooklyn neighborhood is bounded by Degraw, Hoyt, and 9th Sts. and the Brooklyn-Queens Expressway. It dates to nineteenth-century Irish settlers and was later named for the only Irish Catholic signer of the Declaration of Independence, Charles Carroll. More recently, a flourishing Italian population has occupied the many brownstones with their large, front gardens. Colorful community celebrations of religious and national holidays are characteristic of the area. Subway: F, G to Carroll St.

Carousels *see* Central Park Carousel, Flushing Meadows-Corona Park, Forest Park.

Castle Clinton Battery Park (212) 344-7220

Now a national monument, original 1811 fortress was built, but never used, to defend New York harbor against possible British assault. Circular red sandstone building has since seen successive incarnations as the Castle Garden concert hall, an immigrant processing center, and the New York

Aquarium. Today the restored fort is a National Park Service visitor center and ticket office for Statue of Liberty and Ellis Island ferries. Subway: 4, 5 to Bowling Green. Open daily 9 a.m.–5 p.m. Admission free.

Cathedral of St. John the Divine 1047 Amsterdam Ave. btw 110th and 113th Sts. (212) 316-7540 www.stjohndivine.org

Begun in 1892 and still unfinished, this mighty Episcopal cathedral is one of the largest in the world and a glorious combination of Romanesque, Byzantine, and French Gothic architecture. The soaring towers, intricate stonework, stained-glass windows, and unique tapestries display the talents of many artisans and artists throughout the years. The cathedral has become a model of ecumenism and community outreach and offers a vast array of programs and services, ranging from secular concerts and exhibitions to a shelter for the homeless. A variety of tours is available. Subway: 1, 9, B, C to Cathedral Pkwy.-110th St.

Celebrate Brooklyn (718) 855-7882

Stages free outdoor multicultural entertainment from June through August, including musical, theatrical, and literary performances at the Prospect Park band shell in Brooklyn at 9th St. and Prospect Park W in the Park Slope neighborhood. Subway: F to Seventh Ave.

Celeste Bartos Forum *see* New York Public Library Celeste Bartos Forum.

Cemeteries *see* Cypress Hills National Cemetery, Moravian Cemetery, New York Marble Cemetery, Trinity Cemetery, Woodlawn Cemetery.

Cendrillon Asian Grill 45 Mercer St. btw Broome and Grand Sts. (212) 343-9012

Modest in price, this tastefully decorated restaurant features delicious Asian barbecue and adobo, the Philippine national dish. Subway: N, R, 6 to Canal St. Lunch and dinner except Mon. Dinner reservations suggested. Major credit cards.

Center for Jewish History 15 W 16th St. btw Fifth and Sixth Aves. (212) 294-8301 www.cjh.org www.centerforjewishhistory.org

This recently opened facility combines the collections and functions of five major organizations and activities: the American Jewish Historical Society, the Genealogy Institute, the Leo Baeck Institute, the Yeshiva University Museum, and the Yivo Institute for Jewish Research. In addition to the collections of books, documents, memoirs, and photos, the center offers a range of exhibitions and schedules many programs in its large auditorium. Subway: 4, 5, 6, N, R to 14th St.-Union Square. Hours of public access to the different services vary, but the center is closed on weekends and Jewish holidays. Phone ahead to learn specific details.

Center Voice *see* Lesbian and Gay Community Services Center.

Central Park bounded by 59th St. (Central Park S), 110th St. and Fifth Ave., and Central Park W (Eighth Ave.) www.centralpark nyc.org

For its vast array of natural and manmade pleasures, Central Park is a must destination for everyone from the daily local user to the occasional out-of-town visitor. Opened in 1876, this great green space separating midtown east from west, was envisioned by designers Frederick Law Olmstead and Calvert Vaux as a distinctly non-urban public refuge from the surrounding frenetic city. Today the 842-acre park remains remarkably faithful to this original conception, with its abundance of woodlands, grassy slopes, and near-wilderness areas interspersed with lakes and ponds, meandering pathways, and formally landscaped spaces. Over the years generous donors and zealous revisionists have introduced modifications to allow for added enjoyment such as multi-use recreation areas, playgrounds, outdoor theatres, and, perhaps most popular of all, a zoo.

Central Park Belvedere Castle 79th St. mid-park (212) 772-0210

Fanciful gray stone castle sits on top of the well-named Vista Rock and offers great rooftop views of various park features and the surrounding city. Operates as a U.S. Weather Bureau station and houses the Central Park Learning Center with its winning child-oriented nature exhibits and programs. Also functions as one of four visitor centers, dispensing helpful maps, literature, and information about happenings around the park. Subway: B, C to 81st St.-Museum of Natural History. Open 10 a.m. Tues–Sun, closing hour varies by season. Admission free.

Central Park Bethesda Fountain and Terrace 72nd St. traverse, mid-park

Central to the original park plan and overlooking the lake, this wide, circular terrace is a perfect setting for the ornate Bethesda Fountain and Angel of the Waters sculpture, which evoke biblical accounts of a healing angel at the Bethesda pool in Jerusalem. This site also provides a favored spot to view activities on the main park lake and reflect on the passing parade. Subway: B, C to 72nd St.

Central Park Bicycle Tours departure from 2 Columbus Circle at 59th St. and Broadway (212) 541-8759

Offers three daily 2-hour guided tours of major and less well-known spots in this famous and beautiful park. Fee includes bike rental and escort services. Subway: A, B, C, D, 1, 9 to 59th St.-Columbus Circle. Major credit cards.

Central Park Carousel 64th St. mid-park (212) 879-0244

Grand old merry-go-round, one of a disappearing species, was transported from Coney Island and features almost-life-size, hand-carved horses jumping to familiar organ tunes. It's every child's delight, over and over and over again. Subway: B, C to 72nd St. Open daily, weather permitting.

Central Park Carriage Tour *see* Horse-Drawn Carriage Rides.

Central Park Charles A. Dana Discovery Center 110th St. btw Fifth and Lenox Aves., edge of Harlem Meer (212) 860-1370 www. centralparknyc.org

Small Swiss chalet focuses on environmental aspects of the park and provides a range of exhibits and programs, including nature tours, summer bird walks, and informative workshops. Kids will enjoy an opportunity to fish with loaned rods and bait in the regularly stocked Harlem Meer. The center also functions as one of four visitor centers, dispensing helpful maps, literature, and information about happenings around the park. Subway: 2, 3 to Central Park N-110th St. Open Tues–Sun 10 a.m.–4 or 5 p.m.

Central Park Chess and Checkers House 64th St. mid-park

Interesting octagonal building provides playing opportunities at twenty-four outside and ten inside tables. If needed, players with photo identification can find free game pieces nearby at the Central Park Dairy. Subway: B, C to 72nd St.

Central Park Cleopatra's Needle btw Metropolitan Museum of Art and Great Lawn

Egypt's 1881 gift to NYC of a 1600 B.C. obelisk required Vanderbilt funding and serious moving and shaking. Although time has worn away its original hieroglyphics, the 71-foot stone needle remains a startling and curious sight. Subway: 6 to 77th St.

Central Park Conservancy The Arsenal, 830 Fifth Ave. (212) 360-2726 www.centralparknyc.org

This nonprofit organization, founded in 1980 to oversee and administer park activities, operates the four visitor centers within the park at Central Park Belvedere Castle, Central Park Charles A. Dana Discovery Center, Central Park Dairy, and Central Park North Meadow Recreation Center. The conservancy also offers an impressive variety of regular and seasonal free walking tours.

Central Park Conservancy Walking Tours of Central Park (212) 360-2726 www.centralparknyc.org

Free walking tours are offered during the week as well as on weekends to explore the park's woodland wonders, glorious gardens, history and design, and other unusual features.

Central Park Conservatory Garden Fifth Ave. btw 103rd and 106th Sts. (212) 360-2766 www.centralparknyc.org

Enter this glorious space through spectacular wrought-iron gates from a Vanderbilt mansion and discover three separate formal gardens with lawns, hedges, blooming trees, flowers, and plantings to delight both eye and soul. Children will enjoy recognizing characters from *The Secret Garden* in a south garden sculpture. Subway: 6 to 110th St.; 2, 3 to Central Park N-110th St. Open daily 8 a.m.–dusk.

Central Park Dairy 65th St. mid-park (212) 794-6564 www.centralparknyc.org

The dairy is now one of four visitor centers, providing helpful maps, literature, and information about happenings around the park. The curious restored 1870 building originally provided the eating spot within a children's area designated by park planners and also dispensed pure milk and other dairy items to needy city families. Subway: 4, 5, 6 to 59th St.; N, R to Fifth Ave. Open Tues–Sun 10 a.m.–5 p.m.

Central Park Delacorte Clock

Near an entrance arch separating the children's and main zoos is the fanciful decorative clock given by a major park donor, philanthropist George T. Delacorte. At half-hour intervals throughout the day an orchestra of bronze animals emerges to play nursery rhymes as they dance around the hours. Subway: Q to Lexington Ave.

Central Park Delacorte Theatre 80th St. mid-park (212) 861-7277 or (212) 539-8750

This open-air theatre, given by generous park donor George T. Delacorte, is home to the well-known summer Shakespeare-in-the-Park Festival, featuring free evening theatre by the celebrated Joseph Papp Company. Lucky ticket holders must line up early at pickup booths for same-day performances. For free tickets (two per person), people line up at midmorning; the booth opens at 1 p.m. for the evening's performance. Tickets are also distributed at the Joseph Papp Public Theatre at 425 Lafayette Ave. at 1 p.m. on performance days. Subway: B, C to 81st St.-Museum of Natural History.

Central Park Friedsam Memorial Carousel *see* Central Park Carousel.

Central Park Grand Army Plaza Fifth Ave. at Central Park S (59th St.)

Grand is the word for this handsome plaza marking the park's southern entrance. Dominated on one block by a fountain and sculpture appropriately celebrating abundance and on the other by the gilded statue of General Sherman on horseback, the space is also bordered by the perennially ritzy Plaza Hotel. Subway: N, R to Fifth Ave.

Central Park Great Lawn 81st St. mid-park

After extensive rehabilitation efforts, this truly great greensward now boasts a well-maintained turf inviting a relaxed snooze on the ground as well as strenuous activity on its many formal playing fields. Picnicking during free New York Philharmonic and Metropolitan Opera concerts is a favorite New Yorker pastime. Subway: B, C to 81st St.-Museum of Natural History.

Central Park Harlem Meer Fifth Ave. and 110th St.

Stocked with a variety of indulgent fish who must realize that they will be released after catch, the Meer welcomes old and young fisher folk and offers a distinctly non-urban experience. During the season rods and bait are available for loan at the nearby Central Park Charles A. Dana Discovery Center. Subway: 2, 3 to Central Park N-110th St. Open Tues–Sun 10 a.m.–4 or 5 p.m.

Central Park Heckscher Playground

Named for August Heckscher, who inaugurated a near-dynasty of park movers and shakers, this playground provides a range of athletic courts, games, and a puppet theatre designed to occupy the young.

Central Park Historic District

This area recalls an earlier time with its well-preserved early-twentieth-century rowhouses. It runs from 75th to 77th Sts. on Central Park W and between Central Park W and Columbus Ave. on 76th St. Subway: B, C to 72nd St.

Central Park Jacqueline Kennedy Onassis Reservoir from 86th to 97th Sts., park center

The stylish former first lady was an enthusiastic park devotee during her NYC residency, and this vast stretch of water with its well-used circular running track is one more tribute to her influence. Joggers and the like rave about the rewarding skyline views along the near-2-mile huffing and puffing route. Subway: B, C to 86th St.

Central Park Lake

When season and weather permit, this irregular 18-acre lake seems to bring out every row-row-row-your-boat enthusiast in town. It's a very pleasant sit-and-watch place too. It is located in the middle of the park from about 72nd to 77th Sts. Subway: B, C to 72nd St.

Central Park Loeb Boathouse 74th St. and East Dr., mid-park (212) 517-4723

Located near the main park lake, the boathouse rents out rowboats and a capacious gondola during the season. Bike rentals are also available here. Subway: 6 to 77th St. Boat rental 11 a.m.–4 p.m. Cash only.

Central Park Mall mid-park around 68th St.

A formal element of the original park plan, this wide promenade was an early-on preserve of the carriage trade but has seen more populist uses in recent times; the quarter-mile stretch now regularly hums with the sound of in-line skaters and street musicians; during the summer free concerts are offered in the area. Tree-lined Literary Walk at the south end of the mall features busts of writers and other recognizable figures. Subway: 6 to 68th St.-Hunter College.

Central Park Model Boat Pond 72nd St. and Fifth Ave.

Remote-controlled miniature craft sail and compete here from spring to fall in a manmade pond, also known as Conservatory Water. Tiny model boats can be rented throughout the season at the nearby boathouse, and the enthusiastic yacht regattas each Saturday morning are a favorite spectator sport for wanna-be mariners of all ages. Subway: 6 to 68th St.-Hunter College.

Central Park Naturalists' Walk W 79th St.

This recently designated nature path provides an informative field trip for confirmed and budding naturalists and birders. Walkway extends to Belvedere Castle and displays rock outcroppings and other geologic features and the great abundance and variety of local flora and fauna. Subway: B, C to 81st St.-Museum of Natural History.

Central Park North Meadow Recreation Center 97th St. mid-park (212) 348-4867

Area recreational facilities include tennis courts and soccer fields. The center also functions as one of the four visitor centers, dispensing helpful maps, literature, and information about happenings around the park. Subway: B, C to W 96th St.; 6 to E 96th St.

Central Park Obelisk *see* Central Park Cleopatra's Needle.

Central Park Ramble

To the west of the Central Park Model Boat Pond and north of Central Park Lake, this distinctly non-urban and isolated 38 acres is heavily forested and features the small streams and twisting dirt paths more characteristic of upstate regions. A large variety of migratory birds make a pit stop here each year, and contacting (888) NYPARKS or www.nyparks.org will yield information about Urban Park Ranger bird watching tours and other park events. Subway: B, C to 81st St.-Museum of Natural History.

Central Park Robert Bendleim Playground 108th St. and Fifth Ave.

This area was specifically designed to be a fun place for physically challenged kids and contains a marvelous array of accessible equipment and facilities. Subway: 2, 3 to Central Park N-110th St.

Central Park Shakespeare Garden north of 79th St. traverse

Well worth looking for, this somewhat hidden garden allows you to check out all of the flowers and plants mentioned in the works of the Bard. During the summer, New York Shakespeare Festival free performances of his dramas are presented at the nearby Central Park Delacorte Theater. Subway: B, C to 81st St.-Museum of Natural History.

Central Park Sheep Meadow W 66th to 69th Sts.

Maintained by lawnmowers rather then grazing sheep since 1934, the pleasant 22-acre meadow remains the largest grassy area in the park. Officially a "quiet zone," the first sign of warm weather brings out crowds of sunbathers and picnickers, but only the muted sound of Frisbee players tends to fill the air. The young find it a natural and multi-use hangout all year long. Subway: B, C to 72nd St.

Central Park South

This avenue, also known to many as 59th St., forms the southernmost border of the park and is notable for its upscale hotels and restaurants. Reminiscent of a more leisurely time, this is the place to rent a horse-drawn carriage for a half-hour ride in the park. They start between Fifth and Seventh Aves. alongside the park. Subway: N, R to Fifth Ave.

Central Park Strawberry Fields 72nd St. and Central Park W

The music and life of the Beatles' John Lennon are recalled in this memorial park designed by his widow, Yoko Ono, to serve as "an international garden of peace." Almost 200 plant species from donors throughout the world grace the garden, and the beautifully landscaped area draws a large crowd of Lennon fans and mourners, as well as park visitors who simply find it a wonderfully relaxing spot. Subway: B, C to 72nd St.

Central Park SummerStage *see* SummerStage.

Central Park Swedish Cottage 79th St. mid-park (212) 988-9093

In 1876 Sweden provided this typical schoolhouse for a Philadelphia exhibition, and after later transport to the park it became the site for skillful puppet show performances of classic children's stories. Days and hours of the shows vary, but early advance reservations are a must. Subway: B, C to 81st St.-Museum of Natural History.

Central Park Tisch Children's Zoo off Fifth Ave. at 64th St. (212) 861-6030

The Central Park Wildlife Conservation Center (or zoo) offers children, even very small ones, this petting zoo with interactive displays that may be a comfortable place for little ones. Subway: N, R to Fifth Ave. Open daily from 10 a.m. Modest admission charge (includes Central Park Wildlife Conservation Center).

Central Park Urban Park Rangers *see* Urban Park Rangers.

Central Park West

Beginning at the point where it branches off Columbus Circle, this street runs uptown in a line of striking residential structures, which are homes to the affluent. Many of the apartment buildings overlooking the park are handsome, and some are strikingly spectacular. Art Deco styles are the design feature of many of these high-rise residences of the rich and famous. Along the cross streets running west are a number of fine brownstones, particularly in the 70s. Subway: B, C to 72nd St.

Central Park Wildlife Conservation Center off Fifth Ave. at 64th St. (212) 861-6030

This small zoo, also known as the Central Park Zoo, is divided by climate regions into three parts: Tropic Zone, Temperate Region, and Polar Zone. It is home to more than 100 animal species. Main attractions are the monkeys, polar bears, and sea lions, and in summer the penguins in the icy room. Subway: N, R to Fifth Ave. Open daily from 10 a.m. Modest admission charge (includes Central Park Tisch Children's Zoo).

Central Park Wollman Memorial Rink 62nd St. mid-park (212) 396-1010

In winter the crowds cavort here on ice skates, and in warm weather it becomes a roller skating and in-line skating center. Equipment is available for rent, or you can bring your own. Subway: B, Q to 57th St.; N, R to Fifth Ave. Days and hours vary by season.

Central Park Zoo *see* Central Park Wildlife Conservation Center.

Central Reservation Service *see* CRS.

Central Synagogue 652 Lexington Ave. at 55th St. (212) 838-5122 www.centralsynagogue.org

This is the oldest continuously operating synagogue in the city. It was constructed in 1872 with a Moorish façade and onion domes and beautifully carved wooden doors; splendid stained glass is displayed within. Subway: 6 to 51st St.

Chamber Music *see* Alice Tully Hall, The Cloisters, Nicholas Roerich Museum.

Chanin Building 122 E 42nd St. btw Third and Park Aves.

This 56-story structure was constructed in 1929 and exemplifies the best of the period's Art Deco design. The façade features bronze and marble with intricate decoration, while the interior lobby contains bas-reliefs depicting the rags-to-riches saga of Irwin Chanin, the real estate developer whose firm was headquartered here. Subway: S, 4, 5, 6, 7 to Grand Central-42nd St.

Channel Gardens Fifth Ave. btw 49th and 50th Sts.

This promenade leads pedestrians from Fifth Ave. to the stairs going down to the Lower Plaza of Rockefeller Center. It takes its name because it is situated between the British building on the north side and the French one on the south. Above each structure's entry can be seen the coat of arms of each nation. Flower beds with seasonal plantings adorn the center along the garden's pathway. Subway: B, D, F, Q to 47th-50th Sts.-Rockefeller Center.

Chanterelle 2 Harrison St. btw Hudson and Greenwich Sts. (212) 966-6960

This is reputed to be one of the city's very finest restaurants for contemporary French food. Everything about it is elegant, from the small beautiful room, to the comfortably spaced tables, to the flawless service, to the sublime and succulent culinary inventions. It is, of course, very expensive but quite extraordinary as a dining experience, and reservations are essential. Subway: 1, 9 to Franklin St. Lunch Tues–Sat, dinner Mon–Sat. Major credit cards.

Chanukah Celebration *see* Hanukkah Menorah.

Chapel of the Good Shepherd at the General Theological Seminary entrance, 175 Ninth Ave. btw 20th and 21st Sts.

This is one of the finest buildings at the seminary and recognized because of its massive bronze doors and striking bell tower that is 161 feet high. Subway: C, E to 23rd St. Open weekday afternoons.

Charles A. Dana Discovery Center *see* Central Park Charles A. Dana Discovery Center, Central Park Conservancy.

Charles' Southern Style Kitchen 2841 Frederick Douglass Blvd. btw 151st and 152nd Sts. (212) 926-4313

This popular and inexpensive Harlem buffet, featuring all you can eat, is celebrated for the excellent and tasty fried chicken. Subway: A, B, C, D to 155th St. Dinner daily until late, Sun 1 p.m.–8 p.m. Major credit cards.

Charlie Parker Place

This block between 10th and 11th Sts., on which the famous jazz musician lived at 151 Ave. B in the East Village during the 1950s, was renamed in 1993 to bear his name. Subway: L to First Ave.

Charlton Street

On the north side of this street, to the west of Sixth Ave. and south of W Houston St., can be seen houses with paneled front doors, high stoops, and lead-glass and dormer windows, in New York's longest line of red brick townhouses, remarkably well preserved from the early part of the nineteenth century. Subway: 1, 9 to Houston St.

Chase Bank Melrose Games Madison Square Garden, Seventh Ave. at 32nd St. (212) 465-6741

This track-and-field contest is held in February and includes long-distance races, sprints, high jumping, pole vaults, and other events by some of the finest competitors in the world. Subway: A, C, E, 1, 2, 3, 9 to 34th St.-Penn Station.

Chase Championships Madison Square Garden, Seventh Ave. at 32nd St. (212) 465-6073

This major indoor professional tennis tournament for women's singles and doubles competitors takes place in November. Subway: A, C, E, 1, 2, 3, 9 to 34th St.-Penn Station.

Chase Manhattan Bank Building 1 Chase Manhattan Plaza on Pine St.

This undistinguished office building was constructed in the financial district in 1961 to serve as the New York center for this important banking company. A sculpture by Jean Dubuffet, *Group of Four Trees,* resides before it. Subway: 2, 3 to Wall St.

Chassidic Art Institute 375 Kingston Ave. btw Carroll and Crown Sts., Brooklyn (718) 774-9149

Located in the heart of the Lubavitch Jewish community, this center exhibits religious folk art and artifacts reflective of this sect. Subway: 3 to Kingston Ave. Open daily except Sat, noon–7 p.m. Admission free.

Chatham Square

Ten streets converge at the southeastern entrance to traditional China-town, frequently called Kim Lau Square because the Kim Lau Arch stands at the center on an island surrounded by constant auto traffic. The arch is a memorial to Chinese-American casualties of World War II. To the east of Chatham Square at Division St. is Confucius Plaza, a high-rise complex of apartments, a school, and an interior park. A large, stone statue of Confucius stands here at the corner of Division St. Subway: B, D, Q to Grand St.

Checkers *see* Central Park Chess and Checkers House.

Cheetah 12 W 21st St. btw Fifth and Sixth Aves. (212) 206-7770

Cheetah prints everywhere in sight and a waterfall add to the glitzy fun of this trendy night spot with expensive drinks and its DJ mixture of every type of music to dance to. Subway: F, N, R to 23rd St. Open nightly from 10 p.m. Admission charge (cash only). Major credit cards except American Express.

Chelsea

Bordered roughly by 14th St. on the south, 29th St. on the north, Fifth Ave. to the east, and stretching west to the Hudson River, this area, like its London namesake, seeks to maintain the look and feel of its quiet residen-tial streets. These days it's in the midst of transformation into a trendy, artistic, gay, and upscale neighborhood, drawing the spillover from the in-creasingly expensive Greenwich Village. It is home more and more to lively stores, restaurants, fashionable night spots and bars, and a growing num-ber of smart galleries. Even with the economic boom, neighborhood deni-zens try hard to retain the friendly and folksy village ambiance. Subway: C, E to 23rd St.

Chelsea Billiards 54 W 21st St. btw Fifth and Sixth Aves. (212) 989-0096

This comfortable establishment makes beer and food available along with billiard games. Subway: F to 23rd St. Open 11 a.m.–4 a.m. 365 days a year. Major credit cards.

Chelsea Brownstone 241 W 24th St. btw Seventh and Eighth Aves. (212) 206-9237, fax (212) 388-9985

Well established on a quiet street, this facility offers a limited number of private apartments; each contains a bathroom, phone, TV, and kitchen. Rates are very inexpensive, with discounts offered for longer stays. Reservations well in advance during busy seasons are suggested. Subway: 1, 9, C, E to 23rd St.

Chelsea Center Hostel 313 W 29th St. near Eighth Ave., NY 10001 (212) 643-0214, fax (212) 473-3945 www.chelseacenterhostel.com

This domicile offers very inexpensive beds with clean sheets and blankets. Breakfast is included in dormitory-arranged spaces for travelers. Bookings well in advance are suggested for peak seasons at this very well-located hostel. Subway: 1, 9 to 28th St.

Chelsea Flea Market

Located between 26th and 27th Sts. on Sixth Ave., this market is open only on Saturdays and Sundays. Everything imaginable is on sale here, from old clothing to jewelry to furniture to tools; it is a happy hunting ground for collecting things. Subway: F to 23rd St.

Chelsea Historic District

The streets from Ninth to Tenth Aves. and from W 20th to W 21st Sts. make up this small nineteenth-century neighborhood of handsome brownstone rowhouses. They are built mostly in Italian and Greek Revival style. The very finest are in a row from 406 to 418 W 20th St. They were built by a banker and merchant around 1840 and are known by his name as Cushman Row. Subway: C, E to 23rd St.

Chelsea Hotel 222 W 23rd St. btw Seventh and Eighth Aves., NY 10011 (212) 243-3700, fax (212) 675-5531 www.hotelchelsea.com

This famous residential hotel has housed innumerable writers, artists, and musicians. Plaques on the front door celebrate some of the most famous of its past residents. It's a bit seedy these days, but that may be part of its ghostly allure as it continues as a reasonable place to stay with well-worn large rooms filled with memories. The lobby displays art works created by residents. Subway: 1, 9, C, E to 23rd St.

Chelsea International Hostel 251 W 20th St. btw Seventh and Eighth Aves., NY 10011 (212) 647-0010, fax (212) 727-7289 www. chelseahostel.com

Dorm accommodations with four or six in a room and hall bathrooms are very inexpensive at this conveniently located place that also has some private double rooms. It's a safe place that offers little more than the basics, but because it's so cheap, reserving in advance is advisable. Subway: C, E to 23rd St.; 1, 9 to 18th St.

Chelsea Market 75 Ninth Ave. btw 15th and 16th Sts. (212) 243-6005

In what was eighteen old buildings, is now a single unusual marketplace with a waterfall and some twenty shops selling meats, wines, produce, flowers, bakery products, and more. Subway: A, C, E to 14th St.

Chelsea Piers 23rd St. and the Hudson River (212) 336-6666 www. chelseapiers.com

With its entrance at 23rd St., this enormous sports and entertainment complex, covering some 1.7 million square feet, extends from 17th to 23rd Sts. and grew out of the transformation of the old buildings at four piers. It is home to the AMF Chelsea Bowl, the Field House, Golf Club, the Roller Rinks, and the Sports Center, as well as numerous shops and places to eat or board cruises. Opened in 1995, it's designed to be a year-round sports village where a combination of very different sports activities can be found. Subway: C, E to 23rd St., then Bus M23 west.

Chelsea Piers AMF Chelsea Bowl btw Piers 59 and 60 at Chelsea Piers (212) 835-BOWL

This bowling center offers forty lanes, a bar, and a big arcade. Subway: 1, 9 to 23rd St., then Bus M23 west. Open daily 9 a.m.–1 a.m. Major credit cards.

Chelsea Piers Golf Club Pier 59 at Chelsea Piers at 18th St. (212) 336-6400

This practice center offers fifty-two sheltered and heated driving positions, a large putting green, an automatic ball-carrying system, and a fairway extending over 200 yards of artificial grass. Subway: C, E to 23rd St.; 1, 9 to 18th St. Open 5 a.m.–midnight daily. Major credit cards.

Chelsea Piers Roller Rinks Pier 62 at 23rd St. at Chelsea Piers (212) 336-6200

There are two outdoor roller skating rinks located here as well as an

Extreme Skate Park for use by in-line skaters offering various height ramps. Subway: C, E to 23rd St., then Bus M23 west. Days and hours vary at the different facilities. Major credit cards.

Chelsea Piers Sky Rink Pier 61 at Chelsea Piers (212) 336-6100

This is the only year-round indoor ice skating rink in Manhattan, offering a range of programs and ice skating performances. Subway: C, E to 23rd St., then Bus M23 west. Days and hours vary. Major credit cards.

Chelsea Piers Sports Center Pier 60 at Chelsea Piers (212) 336-6000

Fitness enthusiasts can find an Olympic-size swimming pool, basketball courts, volleyball courts, weights, exercise machines, steam room, sauna, and a climbing wall here. Subway: C, E to 23rd St., then Bus M23 west. Hours vary, open daily. Major credit cards.

Chen and the Dancers 70 Mulberry St. at Bayard St. (212) 349-0126

This troupe is among the most highly regarded Asian-American dance companies, giving performances at various venues in New York, at their theatre on Mulberry Street, and elsewhere around the country.

Cherry Blossom Festival (718) 623-7200

This two-day weekend event takes place in May with the blossoming of the Brooklyn Botanic Garden's many cherry trees and is celebrated with music, art, dance, and craft demonstrations. Subway: 2, 3 to Eastern Pkwy.-Brooklyn Museum.

Cherry Lane Theatre 38 Commerce St. btw Hudson and Bedford Sts. (212) 727-3673 www.cherrylanetheatre.com

Dating from the 1920s to showcase innovative new productions, this small house continues as a leading off-Broadway performance venue. Subway: A, B, C, D, E, F, Q to W 4th St.

Chess and Checkers House *see* Central Park Chess and Checkers House.

Cheyenne Diner 411 Ninth Ave. at 33rd St. (212) 465-8750

This place looks like a diner is supposed to look and serves big portions at inexpensive prices. Subway: A, C, E to 34th St.-Penn Station. Open daily 24 hours. Major credit cards.

Chicago B.L.U.E.S. 73 Eighth Ave. btw 13th and 14th Sts. (212) 924-9755

This relaxed place draws sophisticated audiences in droves to hear Manhattan's best blues from some of the finest performers. Subway: A, C, E, L to 14th St.-Eighth Ave. Open nightly. Admission charge varies.

Chicago City Limits 1105 First Ave. btw 60th and 61st Sts. (212) 888-5233

This company performs in a renovated movie house and has been doing often-hilarious improvisational comedy from audience-proposed themes for more than twenty years. Subway: 4, 5, 6 to 59th St.; N, R to Lexington Ave. Performance days and hours vary.

Children in New York *see* Amusement Parks, Baby-sitting, Carousels, *Kid's Culture Calendar,* Museums of Particular Interest to Children and Teens, Parks and Playgrounds, Places That Appeal to Children and Teens.

Children's Museum of Manhattan W 83rd St. btw Broadway and Amsterdam Ave. (212) 721-1223 www.cmom.org

This 5-story space is designed to be experienced by kids from under 1 to around 12 years old and is filled with imaginative displays and interactive exhibits where they can touch and experiment with everything. There's a media center, where older children can work up their own TV shows, an early childhood play area, a place for the youngest children that deals with developing language skills, and much more to delight any child. Subway: 1, 9 to 86th St. Open Wed–Sun 10 a.m.–5 p.m. Tues also in summer. Modest admission charge.

Children's Museum of the Arts 182 Lafayette St. btw Broome and Grand Sts. (212) 941-9198 www.cmany.org

This is a place for kids to experience and learn about the arts. Children receive encouragement to experiment with clay, paints, plaster of paris, paper, beads, and other materials. It is more a giant playground than a museum but a nifty spot for allowing the under-8-year-olds to try their hands at creating their own something. Subway: 6 to Spring St. Open Wed–Sun 10 a.m.–5 p.m. Modest admission charge. Cash preferred.

Chin Chin 216 E 49th St. btw Second and Third Aves. (212) 888-4555

This upscale Chinese dining spot features a wide range of choices from many regions, including a number of unique concoctions. The food is excellent and moderately expensive. Subway: 4, 5, 6 to 59th St. Lunch Mon–Fri, dinner daily. Major credit cards.

China Club 268 W 47th St. btw Broadway and Eighth Ave. (212) 398-3800

This giant place is very popular, very much in. Fine acoustics and lighting attract the famous and beautiful as well as the less well endowed for rock dancing to disco music played by disc jockeys and the occasional live group. Getting in may not be easy on some nights. Subway: 1, 9, C, E to 50th St. Open nightly from 10 or 11 p.m. Cover charge varies.

China Institute Gallery 125 E 65th St. btw Park and Lexington Aves. (212) 744-8181 www.chinainstitute.org

In two small rooms within the institute are interesting changing shows featuring Chinese art and artifacts, including ceramics, illustrations, calligraphy, historic works, and contemporary creations of Chinese artists. The institute also sponsors a range of lectures, performances, films, educational offerings, language courses, and tours. Subway: 6 to 68th St. Open daily, hours vary. Modest admission charge.

Chinatown

This exotic part of town is home to about half the city's 300,000 Chinese people. It is by far Manhattan's most popular ethnic enclave with tourists. Most visit the neighborhood to feast on Chinese cuisine, which is invariably tasty, bountiful, and inexpensive. It is a noisy, colorful, aromatic, and crowded part of town. Chinatown is most pleasurable to visit during daylight hours when its streets are busiest since after dark it is pretty deserted, although still safe to be about. Mott St. is the main thoroughfare, where along with Canal St., Pell St., Bayard St., and the Bowery, are found restaurants; tea and rice stores; herb shops; fish markets; bargain stores selling leather goods, clothing, and electronic equipment; as well as souvenir emporiums. Subway: J, M, N, R, Z, 6 to Canal St.

Chinese Community Cultural Center 10 Confucius Plaza in Chinatown (212) 925-2245 or (212) 925-3538

The Chinese Consolidated Benevolent Association began its support of this activity in the 1880s and still sponsors this community resource. Subway: B, E, Q to Grand St.

Chinese in New York *see* Bay Ridge, Chinatown, Flushing.

Chinese New Year

Sometime between January 21 and February 21, beginning with the first full moon after January 21, Chinatown is the place to witness this spectacular ten-day event from noon until sunset. Parades, slithering dragons, floats, loud music, firecrackers, and eating are all part of the festivities on Mott St. Subway: J, M, N, R, Z, 6 to Canal St.

Chinese Restaurants *see* Bo Ky, Canton, Chin Chin, Excellent Dumpling House, Golden Unicorn, Hunan Park, Joe's Shanghai,

New York Noodletown, Ollie's Noodle Shop, Oriental Garden, Pig Heaven, Shun Lee Palace, Tai Hong Lau, Tang Pavilion, Tse Yang, 20 Mott Street, Zen Palate.

Christ Church 520 Park Ave. at 60th St. (212) 838-3036

Built some 70 years ago, this Methodist house of worship appears to have a longer history, with its blend of external Romanesque and Byzantine features, mosaics, and marble columns. It sometimes offers concerts of classical music. Subway: N, R to Lexington Ave.; 4, 5, 6 to 59th St.

Christie's 20 Rockefeller Plaza btw Fifth and Sixth Aves. (212) 636-2000 www.christies.com

This internationally respected British auction house has been in the business for more than 200 years. Its high seasons are in May and November. Goods on auction are available for free viewing five days in advance of the auction. Telephone to learn what's on display. Catalogues of particular sales events are sold. Attendance at auctions is free on a space-available basis, but evening auctions may require a reservation. Christie's East at 219 E 67th St. between Second and Third Aves. (212) 606-0400 features somewhat less expensive merchandise in June and December. Subway: (Rockefeller Plaza) B, D, F, Q to 47th-50th Sts.-Rockefeller Center; (E 67th St.) 6 to 68th St.-Hunter College.

Christmas Decorations *see* Christmas Window Displays.

Christmas Spectacular at Radio City Music Hall (212) 247-4777

From mid-November to early January the famous Rockettes kick up their heels as part of a great extravaganza on the stage of this classic tourist venue at 1260 Sixth Ave. at 50th St., which has been drawing crowds for this special show for a long time. Subway: B, D, F, Q to 47th-50th Sts.-Rockefeller Center.

Christmas Tree-Lighting Ceremony *see* Tree-Lighting Ceremony.

Christmas Window Displays

Each year from late November until early January, Fifth Ave. is a festive spectacle. Have a peek at the mannequins in imaginative display in windows at Saks Fifth Ave. at 611 Fifth Ave. between 49th and 50th Sts. and Lord & Taylor at 424 Fifth Ave. between 38th and 39th Sts. The wreaths around the necks of the celebrated New York Public Library lions on Fifth Ave. at 41st St. are another colorful and endearing sight.

Christopher Street

This is a main cross street that cuts across the center of the West Village.

It is celebrated as the heartland of gay and lesbian New York City but is frequented these days by others for whom the neighborhood is less exotic than when the first protest by gay men at the Stonewall Inn in 1969 heralded the beginning of the gay rights movement. The street is lined with every manner of shops, bars, and bookstores. Subway: 1, 9 to Christopher St.-Sheridan Square.

Chrysler Building 405 Lexington Ave. at 42nd St. (212) 682-3070

This famous and beloved 1,000-foot Art Deco building was the world's highest when it was constructed in 1930, until the Empire State Building surpassed it three years later. Its tower is at its best at sunset, when its spire glows, and after dark when its illumination is a glorious sight. The striking lobby with its marble and granite decoration, the exterior building gargoyles on the upper stories, the wings from the 31st floor, and the eagle heads from the 61st floor, all shaped like 1929 Chrysler car ornaments, add to the structure's charm. The Chrysler Company is long gone, but the building and its lobby are clearly worth a look. Subway: S, 4, 5, 6, 7 to Grand Central-42nd St.

Church of St. Luke in the Fields 487 Hudson St. at Barrow St. (212) 924-0562

When this third-oldest church in Manhattan was constructed in 1821 as a country chapel for the Trinity Church in Wall Street, this area was then literally located in the fields. Particularly attractive is the Barrow Street Garden on the chapel's grounds. Subway: 1, 9 to Christopher St.-Sheridan Square. *See also* St. Luke's Garden.

Church of St. Paul the Apostle 415 W 59th St. at Ninth Ave. (212) 265-3495

This lovely Roman Catholic Gothic church contains fine interior features; perhaps the finest is the altar designed by Stanford White. Subway: A, B, C, D, 1, 9 to 59th St.-Columbus Circle.

Church of St. Vincent Ferrer Lexington Ave. at 66th St. (212) 744-2080

This Roman Catholic worship center boasts a handsome exterior as well as beautiful interior features, including lovely stained-glass windows and reredos. Subway: 6 to 68th St.-Hunter College.

Church of Sea and Land *see* First Chinese Presbyterian Church.

Church of the Ascension 36-38 Fifth Ave. at W 10th St. (212) 254-8620

This 1841 Gothic Episcopal church was recently restored and features a marble altar sculpture by Saint-Gaudens, lovely stained-glass windows, and a mural depicting the Ascension of Jesus by John La Farge. Subway: N, R to 8th St.-NYU.

Church of the Holy Trinity 316 E 88th St. btw First and Second Aves. (212) 289-4100

Constructed in 1889 of brick and terra-cotta in French Gothic style, this Episcopal church features a richly elaborated arched doorway, one of the city's finest bell towers, and a picturesque small garden. It offers very popular musical programs and concerts. Subway: 4, 5, 6 to 86th St.

Church of the Incarnation 205 Madison Ave. at 35th St. (212) 689-6350

This dark brownstone Gothic structure was constructed in 1864. The Episcopal church contains beautiful stained-glass windows, one executed by Tiffany and two others by the celebrated British designer William Morris. Subway: 6 to 33rd St.

Church of the Intercession 550 W 155th St. (212) 283-6200

Just below Audubon Terrace in Harlem is the very large Gothic Revival structure housing this church. It is surrounded by the quiet and tranquil Trinity Cemetery, making this spot an unusual peaceful country scene in the fast-paced city. Subway: 1 to 157th St.

Church of the Transfiguration 1 E 29th St. btw Fifth and Madison Aves. (212) 684-6770 www.littlechurch.org

Better known as the "Little Church Around the Corner," this Episcopal house of worship has been favored by theatre people since 1870. It is set back from the street past a little garden in a small, brown brick Gothic building. It sponsors popular concerts and recitals. Subway: 6 to 28th St.

Churches *see* Abyssinian Baptist Church, Canaan Baptist Church of Christ, Cathedral of St. John the Divine, Chapel of the Good Shepherd, Christ Church, Church of St. Luke in the Fields, Church of St. Paul the Apostle, Church of St. Vincent Ferrer, Church of the Ascension, Church of the Holy Trinity, Church of the Incarnation, Church of the Intercession, Church of the Transfiguration, Columbia University St. Paul's Chapel, Elias Greek Rite Church, First Chinese Presbyterian Church, First Presbyterian Church, Grace Church, Jan Hus Presbyterian Church, John Street Church, Judson Memorial Church, Marble Collegiate Reformed Church, Mother

A.M.E. Zion Church, Mount Olivet Baptist Church, Old St. Patrick's Cathedral, Plymouth Church of the Pilgrims, Riverside Church, Russian Orthodox Cathedral of Transfiguration, St. Ann and the Holy Trinity Church, St. Bartholomew's Church, St. Charles Borromeo Roman Catholic Church, St. Frances X. Cabrini Shrine, St. George's Episcopal Church (two listings), St. George's Ukrainian Catholic Church, St. James Church, St. John the Baptist Church, St. John's Episcopal Church, St. Luke's Church, St. Mark's-in-the-Bowery Church, St. Martin's Episcopal Church, St. Nicholas Russian Orthodox Church, St. Patrick's Cathedral, St. Paul's Chapel, St. Peter's Episcopal Church, St. Peter's Lutheran Church, St. Thomas Church, Shrine of St. Mother Elizabeth Ann Seton, Trinity Church, Zion St. Mark's Evangelical Lutheran Church.

Churrascaria Plataforma 316 W 49th St. btw Eighth and Ninth Aves. (212) 245-0505

One should bring a ravenous appetite along to this Brazilian temple of meat, which begins with a visit to a bountiful salad bar followed by an endless range of lamb, beef, chicken, sausage, and ham offerings, and ends only when the diner signals an end to the continuously returning procession. Moderate prices make this eating orgy one of the town's great bargains. Subway: C, E to 50th St. Lunch and dinner daily. Major credit cards.

Cinema *see* Film Festivals, Film Groups, Film Revivals, Foreign and Independent Films.

Cinema Classics 332 E 11th St. btw First and Second Aves. (212) 677-6309 or (212) 971-1015

This is the place in the East Village for seeing old-fashioned double-feature shows of dated films with a very cheap admission ticket. Subway: L to First Ave. Open Mon–Sat, hours vary. Closed Sun. Cash only.

Cinema Village 22 E 12th St. btw Fifth Ave. and University Pl. (212) 924-3363

Schedules a wide range of independent American and foreign features and documentaries and sometimes runs a series of Hong Kong action films. Very comfortable seating. Subway: L, N, R, 4, 5, 6 to 14th St.-Union Square. Cash only.

Circle in the Square Theatre 1633 Broadway at 50th St. (212) 239-6200

Still bearing the name of the celebrated repertory ensemble from its Village history, this is now simply another Broadway theatre venue for current theatrical performances. Subway: 1, 9 to 50th St.

Circle Line Cruises departing from Pier 83, W 42nd St. at Twelfth Ave. and from Pier 16, South St. Seaport at Water St. (212) 563-3200 www.circleline.com

Best known for its 3-hour cruise, which circumnavigates Manhattan and takes it all in—three rivers, seven major bridges, five boroughs, and more than twenty-five landmarks, including a close-up of the Statue of Liberty—this company has a wide range of water trips, some of 1 or 2 hours' duration, some by speedboat, and some with live music and harbor light viewing at night. For schedules and prices, call, check the Web site, or drop in at the sales office at the Times Square Visitors Center at 1560 Broadway between 46th and 47th Sts. for full details.

Circuses *see* Big Apple Circus, Ringling Brothers and Barnum & Bailey Circus.

Le Cirque New York Palace Hotel, 455 Madison Ave. btw 50th and 51st Sts. (212) 303-7788

Considered by many to be the city's finest restaurant, this very elegant and very expensive French dining spot frequented by celebrities and the elite is now situated in a fantastic new setting of futuristic design, but the food and service remain sublime. Reservations far in advance are a good idea. Subway: 6 to 51st St. Lunch Mon–Sat, dinner daily. Major credit cards.

Citicorp Center 153 E 53rd St. btw Third and Park Aves.

This 59-story structure occupies the area from 53rd to 54th Sts. between Lexington and Third Aves. Constructed in 1959, it is conspicuous for its slanted roof and because it rises above 10-story stilts. It is home to a pleasing indoor atrium mall lined with shops and eating spots and is sometimes the setting for lunchtime concerts and other events. Subway: 6 to 51st St.; E, F to Lexington Ave.

City Center of Music and Drama 131 W 55th St. btw Sixth and Seventh Aves. (212) 581-1212 or (212) 581-7907

Once a mosque, this theatre now functions as a premier performing arts venue for some of the major modern dance groups including the Alvin Ailey American Dance Theater, the Merce Cunningham, the Paul Taylor, the Joffrey Ballet, the Dance Theatre of Harlem, and other companies. Subway: B, D, E to Seventh Ave.

City College of the City University of New York main entrance at
Convent Ave. and W 138th St. (212) 650-7000

Begun in the mid-nineteenth century as a free college for capable young
men, City College has grown into a major university, City University of
New York, of which it is the original base. City College itself is on a rustic
campus of Gothic buildings with spires made of stone, arched gateways,
and green lawns, centering around Convent Ave. between 130th and 140th
Sts. No longer free, the college now enrolls some 15,000 male and female
students, most of whom are from minority families, with tuition rates very
low compared to those at private institutions. Subway: 1, 9 to 137th St.-
City College.

City Hall

Built in 1811, this architectural treasure is situated at the northern end
of City Hall Park between Broadway and Park Row. A blend of French and
Federal styles, the building is still used for its original purpose, and the
Rotunda and Governor's Room are often open to the public. A lovely marble circular staircase leads from the domed Rotunda to the rooms on the
2nd floor. Free tours of the building are offered with advance reservations,
with details at (718) 788-6879. Subway: J, M, Z to Chambers St.; 4, 5, 6 to
City Hall; 2, 3 to Park Pl. Open Mon–Fri 10 a.m.–4 p.m. Admission free.

City Hall Park

Situated between Broadway and Park Row and Chambers Street, this
has been a public space as far back as the seventeenth century. No longer
the site of public executions as it once was, this remains a tree-shaded triangular strip, with the classic City Hall structure looming at its northern
end. The park is the place where many civic celebrations and public pro-
tests are often staged. At other times, its many benches are used by neighborhood building occupants on their lunch breaks. Subway: J, M, Z to
Chambers St.; 4, 5, 6 to City Hall; 2, 3 to Park Pl.

City Island

Located just off the northeast shore of the Bronx and sticking out into
Long Island Sound is this island stretching across 230 acres. It was once
home to New York's shipbuilding industry and still retains its nautical flavor and something of a New England feel with its clapboard houses, scenic
marinas, and seafood eateries all contributing to its small-town fishing village atmosphere. City Island Ave. is its only real street, and the place seems
totally detached from the rest of the city. Subway: 6 to Pelham Bay Park,
then Bus BX21 to City Island.

City Lights Bed and Breakfast (212) 737-7049, fax (215) 535-2755
www.citylightsbandb.com

This firm arranges accommodations at several hundred locations in Manhattan and Brooklyn with a minimum stay of two nights. Prices range widely, based on the specific accommodations, running from hosted singles and doubles to unhosted apartments of different sizes. Call Mon–Fri 9 a.m.–5:30 p.m. or leave a message at other times.

City Pass (707) 256-0490 www.citypass.net

With this pass, visitors can enjoy five major New York City attractions for 50 percent of the usual price and avoid ticket lines at the American Museum of Natural History, the Empire State Building Observatory, the Guggenheim Museum, the Intrepid Sea–Air–Space Museum, and the Museum of Modern Art. City Pass booklets can be purchased at visitor information centers, many hotels, and any of the participating attractions. Tickets are valid for nine days from the first day of use.

City Sightseeing main office at Port Authority Terminal at 42nd St. and Eighth Ave. (212) 944-9200 or (800) 876-9868

This is the successor to New York Big Apple Tours. It is a competitor to the Gray Line, with double-decker hop-on, hop-off bus riding, which permits unlimited stops and reboardings as it loops around Manhattan at various locations during the 48-hour period for which the ticket is valid. Subway: A, C, E to Port Authority-42nd St.

City Sonnet Village Station, P.O. Box 347, NY 10014 (212) 614-3034, fax (212) 674-3393 www.citysonnet.com

This bed-and-breakfast agency offers fully furnished private accommodations everywhere in Manhattan. Hosts provide continental breakfast and offer helpful neighborhood details. Prices range widely based on number of guests, size of room, and private or shared bath arrangements.

City Tours *see* Boat Tours, Bus Tours, Helicopter Tours, Limousine Tours, Special Interest Tours, Walking Tours.

City University of New York *see* City College of the City University of New York.

Claremont Riding Academy 175 W 89th St. btw Columbus and Amsterdam Aves. (212) 724-5100

The oldest commercial stable in New York provides horseback riding instruction as well as the rental of horses with English saddles for experienced riders to use on the bridle paths of nearby Central Park. Subway: B, C to 86th St. Open daily from 6:30 a.m.

Classic Stage Company Repertory 136 E 13th St. btw Third and Fourth Aves. (212) 677-4210

This group presents performances of classic theatre productions with adaptations and new slants. Subway: L to Third Ave.

Classical Music *see* Alice Tully Hall, Avery Fisher Hall, Bargemusic, Beacon Theatre, Brooklyn Academy of Music, Brooklyn Center for the Performing Arts, Carnegie Hall, Cathedral of St. John the Divine, Colden Center for the Performing Arts at Queens College, Harlem School of the Arts, Hunter College, Juilliard School of Music, Lehman Center for the Performing Arts, Lincoln Center for the Performing Arts, Lincoln Center Library for the Performing Arts, Merken Concert Hall, Messiah Sing-In, Metropolitan Museum of Art, Mostly Mozart Festival, New York Philharmonic, Nicholas Roerich Museum, 92nd Street Y, St. Bartholomew's Church, St. Paul's Chapel, St. Peter's Lutheran Church, St. Thomas Church, Symphony Space, Town Hall, Wave Hill. *See also* Opera Music.

Clay Pit Ponds State Park Preserve 83 Nielsen Ave. at Sharrots Rd., Staten Island (718) 967-1976

More than 250 acres of wetlands with lovely hiking trails can be found in this parkland without playgrounds or ball fields, where the sole attraction is the pleasure of rustic hiking. Subway: 1, 9 to South Ferry; N, R to Whitehall St., then ferry to Staten Island. From Staten Island St. George Ferry Terminal, take Bus S74 to Sharrots Rd., then walk one quarter mile and turn left onto Carlin St. to its end. Open daily 9 a.m.–5 p.m.

Clementine 1 Fifth Ave. at 8th St. (212) 253-0003

The main dining room boasts a charming rock garden and pool, the service is congenial, and delectable American-style dishes at only moderately expensive prices are served at this popular restaurant, where reservations are essential. Subway: A, B, C, D, E, F, Q to W 4th St.; 6 to Astor Pl.; N, R to 8th St.-NYU. Open Mon–Sat for dinner. Major credit cards.

Cleopatra's Needle in Central Park *see* Central Park Cleopatra's Needle.

Climbing *see* Chelsea Piers Sports Center.

Clinton District *see* Hell's Kitchen.

The Cloisters Fort Tryon Park, Fort Washington Ave. at Margaret Corbin Dr., Washington Heights (212) 923-3700

This celebrated building incorporates cloisters, chapels, and halls housing the Metropolitan Museum of Art's rich collection of medieval art in a lovely tranquil setting that looks out over the Hudson River. The choicest treasures are the sixteenth-century unicorn tapestries hung in a room of their own. The Cloisters' enclosed gardens are home to more than 250 varieties of herbal and cooking plants and flowers grown in the middle ages. Subway: A to 190th St. Open Tues–Sun. Admission charge. No credit cards.

Clubs *see* Grolier Club, Metropolitan Club, Montauk Club, National Arts Club, New York Road Runners Club, New York Sports Clubs, Pen and Brush Club, Players Club, Printing House Racquet and Fitness Club, Salmagundi Club, University Club.

Clubs for Dancing *see* Dance Clubs.

Cobble Hill

Just across Atlantic Ave. from Brooklyn Heights in Brooklyn is a lovely, quiet, residential area of tree-lined streets and brownstone houses constructed in the nineteenth century that is growing in popularity with young professionals. Principal streets here are Congress, Amity, and Warren. Just off Clinton St. south of Congress St. is a lovely alleyway, Verandah Pl., replete with beautifully restored carriage houses. Subway: F, G to Bergen St.

Coco Roco 392 Fifth Ave. btw 6th and 7th Sts., Park Slope, Brooklyn (718) 965-3376

This moderate-priced Peruvian restaurant masterfully prepares a wide range of Latin American specialty dishes, from skewered chicken to imaginatively conceived delicious seafood creations. Subway: F, M, N, R to Fourth Ave.-9th St. Lunch and dinner daily. Major credit cards.

Coffee and Cakes *see* Café Gitane, Caffé Bianco, Caffé Dante, Caffé Ferrara, Caffé La Fortuna, Caffé Reggio, Caffé Roma, Hungarian Pastry Shop, Payard Patisserie and Bistro.

Colden Center for the Performing Arts at Queens College 65-30 Kissena Blvd., Flushing, Queens (718) 793-8080

A performance venue for theatre, jazz, classical, and popular music, opera, and children's programs, as well as the Queens Philharmonic Orchestra. Subway: F to Parsons Blvd., then Bus Q25 or Q34 to Queens College campus.

Coliseum Books 1775 Broadway at 57th St. (212) 757-8381 www.coliseumbooks.com

This is a large bookshop with a strong inventory in virtually every subject area, with ample space and location marks for finding things and a good choice of discounted paperbacks and hardcover works for sale down-stairs. Subway: A, B, C, D, 1, 9 to 59th St.-Columbus Circle. Open daily, hours vary. Major credit cards.

Collective Unconscious 145 Ludlow St. (212) 254-5277 www. weird.org

This limited space features high creativity and surprise in its theatre of-ferings, with a constantly changing schedule of events. Subway: F to E Broadway.

Colleges *see* Universities and Colleges.

Colombian Independence Day Festival

On the Sunday closest to July 20, this annual event with music, food, and dancing to celebrate the occasion takes place at Flushing Meadows-Corona Park in Queens. Subway: 7 to Willets Pt.-Shea Stadium.

Colombians in New York *see* Jackson Heights.

Le Colonial 149 E 57th St. btw Third and Lexington Aves. (212) 752-0808

This Vietnamese restaurant with a decor strongly suggestive of South-east Asia of the colonial period serves moderately expensive fare that is well prepared and delicious. Reservations suggested. Subway: 4, 5, 6 to 59th St.; N, R to Lexington Ave. Lunch Mon–Fri, dinner daily. Major credit cards.

Colonnade Row 428-434 Lafayette St. at 4th St.

Originally a row of nine splendid, Greek-style, columned houses were built here in 1833 as homes for some of the city's financially elite families. Today only four of these once-magnificent townhouses remain, and they have suffered from neglect and look somewhat dilapidated. Subway: 6 to Astor Pl.

Columbia University (212) 854-1754 www.columbia.edu

The campus covers the area bounded by 114th and 120th Sts. and be-tween Amsterdam and West End Aves., but the university's presence ex-tends beyond into the entire community with its students and as the neighborhood's major landlord. The main entrance to the campus is at 116th St. and Broadway. There is an information office at this corner where tours of the campus, one of the oldest and finest private American univer-sities, are offered. Subway: 1, 9 to 116th St.-Columbia University.

Columbia University Low Memorial Library

This imposing late-nineteenth-century structure with its lofty dome and columned entry above three flights of stone steps dominates the main quadrangle of the campus at 116th St. It is now used as university offices, with the inner rotunda serving as the setting for a range of ceremonial and academic activities. Subway: 1, 9 to 116th St.-Columbia University.

Columbia University St. Paul's Chapel (212) 854-1487

This, one of the most handsome buildings on the campus, is a beautiful church built in 1904 in a blend of Byzantine and Gothic styles, laid out in the shape of a cross with a lovely dome and splendid tiled interior vaulting. Free organ concerts are given here. It is usually open, but because it is reserved for special functions, it is advisable to call first. Subway: 1, 9 to 116th St.-Columbia University.

Columbus Avenue

This street is a continuation uptown of Ninth Ave. starting at 66th St. Beginning some 20 years ago, it has blossomed as a thriving Upper West Side district jammed with upscale boutiques and restaurants, coffee bars, ice cream parlors, and clothing and specialty stores that cater to young professional clients, many of whom reside in the area. Subway: 1, 9 to 66th St.-Lincoln Center.

Columbus Avenue Flea Market (212) 721-0900

Every Sunday between 76th and 77th Sts. and at the P.S. 44 schoolyard, this market with some 300 stalls of various types of new and used jewelry, clothing, odds and ends, and even some fresh produce draws shoppers between 10 a.m. and 6 p.m. Subway: 1, 9 to 79th St.

Columbus Circle

Located at the intersection of Broadway, Central Park West, and 59th St., this windswept circle is the southwest corner of Central Park and strikes fear in the heart of pedestrians. There is a granite monument with a statue of Christopher Columbus at the top standing a lonely vigil in the midst of the endless sea of traffic on all sides. Subway: A, B, C, D, 1, 9 to 59th St.-Columbus Circle.

Columbus Day Parade

On Fifth Ave. from 44th to 86th Sts. on or around October 12, Italian schoolchildren, marching bands, union members, and recent arrivals from Italy, led by a big contingent of politicos stride proudly in this procession celebrating the famous explorer and their Italian heritage, while crowds of viewers in the thousands line the sidewalks.

Columbus Park

Located between Mulberry and Mott Sts. and Bayard and Baxter Sts., this park is the only open space in Chinatown. It is filled with older Chinese in the mornings carrying out their graceful Tai Chi motions. Subway: J, M, N, R, Z, 6 to Canal St.

Comedy Cellar 117 MacDougal St. btw Bleecker and W 3rd Sts. (212) 254-3480 www.comedycellar.com
This dark and cozy underground spot has been a Greenwich Village favorite for more than 20 years, showcasing fine jokesters. Subway: A, B, C, D, E, F, Q to W 4th St.-Washington Square. Open nightly. Admission charge. Minimum drink charge. Major credit cards.

Comedy Clubs *see* Astor Place Theatre, Boston Comedy Club, Caroline's Comedy Club, Chicago City Limits, Comedy Cellar, Comic Strip Live, Gladys' Comedy Room at Hamburger Harry's, Gotham Comedy Club, Luna Lounge, New York Comedy Club, Stand-Up New York, Surf Reality. *See also* Night Clubs.

Comfort Diner 214 E 45th St. btw Second and Third Aves. (212) 867-4555
An amiable eatery that's furnished like a 1950s diner, where old-fashioned dishes like macaroni and cheese, meatloaf, fried chicken, and good coffee are some of the attractions of this inexpensive place. Subway: S, 4, 5, 6, 7 to 42nd St.-Grand Central. Open 7:30 a.m.–11 p.m. weekdays, 9 a.m.–11 p.m. Sat and Sun. Major credit cards.

Comfort Inn Manhattan 42 W 35th St. btw Fifth and Sixth Aves., NY 10001 (212) 947-0200 or (800) 228-5150, fax (212) 594-3047 www.hotelchoice.com
This moderate-priced, comfortable, recently renovated hotel conveniently near Macy's provides its guests with fine continental breakfasts and newspapers. Subway: B, D, F, N, Q, R to 34th St.-Herald Square.

Comic Strip Live 1586 Second Ave. btw 81st and 82nd Sts. (212) 861-9386 www.comicstriplive.com
A long-lived venue showcasing stand-up comic talent, it has the flavor of a neighborhood watering hole, featuring knowns and promising unknowns with Monday nights open to amateur wanna-bes. Subway: 4, 5, 6 to 86th St. Open nightly. Admission charge varies. Drink minimum varies. Major credit cards.

Commerce Street
This is one of the city's tiniest streets, forming a small curve between Seventh Ave. South and Barrow St. On it can be found the Cherry Lane

Theatre at 38 Commerce St. Subway: 1, 9 to Christopher St.-Sheridan Square.

Complete Traveller Bookstore 199 Madison Ave. at 35th St. (212) 685-9007, fax (212) 982-7628

This is the place to locate every possible type of book or map on travel in New York and every other place in the world. Subway: 6 to 33rd St. Open daily. Major credit cards.

Con Ed Building *see* Consolidated Edison Building.

Con Ed Museum *see* Consolidated Edison Building.

Conan O'Brien Late Show *see Late Night with Conan O'Brien.*

Concert Halls *see* Classical Music.

Coney Island

In the 1920s Coney Island was describing itself as the world's largest playground. It's still a major Atlantic Ocean seaport pleasure center, with its 3-mile boardwalk and beaches that are jammed with sunbathers, swimmers, and boardwalk strollers on summer weekends. Some of its principal attractions include the amusement rides at Astroland and the Coney Island Cyclone, a hot dog from Nathan's, or simply eating cotton candy or munching on a corn dog while enjoying the ocean breeze. Subway: B, D, F, N to Stillwell Ave.-Coney Island.

Coney Island Cyclone 834 Surf Ave. and W 10th St., Coney Island, Brooklyn (718) 266-3434

This 1927 seaside landmark attraction lasts 100 terrifying seconds in a wooden roller coaster over nine slopes of old tracks while your digestive system feels every bit of the ups and downs. It is located in Astroland. Subway: B, D, F, N to Stillwell Ave.-Coney Island. Open daily from midday in summer season, weather permitting. No credit cards.

Coney Island Mermaid Parade (718) 372-5159

Usually held on the last Saturday in June, this colorful costume and float parade moves in a bizarre procession as participants outfitted as sea monsters, mermaids, Father Neptune, and other weird get-ups pass before the ecstatic crowds. Subway: B, D, F, N to Stillwell Ave.-Coney Island.

Coney Island Museum 1208 Surf Ave., Coney Island, Brooklyn (718) 372-5159 www.coneyisland.com

Run by the nonprofit organization Sideshows by the Seashore, located at W 12th St. and Surf Ave., this place is actually upstairs from Sideshows.

It contains considerable memorabilia about Coney Island. Sideshows offers a number of actors and performing artists playing roles like Snake Woman, Fire Eater, Escape Artist, and others to remind viewers of Coney Island's halcyon days. Subway: B, D, F, N to Stillwell Ave.-Coney Island. Open weekends during summer season, weather permitting. Modest admission charge.

Coney Island Wonder Wheel 1000 Surf Ave. at W 8th St., Coney Island, Brooklyn (718) 372-0275

Located in Astroland amusement park is this 1920 Ferris wheel that is said to be the tallest in the world and remains a treat for children of all ages. Subway: D, F to W. 8th St.-NY Aquarium. Open from midday during summer season, weather permitting. No credit cards.

Conference House National Historic Landmark (718) 984-2086

Located at the foot of Hylan Blvd. in Conference House Park in Totten-ville, Staten Island, this building is the historic place where the only peace conference ever took place between the American revolutionaries and the English military in September 1776. The building holds furnishings from the period and materials about the Revolutionary War. Guided tours are available when the house is open. Subway: 1, 9 to South Ferry; N, R to Whitehall St., then ferry to Staten Island. From Staten Island St. George Ferry Terminal, take Bus S79 to the last stop at Craig Ave. in Tottenville. Open Fri–Sun 1 p.m.–4 p.m. Modest admission charge.

Confucius Plaza *see* Chatham Square.

Congregation Shearith Israel 8 W 70th St. at Central Park W (212) 873-0300 www.sephardichouse.org/csi.html

This house of worship dates only to 1897, but the congregation can be traced to the mid-seventeenth century. The stained-glass windows of the synagogue are Tiffany creations. Subway: 6 to 68th St.-Hunter College.

Conservatory Garden *see* Central Park Conservatory Garden.

Conservatory Water *see* Central Park Model Boat Pond.

Consolidated Edison Building 4 Irving Pl. at 14th St.

This headquarters structure for Con Edison is best known for the strik-ing clock tower completed in 1926 with its bright illumination designed by Douglas Leigh of Times Square display renown. The small Con Ed Mu-seum on the ground floor is free and offers displays and interactive exhibits of how electricity works and the history of its development in the United States. Subway: L, N, R, 4, 5, 6 to 14th St.-Union Square.

Contemporary Restaurants *see* An American Place, Arizona 206, B. Smith's, Bouley Bakery, Clementine, Four Seasons Restaurant, Gotham Bar and Grill, Halcyon in the Rihga Hotel, Jean Georges, March, Odeon, The Park, River Café, Tavern on the Green, TriBeCa Grill, Water Club, Water's Edge, Zoë.

Continental Restaurants *see* Ambassador Grill, Café des Artistes, Jean Claude, Petrossian, Tavern on the Green.

Contrapunto 200 E 60th St. at Third Ave. (212) 751-8616 www.con trapuntonyc.com
A popular pasta restaurant favorite, offering good seafood and other dishes at reasonable prices, it's busy and noisy most of the time. Subway: N, R to Lexington Ave.; 4, 5, 6 to 59th St. Lunch and dinner daily. Major credit cards.

Convention and Visitors Bureau *see* New York Convention and Visitors Bureau.

Cooper Gallery *see* Paula Cooper Gallery.

Cooper-Hewitt Design Museum 2 E 91st St. at Fifth Ave. (212) 849-8400 www.si.edu/ndm
This branch of the Smithsonian Museum relocated into what was Andrew Carnegie's spacious mansion in 1976. It boasts an enormous collection of every aspect of design and the decorative arts and features frequently changing exhibitions. Programs of lectures, gallery talks, and workshops are offered, often treating the exhibition themes. The museum sponsors walking tours of NYC areas, and free musical concerts in the lovely rear garden are sometimes presented in summer. Subway: 4, 5, 6 to 86th St. Open Tues–Sun, hours vary. Admission charge. No credit cards.

Cooper Union 51 Astor Pl. (212) 353-4100
Located in what must be the largest brownstone building in New York at the triangle between Astor Pl. and Third and Fourth Aves., this 1859 building was constructed as a free college to provide technical education for students of promise in architecture, engineering, and art, and it continues in the tradition today. On the 2nd floor can be found the Houghton Gallery, which exhibits works on design and American history as well as student-created efforts. The Great Hall is where Abraham Lincoln made the 1860 speech said to have won him the Republican presidential nomination. Subway: 6 to Astor Pl.

Copacabana 34th St. at Eleventh Ave. (212) 239-2672 www.copaca banany.com

This legendary night club decked out in tropical decor is the spot for dancing to disco or live Latin bands on some nights and to the beat of some of the hottest sounds of different types of music from south of the border. Occupying this new site in spring 2002, the best current information on performances, nights open, and prices is available by telephone or at the Web site. Subway: A, C, E to 34th St.-Penn Station.

Copeland's 549 W 145th St. btw Broadway and Amsterdam Ave. (212) 234-2357

Fine soul food is the specialty here at moderate prices at dinner or the Sunday gospel brunch. There's cafeteria-style service at lower prices right next door. Subway: 1 to 145th St. Open for dinner Tues–Sun. Cafeteria open seven days from 8 a.m. Major credit cards.

Cornelia Street Café 29 Cornelia St. btw Bleecker and W 4th Sts. (212) 989-9319

A café/restaurant/cabaret featuring moderately priced American and country French meals, where small jazz groups often perform. Subway: A, B, C, D, E, F to W 4th St.; 1, 9 to Christopher St.-Sheridan Square. Open seven days from 10 a.m. Major credit cards.

Corner Billiards 85 Fourth Ave. at 11th St. (212) 995-1314

Twenty-eight tables are available here for those drawn to its pool tables. Subway: 4, 5, 6, L, N, R to 14th St.-Union Square. Open daily, hours vary. Major credit cards.

Cort Theatre 138 W 48th St. btw Sixth and Seventh Aves. (212) 239-6200

With a lobby of beautiful marble, this thousand-seat house has been the showcase for countless Broadway successes for three quarters of a century. Subway: N, R to 49th St.; B, D, F to 47th-50th Sts.-Rockefeller Center.

La Côte Basque 60 W 55th St. btw Fifth and Sixth Aves. (212) 688-6525

Dining at this outstanding restaurant is memorable for the gracious and lovely decor and comfort as well as the unsurpassed excellence of the French cuisine and superb service. It is, of course, very expensive and reservations are required. Subway: E, F to Fifth Ave. Lunch Mon–Sat, dinner daily. Major credit cards.

Cotton Club 666 W 125th St. btw Broadway and Riverside Dr. (212) 663-7980 www.cottonclubnewyork.com

Not the original, but this jazz hall still delivers good blues, jazz, and soul food in the evening and features a real gospel brunch on weekends. Subway: 1, 9 to 125th St. Open Thurs–Mon. Cover charge varies. Visa and MasterCard.

Country Music *see* The Bottom Line, Cowgirl Hall of Fame, Midsummer Night Swing.

Cowgirl Hall of Fame 519 Hudson St. at W Tenth Ave. (212) 633-1133

Tex-Mex food plus barbecue and other Southwestern favorites are served in bountiful portions with country music wailing and pictures of celebrated cowgirls hanging on the walls in this inexpensive and lively place. Subway: 1, 9 to Christopher St.-Sheridan Square. Lunch Mon–Fri, dinner daily, brunch on weekends. Major credit cards.

Criminal Courts Building *see* The Tombs.

Crossland Bank Building

Located just north of Herald Square where Broadway joins 36th St. is this structure with its unimpressive exterior but extremely attractive lobby and lovely skylight well worth having a peek at. Subway: B, D, F, N, R to 34th St.-Herald Square.

Crown Building 730 Fifth Ave. at 57th St.

This structure built in 1924 is best known for its very elaborate peak with a brightly shining upper section adorned in gold leaf, which reflects gloriously in the fading rays of the evening sun to form a brilliant crown. Subway: E, F, N, R to Fifth Ave.

Crown Heights

This Brooklyn residential area combines portions of Prospect Heights, Bedford-Stuyvesant, and East New York. The boundaries are hard to find for this community, but Fulton St. and Atlantic Ave. form something of a dividing line between Crown Heights and Bedford-Stuyvesant. The neighborhood is home to two distinct ethnic groups that live, at times very stormily, side by side. The West Indians hereabouts are drawn primarily from Haiti and Jamaica and form the city's largest concentration of Afro-Caribbean people. The Lubavitch Hasidic Jewish sect, while considerably fewer in number, is the other sizable local population, with the world headquarters for the Hasidic located at 770 Eastern Pkwy. in this neighborhood. Eastern Pkwy. is the main thoroughfare running through the center of Crown Heights. Subway: 3 to Kingston Ave.

Cruises *see* Boat Tours.

Cunard Building 25 Broadway at Bowling Green (212) 363-9490

This building now serves as a post office, but when constructed in 1921 it was the headquarters of the greatest passenger ship company of its time. The elaborate domed entry hall features lovely frescoes and murals of sailing ships and maps showing the routes of earlier sea explorers. Subway: 4, 5 to Bowling Green.

Cunningham Park 196-00 Union Turnpike, Queens (718) 217-6452

Most of this 324-acre park is situated between the Long Island Expressway and Grand Central Parkway in northeastern Queens and consists of native forest, meadows, and ponds. It is a favorite place for family picnics and concerts and offers many baseball fields, a number of tennis courts, soccer fields, and bicycle and jogging paths. It remains open daily from early morning until sunset. Subway: E, F to Kew Gardens-Union Turnpike, then Bus Q46 east to 193rd St.

Cushman Row *see* Chelsea Historic District.

Custom House 1 Bowling Green, Broadway at Bowling Green (212) 668-6624

This striking granite building, former home of the U.S. Custom House, was constructed in 1907 in the grand Beaux Arts style. It is handsomely embellished inside and out with symbolic representations of the world of maritime trade. The rotunda ceiling inside features a series of murals by Reginald Marsh brought into being under the sponsorship of the Depression era's Works Progress Administration. This building is now home to the National Museum of the American Indian. Subway: 4, 5 to Bowling Green.

Cycling *see* Bicycling.

Cyclone *see* Coney Island Cyclone.

Cypress Hills National Cemetery

Located in Brooklyn at Jamaica and Hale Aves., this final resting place is home to the original 3,000-some graves of Civil War casualties who died in hospitals around New York City. Subway: J to Cypress Hills. Open daily 9 a.m.–4:30 p.m. Admission free.

Czechoslovak Festival (718) 274-4925

At Bohemian Hall, 29-19 24th Ave. in Astoria, Queens, on Memorial Day weekend, this celebration is held; it includes music, dancing, and ethnic food. Subway: N to Astoria Blvd.

Da Umberto 107 W 17th St. btw Sixth and Seventh Aves. (212) 989-0303

Excellent Tuscan dishes and antipastos as well as fine service in an attractive restaurant in which the kitchen is on view behind glass in the rear, make this moderately expensive place a good choice for serious Italian dining. Subway: 1, 9 to 18th St. Lunch Mon–Fri, dinner Mon–Sat. American Express only.

Dahesh Museum 601 Fifth Ave. btw 48th and 49th Sts. (212) 795-0606 www.daheshmuseum.org

This small 2nd-floor space is a museum devoted exclusively to nineteenth- and early-twentieth-century European academic art. Changing exhibitions from its collection and elsewhere include paints, sculptures, prints, drawings, and decorative arts. Tours, lectures, symposia, musical evenings, and special children's activities supplement and complement the shows. Subway: 6 to 51st St.; B, D, F, Q to 47th-50th Sts.-Rockefeller Center. Open Tues–Sat 11 a.m.–6 p.m. Admission free.

Daily News

This tough tabloid newspaper with its screaming headlines covers local news thoroughly and has popular regular features and reviews that appeal to a mass audience.

Daily News Building 220 E 42nd St. btw Second and Third Aves.

This towering skyscraper has an Art Deco lobby featuring a giant illuminated globe that revolves slowly and recalls the Superman movies of the 1980s when this building was the site of the *Daily Planet* newspaper. Subway: S, 4, 5, 6, 7 to Grand Central-42nd St. Open Mon–Fri 8 a.m.–6 p.m.

The Dairy *see* Central Park Conservancy, Central Park Dairy.

The Dakota 1 W 72nd St. at Central Park W

Perhaps the most famous apartment building in New York, this luxury prestigious address has been home to innumerable celebrities and was so far from city center when it was constructed in 1884 that it might have been in the Dakota Territory. It recently underwent an exterior cleansing so that the external building's innumerable details are more clearly visible. Subway: B, C to 72nd St.

Dallas BBQ 27 W 72nd St. btw Columbus Ave. and Central Park W (212) 873-2004 www.bbqnyc.com

Crowded with enthusiasts for the barbecued chicken, ribs, burgers, and other tasty inexpensive treats, this restaurant has other locations at 1265 Third Ave. at E 73rd St. (212) 772-9393; 21 University Pl. at E 8th St. (212) 674-4450; 132 Second Ave. at St. Marks Pl. (212) 777-5574; 132 W 43rd St. between Sixth and Seventh Aves. (212) 221-9000; and 3956 Broadway at 166th St. (212) 568-3700. Subway: (W 72nd St.) B, C to 72nd St.; (Third Ave.) 6 to 77th St.; (University Pl.) N, R to 8th St.-NYU; (Second Ave.) 6 to Astor Pl.; (W 43rd St.) N, R, S, 1, 2, 3, 7, 9 to Times Square-42nd St.; (Broadway) 1, 9 to 168th St.-Washington Heights. Open daily 11:30 a.m.–midnight. Major credit cards.

Dana Discovery Center *see* Central Park Charles A. Dana Discovery Center.

Dance *see* Alvin Ailey American Dance Theater, American Ballet Theatre, Brooklyn Academy of Music, Chen and the Dancers, City Center of Music and Drama, Dance Theatre of Harlem, Dance Theatre Workshop, Danspace Project, Henry Street Settlement Abrons Art Center, Hunter College, Joyce Theatre, Judson Memorial Church, The Kitchen, Lincoln Center for the Performing Arts, Merce Cunningham Dance Studio, Metropolitan Opera House, Midsummer Night Swing, New York City Ballet, New York State Theatre, Next Wave Festival, O'Bon Festival, Out-of-Doors Festival, P.S. 122, Paul Taylor Dance Company, Performing Garage, Queens Theatre in the Park, Riverside Church, Surf Reality, Town Hall, Wave Hill. *See also* Dance Clubs.

Dance Clubs *see* Boca Chica, Bowlmor Lanes, Cheetah, China Club, Copacabana, Decade, Hell, Irving Plaza, Latin Quarter, Life, Nell's, Odessa, Ohm, Rasputin, Roxy, S.O.B.'s, Supper Club, Tunnel, Webster Hall.

Dance Theatre of Harlem 466 W 152nd St. btw Amsterdam Ave. and Convent St. (212) 690-2800 www.dancetheatreofharlem.com

The center for the highest standard of ballet performances, this is also an important school for dancers. It has been hosting a street dance festival for many years during the month of August, which is held on 152nd St. between Amsterdam Ave. and Convent St. Subway: C to 155th St.

Dance Theatre Workshop 219 W 19th St. btw Seventh and Eighth Aves. (212) 691-5829 or (212) 924-0077 www.dtw.org

Performing in the Bessie Schonberg Theatre, this group has been staging many alternative dance productions and has been a premier laboratory for showcasing emerging dance talent for many years at very modest prices. Subway: C, E to 23rd St.

Daniel 60 E 65th St. btw Park and Madison Aves. (212) 288-1033 www.danielnyc.com

To dine here is to enjoy extraordinary French country-style food raised to a fine art in an elegant formal setting where service and hospitality are gracious and thoughtful. The delightful meal will be quite expensive, and reservations long in advance are required. Subway: 6 to 68th St.-Hunter College. Lunch and dinner Mon–Sat. Major credit cards.

Danspace Project St. Mark's-in-the-Bowery Church, 131 E 10th St. at Second Ave. (212) 674-8112 www.danspaceproject.org

In one of the loveliest downtown dance spaces, avant-garde and experimental dance performances showcase choreographic works from September through June. Subway: 6 to Astor Pl.

Dante Park

Located on the triangular space just south of where Broadway and Columbus Ave. intersect across from Lincoln Center is this tiny park. The bronze statue in the park celebrates the famous Italian poet. Subway: 1, 9 to 66th St.-Lincoln Center.

David Letterman Show *see Late Show with David Letterman.*

Dawat 210 E 58th St. btw Second and Third Aves. (212) 355-7555

Billing itself as Dawat Haute Indian Cuisine, this restaurant has long been thought of as one of Manhattan's best for its unusual and tasty meat and vegetarian dishes that are creatively prepared. It is moderately expensive, and reservations are advisable. Subway: N, R to Lexington Ave.; 4, 5, 6 to 59th St. Lunch Mon–Sat, dinner daily.

de Hirsch Residence at the 92nd Street Y 1395 Lexington Ave. btw 91st and 92nd Sts., NY 10128 (212) 415-5650 or (800) 858-4692, fax (212) 415-5578 www.92ndsty.org

This clean, attractive spot has a three-day minimum but offers moderate prices for longer-term accommodations in dormitory and single rooms with shared bathrooms and laundry and cooking arrangements on each floor. The Y also sponsors classes, lectures, concerts, poetry readings, and other activities. Reservations here must be arranged far in advance. Subway: 4, 5, 6 to 86th St.

Dean & DeLuca 560 Broadway at Prince St. (212) 226-6800 www. dean-deluca.com

This is a fine and celebrated gourmet specialty store with a wide range of high-quality baked goods; fresh produce; wonderful cheeses; all sorts of meat, fish, and poultry products; dried fruits and nuts; great coffee bean selection; patés; and much more. There are several Dean & DeLuca cafés around town, but this location is quality food headquarters. Subway: N, R to Prince St. Mon–Sat 9 a.m.–8 p.m., Sun 9 a.m.–7 p.m. Major credit cards.

Decade 1117 First Ave. at 61st St. (212) 835-5979

This is an upscale place where well-dressed and established over-35-year-olds come on certain nights to sip champagne and dance to classic tunes. On other nights the tempo is livelier with jazz and younger patrons. Subway: 4, 5, 6 to 59th St.; N, R to Lexington Ave. Cover varies with the entertainment. Major credit cards.

Delacorte Clock *see* Central Park Delacorte Clock.

Delacorte Theatre *see* Central Park Delacorte Theatre.

Delancey Street

This once-majestic boulevard, which leads to the Williamsburg Bridge, is a major east–west cross street in the Lower East Side. Home in the past to crowds of people and peddlers' carts, today it is badly run down and lined only with tawdry stores and fast-food eateries. Subway: F, J, M, Z to Delancey-Essex St.

Delicatessens *see* Carnegie Delicatessen, Ess-A-Bagel, Katz's Delicatessen, Stage Delicatessen. *See also* Jewish Restaurants, Kosher Restaurants.

Deno's Wonderwheel Park 3059 W 12th St. at the Boardwalk, Coney Island, Brooklyn (718) 372-2592

This is an old-fashioned outdoor playground in Coney Island, where children of all ages can enjoy the rides. Subway: B, D, F, N to Coney Island-Stillwell Ave. Open daily from noon in warm season, weather permitting.

Department Stores *see* Barney's New York, Bergdorf Goodman, Bloomingdale's, Felissimo, Henri Bendel, Lord & Taylor, Macy's, Saks Fifth Ave., Takashimaya. *See also* Shopping Malls.

Dia Center for the Arts 548 W 22nd St. btw Tenth and Eleventh Aves. (212) 229-2744 www.diacenter.org

This large SoHo exhibition area on four floors offers changing shows of innovative modern works by contemporary artists using a wide range of styles and media, with a permanent rooftop installation as well. There are poetry readings, seminars, and lectures available here also. Subway: C, E to 23rd St. Wed–Sun noon–6 p.m. Modest admission charge.

Diamond District

On West 47th St. between Fifth and Sixth Aves. can be found jewelry stores and jewelry exchanges lining both sides of the street. Upstairs in the buildings, millions of dollars' worth of gold, pearls, and other gems are bought and sold daily. It is a grand bazaar of wheeling and dealing and is made more colorful and exotic by the ubiquitous sight of countless Hasidic Jews garbed in black frock coats and sporting beards and side locks. Subway: B, D, F, Q to 47th-50th Sts.-Rockefeller Center.

Diner 85 Broadway at Berry St., Williamsburg, Brooklyn (718) 486-3077

This is a genuine old dining car that attracts trendy crowds for the burgers and drinks served at modest prices. Subway: J, M, Z to Marcy Ave. Lunch and dinner daily. Visa and MasterCard.

Diners *see* Broadway Diner, Cheyenne Diner, Comfort Diner, Diner, EJ's Luncheonette, Empire Diner, Jackson Diner, Jones Diner, M&G Soul Food Diner, Moondance Diner, Tom's Restaurant.

DiPalo's 206 Grand St. at Mott St. (212) 226-1033

This store began in Little Italy in 1910 selling only fresh cheese, milk, and butter. Today it carries other specialty gourmet products like fine sausage and dried figs, but what it's most noted for is its superb selection of cheeses, which certainly rank with the finest that can be found anywhere in the city. Subway: B, D, Q to Grand St.; 6 to Spring St. Mon–Sat 9 a.m.–6:30 p.m., Sun 9 a.m.–3 p.m. Major credit cards.

Disabled Services *see Access for All, Access Guide to New York City,* Big Apple Greeter, Mayor's Office for People with Disabilities.

Discount Theatre Tickets *see* TKTS.

Discover NY City Walking Tours (917) 364-6047

Native New Yorkers lead informative tours ranging from 3 hours to all day to some of the city's most interesting places.

Discovery Tour (212) 665-8363

Offers a wide range of informative bus tours lasting 3 to 4 hours all through the week in foreign languages as well as English, focusing on some of New York's oldest neighborhoods and trendy newer areas in groups from four to thirty-four and starting at 489 Fifth Ave. between 41st and 42nd Sts.

Diwan Grill 148 E 48th St. btw Third and Lexington Aves. (212) 593-5425

Excellent meat, vegetarian dishes, and tandoori bread are served at this fine Indian restaurant with comfortable booth seating and moderate prices. Subway: 6 to 51st St.; N, R to Lexington Ave. Lunch and dinner daily. Major credit cards.

Dojo Restaurant 24 St. Marks Pl. btw Second and Third Aves. (212) 674-9821

The choices are between vegetarian and Japanese dishes at this very popular East Village spot where the food is healthy, delicious, and very inexpensive. There's another location at 14 W 4th St. between Broadway and Mercer St. (212) 505-8934. Subway: (St. Marks Pl.) 6 to Astor Pl.; (W 4th St.) A, B, C, D, E, F, Q to W 4th St. Daily 11 a.m.–midnight. No credit cards.

Dominicans in New York *see* Washington Heights.

Douglas Fairbanks Theatre 432 W 42nd St. btw Ninth and Tenth Aves. (212) 239-4321

One of several small houses with 100 or fewer seats located in 42nd St.'s off-Broadway Theatre Row. Subway: A, C, E to 42nd St.-Port Authority.

Downtown Arts Festival (212) 243-5050

Held in mid-September each year at various locations, this is a large-scale program featuring gallery tours, art exhibitions, performance art events, poetry and fiction readings, media showings, and more.

Downtown Athletic Club 19 West St. close to Battery Park (212) 425-7000 www.dacnyc.org

This is one of the downtown area's most interesting Art Deco constructions, dating from the 1920s. The front is an arcade of Moorish-style arches, and the façade features glazed, colored tiles. Subway: 1, 9 to South Ferry; 4, 5 to Bowling Green.

Doyle Auctions *see* William Doyle.

Drama Bookshop 723 Seventh Ave. btw 48th and 49th Sts., 2nd Floor (212) 944-0595 www.dramabookshop.com

Located in the heart of New York's theatrical district, where it obviously belongs, this is the place to find every type of book that would appeal to avid theatregoers and readers. Subway: N, R to 49th St.; 1, 9 to 50th St. Open daily, hours vary. Major credit cards.

Drawing Center 35 Wooster St. btw Broome and Grand Sts. (212) 219-2166 www.drawingcenter.org

This art gallery in SoHo is a big airy space where kids can interact with art, puppets, and objects. It is also a place for author readings combined with performance and visuals. Call to learn what's being scheduled. Subway: A, C, E to Canal St. Tues–Fri 10 a.m.–6 p.m., Sat 11 a.m.–6 p.m. Admission free.

Duffy Square *see* Father Duffy Square.

Duplex Cabaret 61 Christopher St. at Seventh Ave. (212) 255-5438 www.geocities.com/Broadway/Alley/6070

This night spot is popular with gays and others, with a lively downstairs piano bar and the cabaret section upstairs. Subway: 1, 9 to Christopher St.-Sheridan Square. Nightly 4 p.m.–4 a.m. Small cover on weekend, drink minimum. No credit cards.

Dyckman Farmhouse Museum 4881 Broadway at 204th St. (212) 304-9422 www.dyckman.org

This is the sole remaining eighteenth-century Manhattan farm building. It has been restored and contains pieces from the period and also displays Revolutionary War artifacts in a relic room. It is the main tourist attraction in Inwood at Manhattan's northmost point. Subway: A to Inwood-207th St. Tues–Sat 10 a.m.–5 p.m., Sun 10 a.m.–4 p.m. Admission free.

Dyckman Fields northern end of Manhattan on the Hudson River

This small, little-frequented park runs along the water and contains four baseball diamonds and a bike path. There's a small concrete pier at water's edge offering striking views south to the George Washington Bridge. Subway: A to Dyckman St., then walk west to the park.

E.A.T. 1064 Madison Ave. btw E 80th and 81st Sts. (212) 772-0022

An East Side version of Zabar's in the form of a café and take-out shop that provides excellent Jewish-style favorites such as soups, salads, sandwiches, and heavenly desserts to crowds of patrons at expensive prices. Subway: 6 to 77th St. Daily 7 a.m.–10 p.m. Major credit cards.

EJ's Luncheonette 1271 Third Ave. at 73rd St. (212) 472-0600

This classy diner satisfies hordes of East Side patrons with tasty and plentiful portions at moderate prices. Two other locations are at 447 Amsterdam Ave. at 81st St. (212) 872-3444 and 432 Sixth Ave. at 10th St. (212) 473-5555. Subway: (Third Ave.) 6 to 77th St.; (Amsterdam Ave.) 1, 9 to 79th St.; (Sixth Ave.) F, L to 14th St. Daily 8 a.m.–11 p.m. Cash only.

Eagle Warehouse 28 Old Fulton St., Brooklyn Heights, Brooklyn

Once home to the now defunct *Brooklyn Eagle* in the nineteenth century, this ancient-looking structure near the Brooklyn Bridge is now an apartment building. Subway: A, C to High St.

East Coast War Memorial

Granite slabs engraved with the names of American sea casualties of World War II can be found at this site at the south end of Battery Park that overlooks the harbor and offers excellent views of the Statue of Liberty and Ellis Island. Subway: 4, 5 to Bowling Green; 1, 9 to South Ferry.

East Midtown

The area from around 34th St. to 59th St. and east of Sixth Ave. is commonly termed East Midtown. This section of the town is characterized by rapidly striding businesspeople propelled to the next appointment, with cell phones in play while noisy taxis often move at a snail's pace through the side-street caverns between skyscrapers and hotels. The frantic and headlong movement and pulsing animation are precisely what the mind conjures as defining busy Manhattan.

East River Esplanade

One of Manhattan's favorite walking and jogging routes, part boardwalk and part promenade, runs beside the East River from 60th to 90th Sts.

East River Park

Running from Jackson St. to 15th St. east of East River Drive is this green oasis in lower Manhattan under the Williamsburg Bridge that fills with families and kids in warm weather, mostly drawn from neighboring housing projects. Subway: A, F, J, M to Delancey St.-Essex St.

East Side

When New Yorkers speak of the East Side, they usually refer to the elite neighborhood stretching from around Fifth Ave. to the East River and running between about 59th and 110th Sts. It is replete with tony residential addresses, excellent restaurants, classy shops, and all the services that cater to the more affluent.

East Side Billiard Club 163 E 86th St. btw Third and Lexington Aves. (212) 831-7665

In addition to playing pool here, customers can also get beer and snacks. Subway: 4, 5, 6 to 86th St. Daily 11 a.m.–4 a.m. Major credit cards.

East Village

This section is very different from its counterpart, Greenwich Village, also know as the West Village. This neighborhood stands between E 14th and E Houston Sts. and the East River and Broadway. Once considered a natural habitat of hippies and punks, it has been undergoing a rediscovery and upgrading its image through attempts at gentrification. It still has its share of seediness, but it also can boast many trendy and inexpensive restaurants and bars, quaint fashion boutiques, and experimental theatres. There's been an influx of artistic and literary residents to complement the earlier Ukrainian and Polish families making the region distinctive with a colorful blend of ethnic, vibrant, and youthful as well as gritty elements. Subway: L to First Ave. (on north side); or F to Second Ave. (on south side).

Easter Flower Show

Macy's department store at W 34th St. and Herald Square is the site of this celebrated, colorful extravaganza of floral displays during the week be-

fore Easter each year. Call Macy's Visitor's Center (212) 494-3827 for precise dates.

Easter Parade

This is not a formal event, but every Easter Sunday, usually in April.
New Yorkers in droves flamboyantly join the procession in extravagant
costumes and millinery creations to stroll along Fifth Ave. from around
Rockefeller Center to 59th St., with the greatest concentrations around St.
Patrick's Cathedral at 50th St., starting about 11 a.m. until about 3 p.m.
Subway: E, F to Fifth Ave.; 6 to 51st St.; B, D, F to 47th-50th Sts.-Rockefeller
Center.

Eastern Parkway

This six-lane roadway in Brooklyn starts at Grand Army Plaza at the
entrance to Prospect Park and stretches for several miles. It is lined on either side by larger residential buildings on one side and the Brooklyn Public Library central building and the Brooklyn Museum on the other side
near the Grand Army Plaza end. As the boulevard winds along, there are
smaller private houses, with the occasional larger public structure. Eastern
Pkwy. is the avenue along which many of Brooklyn's cultural events and
processions are held. Subway: 2, 3 to Grand Army Plaza (on west side); 3,
4 to Crown Heights-Utica Ave. (on east side).

Eastern States Buddhist Temple of America 64 Mott St. (212) 699-6229

Curious tourists who frequent this house of worship will find numerous
residents of Chinatown in prayer or meditation in pews before the altar
with its golden statues of Buddha. Subway: J, M, N, R, Z, 6 to Canal St.

Economy Candy 108 Rivington St. btw Essex and Ludlow Sts. (212) 254-1531 www.economycandy.com

Sugar products in all their irresistible forms, including imported jams,
chocolates, and other tempting confectionary products, are sold here at
very low prices. Subway: F, J, M, Z to Delancey St.-Essex St. Open daily
until 6 p.m. Major credit cards.

Ecuadorian Festival

On the Sunday nearest August 10, Ecuador's independence day from
Spain is celebrated with music, colorful dancing, and food at Flushing
Meadows-Corona Park in Queens. There is also a parade on Thirty-Seventh
Ave. from 70th to 94th Sts. in Jackson Heights. Subway: (Flushing Meadows-
Corona Park) 7 to Willets Pt.-Shea Stadium; (Jackson Heights) E, F, G, R
to Jackson Heights-Roosevelt Ave.

Ecuadorians in New York *see* Jackson Heights.

Edgar Allan Poe Cottage 2640 Grand Concourse at E Kingbridge Rd., Bronx (718) 881-8900

This small, white clapboard structure included in the National Register of Historic Places is where Poe spent his final years. It contains a kitchen and sitting room downstairs with a tiny office and bedroom above. The house is as bleak an abode as one might expect Poe to occupy. On display are Poe manuscripts and memorabilia, and one can view a short video about the man. Subway: B, D, 4 to Kingsbridge Rd. Open only on weekends. Modest admission charge.

Edward Mooney House 18 Bowery at Pell St.

This building constructed in 1785 is the city's oldest dwelling place. It began as a private home but was put to many different commercial uses from early in the nineteenth century on. Subway: J, M, N, R, Z, 6 to Canal St.

Eichenbaum Tours *see* Jack Eichenbaum Tours.

Elaine's 1703 Second Ave. btw 88th and 89th Sts. (212) 534-8103

The attraction of this dining spot is clearly not the expensive Italian food but the passion to ogle the celebrities from the entertainment, political, and media worlds who enter its doors to be greeted by the irrepressible Elaine herself. Subway: 4, 5, 6 to 86th St. Dinner nightly. Major credit cards.

El Barrio *see* El Barrio under B.

El Dorado Apartments 300 Central Park W btw 90th and 91st Sts.

This attractive Art Deco 1931 twin-towered luxury apartment building graciously overlooks the park. Subway: B, C to 86th St.

El Faro *see* El Faro under F.

El Museo del Barrio *see* El Museo del Barrio under M.

El Pollo *see* El Pollo under P.

El Quijote 226 W 23rd St. btw Seventh and Eighth Aves. (212) 929-1855

Spanish food is served in tasty abundance at moderate prices in this old-fashioned restaurant with its murals featuring the place's namesake. Subway: 1, 9 to 23rd St. Lunch and dinner daily. Major credit cards.

Eldridge Street Synagogue 12 Eldridge St. btw Canal and Division Sts. (212) 219-0888 www.eldridgestreet.org

This was the first New York synagogue, constructed by eastern European Jews in 1887, and is a national historic landmark. It is a large, elaborate structure with lovely carved wooden doors, an Italian hand-carved ark, and a sculpted wooden balcony. It is undergoing renovation but still open for very interesting tours and special events. Subway: F to E Broadway; B, D, Q to Grand St. Open for guided tours Tues and Thurs at 11:30 a.m. and 2:30 p.m. and Sun 11 a.m.–4 p.m. for hourly tours at a modest charge.

Elephant and Castle 68 Greenwich Ave. btw Sixth and Seventh Aves. (212) 243-1400 www.elephantcastle.com

A popular SoHo and Village dining spot and bar serving fine hamburgers and salads, excellent omelets as well as tasty other choices at reasonable prices. Subway: 1, 2, 3, 9 to 14th St. Open for breakfast, lunch, and dinner. Major credit cards.

Elias Greek Rite Church Kent St. btw Manhattan and Franklin Aves., Greenpoint, Brooklyn

This Gothic-inspired historic structure is located in the predominantly residential neighborhood of Greenpoint. Subway: G to Greenpoint Ave.

Ellis Island (212) 363-3200 www.ellisisland.org

During the years from 1892 to 1924 this was the entry point to America for some 12 million immigrants, and this small island in the New York Harbor is one of the city's favorite tourist destinations. After many years of decay and neglect, a multimillion-dollar restoration led to the main building on the island being opened as a museum in 1990. Ferries serve the Statue of Liberty and Ellis Island on the same run. Subway: 1, 9 to South Ferry; 4, 5 to Bowling Green, then Statue of Liberty Ferry, leaving from Battery Park pier 9 a.m.–5 p.m.

Ellis Island Museum of Immigration (212) 363-3200 www.ellisis land.com

This fascinating place dramatically displays artifacts, photographs, maps, exhibitions, and documentary films about the island's history. A special feature with a modest charge is offered from April to September: *Ellis Island Stories,* a moving, live dramatic reenactment of immigrant experiences. The Wall of Honor identifies many of those who came through Ellis Island, and "Treasures from Home" is a collection of touching photos and other artifacts contributed by descendants of the immigrants. Subway: 1, 9 to South Ferry; 4, 5 to Bowling Green, then Statue of Liberty Ferry leaving from Battery Park pier 9 a.m.–5 p.m. Admission to the museum is free.

Emergencies

Dial 911 in emergencies for response by police, fire department, or ambulance. If you require emergency treatment and can go to the emergency room of a hospital, the private hospitals are preferable to the overtaxed public hospitals. In Manhattan, the private hospitals with twenty-four-hour emergency rooms include St. Vincent's Hospital, Seventh Ave. at 11th St. (212) 604-7000; Beth Israel Medical Center, First Ave. at 16th St. (212) 420-2000; New York University Medical Center, First Ave. at 34th St. (212) 263-7300; St. Luke's-Roosevelt Hospital, Ninth Ave. at 58th St. (212) 523-4000; New York Presbyterian Hospital, 622 W 168th St. (212) 305-2500; and Mount Sinai Hospital, Fifth Ave. at 100th St. (212) 241-6500.

Emily's Restaurant 1325 Fifth Ave. at E 111th St. (212) 996-1212

This pleasant spot serves excellent ribs and barbecued chicken at moderate prices. Subway: 2, 3 to 110th St.-Central Park N. Open daily for lunch and dinner, hours vary. Major credit cards.

Empire Diner 210 Tenth Ave. btw W 22nd and W 23rd Sts. (212) 243-2736

The authentic diner atmosphere is the charm of this Art Deco restaurant, with its stainless steel counter and black and chrome trim. Open 24 hours every day, it is often crowded and offers simple dishes like hamburgers and sandwiches at moderate prices. Subway: C, E to 23rd St. Major credit cards.

Empire Fulton Ferry State Park *see* Fulton Ferry District.

Empire Hotel 44 W 63rd St. at Broadway, NY 10023 (212) 265-7400 or (888) 822-3555, fax (212) 245-3382 www.empirehotel.com

This moderately priced establishment, close to Lincoln Center, offers quite small, cheerfully furnished rooms. Subway: 1, 9 to 66th St.-Lincoln Center.

Empire State Building 34th St. and Fifth Ave. (212) 736-3100 www.esbnyc.com

Since it was constructed in 1931, this has been the symbol of New York. Its 102 stories soar high above and it draws some 3 million visitors a year. The favorite viewing sites for everything for up to 80 miles around on a clear day are from its 86th-floor exterior observation deck or its 102nd-floor indoor observatory, reached by swift elevators climbing 1,200 feet a minute. There's also a free tour around the neighborhood of the building offered by the 34th Street Partnership. Call for details at (212) 868-0521.

Subway: B, D, F, Q, N, R to 34th St.-Herald Square. Observatories open daily 9:30 a.m.–midnight. Admission charge. *See also* City Pass.

Empire State Building Run-Up (212) 736-3100

In mid-February each year, runners race up the more than 1,500 steps from the lobby floor to the 86th-floor observation deck. Subway: B, D, F, Q, N, R to 34th St.-Herald Square.

Enchanted Forest 85 Mercer St. btw Spring and Broome Sts. (212) 925-6677

An extraordinarily imaginative toy store, where many unusual playthings in the form of charming stuffed animals, puppets and marionettes, masks, and more dwell in a magical forest that appeals as much to adults as to kids. Subway: 6 to Spring St. Open daily 11 a.m.–7 p.m. Major credit cards.

Engine Company No. 31 87 Lafayette St. at White St. (212) 966-4510

Now occupied by the Downtown Community Television Center, which provides courses, seminars, and exhibitions of the work of artists and film makers, this 1895 building is a splendid example of the best of nineteenth-century firehouse construction, with its impressive French-chateaulike features. Subway: J, M, N, R, Z, 6 to Canal St.

Engine Company No. 55 363 Broome St. btw Mott and Elizabeth Sts.

This city landmark fire station was constructed in 1898 and is a richly ornamental, well-preserved brick and limestone structure featuring a great archway and lovely oval windows. Subway: J, M to Bowery.

Enrico Fermi Cultural Center 610 E 186th St., Bronx (718) 933-6410 www.nypl.org/branch/bx/ber.html

Located within the Belmont Regional Library of the New York Public Library in the heart of the Belmont neighborhood, home to a large Italian population, this is one of the city's leading resources for information about the cultural traditions of Italian-Americans and offers a substantial collection of publications in Italian. It also sponsors special events and programs on Italian themes. Subway: B, D to Fordham Rd., then Bus BX12 east. Mon–Sat, hours vary. Admission free.

Ensemble Studio Theatre 549 W 52nd St. btw Tenth and Eleventh Aves. (212) 247-3405 www.ensemblestudiotheatre.org

This acting group showcases promising new dramatic works and sponsors an annual one-act play series. Subway: C, E to 50th St.

Episcopal Church of the Transfiguration *see* Church of the Transfiguration.

The Esplanade *see* The Promenade.

Ess-A-Bagel 831 Third Ave. btw 50th and 51st Sts. (212) 980-1010
Twelve types of bagels are baked daily and sold here. They are big with chewy crusts, and they taste delicious. Different types of sandwiches are available as well for carryout or dining in, all at modest prices. A second location is at 359 First Ave. at 21st St. (212) 260-2252. Subway: (Third Ave.) 6 to 51st St.; E, F to Lexington Ave.; (First Ave.) 6 to 23rd St. Daily 6:30 a.m.–10 p.m., except Sun until 5 p.m. Major credit cards.

Essex Street Market Essex St. btw Rivington and Delancey Sts. (212) 388-0449
When pushcarts became illegal in 1939, this covered market took their place in what is now an old municipal building. It's filled with stalls selling traditional Jewish and Italian food specialties, but there's also a great deal of Latin American and Chinese groceries and produce to meet the requirements of the Lower East Side's current ethnic diversity. Subway: F, J, M, Z to Delancey St.-Essex St. Mon–Fri 9 a.m.–6 p.m.

Estiatorio Milos Restaurant 125 W 55th St. btw Sixth and Seventh Aves. (212) 245-7400
This fashionable Greek seafood house prepares diner-selected fresh fish and then serves it in a relaxed manner in a lively and cheerful ambiance where prices are moderately expensive. Subway: B, D, E to Seventh Ave. Lunch Mon–Fri, dinner daily. Major credit cards.

Ethel Barrymore Theatre 243 W 47th St. btw Broadway and Eighth Ave. (212) 239-6200
Since its construction in the 1920s to attract Ms. Barrymore to perform there, this house has been the setting for innumerable Broadway dramatic productions. Subway: 1, 9 to 56th St.; N, R to 49th St.

Ethiopian Restaurants *see* Ghenet, Massawa, Meskerem.

Ethnic and Community Museums *see* African American Wax Museum, Alliance Française, Americas Society, Asian Society, Chassidic Art Institute, China Institute Gallery, Garibaldi-Meucci Museum, Goethe House German Cultural Institute, Hispanic Society of America, Jacques Marchais Museum of Tibetan Art, Japan Society, Jewish Museum, Kurdish Library and Museum, Lower East Side Tenement Museum, El Museo del Barrio, Museum for African Art,

Museum of Jewish Heritage, Museum of the Chinese in the Americas, National Museum of the American Indian, Neue Galerie, Schomburg Center for Research in Black Culture, Studio Museum in Harlem, Ukrainian Museum. *See also* Art and Design Museums, Historical Museums, Major New York City Museums, Media Museums, Military Museums, Museums of Particular Interest to Children and Teens, Science and Technology Museums, Specialized City Museums.

Ethnic Music *see* Rock, Alternative, and Ethnic Music.

Ethnic Neighborhoods *see* Aleppo in Flatbush, Astoria, Atlantic Avenue, Bainbridge, El Barrio, Bay Ridge, Belmont, Bensonhurst, Borough Park, Brighton Beach, Carroll Gardens, Chinatown, Crown Heights, Flatbush, Flushing, Fort Greene, Greenpoint, Howard Beach, The Italian Village, Jackson Heights, Jamaica, Little India, Little Italy, Little Korea, Little Lebanon in Bay Ridge, Little Ukraine, Lower East Side, La Saline, Sunnyside Queens, Washington Heights, Williamsburg, Woodside, Yorkville.

Eugene O'Neill Theatre 230 W 49th St. btw Broadway and Eighth Ave. (212) 239-6200
Originally known as the Forrest when it was built in 1925, this house was later renamed for the celebrated playwright in 1959. It has since been the showcase for many hit plays by some of Broadway's most stellar dramatists and musical producers. Subway: N, R to 49th St.; 1, 9 to 50th St.

Events in New York *see* African-American Day Parade, African Arts Festival, American Crafts Festival, Antiquarian Book Fair, The Art Show, Atlantic Antic Street Festival, Bang On a Can Festival, Baseball Season, Basketball Season, Bastille Day, Belmont Stakes, Big Apple Circus, Bike New York: The Great Five Boro Bike Tour, Black Film Festival, Black History Month, Black World Championship Rodeo, Blessing of the Animals, Brazilian Carnival, Broadway on Broadway, Brooklyn Beerfest, Brooklyn Bridge Day, Bryant Park Film Festival, Celebrate Brooklyn, Chase Bank Melrose Games, Cherry Blossom Festival, Chinese New Year, Christmas Spectacular at Radio City Music Hall, Christmas Window Displays, Colombian Independence Day Festival, Columbus Day Parade, Coney Island Mermaid Parade, Czechoslovak Festival, Easter Parade, Ecuadorian

Festival, Empire State Building Run-Up, Fall Antiques Show, Feast of St. Anthony, Feast of San Gennaro, Feast of Santa Rosalia, Feast of the Giglio, Festa Italiana, Festa of Our Lady of Mt. Carmel, Fleet Week, Football Season, Golden Gloves Boxing Championships, Goldman Memorial Band Concerts, Great Irish Fair, Greater New York International Auto Show, Greek Heritage Festival, Greek Independence Day Parade, Greenwich Village Jazz Festival, Halloween Parade in Greenwich Village, Hanukkah Menorah, Harlem Meer Performance Festival, Harlem Week, Hispanic Day Parade, Hong Kong Dragon Boat Festival, Ice Hockey Season, India Day Parade, India Festival, International Asian Fine Arts Fair, International Cat Show, International Cultures Expo Fest, International Cultures Parade, International Fine Arts and Antiques Dealers Show, JVC Jazz Festival, Lesbian and Gay Film Festival, Lesbian and Gay Pride Parade, Lincoln Center Festival, Lincoln Center Out-of-Doors, Lower East Side Festival of the Arts, Lower East Side Jewish Festival, Macy's Fireworks Display, Macy's Flower Show, Macy's Thanksgiving Day Parade, Martin Luther King Jr. Day Parade, Medieval Festival, Messiah Sing-In, Metropolitan Opera Parks Concerts, Midsummer Night Swing, Mini Marathon, Mostly Mozart Festival, Museum Mile Festival, National Boat Show, National Horse Show, New Directors New Films, New Year's Eve Celebrations, New York City Ballet Spring Season, New York City Marathon, New York City Opera Season, New York Film Festival, New York Flower Show, New York Fringe Festival, New York Is Book Country, New York Jazz Festival, New York Jewish Film Festival, New York Philharmonic Parks Concerts, New York Underground Film Festival, New York Video Festival, Next Wave Festival, Ninth Avenue Street Festival, Norwegian Day Parade, O'Bon Festival, One World Festival, Out-of-Doors Festival, Out of the Darkness, Outsider Art Fair, Philippine Independence Day Parade, Presidents Day Sales, Promenade Art Show, Puerto Rican Day Parade, Pulaski Day Parade, Queens Ethnic Folk Festival, Restaurant Week, Richmond County Fair, Ringling Brothers and Barnum & Bailey Circus, St. Patrick's Day Parade, Salute to Israel Parade, Shakespeare in the Park, Small Press Book Fair, Summer Festival at Snug Harbor Cultural Center, Summer Garden Concerts, SummerStage, Tap City Festival, Tree-Lighting Ceremony, Triple Pier Expo, Tugboat Challenge, U.S. Open Tennis Championships,

Valentine's Day Marriage Marathon, Veterans Day Parade, Virginia Slims Championships, Von Steuben Day Parade, Washington Square Music Festival, Washington Square Outdoor Art Exhibit, Welcome Back to Brooklyn Festival, West Indian Carnival, Westminster Kennel Club Dog Show, Wigstock, Winter Antiques Show, World Financial Center Arts and Events.

Events in New York by Month

January *see* Chinese New Year, National Boat Show, New York Jewish Film Festival, Outsider Art Fair, Winter Antiques Show.

February *see* The Art Show, Black History Month, Chase Bank Melrose Games, Empire State Building Run-Up, International Cat Show, New York City Opera Season, Presidents Day Sales, Valentine's Day Marriage Marathon, Westminster Kennel Club Dog Show.

March *see* Greek Independence Day Parade, New Directors New Films, New York Flower Show, New York Underground Film Festival, Ringling Brothers and Barnum & Bailey Circus, St. Patrick's Day Parade, Small Press Book Fair, Triple Pier Expo.

April *see* Antiquarian Book Fair, Baseball Season, Easter Parade, Golden Gloves Boxing Championships, Greater New York International Auto Show, Macy's Flower Show, New York City Ballet Spring Season.

May *see* Bike New York: The Great Five Boro Bike Tour, Black World Championship Rodeo, Brooklyn Bridge Day, Cherry Blossom Festival, Czechoslovak Festival, Fleet Week, Harlem Meer Performance Festival, International Asian Fine Arts Fair, International Fine Arts and Antique Dealers Show, Lesbian and Gay Film Festival, Lower East Side Festival of the Arts, Martin Luther King Jr. Day Parade, Ninth Avenue Street Festival, Norwegian Day Parade, Washington Square Outdoor Art Exhibit.

June *see* African Arts Festival, American Crafts Festival, Belmont Stakes, Bryant Park Film Festival, Celebrate Brooklyn, Coney Island Mermaid Parade, Feast of St. Anthony, Goldman Memorial Band Concerts, Greek Heritage Festival, International Cultures Expo Fest, JVC Jazz Festival, Lesbian and Gay Pride Parade, Lower East Side Jewish Festival, Midsummer Night Swing, Mini Marathon, Museum Mile Festival, New York Jazz Festival, Philippine Independence Day Parade, Puerto Rican Day Parade, Restaurant Week, Salute to Israel Parade, Shakespeare in the Park, SummerStage, Welcome Back to Brooklyn Festival, World Financial Center Arts and Events.

July *see* Bastille Day, Colombian Independence Day Festival, Feast of the Giglio, Festa Italiana, Festa of Our Lady of Mt. Carmel, Lincoln Center Festival, Macy's Fireworks Display, Metropolitan Opera Parks Concerts,

Mostly Mozart Festival, New York Philharmonic Parks Concerts, New York Video Festival, O'Bon Festival, Summer Festival at Snug Harbor Cultural Center, Summer Garden Concerts, Tap City Festival, Washington Square Music Festival.

August *see* Black Film Festival, Ecuadorian Festival, Feast of Santa Rosalia, Greenwich Village Jazz Festival, Harlem Week, Hong Kong Dragon Boat Festival, India Day Parade, India Festival, Lincoln Center Out-of-Doors, New York Fringe Festival, Out-of-Doors Festival, U.S. Open Tennis Championships.

September *see* African-American Day Parade, Atlantic Antic Street Festival, Brazilian Carnival, Broadway on Broadway, Brooklyn Beerfest, Feast of San Gennaro, Great Irish Fair, International Cultures Parade, New York Film Festival, New York Is Book Country, Next Wave Festival, One World Festival, Queens Ethnic Folk Festival, Richmond County Fair, Tugboat Challenge, Von Steuben Day Parade, West Indian Carnival, Wigstock.

October *see* Bang On a Can Festival, Blessing of the Animals, Basketball Season, Columbus Day Parade, Football Season, Halloween Parade in Greenwich Village, Hispanic Day Parade, Ice Hockey Season, International Fine Arts and Antique Dealers Show, Medieval Festival, Promenade Art Show, Pulaski Day Parade.

November *see* Big Apple Circus, Christmas Spectacular at Radio City Music Hall, Christmas Window Displays, Fall Antiques Show, Macy's Thanksgiving Day Parade, National Horse Show, New York City Marathon, Triple Pier Expo, Veterans Day Parade, Virginia Slims Championships.

December *see* Hanukkah Menorah, Messiah Sing-In, New Year's Eve Celebrations, Out of the Darkness, Tree-Lighting Ceremony.

Excellent Dumpling House 111 Lafayette St. just south of Canal St. (212) 219-0212

Truly celebrated for its splendid vegetarian and meat dumplings prepared fried, steamed, or boiled, this small, crowded restaurant offers a range of other fine noodle, chicken, and fish dishes, all at modest prices. Subway: M, N, R, Z, 5, 6 to Canal St. Lunch and dinner daily. No credit cards.

Excelsior Hotel 45 W 81st St. btw Columbus Ave. and Central Park W, NY 10024 (212) 362-9200 or (800) 368-4575, fax (212) 721-2994 www.excelsiorhotelny.com

Close to both the American Museum of Natural History and Central Park, this comfortable, moderate-priced hotel has undergone recent renovation. Subway: B, C to 81st St.; 1, 9 to 79th St.

Exercise *see* Fitness Centers, Participatory Sports Activity.

Exit Art 548 Broadway btw Spring and Prince Sts., 2nd Floor (212) 966-7745 www.exitart.org

In two exhibit areas and a performance space this organization features alternative and experimental works by emerging and recognized artists. Subway: N, R to Prince St. Open Tues–Sat, hours vary. Admission charge.

Express Reservations (800) 356-1123 (weekdays only, 9 a.m.–6:30 p.m.), fax (303) 440-0166 www.expressreservations.com

This company features a good range of Manhattan hotels at a discount.

F.A.O. Schwarz 767 Fifth Ave. at 58th St. (212) 644-9400 www.
fao.com

America's favorite and most loved toy store beguiles children of all ages.
An enormous inventory of ingenious, colorful, imaginative, and conventional playthings that is hard to resist and almost impossible to leave without buying something. Fun for young and old. Subway: N, R to Fifth Ave.
Open daily, hours vary.

FDNY Fire Zone 34 W 51st St. btw Fifth and Sixth Aves. (212) 698-4520 www.fdnyfirezone.org

This program of the city's fire department is a lively multimedia presentation of real fire fighting. The viewers are seated on a full-size fire truck while they watch a film showing a fire company headed for a fire. Subway: B, D, F, Q to 47th-50th Sts.-Rockefeller Center. Open daily, hours vary. Modest admission charge.

Fairbanks Theatre *see* Douglas Fairbanks Theatre.

Fall Antiques Show (212) 452-3067

In mid-November each year some 100 dealers from around the country display their wares for collectors of American antiques in perhaps the foremost show of its type in the United States at the Seventh Regiment Armory, 643 Park Ave. at 66th St. Subway: 6 to 68th St.

El Faro 823 Greenwich St. at Horatio St. (212) 929-8210

This venerable restaurant offers some of the finest Spanish food in the city at moderate prices. Subway: A, C, E to 14th St.; L to Eighth Ave. Lunch and dinner Mon–Sat. Major credit cards.

Fashion Avenue

This is simply another designation for Seventh Ave. along the stretch from around 34th St. to 42nd St., which is the heart of New York's garment industry. Subway: 1, 2, 3, 9 to 34th St.-Penn Station.

Fashion Institute of Technology Seventh Ave. at 27th St. (212) 217-5800 www.fitnyc.suny.edu

This is the city's center for instruction in fashion, art, design, and manufacturing for the garment trade. Its museum gallery features striking exhibitions that focus on some facet of the fashion world or the work of outstanding designers and are open to the public. Subway: 1, 9 to 28th St. Tues–Sat, hours vary. Admission free.

Father Duffy Square Traffic Island btw Broadway and Seventh Ave. and W 46th and 47th Sts.

This triangle at the north end of Times Square features a statue of the famous "Fighting Priest" of World War I as well as one of George M. Cohan of "Yankee Doodle Dandy" fame. Here's where the lines form to buy discounted tickets for Broadway and off-Broadway shows at the TKTS booths at the northmost end of the triangle. Subway: N, R, S, 1, 2, 3, 7, 9 to Times Square-42nd St.

Feast of St. Anthony

On the last day of this festival, June 15, the image of St. Anthony of Padua is carried along in procession along Sullivan St. in Little Italy. It is a smaller event than the San Gennaro festival, but there are food stands and games of chance to engage the many spectators. In the Bronx, St. Anthony is also celebrated from June 5 to June 15 every evening along 187th St. with a carnival of food stalls, music, and other activities. Subway: (Sullivan St.) 6 to Spring St.; (187th St.) B, D to Fordham Rd.

Feast of St. Francis see Blessing of the Animals.

Feast of San Gennaro

For more than 75 years along Mulberry St. north of Canal St. in Little Italy this patron saint of Naples has been celebrated for ten days around the third week of September. This is the city's biggest, best known, and most crowded festa, with hundreds of vendors selling food, music and games, and the annual parade of the statue of the saint through the streets usually following a Mass at Most Precious Blood Catholic Church at 113 Baxter St. (212) 226-6427, where the statue resides. Subway: 6 to Spring St.

Feast of Santa Rosalia

This event at the end of August takes place for one week along Eighteenth Ave. in Bensonhurst, Brooklyn, when the Sicilian patron saint is celebrated with lights, music, and food stalls selling Italian specialties. Subway: N to Eighteenth Ave.

Feast of the Giglio

The high point of this twelve-day Italian festival is the Dance of the Giglio, when a platform bearing a tremendous structure is carried through the streets on the shoulders of an army of men. It all takes place in mid-July in Williamsburg, Brooklyn, around Our Lady of Mt. Carmel Church, 1 Havemeyer St. at N 8th St. (718) 384-9848. Subway: L to Lorimer St.

Federal Hall National Memorial 26 Wall St. at Broad St. (212) 825-6888 www.nps.gov/feha

This fine Greek Revival structure is the place where George Washington was sworn in and the nation had its beginning. It also served as the home to the federal government and Congress. The hall features a handsome rotunda with a bronze statue of George Washington beside the staircase. It is open to visitors Mon–Fri 9 a.m–5 p.m. and is free, with exhibits displaying the history of the site and the downtown area. Subway: J, M, Z to Broad St.; 4, 5 to Wall St.

Federal Reserve Bank of New York 33 Liberty St. btw Nassau and William Sts. (212) 720-6130 www.ny.frb.org

Occupying an entire block, this massive fortress holds in its below-ground vaults the world's largest gold hoard. Free tours are offered Mon–Fri (which should be arranged at least five days in advance or longer during busy periods). They take one hour and offer visual details of the bank's operations and views of the gold vaults and other features of the institution. Subway: 4, 5 to Fulton St.-Broadway Nassau.

Felidia 243 E 58th St. btw Second and Third Aves. (212) 758-1479

A celebrated authentic Italian dining spot with different decor styles in the comfortable rustic room and bar area or the balcony with its skylight. Delicious regional and seasonal dishes are featured in this moderately expensive restaurant where reservations are required. Subway: 4, 5, 6 to 59th St.; N, R to Lexington Ave. Lunch Mon–Fri, dinner Mon–Sat. Major credit cards.

Felissimo 10 W 56th St. btw Fifth and Sixth Aves. (212) 247-5656 www.felissimo.com

This Japanese-operated store offers a stock of tempting things for the home as well as jewelry and clothing in an attractive renovated townhouse close to Fifth Ave. On the top floor a calm and peaceful café dispenses

sandwiches and tea. Subway: N, R to Fifth Ave.; 2 to 57th St. Open Mon–
Sat, hours vary. Major credit cards.

Fermi Cultural Center *see* Enrico Fermi Cultural Center.

Ferries *see* Circle Line Cruises, Ellis Island, Staten Island Ferry,
Statue of Liberty/Ellis Island Museum Ferry.

Festa de San Gennaro *see* Feast of San Gennaro.

Festa Italiana

This event is held from July 20 to July 30 on Carmine St. in Little Italy.
The Church of Our Lady of Pompeii offers special Masses, the band delights
the street crowds, and there are numerous food stands selling Italian treats,
as well as children's rides and games of chance. Subway: 6 to Spring St.

Festa of Our Lady of Mt. Carmel

This celebration has been going in the Belmont Little Italy neighborhood of the Bronx since 1906. The procession takes place on the Sunday
following the saint's day on July 16. Men carry the statue on her altar, and
women lead the parade followed by a band and church dignitaries as the
march moves through the neighborhood. Food stands and games of
chance add to the festive atmosphere. The church is located at 627 E 187th
St. (718) 295-3770. Another procession takes place around the Church of
Our Lady of Mt. Carmel in East Harlem at 448 E 116th St. (212) 534-0681,
where the celebrants are Haitians who venerate Mary with music and pray-
ers in the Caribbean tradition. Subway: (Belmont) B, D to Fordham Rd.;
(East Harlem) 6 to 116th St.

Festival of Lights *see* Hanukkah Menorah.

Festivals *see* Events in New York, Events in New York by Month.

Fez inside Time Café, 380 Lafayette Ave. at Great Jones St. (212)
533-2680 www.feznyc.com

At the dividing point between the East and West Village is this lively
Moroccan-inspired spot offering nightly events ranging from readings to
comedy to excellent jazz performances for which reservations are necessary. The Time Café is open seven days a week from morning until late
night. Fez is open nightly with varying hours. Admission prices vary with
the entertainment. Subway: B, D, F, Q to Broadway-Lafayette St.; 6 to
Bleecker St. Major credit cards. Drink minimum.

Field House *see* Chelsea Piers.

Fifth Avenue

Just as Paris has its Champs-Élysées, and Rome the Via Veneto, New York has Fifth Ave. The streets from 42nd to 59th Sts. are the main line of confident consumerism, but the portion between 49th and 59th Sts. from Rockefeller Center to the Plaza Hotel is its loftiest point. Fifth Ave. is synonymous with luxury goods, and the shops, hotels, boutiques, and other establishments that line both sides of this street make it one of the favorite tourist destinations for window shopping and people watching in town. On days when the avenue is reserved for celebrations, thousands of spectators line the streets to watch the colorful parades. Subway: (northern end) N, R to Fifth Ave.; (southern end) Grand Central-42nd St.

Fifth Avenue Presbyterian Church 7 W 55th St. at Fifth Ave. (212) 247-0490 www.fapc.org

This awe-inspiring structure constructed in 1875 is the largest Presbyterian house of worship in the city, with seats for 1,800 worshippers. Its interior with its austere pulpit and pews is a sharp contrast with the glitz of most of the neighborhood. Subway: E, F to Fifth Ave.

55 Bar and Grill 55 Christopher St. btw Sixth and Seventh Aves. (212) 929-9883

This is a pleasant, intimate night spot where one can count on finding excellent live musical entertainment every night of the week. Jazz is featured most nights. The bar opens at 1 p.m., and music starts in the evening. Subway: 1, 9 to Christopher St.-Sheridan Square. Modest admission charge, except for well-known performers. No credit cards.

52nd Street

Between Fifth and Sixth Aves. was "The Street" for the finest jazz music in the world with all the famous names during the fabled 1930s and '40s performing in night spots in old brownstone buildings. It's all gone now except for the street signs still proclaiming this as "Swing Street" and the plaques in the sidewalk close to Sixth Ave. paying tribute to some of the jazz greats. Subway: E, F to Fifth Ave.

57th Street

This important wide street runs across town from river to river. From about Sixth Ave. east can be found some of the city's most opulent shops as well as major art galleries, and farther east are many luxury doorman-attended apartment buildings, which are home to some of the city's elite.

West of Sixth Ave. there is a great miscellany of activities, structures, and people conforming to no single defining theme.

59th Street Bridge *see* Queensboro Bridge.

Film Center Building 630 Ninth Ave. btw 44th and 45th Sts.

Many film companies maintain offices in this structure, but its most stunning feature is the Art Deco lobby and interior entryway, designed by a gifted decorative architect of the modernist period of the earlier part of the twentieth century, which can be seen during the business day. Subway: A, C, E to 42nd St.-Port Authority.

Film Festivals *see* Events in New York, Events in New York by Month.

Film Forum 209 W Houston St. btw 6th and Varick Sts. (212) 727-8100

This venue with its three screens is the place to find independent and foreign films, documentaries, and classic revivals sometimes presented as part of a series on directors, other cinematic artists, or film genres. Subway: 1, 9 to Houston St.; A, B, C, D, E, F, Q to W 4th St. No credit cards.

Film Groups *see* Cinema Classics, Ocularis, River Flicks at Chelsea Piers. *See also* Film Revivals, Foreign and Independent Films.

Film Revivals *see* American Museum of the Moving Image, Angelika Film Center, Anthology Film Archives, BAM Rose Cinemas, Cinema Classics, Cinema Village, Film Forum, Millennium Film Workshop, Museum for African Art, Museum of Modern Art, Museum of Television and Radio, P.S. 122, Walter Reade Theatre. *See also* Foreign and Independent Films.

Films *see* Film Groups, Film Revivals, Foreign and Independent Films.

Finley Walk *see* John H. Finley Walk.

Fire Museum *see* New York City Fire Museum.

Firebird 365 W 46th St. btw Eighth and Ninth Aves. (212) 586-0244 www.firebirdrestaurant.com

A lavish dining spot featuring outstanding Russian specialties, decorated handsomely with paintings, art objects, and antiques where the dining is grand and expensive. Next door at 367 is the Firebird Café, an intimate cabaret serving desserts and fine vodkas to accompany the performance. Subway: A, C, E to 42nd St.-Port Authority. Lunch Tues–Sat, dinner daily.

Fireworks *see* Macy's Fireworks Display, New Year's Eve Celebrations.

First Chinese Presbyterian Church 61 Henry St. at Market St. (212) 964-5488 www.fcpc.org

Built in 1817 and frequented by dockworkers and sailors, this was long known as the Church of Sea and Land. It is a stone, Gothic-arched landmark structure. Subway; F, J, M, Z to Delancey St.-Essex St.

First Night *see* New Year's Eve Celebrations.

First Presbyterian Church Fifth Ave. btw 11th and 12th Sts. (212) 675-6150 www.firstpresnyc.org

Constructed in 1846, this church, with its lovely brownstone tower, came to be the congregation's home after being moved from downtown. It is said to be descended from the first Presbyterian worship group in the country. The interior blends beautifully with wooden pews and pulpit and its lovely colored windows. Subway: L, N, R, 4, 5, 6 to 14th St.-Union Square.

First Shearith Israel Cemetery 55 St. James Pl. south of Chatham Square

This small burial ground dates to the 1680s and holds the remains of Sephardic Jews who came from Brazil during the seventeenth century. It was originally well outside the city limits. Subway: 4, 5, 6 to Brooklyn Bridge-City Hall.

Fish Restaurants *see* Seafood and Fish Restaurants.

Fisher Hall *see* Avery Fisher Hall at Lincoln Center.

Fitness Centers *see* Anushka Day Spa, Asphalt Green, Aveda Institute, Avon Center Spa and Salon, Away Spa and Gym at W Hotel, Bliss Spa, Carapan, Chelsea Piers Sports Center, Frédéric Fekkai Beauté de Provence, Georgette Klinger, 92nd Street Y, Printing House Racquet and Fitness Club, SoHo Sanctuary, Spa at Equinox, Suite 303, Woodstock Spa and Wellness Center, YMCA/YWCAs.

Flatbush

This is a predominantly residential and shopping area southeast of Prospect Park in Brooklyn and currently home to many West Indians. Two of its premier features are the Protestant Dutch Church of Flatbush on Church St. at the corner of Flatbush Ave., with its small backyard and cemetery holding the remains of early Dutch settlers. Right across the street on

Flatbush Ave. is the huge structure housing Erasmus Hall High School, which began as a private church school in the late eighteenth century. Subway: D, Q to Church Ave.

Flatiron Building 175 Fifth Ave. at intersection of Broadway, 23rd St., and Fifth Ave.

Called what it is because of its triangular flat, ironlike shape, this 22-story steel frame structure is one of Manhattan's famous landmarks. When it was built in 1902, it was the tallest building in the world at 286 feet. Subway: N, R to 23rd St.

Flea Markets *see* Annex Antiques Fair and Flea Market, Antique Flea and Farmers Market, Antiques Fair and Collectibles Market, Chelsea Flea Market, Columbus Avenue Flea Market, The Garage, Green Flea Market, Malcolm Shabazz Harlem Market, P.S. 183 Flea Market, Tower Market, Triple Pier Expo, Winter Antiques Show.

Fleet Week

Sailors descend upon the city from the United States and elsewhere at the end of May, when many naval ships and aircraft carriers are docked at piers on the west side of Manhattan and open for viewing during certain hours. The Intrepid Sea–Air–Space Museum is the source of information about all activities, so call (212) 245-0072 for details of events.

Flower District

This district around Sixth Ave. and 27th to 28th Sts. is home to the city's colorful wholesale flower neighborhood, where glorious scented wares during the early morning hours are presented by vendors for sale. Later in the day, the stores show their floral arrays drawn from many regions of the world for purchase by retail customers. Subway: 1, 9 to 28th St.

Floyd Bennett Field

This early airfield northeast of Sheepshead Bay no longer handles air traffic and is the main office of the Gateway National Recreation Area in Jamaica Bay (718) 338-3799. Its large airstrip is now given over to bicyclists and skating enthusiasts. Subway: 2, 5 to Flatbush Ave.-Brooklyn College, then Bus Q35 to Visitors Center opposite the marina.

Flushing

With the influx of recently arrived immigrants, this Queens neighborhood has come to be known as Little Asia. The section is bounded by Northern Blvd. on the north, Sanford Ave. on the south, College Point Blvd. on the west, and Union St. on the east. The principal active streets are

Union St., where much Korean activity can be found; the Chinese region, centering around the northern stretch of Main St.; and the Indians, who tend to be concentrated at the southern portion of Main St. There is a plethora of lively and colorful restaurants and shops here sporting signs in many exotic languages. Subway: 7 to Flushing-Main St.

Flushing Council on Culture and the Arts Flushing Town Hall, 137-35 Northern Blvd., Flushing, Queens (718) 463-7700 www. queensnewyork.com/cultural/flushing/hall.html

This is the newest arts center in Queens and offers programs that include biweekly live jazz performances, classical concerts, and a variety of visual arts presentations. Fees for concerts and special events vary. Subway: 7 to Main St., then walk north to Northern Blvd.

Flushing Meadows

This green park is a tranquil area in Queens much frequented on weekend outings by families. It is contiguous with Corona Park and is usually referred to as Flushing Meadows-Corona Park. Subway: 7 to Willets Pt.-Shea Stadium.

Flushing Meadows-Corona Park

Once the site for the 1939 and 1964 World Fairs, this section of Queens between Northern Blvd. and Grand Central Pkwy. has been transformed into this attractive 1,200-acre parkland, which includes sports facilities, botanical gardens, and museums. It is known as the home of the U.S. Tennis Center, where the U.S. Open Tournament matches take place, and of the 50,000-seat Shea Stadium, where the New York Mets play their home games and popular music concerts are held. The area includes several playgrounds, two lakes, a historic still-operating carousel, and a miniature golf course. Urban Park Rangers offer free tours (718) 699-4204. Subway: 7 to Willets Pt.-Shea Stadium

Foley Square

To the north and a bit east of City Hall Park is this site named for a Tammany Hall politician. Looming over it are the U.S. Courthouse, with an imposing tower at its peak, and the New York County Courthouse, with a rotunda featuring fading murals produced by WPA artists in the 1930s. Subway: N, R to City Hall.

Follonico 6 W 24th St. btw Fifth and Sixth Aves. (212) 691-6359

Delicious Italian dishes are served in this tastefully arranged, welcoming restaurant serving flavorful Tuscan food at moderately expensive prices. Reservations suggested. Subway: F, N, R to 23rd St. Lunch Mon–Fri, dinner Mon–Sat. Closed Sun. Major credit cards.

Fonthill Castle Riverdale Ave. at W 261st St., Riverdale, Bronx
(718) 405-3230

To the north of Wave Hill is a tiny castle that houses the administrative
offices of the College of Mt. St. Vincent. Barely 70 feet tall with six towers,
the structure's interior, with its lovely floors, carved gargoyles, and sky-
lights is beautiful to behold. Tours of the castle are available by appointment. To Wave Hill from Grand Central Terminal take Metro North train
to Wave Hill. Then take Bus BX7 or BX10 to the last stop.

Food Specialties *see* Specialty Food Stores and Bakeries.

Football *see* New York Giants, New York Jets.

Football Season

The New York Giants and the New York Jets begin their seasons in October but they play their home games at Giants Stadium, in East Rutherford,
N.J. (201) 935-8222. The Jets box office can be reached at (516) 560-8200.
To Giants Stadium take bus from Port Authority Bus Terminal at 42nd St.
and Eighth Ave. Subway: A, C, E to Port Authority-42nd St.

Forbes Magazine Galleries 62 Fifth Ave. at 12th St. (212) 206-5549

Located on the ground floor of the Forbes Building, this museum boasts
the world's greatest collection of Fabergé eggs, 500-some model boats, innumerable toy soldiers, several thousand historical documents, a collection
of presidential memorabilia, and an odd collection of trophies. Subway: 4,
5, 6, L, N, R to 14th St.-Union Square. Open Tues–Sat 10–4. Admission
free.

Forbidden Planet 840 Broadway at 13th St. (212) 473-1576

One can find here Manhattan's biggest collection of science fiction literature from comic books to graphic works, both used and new, as well as
games, toys, and other collectors' material devoted to this genre. Subway:
4, 5, 6, L, N, R to 14th St.-Union Square. Open daily, hours vary. Major
credit cards.

Ford Center for the Performing Arts 213-215 W 42nd St. btw Seventh and Eighth Aves. (212) 307-4100

Opened in 1998, this house arose out of elements of the former Apollo
and Lyric Theatres and was designed to showcase major musical productions in the lush performance site, with a great stage that seats 1,800 or so
theatregoers. Subway: N, R, S, 1, 2, 3, 7, 9 to Times Square-42nd St.

Ford Foundation Building 320 E 43rd St. btw First and Second
Aves.

Containing a lovely glass enclosed multi-level greenhouse with trees and beautiful flowers in its lobby, this 1967 structure was a forerunner of the many buildings featuring atriums in Manhattan. It is open to visitors and is one of the city's most beautiful and tranquil building interiors. Subway: S, 4, 5, 6, 7 to Grand Central-42nd St.

Fordham University Lincoln Center Campus, 113 W 60th St. (212) 636-6000 www.fordham.edu

This campus is in midtown Manhattan and in the Jesuit tradition offers personal attention in small class groups in a wide range of subject areas and professional schools. The Rosemont Campus is at 441 East Fordham Rd. (718) 817-1000 on 85 acres of rolling lawns, tree-lined walkways, and Gothic buildings in a fenced-in area in the north Bronx. Subway: (Lincoln Center campus) A, B, C, D, 1, 9 to 59th St.-Columbus Circle; (Rosemont campus) B, D to Fordham Rd.

Foreign and Independent Films *see* Alliance Française, Angelika Film Center, Anthology Film Archives, Asia Society, BAM Rose Cinemas, Cinema Village, Goethe House German Cultural Institute, Japan Society, Lincoln Plaza, Museum of Modern Art, Quad Cinema, Sony Lincoln Square, Symphony Space, Walter Reade Theatre, Whitney Museum of American Art. *See also* Film Groups, Film Revivals.

Forest Hills

This section of Queens remains a fashionable residential area, even though its West Side Tennis Club no longer hosts the U.S. Open Tournament. The private residences in Forest Hills Gardens form an English garden-style community of mock Tudor houses, and the strip along Austin St. between Ascan Ave. and Yellowstone Blvd. features many upscale shops. Subway: E, F, G, R to Forest Hills-71st Ave.

Forest Park

Located west of Jamaica is this thickly wooded region with its miles of walking trails, golf courses, baseball fields, tennis courts, horseback riding, and even an old-fashioned carousel ride. To learn about park activities and special events, call (718) 235-4100 or (718) 520-5941. Subway: J, Z to Woodhaven Blvd.

Forest Park Golf Course (718) 296-0999

Located in Woodhaven, Queens, is this 6,300-yard course at Park Lane S and Forest Pkwy. Subway: J to 85th St.-Forest Pkwy.

Fort Greene

This Brooklyn community is between the Brooklyn Navy Yard and Atlantic Ave. on the north and south and Flatbush Ave. Extension and Clinton Ave. on its east and west sides. It is a thriving neighborhood comprised predominantly of affluent professional and artistic African-American and other minority families, who occupy the attractive brownstone buildings on tree-lined streets. Subway: G to Fulton St.

Fort Greene Park

On DeKalb St. between St. Edwards St. and Washington Park in Brooklyn is a hilly parkland designed in 1860 by Frederick Law Olmstead of Central Park fame. At its center is the Prison Ship Martyrs Monument commemorating the more than 10,000 American sailors who died while prisoners on English ships during the American Revolution, many of whom are buried beneath the monument. Subway: D, M, N, Q, R to DeKalb Ave.

Fort Tryon Park

Located at 192nd St. between Broadway and Riverside Dr. with its entrance on Fort Washington St., this park is the site of the Cloisters but also provides a lovely, wooded, hilly parkland affording splendid views of the Hudson River. It is also home to the largest public garden in the city, the splendid Heather Garden. Subway: A to 190th St.

Fort Washington Park Hudson River from 145th to 181st Sts.

The celebrated sight here is the Little Red Lighthouse, but there's more to this little-known park, with its walking paths and tennis courts. The park runs along the river's edge in well-tended grassy stretches. Subway: A to 181st St.

42nd Street *see* West 42nd Street.

47th Street Theatre 304 W 47th St. btw Eighth and Ninth Aves. (212) 265-1086

Another Broadway house, a bit west of the main district of legitimate theatres. Subway: A, C, E to Port Authority-42nd St.

Four Seasons Hotel 57 E 57th St. btw Madison and Park Aves., NY 10022 (212) 758-5700 or (800) 332-3442, fax (212) 758-5711 www.fourseasons.com

This hotel is the world's most lavish and elegant hostelry, featuring Art Deco rooms of 600 or so square feet, many at the higher levels with spectacular views of the city. Everything is lush and comfortable, and the service is superb. All is here to make for a memorable stay from the excellently equipped exercise facility to the fine dining spots within the establishment. Naturally it's ultra-expensive. Subway: N, R to Lexington Ave.; 4, 5, 6 to 59th St.

Four Seasons Restaurant 99 E 52nd St. btw Park and Lexington Aves. (212) 754-9494 www.fourseasonsrestaurant.com

This notable restaurant is a genuine New York landmark, where the decor complements the excellent contemporary American cuisine and service. It features the grill room, its masculine leather style suited to deal-making lunches, and the pool room with its marble reflecting pool at the center for more romantic evenings of dining. Naturally service is superb, but it's a very expensive spot and reservations are essential. Subway: E, F to Lexington Ave.; 6 to 51st St. Lunch Mon–Fri, dinner Mon–Sat. Major credit cards.

14th Street *see* Union Square.

Fourth of July Fireworks *see* Macy's Fireworks Display.

Foy House Carroll St. btw Eighth Ave. and Prospect Park (718) 636-1492

This historic brownstone bed-and-breakfast in Brooklyn's attractive Park Slope neighborhood offers modestly priced rooms with shared bath and private bath. Subway: 2, 3 to Grand Army Plaza. No credit cards.

Frank E. Campbell Funeral Chapel 1076 Madison Ave. at 81st St. (212) 288-3500 www.frankecampbell.com

The celebrated funeral home of wealthy and well-known figures from public life and the entertainment world is found at this modest-sized building. Subway: 6 to 77th St.

Fraunces Tavern Museum 54 Pearl St. at Broad St. (212) 425-1779 www.frauncestavernmuseum.org

On the 2nd and 3rd floors of this landmark building can be found one of the oldest museums in New York, offering rotating exhibits of artifacts in rooms that reflect the colonial and early American period of U.S. history. Downstairs is the moderately priced and charming Fraunces Tavern, which combines a historic and comfortable ambiance with good American food (212) 269-0144. Subway: 4, 5 to Bowling Green; 1, 9 to South Ferry. Museum open daily, hours vary. Modest charge. Restaurant open Mon–Fri for breakfast, lunch, and dinner.

Fred F. French Building 521 Fifth Ave. at 44th St.

This beautiful structure was constructed in 1927. It combines elements of Greek and Egyptian construction characteristics with Art Deco features. The lovely vaulted lobby and its elaborately designed ceiling and striking bronze doors clearly deserve a look. Subway: S, 4, 5, 6, 7 to Grand Central-42nd St.

Frédéric Fekkai Beauté de Provence 15 E 57th St. btw Madison and Fifth Aves. (212) 753-9500

This chic salon is a favorite of celebrity patrons and others, drawn by the hair styling reputation of Fekkai but as well by the other spa services, which pamper the clients from head to toe. Subway: N, R to Fifth Ave.; 4, 5, 6 to 59th St. Open Mon–Sat, hours vary. Major credit cards.

French Building *see* Fred F. French Building.

French Institute *see* Alliance Française.

French Restaurants *see* Alison on Dominick, Balthazar, Le Bernardin, Bouley Bakery, Bouterin, Café Boulud, Café des Artistes, La Caravelle, Chanterelle, Le Cirque, La Côte Basque, Daniel, Le Jardin Bistro, Jean Georges, Jo Jo, Les Halles, Lutèce, Le Marais, Marichu, Montrachet, Payard Patisserie and Bistro, Peacock Alley, Le Périgord, Petrossian, Provence, Raoul's, Le Refuge, Le Régence, Savanna, West Bank Café.

The Frick Collection 1 E 70th St. at Fifth Ave. (212) 288-0700 www. frick.org

Located in one of New York's most exquisite Beaux Arts mansions, the former home of tycoon Henry Clay Frick contains a world-class collection of European masterpieces, including paintings, furnishings, sculptures, and decorative arts. The experience of visiting is akin to entering an extraordinarily beautiful private home arranged with the utmost taste, where expense was no obstacle. The indoor garden court with reflecting pool is a particularly delightful feature. Subway: 6 to 68th St. Open Tues–Sun, hours vary. Admission charge. No credit cards.

Friends Meeting House 137-16 Northern Blvd. at 15th St., Queens (718) 358-9636

This building is a national historic landmark and was constructed at the end of the seventeenth century. It still is used by Quakers for worship services in its unpretentious central meeting hall. Visitors are welcome for the

Sunday service. To visit the building at other times, call the caretaker at (718) 429-7830. Subway: 7 to Flushing-Main St.

Fujianese

The area along East Broadway toward the Manhattan Bridge is the heart of New York's Fuji community. The section right around the bridge is the site of their noodle shops, herbal stores, beauty parlors, and outdoor markets. Subway: F to E Broadway.

Fujiyama Mama 467 Columbus Ave. btw 82nd and 83rd Sts. (212) 769-1144

This popular Japanese restaurant is decorated to capture the tech tempo of the times, with loud music and wide-ranging, colorfully named dining selections at moderate prices where reservations are a good idea. Subway: 1, 9 to 86th St. Dinner daily. Major credit cards.

Fuller Building 41 E 57th St. btw Park and Madison Aves.

This stylish black Art Deco construction built in 1929 is home to 12 floors of art galleries. The entryway, with intricately designed mosaic tile floors and statues on each side of the clock above the entrance, are particularly striking. Subway: 4, 5, 6 to 59th St.

Fulton Ferry District

At Brooklyn Heights' northernmost point is this historic district, virtually under the Brooklyn Bridge centering around Old Fulton St. Hereabouts can be found cobblestone streets and old buildings. Empire Fulton Ferry State Park is not very much of a park, but it affords unsurpassed views of the East River and Manhattan. Subway: A, C to High St.

Fulton Fish Market South and Fulton Sts.

Next to Pier 17, and dating from the early nineteenth century, this is the country's biggest wholesale fish market. Here hundreds of types of fish are sold during early morning hours to buyers from the city's restaurant industry. It's all very messy, very lively, and very smelly. Subway: A, C, J, M, Z, 2, 3, 4, 5 to Fulton St.-Broadway Nassau.

Fur District

Just below the Garment District is another specialized venue, where fur manufacturers carry out their activities. The region is concentrated in the section running from W 27th to W 30th Sts., where many factories and showrooms are clustered between Sixth and Eighth Aves. Subway: 1, 9 to 28th St.

G

Gabriela's 686 Amsterdam Ave. at 93rd St. (212) 961-0574

Inexpensive and tasty Mexican dishes featured here are more authentic than what's found at typical Tex-Mex spots. It's a busy, unpretentious place that enjoys great popularity. Subway: 1, 2, 3, 9 to 96th St. Lunch and dinner daily. Major credit cards.

Gage & Tollner 372 Fulton St. btw Jay and Boerum Sts., Brooklyn (718) 875-5181 www.gageandtollner.com

One of the city's venerable restaurants located in downtown Brooklyn, Gage & Tollner has a well-deserved reputation for serving excellent seafood at moderately expensive prices. Subway: A, C, F to Jay St.-Borough Hall. Lunch and dinner Mon–Sat. Major credit cards.

Gallagher's 228 W 52nd St. btw Broadway and Eighth Ave. (212) 245-5336 www.gallaghersnysteakhouse.com

This comfortable and unpretentious steakhouse delivers excellent steak and lobster dishes with fine potato accompaniments at fairly expensive prices; reservations are advisable. Subway: 1, 9, C, E to 50th St. Lunch and dinner daily. Major credit cards.

Galleries *see* Art Galleries.

Gamut Realty Group 301 E 78th St., NY 10021 (212) 879-4229 or (800) 437-8353, fax (212) 517-5356 www.gamutnyc.com

This agency offers listings of varying size accommodations for short or long stays, hosted or unhosted, at various Manhattan locations across a wide price range.

Gansevoort Market (212) 924-2211

From around 5 a.m. to 8 a.m. on weekdays between the Hudson River and Ninth Ave. and from Gansevoort St. north to 14th St., the meat market for restaurants and retail stores of the city makes fascinating viewing if one has an interest in seeing large numbers of animal carcasses on display. Subway: A, C, E to 14th St.; L to Eighth Ave.

The Garage 112 W 25th St. btw Sixth and Seventh Aves.

An indoor flea market located in a former parking garage on two levels open year-round on weekends. Subway: F, 1, 9 to 23rd St.

Gardens *see* Brooklyn Botanic Garden, Central Park Conservatory Garden, Central Park Shakespeare Garden, Central Park Strawberry Fields, The Cloisters, Japan Society, Jefferson Market Courthouse, King Manor Museum, Metropolitan Museum of Art, Morris-Jumel Mansion and Museum, Mount Vernon Hotel Museum and Garden, New York Botanical Garden, Ninth Street Community Garden and Park, Noguchi Museum, Queens Botanical Garden, St. Luke's Garden, Snug Harbor Cultural Center, Staten Island Botanical Garden, United Nations, Van Cortlandt House, Wave Hill, World Financial Center.

Garibaldi-Meucci Museum 420 Tompkins Ave. at Chester St., Rosebank, Staten Island (718) 442-1608

This was the home of Antonio Meucci, who invented a crude form of telephone in 1851, 20 years before Alexander Graham Bell. Giuseppi Garibaldi, the Italian statesman, escaped to spend some time here after being defeated by Napoleon III around 1850. The museum features exhibits about Meucci's inventions and his friendship with Garibaldi. Subway: 1, 9 to South Ferry; N, R to Whitehall St., then ferry to Staten Island. From Staten Island St. George Ferry Terminal, take Bus S52. Open Tues–Sun afternoons. Modest admission charge.

Garment District

Once this neighborhood spanned the district from around 25th to 42nd St. between Fifth and Ninth Aves., but in recent years it has been reduced to a smaller area from roughly 34th to 42nd St. between Sixth and Eighth Aves. This is home to Manhattan's fashion industry, where Seventh Ave., its epicenter, is named "Fashion Avenue." This neighborhood features sample sales at some showrooms, where designer clothes are sold at a discount. The side streets bustle with workers and bosses, particularly during lunch hour, and delivery trucks and garment racks are wheeled by young men on handcarts between factories, contractors, and showrooms. Subway: 1, 2, 3, 9, A, C, E to 34th St.-Penn Station.

Gateway National Recreation Area www.nps.gov/gate

This is a 26,000-acre region of forest, beach, and wetlands extending from Sandy Hook in New Jersey all the way to the Rockaways in Queens. It is managed by the National Park Service. Gateway's office is at Floyd Bennett Field, Brooklyn's first municipal airport. More details about the area are available at (718) 388-3799.

Gay and Lesbian Community Services Center 208 W 13th St. btw Seventh and Eighth Aves. (212) 620-7310 www.gaycenter.org

Provides helpful information to gay men and women on various aspects of life in New York, such as restaurants, living accommodations, and night life, as well as referrals to legal resources.

Gay Pride Day Parade *see* Lesbian and Gay Pride Parade.

Gelfand's Walk of the Town *see* Marvin Gelfand's Walk of the Town.

Genealogy Institute *see* Center for Jewish History.

General Electric Company Building 570 Lexington Ave. at 51st St.

Originally built as a site for Radio Corporation of American (RCA) headquarters, this red brick skyscraper constructed in 1931 has a spiked tower crowned with what looks like radio waves. The chrome and marble Art Deco lobby is another handsome feature. Subway: N, R to Lexington Ave.; 4, 5, 6, to 59th St.

General Grant National Memorial *see* Grant's Tomb.

General Post Office 421 Eighth Ave. at 33rd St. (212) 967-8585

Built in 1913 to complement what was then Pennsylvania Station across the street, this is the city's main post office and is open 24 hours a day. It is an impressive two-block-long structure lined with massive Corinthian columns and is also known as the James A. Farley Building. It contains a one-room post office museum displaying artifacts of postal history. Subway: A, C, E to 34th St.-Penn Station.

General Theological Seminary 175 Ninth Ave. at W 20th St. (212) 243-5150 or (888) GTS-5649 www.gts.edu

This one-block-square campus in Chelsea can be entered only from Ninth Ave. The lovely inner garden is a serene grassy oasis in the midst of ivy-covered buildings. The seminary's library is one of America's finest ecclesiastical collections, particularly noted for its renowned Latin Bibles. Subway: C, E to 23rd St. Grounds open afternoons, library by special arrangement.

Gennaro 665 Amsterdam Ave. btw 92nd and 93rd Sts. (212) 665-5348

A tiny, moderately priced Italian restaurant that is extremely popular for its splendid service and extraordinary well-prepared dishes. Subway: 1, 2, 3, 9 to 96th St. Dinner daily. Cash only.

George Washington Bridge

This fourteen-lane, 3,500-foot suspension bridge spans the Hudson River from Manhattan to New Jersey. It was constructed in 1931 and, while not so famous a city landmark, rivals the Brooklyn Bridge for first place in the architectural beauty contest of city bridges. Located beneath the bridge is the lighthouse celebrated as the children's favorite *Little Red Lighthouse*. Subway: A to 175th St.

Georgette Klinger 501 Madison Ave. btw 52nd and 53rd Sts. (212) 838-3200 www.georgetteklinger.com

Features discreet, expert facial treatments and body skin revitalization. Subway: E, F to Fifth Ave. Open daily, hours vary. Major credit cards.

German Cultural Center *see* Goethe House German Cultural Institute.

German Restaurants *see* Zum Stammtisch.

Germans in New York *see* Yorkville.

Gershwin Hotel 7 E 27th St. btw Madison and Fifth Aves., NY 10016 (212) 545-8000, fax (212) 684-5546 www.gershwinhotel.com

The Flatiron district's large building is full of pop art and offers dorm accommodations as well as private rooms with very modest furnishings at budget prices. It's popular with young people and international visitors, and the roof terrace serves as party headquarters during the warm weather. Credit cards accepted. Subway: 6 to 28th St.

Gershwin Theatre 222 W 51st St. btw Broadway and Eighth Ave. (212) 586-6510

This house began as the Uris in 1972 before its name change and has been the showcase for many Broadway musical successes. Subway: 1, 9, C, E to 50th St.

Ghenet 284 Mulberry St. btw Houston and Prince Sts. (212) 343-1888

This budget-priced restaurant serves genuine Ethiopian fare. It has atmosphere and style to go with the good eating. Subway: B, D, E, Q to

Broadway-Lafayette St.; N, R to Prince St. Lunch and dinner Tues–Sun. Major credit cards.

Ginter Walking Tours *see* Val Ginter Walking Tours.

Gladys' Comedy Room at Hamburger Harry's 145 W 45th St. btw Broadway and Sixth Aves. (212) 832-1762 or (212) 840-0566

Gladys' features a large range of comics performing in this small room behind Hamburger Harry's. Subway: N, R to 49th St.; B, D, F, Q to 47th-50th Sts.-Rockefeller Center. Open Thurs–Sun nights. Wed night mike is open. Cover charge and minimum drink charge.

Godwin-Ternback Museum at Queens College 65-30 Kessena Blvd., Flushing, Queens (718) 997-4747

The permanent collection holds more than 2,000 works from ancient to modern times. The museum also mounts exhibitions during the academic year on contemporary art themes. Subway: E, F to Union Turnpike, then Bus Q74 to campus. Mon–Thurs 11 a.m.–7 p.m. September–May. Admission free.

Goethe House German Cultural Institute 1014 Fifth Ave. btw 82nd and 83rd Sts. (212) 439-8700

This educational and cultural center offers exhibitions showing works of German artists, sponsors lectures and workshops, maintains an extensive library including German magazines, newspapers, and other media, and shows German films (usually with English subtitles) at various locations around the city as well as in its own auditorium. Subway: 4, 5, 6 to 86th St. Tues–Sat, hours vary. Admission free.

Gold Tours *see* Joyce Gold Tours.

Golden Gloves Boxing Championships Madison Square Garden, Seventh Ave. at 32nd St. (212) 465-6741

Each April this celebrated New York amateur boxing competition takes place. Subway: A, C, E, 1, 2, 3, 9 to 34th St.-Penn Station.

Golden Theatre 252 W 45th St. btw Broadway and Eighth Ave. (212) 239-6200

This 800-seat house has been showing Broadway theatrical productions since it opened with the long-running *Angel Street*. Subway: N, R, S, 1, 2, 3, 7, 9 to Times Square-42nd St.; A, C, E to 42nd St.-Port Authority.

Golden Unicorn 18 E Broadway btw the Bowery and Catherine St. (212) 941-0911

One of the finest Cantonese restaurants in the city, with excellent dim sum and Hong Kong dishes prepared imaginatively in a noisy setting frequented by many Chinese family diners; prices are moderately expensive. Subway: F to E Broadway. Open daily 9 a.m.–11 p.m. Major credit cards.

Goldman Memorial Band Concerts 80 Eighth Ave., Suite 1107, NY 10011 (212) 924-5171 www.goldmanmemorialband.org

Every summer traditional band concerts are performed at various venues around the city by the celebrated Goldman Memorial Band with no admission charge. For schedule information fax request to (212) 924-5171.

Golf *see* Chelsea Piers Golf Club, Forest Park Golf Course, Jacob Riis Park, Kissena Park Golf Course, Pelham Bay Golf Course, Silver Lake Golf Course, Van Cortlandt Park Golf Course. *See also* Miniature Golf.

Gospel Music *see* Abyssinian Baptist Church, Canaan Baptist Church of Christ, Copeland's, Cotton Club, Harlem Spirituals, Sylvia's.

Gotham Bar and Grill 12 E 12th St. btw Fifth Ave. and University Pl. (212) 620-4020 www.gothambarandgrill.com

Serving exciting American fare in a spacious former warehouse, this moderately expensive spot is one of the city's most acclaimed restaurants for its excellent food and service. Reservations are required. Subway: L, N, R, 4, 5, 6 to 14th St.-Union Square. Lunch Mon–Fri, dinner daily. Major credit cards.

Gotham Book Mart 41 W 47th St. btw Fifth and Sixth Aves. (212) 719-4448

This is a long-treasured bookstore that has been a landmark for book lovers since it opened in 1920. It has a celebrated stock of new and used twentieth-century works, with an emphasis on literature, poetry, and the arts. Subway: B, D, F, Q to 47th-50th Sts.-Rockefeller Center. Mon–Sat, hours vary. Major credit cards.

Gotham Comedy Club 34 W 22nd St. btw Fifth and Sixth Aves. (212) 367-9000 www.gothamcomedy.com

In a historic building in the Flatiron neighborhood, this is a well-designed and roomy sophisticated venue showcasing talented comic headliners. Subway: F, N, R to 23rd St. Open nightly. Cover charge, drink minimum.

Gourmet Garage 453 Broome St. at Mercer St. (212) 941-5850

Converted from a garage to market fine foods at discount prices, the range of sale items here includes fruit and vegetables, breads, cheeses, meats, coffee, and organic foods. Various other locations around Manhattan. Check phone book for addresses. Subway: N, R to Prince St. Open daily 7 a.m.–9 p.m. Major credit cards.

Governor's Island

Until recently this small island lying south of Manhattan was a Coast Guard installation. It has now been abandoned, but it remains a very picturesque location and is destined to be sold by the U.S. General Services Administration. It is not accessible to the public at this time.

Grace Church 802 Broadway btw E 10th and E 11th Sts. (212) 254-2000

This Gothic Revival structure is Manhattan's leading Episcopal church and one of New York's most beautiful. It has splendid stained-glass windows, a mosaic floor, and a beautifully carved pulpit. It is also noted for its concert programs. Subway: N, R to 8th St.-NYU. Open Mon–Sat, hours vary.

Gracie Mansion East End Ave. at 88th St. (212) 570-4751

Since the administration of Fiorello LaGuardia in 1942, this has been the residence of New York City's mayors. The historic 2-story colonial-era building was constructed in 1799 as a country estate and is one of the best preserved of its period in the city. Subway: 4, 5, 6 to 86th St., then Bus M86.

Gracie Mansion Conservancy Tour (212) 570-4751 or (212) 570-0985

The lovely 2-story mansion that is home to the mayor of New York is open to the public and chock-full of beautiful historic artifacts. Reservations in advance are essential for the guided tours given from fall until spring for a modest admission charge. Subway: 4, 5, 6 to 86th St., then Bus M86.

Graffiti Hall of Fame 106th St. btw Madison and Park Aves. www. graffitihalloffame.com

In a schoolyard here can be found the imaginative creations of some of the city's premier graffiti artists, which exemplify this spontaneous and colorful form of artistic expression. Subway: 6 to 103rd St.

Gramercy Park

This square was planned in the 1830s to attract residential houses all around it. It is the city's only private park, an immaculately kept, beautifully planted space, accessible only to those with keys who live in the surrounding buildings. The park itself is located at the north end of Irving Pl. between 20th and 21st Sts. Many lovely buildings surround the park, including the Players Club at 16 Gramercy Park S and the National Arts Club next door. Gramercy Park is also the name of the predominantly residential neighborhood surrounding the park from around 16th to 23rd Sts. and east from Park Ave. S to Second Ave. Subway: 6 to 23rd St.

Gramercy Park Hotel 2 Lexington Ave. at 21st St., NY 10010 (212) 475-4320 or (800) 221-4083, fax (212) 505-0535 www.gramercy parkhotel.com

This mid-range priced hotel offers quiet surroundings next to the private park to which hotel residents can receive a key. It attracts a wide range of guests, from business travelers to European tourists. Subway: 6 to 23rd St.

Gramercy Tavern 42 E 20th St. btw Broadway and Park Ave. S (212) 477-0777 www.gramercytavern.com

This moderately expensive, charming nineteenth-century-style inn setting enjoys wide popularity for its fine American cuisine served in the formal dining room, which requires reservations, or the comfortable, couch-filled tavern, which does not. Service is friendly, relaxed, and yet professional. Subway: 6 to 23rd St. Lunch Mon–Fri, dinner daily. Major credit cards.

Grand Army Plaza Prospect Park W, Eastern Pkwy., Flatbush Ave., and Vanderbilt Ave., Brooklyn

This is the main entrance to Prospect Park. At its center is the Soldiers' and Sailors' Monument, reminiscent of the Parisian Arc de Triomphe. The monument honors Civil War veterans and is adorned with sculptural groupings. On some weekends in spring and fall, the top of the arch is open. Subway: 2, 3 to Grand Army Plaza.

Grand Army Plaza (Central Park) *See* Central Park Grand Army Plaza.

Grand Central Oyster Bar *see* Oyster Bar at Grand Central.

Grand Central Partnership Business Improvement District at Grand Central Station, E 42nd St. at Vanderbilt Ave. (212) 883-2420

Offers free tourist information inside the terminal at a booth Sun–Fri 9 a.m.–9 p.m. and Sat until 6 p.m. Sponsors free weekly ninety-minute tour of the historic 42nd St. neighborhood. The group gathers at 12:30 p.m. on Fri in front of the Philip Morris Building at the corner of Vanderbilt Ave. and E 42nd St. Subway: S, 4, 5 6, 7 to Grand Central-42nd St.

Grand Central Station Tours (212) 935-3960

The Municipal Art Society leads a free tour of this beautifully renovated landmark structure. The group meets in front of the information booth on the main level of the terminal on Wed at 12:30 p.m., and the tour lasts about ninety minutes. Subway: S, 4, 5, 6, 7 to Grand Central-42nd St.

Grand Central Terminal www.grandcentralterminal.com

The strikingly beautiful Beaux Arts station, the world's largest, opened in 1913 and has been a symbol of New York ever since. It sits between Madison and Lexington Aves. where Park Ave. stops at E 42nd St. and contains 49 acres. Countless commuters and subway riders pass daily through the recently renovated beautiful landmark structure, with its high concourse, grand staircase, and starry ceiling. Numerous shops and restaurants can be found as well, but they blend well into the breath-taking ambiance. Connected to the station are the miles of track stretching underneath Park Ave. up to 50th St. and leading trains north to upstate New York and Connecticut. Subway: S, 4, 5, 6, 7 to Grand Central-42nd St.

Grand Concourse

Once a glamorous boulevard stretching more than 4 miles through rural areas of the Bronx, the avenue has declined severely, and while many striking Art Deco apartment buildings still line its sides, they are now for the most part run down and dilapidated. Subway: (northern end) B, D to Bedford Park Blvd.; (southern end) 149th St.-Grand Concourse.

The Grand Hyatt www.newyork.hyatt.com

Right next to Grand Central Station to the east can be found the glitzy hotel that was built over the old Commodore Hotel. It is thought by many to illustrate all the excesses of vulgar contemporary interior hotel design. Subway: S, 4, 5, 6, 7 to Grand Central-42nd St.

Grand Union 34 E 32nd St. btw Madison and Park Aves., NY 10016 (212)-683-5890, fax (212) 689-7397

Even with recent renovations, this hotel is still rather drab, but the rooms are comfortable, the prices are budget level, and the location is convenient. Subway: 6 to 33rd St.

Grant's Tomb 122nd St. and Riverside Dr. (212) 666-1640

In a high commanding position overlooking the Hudson River is a massive granite building that contains the remains of General and later President Ulysses S. Grant and his wife Julia. The site is administered by the

National Park Service and was recently renovated inside and outside. It is open daily 9 a.m.–5 p.m. Admission free. Tours are available by park rangers. Subway: 1, 9 to 125th St.

Gray Line Sightseeing Port Authority Terminal, Eighth Ave. and 42nd St. (212) 397-2600 www.graylinenewyork.com

This firm offers many different sightseeing tour bus possibilities for seeing the city year-round and hearing information in various languages. Perhaps most popular are the double-decker buses, which run around town allowing hop on, hop off, with tickets valid for two days. Call for information on the many different options offered or stop in at the office in the Times Square Visitors Center at 1560 Broadway between 46th and 47th Sts.

Great Hudson Sailing Center Chelsea Pier, 23rd St. and Hudson River (212) 741-7245 www.greathudsonsailing.com

Cruises are available during pleasant weather on the Hudson River by sailboat with this outfit. Call for details. Subway: C, E to 23rd St., then Bus M23 to West River.

The Great Irish Fair (718) 891-6622

On the second weekend of September this Hibernian celebration takes place each year in Coney Island, Brooklyn, with the boardwalk filled with families and food concessions, while music and athletic events abound. It is all arranged by the Ancient Order of Hibernians, which also organizes the St. Patrick's Day Parade. Subway: B, D, F, N to Coney Island-Stillwell Ave.

Great Jones Café 54 Great Jones St. btw Lafayette St. and Bowery (212) 674-9304

Fine Cajun food is the specialty of this colorful spot, which offers the dishes you might expect to find in New Orleans at modest prices. Subway: 6 to Bleecker St. Dinner Mon–Sat, Sun brunch. Cash only.

Great Lawn in Central Park *see* Central Park Great Lawn.

The Great White Way *see* Broadway, Times Square.

Greater New York International Auto Show (212) 216-2000 or (800) 282-3336

For one week in early or mid-April, the Jacob R. Javitz Convention Center at 655 W 34th St. at Eleventh Ave. hosts America's biggest car extravaganza. Subway: A, C, E to 34th St.-Penn Station.

Greek Heritage Festival (718) 626-7896

Each year on a weekend in June or July there is picturesque folk dancing, Greek music, and lots of tasty food specialties at the Bohemian Hall, 29-19 Twenty-Fourth Ave., Astoria, Queens. Subway: N to Astoria-Ditmers Blvd.

Greek Independence Day Parade (718) 204-6500

This procession down Fifth Ave. from 59th to 49th Sts. in the afternoon usually on or around March 25 celebrates Hellenic freedom, with bands and colorfully garbed Greeks patriotically striding down the avenue.

Greek Orthodox Cathedral of the Holy Trinity 337 E 74th St. btw First and Second Aves. (212) 288-3215

Behind the beautiful wooden doors, the visitor comes upon a lovely interior, which captures the essence of the Hellenic past. Subway: 6 to 77th St.

Greek Restaurants *see* Estiatorio Milos Restaurant, Karyatis, Meltemi, Molyvos, Periyali, Uncle Nick's.

Greeks in New York *see* Astoria, Washington Heights.

Green Flea Market

This group runs two markets. One is located on the East Side on E 67th St. between First and York Aves. (212) 721-0900; and one is on the West Side on Columbus Ave. between 76th and 77th Sts. (212) 721-0900. The East Side market runs 6 a.m.–6 p.m. on Sat and features wares from food to clothes and jewelry. The West Side market has more vendors and thus a bigger selection and wider range of merchandise being sold. It is open on Sun 10 a.m.–6 p.m. Subway: (E 67th St.) 6 to 68th St.-Hunter College; (Columbus Ave.) 1, 9 to 79th St.

Green-Wood Cemetery main entrance at Fifth Ave. and 25th St., Brooklyn (718) 768-7300 www.green-wood.com

This 478-acre hilly parkland, larger than Prospect Park, is the final resting place for many nineteenth-century notables. It contains many ornate mausoleums and picturesque and elaborate headstones and memorials. It is open daily 8 a.m.–4 p.m., and guided tours are offered by the Brooklyn Center for the Urban Environment with details at (718) 788-8500. Subway: M, N, R, to 25th St.

The Greenbelt (718) 667-2165

In the middle of Staten Island can be found a 2,500-acre scenic park of wetlands, open meadows, and wooded areas. It is a controlled region that puts any development within its bounds off limits. It is home to two beautiful hiking trails. One runs 8½ miles and is marked with blue dots from the College of Staten Island east to the William Davis Wildlife Refuge. It begins on Milford St. where a sign is located. The second is the White Trail, which is 4 miles long and marked with white dots. It begins at High Rock Park running north to Willowbrook Park. Both are exceptionally pleasurable trails, with distinctive features nowhere else to be found. Open daily until 5 p.m. Subway: 1, 9 to South Ferry; N, R to Whitehall St., then ferry to Staten Island. From Staten Island St. George Ferry Terminal, take Bus S62 to Victory Blvd., then transfer to Bus S54 to Rockland Ave. and walk to the park entrance.

Greene Street

This is the place in SoHo where New York's finest cast-iron architectural structures can be found. Along five cobblestoned streets stand some fifty of these structures from the second half of the nineteenth century. The block between Broome and Spring Sts. has thirteen cast-iron fronts, and at the Canal St. end of Greene St. there is the city's longest continuous row of cast-iron façades. The lampposts on Greene St. are lovely cast-iron construction. Subway: C, E to Spring St.

Greenhouses *see* Gardens.

Greenmarkets

Open-air markets where farmers from outside the city and cheesemakers and bakers sell their wares several days a week are part of the twenty-eight greenmarkets network in the city. Most are seasonal, although a few operate year-round. The best known is the one at Union Square on E 14th St., which is open 8 a.m.–6 p.m. Mon, Wed, Fri, and Sat. Everything is fresh, and prices are lower than those in regular stores. For locations and hours of any market in a neighborhood nearest you, call the Greenmarket office at 130 E 16th St. (212) 477-3220 during business hours Mon–Fri.

Greenpoint

This neighborhood across the East River in Brooklyn has been predominantly Polish for a long time. The community is rectangular, with Manhattan and Franklin Ave. on the eastern and western sides and Noble St. and Greenpoint Ave. bordering the north and south ends. A lot of the area still reflects the industrial character of its past when a considerable number of manufacturing plants operated here. The neighborhood continues to be pleasant, with most of the shops and stores to be found along Manhattan Ave. and Nassau St. Subway: G to Greenpoint Ave.

Greenwich Village

This neighborhood used to be the center of iconoclastic and bohemian life and now it is more predominantly home to the well-to-do, but it still maintains the flavor of its artistic heritage in many of its quaint shops, jazz clubs, and dining spots. Known also as the West Village, it is located between W 14th St. and Houston St. and Broadway and the Hudson River. It is a neighborhood with tree-lined cobblestone streets, coffeehouses, and a relaxed life style. The site of Washington Square Park and New York University, it remains attractive to nonconformists except for those more radically inclined or in search of the cheaper everything who have gravitated to the East Village. Subway: 1, 9 to Christopher St.-Sheridan Square; A, B, C, D, E, F, Q to W 4th St.

Greenwich Village Halloween Parade *see* Halloween Parade in Greenwich Village.

Greenwich Village Historic District

This section of the city boasts particularly attractive and fine nineteenth-century buildings set on streets of cobblestone with houses painted in colorful hues. At its heart is the very picturesque and scenic Bank St. Subway: A, C, E to 14th St.

Greenwich Village Jazz Festival

At various jazz spots around the Village, this ten-day event takes place each year in late August, ending with a concert in Washington Square Park that is free to the public.

Greenwich Village Literary Pub Crawl (212) 613-5796

This walking tour of four Village watering holes that have been frequented by literary celebrities is led by actors who read from pertinent writings along the way. The tour starts at the White Horse Tavern at 567 Hudson St. at 11th St. every Saturday afternoon. Call for prices and reservations. Subway: 1, 9 to Christopher St.-Sheridan Square.

Grey Art Gallery and Study Center at New York University 100 Washington Square E (212) 998-6780 www.nyu.edu/greyart

Changing exhibitions of contemporary art in various media are displayed in this relatively small exhibit space. Subway: N, R to 8th St.-NYU. Open Tues–Sat, hours vary. Suggested donation.

Groceries *see* Produce.

Grolier Club 47 E 60th St. btw Madison and Park Aves. (212) 838-6690 www.grolierclub.org

This elegant private club, founded in 1884, is devoted to book-making arts and crafts and presents public exhibitions of book-related topics. It maintains a large library that is open only by appointment. The exhibit gallery is open Mon–Sat. Admission free. Subway: N, R to Lexington Ave.; 4, 5, 6 to 59th St.

Group Health Insurance Building 330 W 42nd St. btw Eighth and Ninth Aves.

This unusually shaped 1931 structure has striking horizontal bands of green terra-cotta. The lobby is designed in Art Deco style with stainless steel and opaque glass. It was earlier known as the McGraw Hill Building. Subway: A, C, E to 42nd St.-Port Authority.

Gryphon Book Shop 2246 Broadway btw 80th and 81st Sts. (212) 362-0706

A treasure trove of used books on jammed shelves that rewards the diligent book lover who conscientiously seeks out items here not available anywhere else. Subway: 1, 9 to 79th St. Open daily 10 a.m.–midnight. MasterCard and Visa.

Guggenheim Museum 1071 Fifth Ave. btw 88th and 89th Sts. (212) 423-3500 www.guggenheim.org

Designed by Frank Lloyd Wright, this white spiral-shaped landmark structure offers galleries on multiple levels. It features modern and contemporary art in changing exhibitions and holds few works prior to the impressionists. A recent addition is the tower, which includes a sculpture gallery offering attractive views of Central Park. It also operates a branch in SoHo. Subway: 4, 5, 6 to 86th St. Open Fri–Wed, hours vary. Admission charge. Major credit cards. *See also* City Pass.

Guggenheim Museum SoHo 575 Broadway at Prince St. (212) 423-3500 www.guggenheim.org

Housed on two large floors of a nineteenth-century landmark building in the Cast-Iron Historic District, this Guggenheim branch provides a downtown showcase for revolving exhibitions complementing the uptown shows. Subway: N, R to Prince St.; 6 to Spring St. Open Thurs–Mon 11 a.m.–6 p.m. Closed Tues and Wed. Admission free.

Guss's Pickles 35 Essex St. btw Grand and Hester Sts. (212) 254-4477

Renowned for more than 80 years as the world's greatest source of sour and half-sour pickles drawn from huge wooden brine-filled barrels. Other specialties include hot peppers, horseradish, sauerkraut, pickled carrots and celery, as well as watermelon rind. Subway: F to E Broadway. Open Sun–Thurs 9 a.m.–6 p.m., Fri 9 a.m.–3 p.m. Major credit cards.

Gymnasiums *see* Fitness Centers.

Gypsy Tea Kettle 137 E 56th St. at Lexington Ave., 2nd Floor (212) 752-5890

This is New York's most popular location frequented by people who seek to learn their future. The readings are conducted by one of a number of readers ready to provide predictions of the future during a 15-minute tarot card reading. Subway: 4, 5, 6 to 59th St. Open Mon–Fri 11 a.m.–6:30 p.m. Readings cost $12 plus tip.

H&H Bagels 2239 Broadway at 80th St. (212) 799-0704 www. hhbagels.com

Some of the finest bagels in town can be found at this establishment dispensing hot fresh bagels anytime. A second location is at 639 W 46th St. between Eleventh and Twelfth Aves. (212) 757-9829. Subway: (Broadway) 1, 9 to 79th St.; (W 46th St.) C, E to 50th St. Open 24 hours a day. Cash only.

Habitat Hotel 130 E 57th St. btw Park and Lexington Aves. (212) 753-8841 or (800) 255-0482, fax (212) 829-9605 www.stayinny.com

Small, comfortable rooms with or without bath in a good location at moderate prices. Subway: 4, 5, 6 to 59th St.

Hacker Art Books 45 W 57th St. btw Fifth and Park Aves. (212) 688-7600 www.hackerartbooks.com

This is the premier bookstore in New York for books on architecture, fine arts, decorative arts, and design. The company has been around a long time and enjoys a fine reputation. Subway: N, R to Fifth Ave. Mon–Sat 9:30 a.m.–6 p.m. Visa and MasterCard.

Haitians in New York *see* El Barrio, Crown Heights, La Saline.

Halcyon in the Rihga Hotel 151 W 54th St. btw Sixth and Seventh Aves. (212) 468-8888

Serving contemporary food, this restaurant offers its diners spacious and tranquil dining with elegant service at fairly expensive prices. Subway: N, R to 57th St. Breakfast, lunch, dinner daily. Major credit cards.

Hall of Fame for Great Americans Bronx Community College, University Ave. and W 181st St., Bronx (718) 289-5100 www.bcc. cuny.edu/hallfame/hallfame.htm

Bronze busts of 100 American notable politicians, educators, and other celebrated persons are to be found in a handsome open-air colonnade built by Stanford White. Subway: 4 to Burnside Ave. Open daily. Admission free.

Hall of Records *see* Surrogate's Court and Hall of Records.

Les Halles *see* Les Halles under L.

Halloween Parade in Greenwich Village

On October 31, thousands of revelers, many in fantastic and creative costumes and make-up, march at sunset up Sixth Ave. from Spring St. to 23rd St. The newspapers carry the precise details. Subway: (south end) C, G to Spring St.; (north end) F to 23rd St.

Hamburger Harry's 145 W 45th St. btw Sixth Ave. and Broadway (212) 840-2756

This diner in the Times Square neighborhood offers juicy big hamburgers and large salads to go at moderate prices. Subway: B, D, F, Q to 47th-50th Sts.-Rockefeller Center; N, R, S, 1, 2, 3, 7, 9 to Times Square-42nd St. 11:30 a.m.–11 p.m. daily. Major credit cards.

Hamburgers *see* Hamburger Harry's, Hard Rock Café, Harley-Davidson Café, Jackson Hole Burgers, Mickey Mantle's, Papaya King, Planet Hollywood, Tom's Restaurant.

Hamilton Grange National Memorial 287 Convent Ave. btw 141st and 142nd Sts. (212) 283-5154 www.nps.gov/hagr

This lovely Federal-style building was Alexander Hamilton's country home from 1802 to 1804, when he was killed in a duel with Aaron Burr. It was moved to this site in 1889. It is managed by the U.S. Park Service and is not open at present because of structural problems. Subway: 1, 9 to 137th St.-City College.

Hamilton Heights Historic District

Just north of City College, along Convent Ave. and running from W 141st to W 145th St. is a handsome row of intricately designed 3- or 4-story brownstone houses constructed between 1886 and 1906 in many different styles. Subway: 1, 9 to 137th St.-City College.

Hammerstein Ballroom at the Manhattan Center 311 W 34th St. btw Eighth and Ninth Aves. (212) 279-7740

A popular showplace for some of Manhattan's best rock performances, the ballroom offers good acoustics and good sight lines from all parts of the house. Subway: A, C, E to 34th St.-Penn Station.

Handball *see* Jacob Riis Park, North River Park, Riverbank State Park.

Handicapped Services *see* Disabled Services.

Hangawi 12 E 32nd St. btw Madison and Fifth Aves. (212) 213-0077 www.hangawirestaurant.com

Vegetarian Korean fare is served in imaginatively prepared succulent dishes at this moderately expensive tranquil place where the kimchi is arguably the best in town. Subway: 6, N, R to 23rd St. Lunch and dinner daily. Major credit cards.

Hanukkah Menorah

A giant menorah is lighted in December at Grand Army Plaza, Fifth Ave. at 59th St. for eight nights to celebrate the annual Festival of Lights. Subway: N, R to Fifth Ave.

The Harbor Islands *see* Ellis Island, Governor's Island, Liberty Island. *See also* Islands In and Around New York.

Hard Rock Café 221 W 57th St. btw Broadway and Seventh Ave. (212) 459-9320 www.hardrock.com

Jammed with rock performance memorabilia, this spot specializes in very loud music and offers tasty burgers, salads, and giant sandwiches at moderately expensive prices. Its greatest appeal is to tourists of the adolescent persuasion. Subway: N, R to 57th St. Lunch and dinner daily. Major credit cards.

Harlem

Beginning from 125th St. on the west and 96th St. on the east and running north between the Hudson and Harlem Rivers, this region is one of New York's most fascinating and is replete with African-American history and architecture. Within it can be found El Barrio (Spanish Harlem), a neighborhood to the east of Fifth Ave. and running between E 110th and E 125th Sts. In Central Harlem, from Fifth Ave. to St. Nicholas Ave., the population is predominantly African-American. West Harlem, which extends to Riverside Dr. and includes Morningside Heights and Hamilton Heights, is made up largely of white residents. Further north, Washington Heights near Manhattan's northern tip, is ethnically mixed. Today Harlem is undergoing revitalization and is becoming far more diverse economically as well as in its ethnic composition.

Harlem Heritage Tours *see* Harlem Spirituals.

Harlem Meer Performance Festival

From late May until October free concerts of jazz and Latin music as well as theatrical and dance productions are offered here in the northeast corner of Central Park. Subway: 2, 3 to Central Park-110th St.

Harlem School of the Arts 645 St. Nicholas Ave. btw 142nd and 143rd Sts. (212) 926-4100 www.harlemschoolofthearts.org

This center is a strong educational and cultural bulwark that grew out of the St. James Presbyterian Church. It is an important training ground for classical music performers and a major venue for public events and performances. Subway: A, B, C, D to 145th St.

Harlem Spirituals 690 Eighth Ave. btw 43rd and 44th Sts. (212) 391-0900 www.harlemspirituals.com

This company specializes in jazz and gospel bus tours of Harlem, which can be combined with a soul food meal or a jazz club visit. The staff is multilingual and can accommodate tourists in several languages. Subway: A, C, E to 42nd St.-Port Authority.

Harlem Studio Museum *see* Studio Museum in Harlem.

Harlem Week (212) 862-8299 www.discover-harlem.com

This annual celebration actually runs for almost a month during August and includes cultural, artistic, and entertainment events including films, music, dance, sports competitions, children's activities, and a food festival. Call for the year's schedule of activities and venues.

Harlem YMCA 180 W 135th St. at Seventh Ave. (212) 281-4101 www.ymcanyc.org/branches/harlem.html

The features here include a sizable swimming pool plus sauna and gymnasium, which can be used with a single-day membership. Subway: B, C to 135th St. Open Mon–Sat.

Harlem Your Way! (212) 690-1687 www.harlemyourwaytours.com

A wide range of scheduled and custom-prepared bus and walking tours of Harlem's sights and sounds, from churches to jazz spots to buildings to soul food eateries and more.

Harley-Davidson Café 1370 Sixth Ave. at 56th St. (212) 245-6000 www.harley-davidsoncafe.com

Packed with bike memorabilia, this theme restaurant serves American-style food at moderate prices in a glitzy setting adorned with leather and cycles and other "hog" decorative displays. Subway: Q to 57th St. Lunch and dinner daily. Major credit cards.

Harrison Houses

Built in the late 1700s and early 1800s, this group of restored Federal townhouses at Harrison and Greenwich Sts. forms a lovely row of land-mark structures with their picturesque dormer windows and pitched roofs. Subway: 1, 2, 3, 9 to Chambers St.

Hart Island

This island near Riker's Island is the city's cemetery for unknown or unwanted deceased. Prisoners from the penal facility at Riker's Island han-dle the arrangements for this potter's field.

Hasidim, Lubavitch *see* Williamsburg.

Hatsuhana 17 E 48th St. btw Fifth and Madison Aves. (212) 355-3345

A very popular Japanese restaurant offering some of Manhattan's best sushi as well as other zesty dining choices at moderate prices. A second location is at 237 Park Ave. (212) 661-3400. Subway: (E 48th St.) 6 to 51st St.; (Park Ave.) S, 4, 5, 6, 7 to Grand Central-42nd St. Lunch Mon–Fri, dinner Mon–Sat. Major credit cards.

Haughtwout Building 488 Broadway at Broome St.

Constructed in 1857, this extraordinary cast-iron edifice includes colon-naded arches and ninety-two windows in its corner location of 5 stories, making it one of the finest illustrations of this type of structure in the city. Subway: C, E to Spring St.

Haveli 100 Second Ave. btw 5th and 6th Sts. (212) 982-0533 www.haveli.com

This is an Indian restaurant serving the full range of tasty dishes in an East Village location where prices are very reasonable. Subway: 6 to Astor Pl. Lunch and dinner daily. Major credit cards.

Hayden Planetarium *see* Rose Center for Earth and Space.

Hayes Theatre *see* Helen Hayes Performing Arts Center.

Health Clubs *see* Fitness Centers.

Heather Garden *see* Fort Tryon Park.

Heckscher Playground *see* Central Park Heckscher Playground.

Helen Hayes Performing Arts Center 240 W 44th St. btw Broad-way and Eighth Ave. (212) 944-9450 www.helenhayespac.org

This venue has been the setting for dramatic productions since it began in 1912, with intermittent periods when it has been used for other performance purposes. Subway: N, R, S, 1, 2, 3, 7, 9 to Times Square-42nd St.

Helena's 432 Lafayette St. btw Astor Pl. and E 4th St. (212) 677-5151 www.helenatapas.com

A lively, pleasantly decorated and moderate-priced Spanish restaurant. Tapas are the main attraction, and an outdoor garden area is an added feature. Subway: 6 to Astor Pl. Dinner daily. Major credit cards.

Helicopter Flight Services (212) 355-0801 www.heliny.com

Sightseeing tours by reservation leave from the downtown Manhattan Heliport at Pier 6 and the East River. Subway: N, R to Whitehall St.; 1, 9 to South Ferry.

Helicopter Tours *see* Helicopter Flight Services, Liberty Helicopter Tours. *See also* Boat Tours, Bus Tours, Limousine Tours, Special Interest Tours, Walking Tours.

Hell 59 Gansevoort St. btw Washington and Greenwich Sts. (212) 727-1666

A comfortably furnished bar and lounge that attracts many gays to this spot in a tough neighborhood. Subway: A, C, E to 14th St. Nightly from 7 p.m. Major credit cards.

Hell's Kitchen

The part of town west of Ninth Ave. between around 34th St. to 59th St. has long been popularly known as Hell's Kitchen because of its violence and notorious slum conditions. With the extensive efforts at cleanup and gentrification in recent years, there has been a major transformation. Today the area is often referred to as Clinton, and with the influx of newer immigrants, theatre people, and some popular and trendy shops and ethnic restaurants, the neighborhood is being revitalized. Subway: (northern end) A, B, C, D, 1, 9 to 59th St.-Columbus Circle; (southern end) A, C, E to 34th St.-Penn Station.

Helmsley Building 230 Park Ave. at 46th St.

This white Beaux Arts structure was built in 1929 and straddles the traffic flowing underneath it on Park Ave. It is particularly striking at night, when its pyramid-shaped gold roof is brightly illuminated. Subway: S, 4, 5, 6, 7 to Grand Central-42nd St.

Helmsley Palace Hotel—Villard Houses *see* New York Palace Hotel.

Henderson Place Historic District

This cul-de-sac on the north side of 86th St. btw East End and York Aves. is home to a charming row of twenty-four small-scale townhouses built in the 1880s in Queen Anne style. They remain picturesque with their gables, dormers, turrets, and parapets beautifully preserved. Subway: 4, 5, 6 to 86th St., then Bus M86 east.

Henri Bendel 712 Fifth Ave. at 56th St. (212) 247-1100 www.henri bendel.com

A classy and attractive upscale shopping destination for the best in fashions and accessories in a store interior with lovely staircases and beautiful Lalique windows. The tearoom overlooking Fifth Ave. is a lovely setting. Subway: N, R to Fifth Ave. Daily, hours vary. Major credit cards.

Henry Street *see* Lower East Side.

Henry Street Settlement 265 Henry St. btw 7th and Montgomery Sts. (212) 766-9200 www.cr.nps.gov/nr/travel/pwwmh/ny31.htm

In the early nineteenth century, a celebrated social reformer, Lillian Wald, was the moving spirit behind the construction of these buildings, now designated as historic landmarks, in which social services and health functions were provided to immigrant families on the Lower East Side. Today it continues to offer a wide range of helpful community programs as well as a very active arts center for recent arrivals. Subway: F to E Broadway.

Henry Street Settlement Abrons Art Center 466 Grand St. at Pitt St. (212) 598-0400 www.henrystreetarts.org

Three indoor professional theatres, an amphitheatre, art galleries, dance and visual arts studios, and an outdoor sculpture garden are located here on the Lower East Side. Subway: F to E Broadway.

Herald Square

At the intersection of Sixth Ave., Broadway, and 34th St. sits this small triangle of asphalt named for the long-defunct *New York Herald,* which once had its headquarters at this site. Subway: B, D, F, N, Q, R to 34th St.-Herald Square.

Herald Square Hotel 19 W 31st St. btw Fifth Ave. and Broadway (212) 279-4017 or (800) 643-9208, fax (212) 643-9208 www.herald squarehotel.com

A recently renovated budget establishment offering rooms with private or shared baths located in a convenient part of midtown. Early reservations are advisable. Subway: N, R to 28th St.; B, D, F, N, Q, R to 34th St.-Herald Square.

Hidden Gardens *see* Gardens.

High 5 Tickets to the Arts (212) 445-8587 www.high5tix.org
Teenagers can buy theatre tickets and museum admission here at a special reduced rate.

High Rock Park Conservation Center Rockland Ave. and Nevada St., Staten Island (718) 667-6042
A twenty-minute walk up the hill at Nevada St. leads to this 72-acre parkland with its miles of lovely walking trails. Tours are led by Urban Park Rangers on weekend afternoons. Subway: 1, 9 to South Ferry; N, R to Whitehall St., then ferry to Staten Island. From Staten Island St. George Ferry Terminal, take Bus S62 to Victory Blvd. and Manna Rd. Transfer to Bus S54 and go to the intersection of Rockland Ave. and Nevada St.

Hindu Temple of New York 45-47 Bowne St. at Holly Ave., Flushing, Queens (718) 460-8484 www.hindusamajtemple.org
This is an ornate, pale blue structure constructed during the 1970s with many rich ornamental details. Subway: 7 to Flushing-Main St.

Hirschl and Adler Galleries 21 E 7th St. btw Fifth and Madison Aves. (212) 535-8810 www.hirschlandadler.com
This gallery shows a wide range and variety of eighteenth- and nineteenth-century American and European art on one level; upstairs Hirschl and Adler Modern features contemporary works. Subway: 6 to 68th St.-Hunter College. Open Mon–Fri 9:30 a.m.–4:45 p.m.

Hispanic Day Parade (212) 242-2360
On a Sunday around the middle of October the city celebrates with its Hispanic population Columbus's discovery of America with a colorful parade on Fifth Ave. from 44th to 72nd Sts. before swinging east. It is another of the festive annual processions that enliven the city.

Hispanic Society of America Audubon Terrace, Broadway btw 155th and 156th Sts. (212) 926-2234 www.hispanicsociety.org
Concentrating on Spanish and Portuguese arts and culture, this museum and library offers paintings by El Greco, Goya, and Valasquez as well as sculpture, furnishings, decorative arts, tiles, and mosaics. It also has a research library collection of more than 100,000 volumes on Iberia. Subway: 1 to 157th St. Museum: Tues–Sun, hours vary. Library: Tues–Sat, hours vary. Admission free.

Hispanics in New York *see* Lower East Side, Washington Heights.

Historic Buildings *see* Alice Austen House, Bartow-Pell Mansion Museum and Garden, Bayard-Condict Building, Bowery Savings Bank Building, Bowne House, Chanin Building, Chrysler Building, Churches, Conference House National Historic Landmark, Dyckman Farmhouse Museum, Edgar Allan Poe Cottage, Edward Mooney House, Flatiron Building, Friends Meeting House, General Post Office, Hamilton Grange National Memorial, Haughtwout Building, Isaacs-Hendricks House, King Manor Museum, Kingsland House, Langston Hughes Residence, Louis Armstrong House, Morris-Jumel Mansion and Museum, Old Merchant's House, One Fifth Avenue, Prospect Park Litchfield Villa, Puck Building, Sara Delano Roosevelt Memorial Home, Singer Building, Sylvan Terrace, Theodore Roosevelt Birthplace, Van Cortlandt House, Vander Ende-Onderdonk House.

Historic Districts *see* Central Park Historic District, Chelsea Historic District, Greenwich Village Historic District, Hamilton Heights Historic District, Henderson Place Historic District, Park Slope, Sniffen Court Historic District, SoHo Cast-Iron Historic District, Striver's Row, Sugar Hill, Tudor City, Weeksville.

Historic Richmond Town 441 Clarke Ave., Staten Island (718) 351-1611 www.historicrichmondtown.org

There are twenty-seven buildings from the rural community of the late 1600s to the busy nineteenth-century Richmond county seat. Many of the structures have been restored and furnished along several streets bustling in summer with costumed guides in period dress and artisans demonstrating early American crafts and trades in a reenactment of daily life. Subway: 1, 9 to South Ferry; N, R to Whitehall St., then ferry to Staten Island. From Staten Island St. George Ferry Terminal, take Bus S74 to St. Patrick's Pl. Open Wed–Sun, hours vary. Modest admission charge.

Historical Museums *see* American Numismatic Society, Brooklyn Historical Society Museum, Edgar Allen Poe Cottage, Ellis Island Museum of Immigration, Fraunces Tavern Museum, Hall of Fame for Great Americans, Intrepid Sea–Air–Space Museum, Lower East Side Tenement Museum, Merchant's House Museum, Morris-Jumel Mansion and Museum, Mount Vernon Hotel Museum and Garden, Museum of American Financial History, Museum of Bronx History,

Museum of the Chinese in the Americas, Museum of the City of New York, New York City Fire Museum, New York City Police Museum, New York City Transit Museum, New York Historical Society, New York Unearthed, Prospect Park Lefferts Homestead Children's Museum, Queens Historical Society in Kingsland Homestead, Queens Museum of Art, Skyscraper Museum, South Street Seaport Museum, Staten Island Ferry Collection, Staten Island Historical Society Museum, Staten Island Institute of Arts and Sciences, Theodore Roosevelt Birthplace, Waterfront Museum. *See also* Art and Design Museums, Ethnic and Community Museums, Major New York City Museums, Media Museums, Military Museums, Museums of Particular Interest to Children and Teens, Science and Technology Museums, Specialized City Museums.

Hockey *see* New York Islanders, New York Rangers.

Hoffman and Swinburne Islands
Originally used as a quarantine area in the 1870s, by the 1920s the islands had been abandoned and remain deserted to this day by all but bird life.

The Hog Pit 22 Ninth Ave. at 13th St. (212) 604-0092 www.hog pit.com
Southern food is the appeal at this noisy, inexpensive West Village honky-tonk that kids would find appealing with its jukebox music and animal skulls on the walls and tasty hush puppies, delicious fried chicken, and excellent ribs. Subway: A, C, E to 14th St. Dinner Tues–Sun. Major credit cards.

Holiday Window Displays *see* Christmas Window Displays.

Holly Solomon Gallery 172 Mercer St. at Houston St. (212) 941-5777
A well-known and well-regarded multi-level exhibition space of avant-garde art in various media from video to illustration to photography and more. Subway: 6 to Bleecker St.; B, D, F, Q to Broadway-Lafayette St.; N, R to Prince St. Open Tues–Sat 10 a.m.–6 p.m.

Holocaust Museum *see* Museum of Jewish Heritage.

Holy Trinity Greek Orthodox Cathedral *see* Greek Orthodox Cathedral of the Holy Trinity.

Home Savings of America Building 110 E 42nd St. btw Third and Park Aves.

Considered by many the finest bank structure of the 1920s, this was originally the uptown office of the downtown Bowery Savings Bank. Between the façade's columns can be found beautifully detailed marble panels with symbolic animal representations. Subway: S, 4, 5, 6, 7 to Grand Central-42nd St.

Hong Kong Dragon Boat Festival (718) 539-8974

On two weekends in August at Flushing Meadow Lake in Flushing Meadows-Corona Park in Queens, this Chinese traditional racing event takes on a festive setting, which also includes demonstrations of Asian arts and crafts and food vending. Subway: 7 to Flushing-Main St.

Honmura An 170 Mercer St. btw Prince and Houston Sts. (212) 234-5253

An elegant, quiet Japanese restaurant offering a lofty standard of service and excellent dining in this expensive place featuring unusual and tasty dishes. Subway: N, R to Prince St. Lunch Wed–Sat, dinner Tues–Sun. Major credit cards.

Horse-Drawn Carriage Rides (212) 246-0520

Carriages line up on Grand Army Plaza at the corner of Fifth Ave. and 59th St. and along 59th St. between Fifth and Seventh Aves. to carry passengers through Central Park or along certain city streets. The cost of the ride is city regulated, just as with taxis. Subway: N, R to Fifth Ave.

Horse Racing see Aqueduct Racetrack, Belmont Park and Race Track, Meadowlands Race Track, Yonkers Raceway.

Horseback Riding see Claremont Riding Academy, Forest Park, Kensington Stables.

Hosteling International–New York 891 Amsterdam Ave. at 103rd St., NY 10025 (212) 932-2300, fax (212) 932-2574 www.hostelling. com

This place offers clean, simple dormitory accommodations for 500 guests in a historic structure on the Upper West Side. Very inexpensive but highly popular, so reservations well ahead of time, especially in busy seasons, are necessary. Major credit cards. Subway: 1, 9 to 103rd St.

Hostels see Aladdin, Blue Rabbit International House, Chelsea International Hostel, Gershwin Hotel, Hosteling International–New York, International House–Sugar Hill, International House of New York, Jazz on the Park, St. George Hotel, Uptown Hostel, Webster Apartments. See also YMCA/YWCAs.

Hotaling's News Agency Warehouse Office, 624 W 52nd St. at Ninth Ave. (212) 840-1868

Since 1905 this firm has been the place where one can find hundreds of foreign and American publications and out-of-town newspapers. Now the firm maintains only a warehouse office, which is open Mon–Fri 6 a.m.– 4 p.m. It is advisable to call in advance to be sure the specific paper is available before visiting the warehouse. Subway: C, E to 50th St.

Hotel Accommodations—Deluxe Hotels *see* Carlyle Hotel, Four Seasons Hotel, Millennium Hilton, Pierre Hotel, Plaza Hotel, Stanhope Hotel, Trump International Hotel and Tower, Waldorf-Astoria, The Warwick.

Hotel Accommodations—First-Class Hotels *see* Algonquin Hotel, Barbizon Hotel, The Benjamin, Iroquois, The Mark, The Michelangelo, Roger Smith.

Hotel Accommodations—Middle-Range Hotels *see* Best Western Manhattan, Comfort Inn Manhattan, Empire Hotel, Excelsior Hotel, Gramercy Park Hotel, Hotel Beacon, Hotel Pennsylvania, Hotel Wellington, Lexington Hotel, Mayflower Hotel, Washington Square Hotel.

Hotel Accommodations—Budget Hotels *see* Broadway Inn, Habitat Hotel, Grand Union, Herald Square Hotel, Hotel Edison, Larchmont Hotel, Malibu Studios Hotel, Murray Hill Inn, Pickwick Arms, Portland Square, Riverside Towers Hotel, Wolcott Hotel, Wyndham Hotel.

Hotel Beacon 2130 Broadway, NY 10023 btw 74th and 75th Sts. (212) 787-1100 or (800) 522-4969, fax (212) 787-8119 www. beaconhotel.com

Clean, roomy, and airy rooms are the prime features of this comfortable, moderately priced hotel located in a good residential area near Central Park and Lincoln Center and close to many of Broadway's near uptown attractions like Zabar's food emporium. Subway: 1, 2, 3, 9 to 72nd St.

Hotel Beverly *see* The Benjamin.

Hotel Conxions (212) 840-8686 or (800) 522-9991, fax (212) 221-8686 www.hotelconxions.com

This broker arranges economic to deluxe accommodations at discount prices at many New York establishments.

Hotel des Artistes 1 W 67th St. btw Central Park W and Columbus Ave. (212) 362-6700

Apartments containing 2 stories were constructed in this 1918 structure designed to serve as studios for working artists. Instead the building has become luxury cooperative apartments with many celebrity tenants. The interior is opulent, and it is here that one finds the famed Café des Artistes (212) 877-3500, a romantic spot with an expensive menu adorned by wall murals of reclining nudes by famed illustrator Howard Chandler Christy. Subway: 1, 9 to 66th St.-Lincoln Center.

Hotel Edison 228 W 47th St., NY 10036 btw Broadway and Eighth Ave. (212) 840-5000 or (800) 637-7070, fax (212) 596-6850 www.edisonhotelnyc.com

This hotel is a moderately priced long-time theatre district favorite with recently renovated rooms and a colorful Art Deco lobby and a coffee shop that is popular with many Broadway denizens. Subway: 1, 9 to 50th St.

Hotel Pennsylvania 401 Seventh Ave. at 33rd St., NY 10001 (212) 736-5000 or (800) 223-8585, fax (212) 502-8712 www.hotelpenn. com

Made famous by Glenn Miller's "Pennsylvania 65000" swing number (it still has the same phone number), this moderately priced hotel directly opposite Madison Square Garden and Penn Station is a big, bustling, conveniently located place. Subway: B, D, F, N, Q, R to 34th St.-Herald Square.

Hotel Reservation Agencies *see* Accommodations Express, CRS, Express Reservations, Hotel Conxions, Hotel Reservations Network, Quikbook.

Hotel Reservations Network (800) 964-0835 www.hoteldiscount. com

This discount hotel booking service offers travelers savings on room rates in all price categories.

Hotel Wellington 871 Seventh Ave. at 55th St., NY 10019 (212) 247-3900 or (800) 652-1212, fax (212) 581-1719 www.wellington hotel.com

A well-located, old-fashioned midtown hotel that's timeworn but comfortable with rooms in the moderate price range. Subway: B, D, E to Seventh Ave.; N, R to 57th St.

Houseman Theatre *see* John Houseman Theatre.

Houses of Worship *see* Churches, Mosques, Synagogues.

Howard Beach

A predominantly Italian neighborhood situated at the southern end of Queens, beyond which lies Jamaica Bay and the Rockaways. Subway: A to Howard Beach-JFK Airport.

Hudson Guild Theatre 441 W 26th St. btw Ninth and Tenth Aves. (212) 760-9800

This performance venue showcases the work of emerging American and international playwrights. Subway: C, E to 23rd St.

Hudson River Club 4 World Financial Center at Vesey St. (212) 786-1500

An American menu is offered along with the extraordinary sweeping views of the lower New York harbor and the Statue of Liberty from virtually every table, at this spot where the prices are moderately expensive and reservations are strongly suggested. Subway: 1, 9 to Cortlandt St. Lunch Mon–Fri, dinner Mon–Sat, brunch Sun. Major credit cards.

Hudson River Park

Running from the World Financial Center to the Museum of Jewish Heritage, this green, landscaped, riverside area offers walkways, bike paths, handball courts, and a sculpture garden as well as grassy spots. It can be reached from the corner of Chamber and West Sts. and offers spectacular views of the New York harbor and the Statue of Liberty. Subway: 1, 2, 3, 9 to Chambers St.

Hunan Park 235 Columbus Ave. btw 70th and 71st Sts. (212) 724-4411

Carefully prepared, inexpensive Chinese dishes with good service in a pleasing environment make this restaurant a recommended spot for Hunan cooking. A second location is at 721 Columbus Ave. at 95th St. (212) 222-6511. Subway: (235 Columbus Ave.) B, C, 1, 2, 3, 9 to 72nd St.; (721 Columbus Ave.) B, C, 1, 2, 3, 9 to 96th St. Lunch and dinner daily. Major credit cards.

Hungarian Pastry Shop 1030 Amsterdam Ave. btw 110th and 111th Sts. (212) 866-4230 www.geocities.com/hungarianpastryshop

Popular coffeehouse featuring excellent inexpensive coffee, pastries, and other home-baked good things that can be enjoyed in an outdoor garden.

Subway: B, C, 1, 9 to Cathedral Pkwy.-110th St. Daily 8 a.m.–10 or 11 p.m. No credit cards.

Hungarians in New York *see* Yorkville.

Hunter College 68th St. btw Park and Lexington Aves. www.hunter. cuny.edu

A complex of buildings houses this branch of the City University of New York. It is the home of the Sylvia and Danny Kaye Playhouse (212) 772-4448, a beautiful concert hall with a schedule of dance, music, operatic, and theatrical performances. Subway: 6 to 68th St.-Hunter College.

IBM Building 590 Madison Ave. btw 57th and 58th Sts.

This is a smart-looking, five-sided granite structure erected in 1983 with a garden plaza and spacious atrium open to the public. Subway: E, F, N, R to Fifth Ave.

ICP *see* International Center of Photography.

Ice Hockey *see* New York Islanders, New York Rangers.

Ice Hockey Season (212) 465-4459

The New York Rangers attract thousands of fans to their home games at Madison Square Garden during the season from October to April. Subway: 1, 2, 3, 9 to 34th St.-Penn Station.

Ice Skating *see* Central Park Wollman Memorial Rink, Chelsea Piers Sky Rink, Riverbank State Park, Rockefeller Center, Wollman Memorial Rink in Prospect Park.

Il Mulino *see* Il Mulino under M.

Imperial Theatre 249 W 45th St. btw Eighth Ave. and Broadway (212) 239-6200

Since its construction in 1923 this Broadway house has been the showplace for innumerable memorable musical and dramatic hits. Subway: A, C, E to 42nd St.-Port Authority; N, R, S, 1, 2, 3, 7, 9 to Times Square-42nd St.

In-Line Skating *see* Central Park Mall, Central Park Wollman Memorial Rink, Chelsea Piers Roller Rinks, East River Esplanade, North River Park, West St. *See also* Roller Skating.

Inagiku Waldorf Astoria Hotel, 111 E 49th St. btw Lexington and Park Aves. (212) 355-0440

Possibly the most beautiful formal Japanese decor in the city is part of the appeal of this venerable and very expensive restaurant serving excellent fish and meat dishes. Subway: 6 to 51st St. Lunch Mon–Fri, dinner daily. Major credit cards.

Independence Day Celebration *see* Macy's Fireworks Display.

Independent Films *see* Foreign and Independent Films.

India *see* Little India.

India Day Parade (212) 732-7678
In this celebratory event in mid-August, events in the history of India are depicted on colorful floats in a procession down Madison Ave. from 34th St. to 21st St. Subway: 6 to 33rd St.

India Festival (212) 732-7678
This annual ethnic celebration takes place during the month of August at South Street Seaport. Subway: J, M, Z, 2, 3, 4, 5 to Fulton St.

Indian Restaurants *see* Dawat, Diwan Grill, Haveli, Jackson Diner, Jewel of India, Madras Mahal, Mavalli Palace, Tabla.

Indians in New York *see* Flushing, Jackson Heights, Little India.

Indochine 430 Lafayette St. btw Astor Pl. and E 4th St. (212) 505-5111
An attractive Southeast Asian ambiance forms the backdrop for the excellent and savory Vietnamese dishes served at this moderately expensive restaurant where reservations are essential. Subway: 6 to Astor Pl. Dinner daily. Major credit cards.

Information for Tourists *see* Tourist Information.

Inn at Irving Place 56 Irving Pl. btw 17th and 18th Sts., NY 10003 (212) 533-4600 or (800) 685-1447 www.innatirving.com
There are only twenty places in this pair of brownstones offering deluxe stays in celebrity-named rooms plus gracious afternoon tea service at steep rates. Subway: L, N, R, 4, 5, 6 to 14th St.-Union Square.

Insider's Hour Programs
Many of New York City's most renowned cultural institutions offer special events and unusual behind-the-scenes tours of interest to families and children of one hour's duration year-round featuring their collections, backstages, gardens, and more. Seasonal brochures describing the organizations and their schedules are available at the New York City Official Visi-

tor Information Center at 810 Seventh Ave. at 53rd St., (800) NYC-VISIT, or www.nycvisit.com. Subway: N, R to 49th St. or 57th St.

International Asian Fine Arts Fair (212) 642-8572

Dealers from many nations show furniture, sculptures, carpets, jewelry, and ceramic objects from Southeast Asia, the Far East, and the Middle East in May at the Seventh Regiment Armory at 66th St. and Park Ave. Subway: 6 to 68th St.-Hunter College.

International Building

This Rockefeller Center structure stands behind the giant statue of Atlas holding up the world. It is at Fifth Ave. between 50th and 51st Sts. and houses many consulates and international airlines. Subway: E, F to Fifth Ave.; 6 to 51st St.

International Cat Show (212) 465-6741

This annual festival of felines drawn from all over the world takes place at Madison Square Garden, Seventh Ave. at 33rd St., for two days in late February or early March. Subway: 1, 2, 3, 9 to 34th St.-Penn Station.

International Center of Photography 1130 Fifth Ave. at 94th St. (212) 768-4682 www.icp.org

Located in an upper Fifth Ave. grand residence, this is the city's premier photography showplace, exhibiting all aspects of the art. The galleries display changing shows featuring works of photographers from all nations as well as pictures drawn from the permanent collection. Subway: 6 to 96th St. Tues–Sun, hours vary. Admission charge.

International Center of Photography–Midtown 1133 Sixth Ave. at 43rd St. (212) 768-4682 www.icp.org

The recently renovated midtown branch features a cascading series of permanent galleries, an atrium, and large murals in its windows. It has been designed to facilitate the growing use of digital photography and other electronic media and offers several exhibitions a year. Subway: B, D, F, Q to 42nd St. Tues–Sun, hours vary. Admission charge.

International Cultures Expo Fest 1435 Broadway (212) 221-7255

This folk festival, sponsored by the International Immigrants Foundation, is held on a Saturday in June on Madison Ave. from 47th to 48th Sts. and celebrates folk arts and crafts with music, food, and festive activities for much of the day. Subway: 6 to 51st St.

International Cultures Parade 1435 Broadway (212) 221-7255

Sponsored by the International Immigrants Foundation, this colorful, multi-ethic annual parade of recent immigrants proceeds along Madison Ave. from 42nd St. to 23rd St. on the second Sunday of September each year in the afternoon. Enthusiastic marchers and performers represent nations both large and small.

International Fine Arts and Antique Dealers Show (212) 642-8572

This fair attracts dealers and collectors from everywhere in mid-October at the Seventh Regiment Armory at 66th St. and Park Ave., where pieces from ancient to modern times are shown. The spring show takes place each year in mid-May and centers on fine art, with paintings, drawings, and sculptures from the Renaissance displayed. Subway: 6 to 68th St.-Hunter College.

International House of New York 500 Riverside Dr. at 122nd St., NY 10027 (212) 316-8400, fax (212) 316-1827

This residence hall for Columbia students is most readily available as a hostel for travelers during the summer and Christmas holiday periods, when rates are at their lowest for rooms with shared baths. Subway: 1, 9 to 125th St.

International House–Sugar Hill 722 St. Nicholas Ave. at 145th St., NY 10031 (212) 926-7030

A well-managed hostel between Harlem and Washington Heights offering a limited number of cheap dormitory accommodations conveniently situated above the subway stop. Reserve well ahead for busy seasons. Subway: A, B, C, D to 145th St.

International Wildlife Conservation Park Fordham Rd. and Bronx River Pkwy. (718) 367-1010 www.wcs.org/zoos/bronxzoo/

The Bronx Zoo, with its 4,000 animals representing some 600 species, is one of the nation's best in which most of its residents roam freely in natural settings. The Children's Zoo offers many hands-on learning experiences and a large petting zoo. Among the special features are a $6^{1}/_{2}$-acre Congo Gorilla Forest and a guided monorail tour through Wild Asia inhabited by elephants, antelope, tigers, and more. Subway: 2, 5 to Pelham Pkwy. Open daily at 10 a.m., closing time varies. Admission charge.

Internet Resources on New York see Web Sites About New York.

Intrepid Sea–Air–Space Museum W 46th St. and Twelfth Ave. at Pier 86 (212) 245-0072 www.intrepidmuseum.org

This enormous World War II and Vietnam War aircraft carrier is now the showplace for displays of fifty aircraft, rockets, and space vehicles.

Guided tours of varying lengths of its many attractions are available, and many audiovisual shows and hands-on exhibits will delight kids. Subway: N, R, S, 1, 2, 3, 7, 9 to Times Square-42nd St., then take Bus M42 west, marked Piers on the front. Open daily 10 a.m., closing time varies. Admission charge. *See also* City Pass.

Inwood Hill Park (212) 360-8111

This expanse of meadows and trees at Manhattan's northwest tip is its second largest park. Wild and rambling and very isolated, this 200-acre area is bordered on the north by the Harlem River and the Hudson River on the east. In it can be found caves once used by the Native Americans as well as many acres of native forest. Entrance at 207th St. and Seaman Ave. Subway: A, 1, 9 to 207th St.

Ipanema 13 W 46th St. btw Fifth and Sixth Aves. (212) 730-5848

This comfortable spot on Brazilians' popular stretch of 46th St. features well-prepared exotic dining specialties like the favorite national dish, *feijoada,* and the drinks that go with it at moderate prices. Subway: B, D, F, Q to 42nd St. Lunch and dinner daily. Major credit cards.

Iridium 44 W 63rd St. at Columbus Ave. (212) 582-2121 www.iridiumjazzclub.com

This spot near Lincoln Center offers good food and fine jazz performed by top names in a strangely designed room. Subway: 1, 9 to 66th St.-Lincoln Center. Open nightly. Cover charge varies, drinks minimum. Major credit cards.

Irish Arts Center 553 W 51st St. btw Tenth and Eleventh Aves. (212) 757-3318 www.irishartscenter.org

Classic as well as contemporary Irish plays are produced here. Subway: C, E to 50th St.

Irish in New York *see* Bainbridge, Carroll Gardens, Sunnyside Queens, Woodside.

Irish Repertory Theatre 132 W 22nd St. btw Sixth and Seventh Aves. (212) 727-2737 www.irishrepertorytheatre.com

This Chelsea performance center showcases works by both contemporary and classic Irish dramatists. Subway: 1, 9, F to 23rd St.

Iroquois 49 W 44th St. btw Fifth and Sixth Aves., NY 10036 (212) 840-3080 or (800) 332-7220, fax (212) 398-1754 www.iroquoisny.com

Recently transformed into a luxury boutique hotel, this midtown hostelry boasts a health center, library, and marble bathrooms as well as expensive room rates. Subway: B, D, F, Q to 42nd St.; 7 to Fifth Ave.

Irving Place

This short seven-block street named for Washington Irving runs south from Gramercy Park to 14th St. and is lined with pretty brownstone row-houses, many of which have been transformed into restaurants and boutiques. Subway: L, N, R, 4, 5, 6 to Union Square-14th St.

Irving Plaza 17 Irving Pl. btw E 15th and E 16th Sts. (212) 777-6800

This one-time ethnic music hall offers a large dance floor and a small balcony with a good view of the stage, where rock, electronic, rap, and other types of bands perform. Subway: L, N, R, 4, 5, 6 to Union Square-14th St. Open nightly. Cover charge. No credit cards.

Irving Trust Company Building 1 Wall St. opposite Trinity Church

Built in 1932, this structure retains the striking and colorful mosaics that brighten its Art Deco lobby. Subway: 4, 5 to Wall St.

Isaacs–Hendricks House 77 Bedford St. at Commerce St.

Remodeled twice since its construction in 1799, this landmark home is the oldest surviving house in Greenwich Village. The brick façade was added in the early nineteenth century, and the 3rd floor was added in the 1920s. It is not open to the public. Subway: 1, 9 to Houston St.

Isamu Noguchi Museum *see* Noguchi Museum.

Islamic Cultural Center and Mosque Third Ave. btw 96th and 97th Sts. (212) 722-5234

The Kuwaiti government was the major contributor to the construction of this modern gold-domed mosque facing Mecca. It can hold 1,000 male worshippers on its main level, while women are accommodated upstairs. Subway: 6 to 96th St.

Island Spice 402 W 44th St. near Ninth Ave. (212) 765-1737

This place is home to some of the finest Caribbean dishes to be found in the city. Because it is also comfortable, friendly, and inexpensive, reservations might be a good idea. Subway: A, C, E to 42nd St.-Port Authority. Lunch and dinner Mon–Sat. Major credit cards.

Islands in and around New York

New York City contains more than just the two best known islands—Manhattan and Staten Island. Beyond the well-known tourist destinations like Ellis Island and Liberty Island and others like Roosevelt Island and Riker's Island, dotting the harbors and rivers around the city are many other small pieces of land, most of which are only accessible to birds and other forms of wildlife. One that bears a familiar designation is in the East River opposite the United Nations, U Thant Island, named for the former UN Secretary General from Burma. *See also* City Island, Coney Island, Governor's Island, Hart Island, Hoffman and Swinburne Islands, Mill Rock Island, North Brother Island, Randall's Island, Riker's Island, South Bronx Island, Ward's Island.

Iso 175 Second Ave. at E 11th St. (212) 777-0361

A warmly welcoming East Village spot offering a full range of moderately expensive, inventively prepared sushi and other Japanese seafood dishes. Subway: L to Third Ave. Dinner Mon–Sat. Major credit cards.

Israelis in New York *see* Aleppo in Flatbush.

Italian Restaurants *see* Babbo, Barbetta, Becco, Bice, Carmine's, Carolina, Caroline's Comedy Club, Contrapunto, Da Umberto, Elaine's, Felidea, Follonico, Gennaro, Le Madri, Manganaro's, Mario's, La Mela, Mezzaluna, Mezzogiorno, Il Mulino, Minetta Tavern, Il Nido, Orso, Palio, Pó, Rao's, Remi, San Domenico, Trattoria dell'Arte. *See also* Pizzerias.

The Italian Village

This enclave south of Washington Square Park was the city's first Italian neighborhood, dating from the mid-nineteenth century. While once among the largest concentrations of Italians in Manhattan, the population here has dwindled, and only the area around Sullivan and Thompson Sts. from Bleecker St. to Spring St. retains its Italian ethnic flavor. Subway: C, E to Spring St.

Italians in New York *see* El Barrio, Bay Ridge, Belmont, Bensonhurst, Carroll Gardens, Howard Beach, The Italian Village, Little Italy.

JVC Jazz Festival (212) 501-1390 or (212) 479-7888

In late June and early July unknown and celebrated jazz musicians perform at various concert halls, clubs, and theatres around town.

Jack Eichenbaum Tours (718) 961-8406

An urban geographer leads informative walking tours of Queens and other city neighborhoods.

Jackie Robinson Park 145th to 152nd St. btw Edgecombe and Bradhurst Sts. (212) 234-9607

This public space in the St. Nicholas area of Harlem is a well-equipped place with a large pool, basketball courts, and majestic oak trees along the walking paths. Subway: A, B, C, D to 145th St.

Jackson Diner 37-03 74th St. btw Thirty-Seventh and Roosevelt Aves., Jackson Heights, Queens (718) 672-1232

Reputed to be the best place in the city for inexpensive Indian food from both the north and south of this giant Asian country. Whatever you select in this plain-looking eatery, from the tandoori chicken to the vegetarian selections, will be tasty and spicy. They serve no alcohol, but you can bring your own. Subway: E, F, G, R to Jackson Heights-Roosevelt Ave. Lunch and dinner daily. Cash only.

Jackson Heights

This section of Queens is home to a large population of Colombians, many Ecuadorians, and a fair number of Argentinians and other Latin American families. The heart of the district runs along Roosevelt and Thirty-Seventh Aves. from 82nd St. to Junction Blvd., and some of the best

Latin restaurants, coffeehouses, and bakeries in the city can be found along Roosevelt and Thirty-Seventh Aves. The region between 7th and 8th Sts. and northwest of Roosevelt Ave. to Thirty-Seventh Ave. has been designated a historic district because of its garden apartment developments and attractively adorned apartment buildings. Little India, with its large Indian community, centers in the area around 74th St. Subway: E, F, G, R to Jackson Heights-Roosevelt Ave.

Jackson Hole Burgers 232 E 64th St. at Second Ave. (212) 371-7187

This spot is popular with kids for its tasty hamburgers and with their parents for the inexpensive prices. Located at a number of other locations: 1270 Madison Ave. (212) 427-2820; 512 Columbus Ave. (212) 362-5177; 1611 Second Ave. (212) 737-8788; and 521 Third Ave. (212) 679-3264. Subway: Q to Lexington Ave. Lunch and dinner daily. Major credit cards.

Jacob K. Javitz Convention Center 655 W 34th St. at Twelfth Ave. (212) 216-2000 www.javits.com

Running along Twelfth Ave. from 34th to 38th Sts. is the nation's largest exhibition space, a striking modernistic glass structure designed by I. M. Pei that hosts some of the largest audiences anywhere for events like the annual auto and boat shows and political conventions. Subway: A, C, E to 34th St.-Penn Station.

Jacob Riis Park

Just west of Rockaway Beach in Queens is this parkland of sandy beach and boardwalk with basketball and handball courts and a golf course. Subway: A, S to Rockaway Park/Beach 116th St., then take Bus Q22; 2, 5 to Brooklyn College/Flatbush Ave., then take Bus Q35.

Jacqueline Kennedy Onassis Reservoir *see* Central Park Jacqueline Kennedy Onassis Reservoir.

Jacques Marchais Museum of Tibetan Art 338 Lighthouse Ave., Staten Island (718) 987-3500 www.tibetanmuseum.com

One of the largest collections of Tibetan art in the Western world is found in one high-ceilinged room containing bronze figures, medical instruments, masks, paintings, and costumes. The building is on a secluded hillside and is a replica of a mountain temple; the garden features stone sculptures and life-size Buddhas. Subway: 1, 9 to South Ferry; N, R to Whitehall St., then ferry to Staten Island. From Staten Island St. George Ferry Terminal, take Bus S78 to Lighthouse Ave. Open April–November Wed–Sun 1 p.m.–5 p.m. Other months phone for open times. Modest admission charge.

Jai-Ya Thai 396 Third Ave. btw 28th and 29th Sts. (212) 889-1330

Bargain dining of tasty Southeast Asian dishes prepared at levels of spiciness from mild to torrid is the appeal of this popular spot. There is another location at 81-11 Broadway in Elmhurst, Queens (718) 651-1330. Subway: 6 to 28th St. Open Mon–Sat for lunch and dinner, Sun dinner only. Major credit cards.

Jamaica

Located in the center of Queens, this neighborhood is home to the borough's principal West Indian and Black residential communities. Jamaica Ave. from 150th to around 168th Sts. is the main street, and the pedestrian mall on 165th St. is the heart of its bustling restaurant and retail activity. Subway: F to 169th St.

Jamaica Bay

This body of water in Queens adjacent to Kennedy Airport and close to the Rockaways contains countless small, untamed islands in the marshlands; the islands are the bay's most picturesque natural feature.

Jamaica Bay Wildlife Refuge Cross Bay Blvd. at Broad Channel, Queens (718) 318-4340

Just south of the Kennedy Airport runways, this area, roughly the size of Manhattan, is a unique urban wildlife refuge and harbors more than 325 species of small creatures and birds, a number of which are classified as endangered. Subway: A, S to Broad Channel. Open daily 8:30 a.m.–5 p.m.

Jamaica Center for Arts and Learning 161-04 Jamaica Ave., Jamaica, Queens (718) 658-7400

Housed in a landmark neo–Italian Renaissance building constructed in 1898, the center presents professional theatre, jazz, and multicultural performances. Subway: E, J, Z to Jamaica Center. Mon–Sat 9 a.m.–6 p.m.

Jamaican Restaurants *see* Caribbean Restaurants.

Jamaicans in New York *see* Crown Heights.

James A. Farley Building *see* General Post Office.

Jan Hus Presbyterian Church 351 E 74th St. btw First and Second Aves. www.janhuspresbyterian.beliefnet.com

Begun in 1914 to serve the Czech residents of the neighborhood once known as Little Bohemia, this church now is best known for hosting dramatic and musical theatrical events. Subway: 6 to 77th St.

Jane Street Theatre Hotel Riverview Ballroom, 113 Jane St. at West Side Hwy. (212) 424-8404

This small, out-of-the-way spot is known for having brought forth *The Angry Inch*, a blockbuster transsexual German rock musical. Subway: A, C, E, L to 14th St.

Japan Society 333 E 47th St. btw First and Second Aves. (212) 752-3015 or (212) 832-1155 www.japansociety.org
Committed to promoting cultural relationships, this organization offers an auditorium, language center, research library, exhibition galleries, and serene Japanese gardens. It sponsors conferences, lectures, concerts, dramatic performances, and several annual series of Japanese films seldom on view elsewhere. Subway: E, F to Lexington Ave.; 6 to 51st St. Gallery open Tues–Sun 11 a.m.–6 p.m. Modest admission charge.

Japanese O'Bon Festival *see* O'Bon Festival.

Japanese Restaurants *see* Bond Street, Fujiyama Mama, Hatsuhana, Honmura An, Inagiku, Iso, Nobu, Sandobe Sushi, Sushisay, Takahachi.

Le Jardin Bistro 25 Cleveland Pl. near Spring St. (212) 343-9599
A welcoming ambiance, splendid and abundant French dishes, and a pleasant back garden and arbor for the warm seasons all add to the appeal of this charming, moderately priced restaurant where reservations are a good idea. Subway: C, E to Spring St. Lunch and dinner daily, brunch on weekends. Major credit cards.

Javitz Convention Center *see* Jacob K. Javitz Convention Center.

Jazz on the Park 36 W 106th St. btw Central Park W and Manhattan Ave. (212) 932-1600 or (888) 609-5299, fax (212) 932-1700 www.jazzhostel.com
Rooms hold two to fourteen people in this clean, bustling hostel replete with coffee bar, game room, rooftop terrace, and jazz den, all at rock-bottom rates. Reservations well in advance are essential. Subway: B, C to 103rd St. Major credit cards.

Jazz Spots *see* Arthur's Tavern, Arturo's, BB King Blues Club and Grill, Birdland, Bitter End, The Blue Note, Cajun, Chicago B.L.U.E.S., Cornelia Street Café, 55 Bar and Grill, Iridium, Jamaica Center for Arts and Learning, The Jazz Standard, Knickerbockers, Knitting Factory, Lola, Nell's, S.O.B.'s, Showman's Café, Small's, Sweet Basil, Terra Blues Bar Restaurant and Music, Village Underground, Zinc Bar.

The Jazz Standard 116 E 27th St. btw Park Ave. S and Lexington Ave. (212) 576-2232 www.jazzstandard.com

A big room featuring mainstream jazz by fine new and seasoned artists, where both the music and the food served upstairs delight the clientele. Subway: 6 to 28th St. Open nightly. Cover charge and minimum drinks charge. Major credit cards.

Jean Claude 137 Sullivan St. btw Houston and Prince Sts. (212) 475-9232

A popular bistro offering continental fare at moderate prices to SoHo diners who like the service, the food, and the trendy ambiance. Subway: C, E to Prince St.; 1, 9 to Houston St. Dinner nightly. Cash only.

Jean Cocteau Repertory Bouwerie Lane Theatre, 330 Bowery at Bond St. (212) 677-0060 www.jeancocteaurep.org

For more than 30 years this performing company has been mounting productions of stage classics. Subway: A, F to Second Ave.; 6 to Bleecker St.

Jean Georges Trump International Hotel, 1 Central Park W btw 60th and 61st Sts. (212) 299-3900 www.trumpintl.com/pages/restaurant.html

Named for its celebrated Alsatian chef, this very expensive, elegant restaurant offers dazzling and creative dining choices to make for a memorable dining experience. Reservations required. Subway: A, B, C, D, 1, 2, 3, 9 to 59th St.-Columbus Circle. Breakfast daily. Lunch Mon–Fri, dinner daily. Major credit cards.

Jefferson Market Courthouse 425 Sixth Ave. at 10th St. (212) 243-4334

This beloved Village landmark has not been a courthouse since the 1940s. Empty and neglected for more than 20 years, it was restored and converted into a branch of the New York Public Library in 1967. Behind the library, a flower garden blooms, nurtured by local volunteers. Subway: L to Sixth Ave.; F to 14th St.

Jehovah's Witnesses

The world center of this religious organization can be found in plain yellow structures in Brooklyn Heights close to the Brooklyn Bridge, where the residence hall is at 124 Columbia Heights and the Jehovah's Witness Library is at 119 Columbia Heights. Subway: A, C to High St.

Jewel of India 15 W 44th St. btw Fifth and Sixth Aves. (212) 869-5544

Northern Indian cooking is the specialty of this dining spot, decorated with attractive sculptures, wall hangings, and screens, and featuring meat dishes and tandoori preparations at moderate prices. Reservations are suggested. Subway: B, D, F to 47th-50th Sts.-Rockefeller Center. Lunch and dinner daily. Major credit cards.

Jewish Museum 1109 Fifth Ave. at 92nd St. (212) 423-3200 www. thejewishmuseum.org

This is the largest museum of its type outside Israel. It contains a permanent exhibition centered on the ideas and cultural development of the entire sweep of Jewish experience as well as changing exhibits of art and artifacts on varying multimedia themes and topical issues. Subway: 6 to 96th St. Open Mon–Thurs, Sun, hours vary. Admission charge. No credit cards.

Jewish Neighborhoods *see* Aleppo in Flatbush, Borough Park, Brighton Beach, Crown Heights, Lower East Side, Washington Heights, Williamsburg.

Jewish Repertory Theatre Playhouse 91, 316 E 91st St. btw First and Second Aves. (212) 831-2000 www.jrt.org

This theatre offers dramatic and musical productions that have aspects of Jewish life as their main theme. Subway: 4, 5, 6 to 86th St.

Jewish Restaurants *see* Ratner's Dairy Restaurant and Bakery, Sammy's Famous Romanian Restaurant. *See also* Delicatessens, Kosher Restaurants.

Jewish Theological Seminary 3080 Broadway at 122nd St. (212) 678-8000 www.jtsa.edu

Begun in the late nineteenth century to prepare rabbis and Jewish scholars, the present building was constructed in 1930. It houses an extraordinary library of more than 250,000 Jewish works that is open to the public. Subway: 1, 9 to 125th St. Library open Sun–Thurs, hours vary. Admission free.

Jo Jo 160 E 64th St. btw Lexington and Third Aves. (212) 223-5656

Moderately expensive French food with an Asian influence is served at this lively bistro, where healthy ingredients and traditional dishes add up to thoroughly pleasurable dining. Reservations suggested. Subway: Q to Lexington Ave.; 6 to 68th St.-Hunter College. Lunch Mon–Fri, dinner Mon–Sat. Major credit cards.

Joe Allen 326 W 46th St. btw Eighth and Ninth Aves. (212) 581-6464 www.joeallenrestaurant.com

This long-time Restaurant Row favorite offers basic, reliable American dishes at moderate prices and is popular for both pre- and post-theatre dining and is frequented by Broadway actors and some aspirants waiting tables. Reservations for pre-theatre seating are essential. Subway: A, C, E to 42nd St.-Port Authority. Lunch and dinner Mon–Fri, brunch and dinner Sat and Sun. Major credit cards.

Joe's Shanghai 9 Pell St. btw Bowery and Mott St. (212) 233-8888

This ever-popular, inexpensive Chinese restaurant is celebrated for its steamy soup dumplings as well as its other excellent Shanghai food favorites. Other locations are at 24 W 56th St. between Fifth and Sixth Aves. (212) 333-3868, 82-74 Broadway between Forty-Fifth and Whitney Aves., Queens (718) 639-6888, 136-21 Thirty-Seventh Ave. between Main and Union Sts., Queens (718) 539-3838. Subway: J, M, N, R, Z to Canal St. Lunch and dinner daily. No credit cards.

Jogging *see* Running.

John F. Kennedy International Airport

This is the largest airport serving the city; it is in Queens. The quickest method of travel to and from this airport is by taxi, but it is also the most expensive. Sharing the taxi with two or three people is more economic. Other means of traveling to Kennedy Airport are

Across from Grand Central Station—Park Ave. and 41st St.
New York Airport Service Express Bus—$13, every 20–30 minutes
5:10 a.m.–10 p.m. (718) 875-8200

Port Authority Bus Terminal—42nd St. and Eighth Ave.
New York Airport Service Express Bus—$13, every 20–30 minutes
5:20 a.m.–8:40 p.m. (718) 875-8200

IND Subway
Subway (A-Train marked "Far Rockaway") $1.50 to Howard Beach Station at JFK transfer to Long Term Parking Lot Bus, free to all terminals. (718) 330-1234

Hotels—Shared Van
SuperShuttle Manhattan Service (midtown hotels) $15 (212) 258-3826
Express Shuttle U.S.A.—service from certain midtown Manhattan hotels, $19 (212) 315-3006

New York Airport Service Express Bus from certain midtown Manhattan hotels. Transfer may be required, $13 (718) 875-8200

Penn Station—33rd St. and Eighth Ave.
Long Island Railroad (LIRR) to Jamaica. Transfer to LIRR, $3.50–$5 (718) 217-5477
New York Airport Service Express Bus, $5 (718) 875-8200

Fares were in effect in fall 2001 and may have changed since then.
For more details on getting to or from Kennedy Airport, call (800) AIR-RIDE.

John H. Finley Walk

This wide, paved esplanade runs above FDR Dr. from 81st to 84th Sts. and offers excellent views of the East River where Long Island and the Harlem River come together. Subway: 6 to 77th St., then Bus M79 east.

John Houseman Theatre 450 W 42nd St. btw Ninth and Tenth Aves. (212) 967-9077

This venue is the showplace for a number of theatrical companies like Studio Theatre, The New Group, Gotham City Improv, and Studio Too. Subway: A, C, E to 42nd St.-Port Authority.

John Jay College of Criminal Justice 899 Tenth Ave. at 58th St. (212) 237-8000 www.jjay.cuny.edu

This neo-Victorian structure built in 1903 once housed the DeWitt Clinton High School before becoming a part of the City University of New York system. Renovations designed by Douglas Leigh added an atrium and an extension, while gargoyles and other statuary enhance the white exterior. Subway: A, B, C, D, 1, 9 to 59th St.-Columbus Circle.

John Street Church 44 John St. (212) 269-0014

The United Methodist Church was begun in the 1760s as Wesley Chapel and lays claim to being the oldest American Methodist society. It was reconstructed twice in the nineteenth century and holds many church relics. Subway: A, C, J, M, Z, 2, 3, 4, 5 to Fulton St.-Broadway Nassau. Open Mon, Wed, Fri noon–4 p.m. Admission free.

John's Pizzeria 278 Bleecker St. btw Sixth and Seventh Aves. (212) 243-1680

Long considered one of the finest brick-oven pizza spots in New York, this restaurant also offers a range of other appetizing pasta dishes at moderate prices. Other locations are 260 W 44th St. between Broadway and Eighth Ave. (212) 391-7560, 408 E 64th St. between First and York Aves.

(212) 935-2895, and 48 W 65th St. between Central Park W and Columbus Ave. (212) 721-7001. Subway: A, B, C, D, E, F, Q to W 4th St.-Washington Square; 1, 9 to Christopher St.-Sheridan Square. Lunch and dinner daily. Major credit cards.

Jones Diner 371 Lafayette St. at Great Jones St. (212) 673-3577

For more than three quarters of a century this dingy-looking place has been serving solid, inexpensive dinner fare to those who frequent it. Subway: 6 to Astor Pl. Mon–Sat 6 a.m.–6 p.m. Cash only.

Joseph L. Papp Public Theatre 425 Lafayette St. btw E 4th St. and Aston Pl. (212) 539-8500

This complex of theatres was once the Astor Library. This is a major off-Broadway showplace for work by new American playwrights as well as new takes on Shakespeare and other classics. In summer it runs the New York Shakespeare Festival in Central Park's outdoor Delacorte Theatre. Subway: 6 to Astor Pl.; N, R to 8th St.-NYU.

Josie's 300 Amsterdam Ave. at 74th St. (212) 769-1212

Specializing in dairy-free dishes, this restaurant prepares nutritious, tasty food that's generally low in fat content at inexpensive prices. Subway: 1, 2, 3, 9, B, C to 72nd St. Lunch Mon–Fri, brunch on weekends. Major credit cards.

Joyce Gold Tours (212) 242-5762 www.nyctours.com

These walking tours around New York are centered on city history, led by a college instructor, and designed around specific themes and neighborhoods.

Joyce Theatre 175 Eighth Ave. at 19th St. (212) 242-0800 www.joyce.org

In what was once a movie house, this has been transformed into one of New York's best dance venues, hosting local, American regional, and imported choreographic productions. There is another showplace of the Joyce in SoHo at 155 Mercer St. between Prince and Houston Sts. (212) 431-9233. Subway: 1, 9 to 18th St.; (Eighth Ave.) A, C, E to 23rd St.; (SoHo) B, D, F, Q to Broadway-Lafayette St.; N, R to Prince St.

Judson Grill 152 W 52nd St. btw Sixth and Seventh Aves. (212) 582-5255

A stylishly designed, airy venue offering American-style dining fare that is well prepared and amiably served at moderately expensive prices. Subway: N, R to 49th St. Lunch Mon–Fri, dinner Mon–Sat. Major credit cards.

Judson Memorial Church 55 Washington Square S btw Thompson and Sullivan Sts. (212) 477-0351 www.judson.org

Built in 1892 and designed by Stanford White, this elaborate structure with stained-glass windows and elegant tower has long been an active political and arts-focused community force and home to avant-garde dance and theatrical performances. Subway: A, B, C, D, E, F, Q to W 4th St. Open daily.

Juilliard School of Music 60 Lincoln Center Plaza btw Broadway and 65th St. (212) 769-5000 www.juilliard.edu

During the school year, students and faculty of this leading training ground for musical talent offer free and inexpensive concerts of many different types of work almost every day, providing viewers some of the city's finest bargain cultural fare. Subway: 1, 9 to 66th St.-Lincoln Center.

Justin's 31 W 21st St. btw Fifth and Sixth Aves. (212) 352-0599

Southern cooking and an ambiance that attracts rap artists are the appeal of this spot, which serves good food at moderately expensive prices. Subway: F to 23rd St. Dinner nightly. Major credit cards.

K

Los Kabayitos Puppet Theatre CSV Cultural Center, 107 Suffolk St. btw Delancey and Rivington Sts. (212) 260-4080

Puppet performances year-round are given in the small, quaint, toy theatre for children and adult audiences. Subway: F to Delancey St.; J, M, Z to Essex St.

Karyatis 35-03 Broadway btw 35th and 36th Sts., Astoria, Queens (718) 204-0666

A spacious, long-standing, attractive place featuring music to accompany the well-prepared and pleasantly served fine Greek dishes at moderate prices. Subway: N to Broadway. Lunch and dinner daily. Major credit cards.

Kate's Joint 58 Ave. B btw 4th and 5th Sts. (212) 777-7059

A relaxed and comfortable family restaurant that offers imaginatively prepared tasty vegetarian food at very modest prices. Subway: F to Second Ave. Open daily 8:30 a.m.–11 p.m. or midnight. Major credit cards.

Katz's Delicatessen 205 E Houston St. btw Essex and Ludlow Sts. (212) 254-2246 www.katzdeli.com

Since 1888 this place has been dispensing classic salami, all-beef hot dogs, enormous pastrami and corned beef sandwiches, and egg cream drinks. It offers cafeteria style or table service from grumpy waiters at reasonable prices. Subway: F to Second Ave. Open daily 8 a.m. to late at night. Major credit cards.

Kaufman-Astoria Studios 34-12 36th St., Astoria, Queens www.kaufmanastoria.com

This is the site of productions of many movies and television programs. Subway: N to Broadway.

Kazimiroff Nature Trail

This trail in Pelham Bay Park, named for a celebrated naturalist, runs through a tranquil area of shrubs, meadows, marshes, and forest in a less frequented part of the park than most visitors experience. Subway: 6 to Pelham Bay Park.

Keen's Steak House 72 W 36th St. btw Fifth and Sixth Aves. (212) 947-3636

Since 1885 this restaurant, formerly Keen's Chop House, has been offering moderately expensive, consistently good dishes, including its well-known mutton chop, in the Herald Square neighborhood, once New York's premier theatre district. There's still the lingering atmosphere of the male bastion of yesteryear, though women have been warmly welcomed for a long time here. Subway: B, D, F, N, Q, R to 34th St.-Herald Square. Lunch Mon–Fri, dinner Mon–Sat. Major credit cards.

Kenmore Hotel 145 E 23rd St. at Lexington Ave.

This building is part of New York's literary history because Stephen Crane once lived here in the late nineteenth century before it was a hotel, while Nathaniel West worked as a desk clerk at the hotel in the 1920s. Now the building contains rental apartments. Subway: 6 to 23rd St.

Kennedy Airport *see* John F. Kennedy International Airport.

Kensington Stables 51 Caton Pl. btw Coney Island Ave. and E 8th St., Brooklyn (718) 972-4588 www.kensingtonstables.com

This is where horses can be rented for riding at the ring or on the trails in nearby Prospect Park. Subway: F to Fort Hamilton Pkwy. Daily 10 a.m. to sundown. Major credit cards.

Kerr Theatre *see* Walter Kerr Theatre.

Kew Gardens

This is one of Queens's most attractive tree-lined neighborhoods, extending south from Queens Boulevard and running along the edge of Forest Park. Subway: E, F to Kew Gardens-Union Turnpike.

Kid's Culture Calendar

This publication by the Alliance for the Arts (212) 947-6340 is published two times a year and can be ordered from the alliance at 330 W 42nd St., NY 10036 for $3.95. It includes information about activities, exhibitions, and programs all over the city, ranging from puppets to storytelling to special events that will delight children.

Kim Lau Square *see* Chatham Square.

King Cole Bar St. Regis Hotel, Fifth Ave. at 55th St. (212) 753-4500
An intimate, attractive room with a 1906 Maxfield Parrish mural, where the excellent service and expertly prepared expensive drinks add to the pleasure of any visit. Subway: E, F to Fifth Ave. Daily 11:30 a.m. to late night. Major credit cards.

King Juan Carlos I Center 53 Washington Square S btw Thompson St. and Sixth Ave. (212) 998-3650
This center, located in the nineteenth-century Stanford White structure Judson Hall, is devoted to the culture of Spain and other Spanish-speaking nations, sponsoring conferences and lectures on topics and themes related to concerns of this constituency. Subway: A, B, C, D, E, F, Q to W 4th St.

King Manor Museum King Park, 150th St. and Jamaica Ave., Jamaica, Queens (718) 206-0545
A handsome 1750 Dutch dwelling offering views of several generally authentic period rooms from the early nineteenth century, considerable historical memorabilia, a library, and a garden park. The house was bought by Rufus King (a signer of the Constitution) in 1805, and he and its successive occupants made alterations and additions to the original structure. Subway: C, E, J to Jamaica Center; F to Parsons Blvd. Open Sat–Sun noon–4 p.m. Modest admission charge.

Kingsland House 143-35 37th Ave., Queens (718) 939-0647
This 1785 English-style building is the place where the Queens Historical Society can be found. It holds frequent exhibitions and sponsors tours of the borough's neighborhoods. Behind the building is a rare "living landmark," a more than 170-year-old beech tree. Subway: 7 to Main St. Open Tues, Sat, Sun 2:30 p.m.–4:30 p.m.

Kissena Park Golf Course 164-15 Booth Memorial Ave. at 164th St., Flushing, Queens (718) 939-4594
This golf course affords some attractive views of Manhattan as a consolation prize for duffers. Subway: 7 to Main St.-Flushing, then Bus Q65. Daily dawn to dusk. Cash only.

The Kitchen 512 W 19th St. btw Tenth and Eleventh Aves. (212) 255-5793
This long-standing Chelsea venue spotlights video, dance, and perform-

ance art of an experimental or avant-garde nature. A, C, E to 14th St.; L to Eighth Ave.

Kitchen Market 218 Eighth Ave. btw 21st and 22nd Sts. (212) 243-4433

The source for Latin American provisions like dried chili, tomatillos, as well as tortillas, salsas, molés, and other south-of-the-border favorites. Subway: 1, 9, C, E to 23rd St. Open daily, hours vary. No credit cards.

Knickerbockers 33 University Pl. at 9th St. (212) 228-8490

This bar and grill features jazz performances showcasing excellent musical artists. Subway: A, B, C, D, F, Q to W 4th St. Open nightly with music Wed–Sat. Cover charge on music nights. Drinks minimum charge. Major credit cards.

Knitting Factory 74 Leonard St. btw Broadway and Church St. (212) 219-3006 www.knittingfactory.com

One of New York's leading centers for theatre and performance art, alternative and experimental musical performances, spoken word and poetry readings, and avant-garde multimedia events. It has four separate spaces and is a favorite TriBeCa showcase for interesting presentations of all kinds. Subway: 1, 9 to Franklin St.

Knoedler & Co. *see* M. Knoedler & Co.

Korea Town *see* Little Korea.

Korean Restaurants *see* Hangawi, New York Kom Tang Soot Bul House.

Koreans in New York *see* Flushing, Little Korea.

Kosher Restaurants *see* Le Marais, Ratner's Dairy Restaurant and Bakery. *See also* Delicatessens, Jewish Restaurants, Schapiro Wine Company.

Kossar's Bialystoker Kuchen Bakery 367 Grand St. at Essex St. (212) 473-4810

Traditional bialies and bagels that are freshly baked and harder and chewier than what is found in most other places can be found here. Subway: F to E Broadway. Open 24 hours daily except 3 p.m.–8 p.m. Sat. No credit cards.

Kramer's Reality Tour (212) 268-5525 www.kennykramer.com

The real-life Kenny Kramer, who was the inspiration for the character in the popular, now-defunct TV series *Seinfeld,* leads a multimedia bus tour of the places where the situation comedy's characters conducted their antics, beginning at the Pulse Theatre, 432 W 42nd St. between Ninth and Tenth Aves. Subway: A, C, E to 42nd St.-Port Authority.

Kurdish Library and Museum 144 Underhill Ave. at Park Pl., Brooklyn (718) 783-7930

The focus of this institution is the culture, crafts, and photographs of this Middle Eastern people. The library's collection centers on the history and politics of the Kurds. Subway: 2, 3 to Grand Army Plaza. Mon–Thurs 1 p.m.–4 p.m., Sun 2 p.m.–5 p.m. Admission free.

La MaMa e.t.c. 74 A East 4th St. btw Bowery and Second Ave. (212) 475-7710

The letters e.t.c. stand for experimental theatre club. This is where off-Broadway got its start. New and experimental drama and music make this nontraditional venue a prime spot for avant-garde performances. Subway: 6 to Astor Pl.; F to Second Ave.

La Marqueta Park Ave. btw 111th and 116th Sts.

Located under the elevated train tracks, this colorful street market is the place to find mangoes, papayas, cassavas, plantains, empanadas, other tropical fruit and vegetables, as well as Latin clothing and handicrafts. It's at its bustling best on Saturday and Sunday. Subway: 6 to 110th St.

La Mela *see* La Mela under M.

La Saline *see* La Saline under S.

Ladder Company 8 btw Varick and N Moore Sts.

Confirmed movie buffs may recognize this venerable firehouse as the site for *Ghostbusters*. The late-nineteenth-century brick and stone façade is covered with white stars. Subway: 1, 9 to Franklin St.

Ladies' Mile

Broadway between 8th and 23rd Sts. and especially between Union Square and Madison Square was in the nineteenth century New York's finest shopping area, with the most elegant department stores located here. Only the cast-iron buildings that housed them, now covered with grime, remain. Subway: L, N, R, 4, 5, 6 to 14th St.-Union Square.

LaGuardia Airport

Located in Queens off the Long Island Expressway, it takes about half the time to reach compared to John F. Kennedy International Airport. The swiftest means of reaching this airport is by using a taxi, but it is also the most expensive. Splitting the fare with two or more people is more economical. Other means of traveling to LaGuardia from Manhattan are the following:

Across from Grand Central Station—Park Ave. and 41st St.
New York Airport Service Express Bus—$10, every 20–30 minutes
5 a.m.–10 p.m. (718) 875-8200

Port Authority Bus Terminal—42nd St. and Eighth Ave.
New York Airport Service Express Bus—$10
5:50 a.m.–9:10 p.m. (718) 875-8200

Subway (7 to 74th St.-Broadway; E, F, R to Roosevelt Ave.-Jackson Heights). Transfer here to Bus Q33 to the CTB and East End terminals or Bus Q47 for the Delta Shuttle, Central Terminal Building, US Airways, Delta, and Marine Air Terminal.

Hotels—Shared Van
SuperShuttle Manhattan Service (midtown hotels) $15 (212) 258-3826
Express Shuttle U.S.A.—service from certain midtown Manhattan hotels, $16 (212) 315-3006
New York Airport Service Express Bus from certain midtown Manhattan hotels. Transfer may be required, $10 (718) 875-8200

Penn Station—33rd St. and Eighth Ave.
Long Island Railroad (LIRR) to Jamaica. Transfer to New York Airport Service Express Bus; LIRR, $3.50–$5 (718) 217-5477
New York Airport Service Express Bus, $5 (718) 875-8200

Downtown (Pier 11 near Wall St.)
Midtown (E 34th St. Pier)
Delta Water Shuttle (ferry service) $15 one way, $25 round trip
Free van service from Wall St. offices to Pier 11 (800) 933-5935

Fares were in effect in fall 2001 and may have changed since then. For more details on getting to or from LaGuardia call (800) AIRRIDE.

The Lake in Central Park *see* Central Park Lake.

Lamb's Theatre 130 W 44th St. btw Sixth and Seventh Aves. (212) 997-1780

This venue has two performing areas, the larger with 349 seats and the other with only 29, where drama and musicals are performed. Subway: N, R, S, 1, 2, 3, 7, 9 to Times Square-42nd St.

Langston Hughes Residence 20 E 127th St. btw Lenox and Fifth Aves.

This brownstone was the home of the celebrated writer and poet of Harlem's Renaissance group for some years at the end of his life. This specific block is named Langston Hughes Place. Subway: 2, 3 to 125th St.

Lansky Lounge *see* Ratner's Dairy Restaurant and Bakery.

Larchmont Hotel 27 W 11th St. btw Fifth and Sixth Aves., NY 10011 (212) 989-9333, fax (212) 989-9496

A comfortable budget hotel on a quiet, tree-lined street in the Village offering small, clean, inexpensive rooms with all but the bathrooms, which are down the hall. Subway: N, R to 8th St.-NYU.

Late Night with Conan O'Brien

For tickets, postcards must be addressed to NBC Tickets, 30 Rockefeller Plaza, NY 10012, four or five months in advance, requesting up to four tickets, including name, address, and telephone number specifying the date when you would like to attend the taping (generally Tues–Fri evenings). Standby tickets may be available on taping days at 9 a.m. in the 49th St. NBC lobby at 30 Rockefeller Plaza. Only those 16 years or older are admitted. Further information at (212) 664-3056 or (212) 664-3057.

Late Show with David Letterman

Tapings are Monday through Thursday at 5:30 p.m., with another taping on Thursday at 8 p.m. For tickets, postcards must be sent six to eight months in advance to Late Show Tickets, 1697 Broadway, NY 10019, with name, address, and telephone number. Only two tickets are available. Audience members must be 16 years or older. More information at (212) 975-1003.

Latin American Restaurants *see* Boca Chica, Coco Roco, La Pequeña Colombia, El Pollo, Patria, Victor's Café. *See also* Brazilian Restaurants, Mexican Restaurants, Peruvian Restaurants.

Latin Americans in New York *see* El Barrio, Jackson Heights, Washington Heights, Williamsburg, Woodside.

Latin Quarter 2551 Broadway btw 95th and 96th Sts. (212) 864-7600

For dancers the giant dance floor here is the most popular spot in town for salsa, merengue, and other Latin steps to the live music of some of the finest bands. Subway: 1, 2, 3, 9 to 96th St. Thurs–Sun nights. Cover charge varies. Major credit cards.

Le Madri *see* Le Madri under M.

Lebanese in New York *see* Little Lebanon in Bay Ridge.

Lectures *see* Public Lectures.

Lefferts Homestead Children's Museum *see* Prospect Park Lefferts Homestead Children's Museum.

L'Eggs Mini Marathon *see* Mini Marathon.

Lehman Center for the Performing Arts Bedford Park Blvd. and Goulden Ave., Bronx (718) 960-8833 www.lehman.cuny.edu/lehmancenter

A fine concert hall in the Bronx on the Lehman College campus, which serves as the setting for performances by many prominent musical artists. Subway: 4 to Bedford Park Blvd.-Lehman College; B, D to Bedford Park Blvd.

Leisure Time Bowling and Recreation Center Port Authority, 625 Eighth Ave. near 40th St., 2nd Floor (212) 268-6909

This is a well-maintained spot with thirty lanes and a bar. Subway: A, C, E to 42nd St.-Port Authority. Open daily at 10 a.m., closing time varies. Major credit cards.

Leo Baeck Institute *see* Center for Jewish History.

Leo Castelli 59 E 79th St. btw Fifth and Park Aves. (212) 249-4470 www.castelligallery.com

Leo Castelli offers shows of works by prominent contemporary American artists. Subway: 6 to 77th St. Tues–Fri 11 a.m.–5 p.m.

Les Halles 411 Park Ave. S btw 28th and 29th Sts. (212) 679-4111 www.leshalles.net

A comfortable bistro offering excellent French dishes at moderately expensive prices. Subway: 6 to 28th St. Lunch and dinner daily. Major credit cards.

Lesbian and Gay Community Services Center 1 Little W 12th St. at Hudson St. (212) 620-7310 www.gaycenter.org

The center offers programs and support activities, including information for tourists, and publishes a free newspaper: *Center Voice*. Subway: A, C, E to 14th St. Open 9 a.m.–11 p.m. daily.

Lesbian and Gay Film Festival

For more than 10 years New York has been the setting for the annual screening of some 200 films on gay themes. It takes place late in May and early June, and the venues are the New School University, 66 W 12th St. (212) 296-5667, and the Cantor Film Center at 36 East 8th St. at University Pl., NYU (212) 875-5600.

Lesbian and Gay Pride Parade (212) 807-7433

Late in June each year a number of happenings take place, culminating in a festive parade midday on Sunday from 52nd St. on Fifth Ave. and continuing down Fifth to Christopher St. in Greenwich Village. Then follows a street festival and a waterfront dance party with fireworks to conclude the day's events.

Lesbian and Gay Services *see* Lesbian and Gay Community Services Center.

Letterman Show *see* Late Show with David Letterman.

Lever House 390 Park Ave. btw 53rd and 54th Sts.

The first of Manhattan's glass-walled office skyscrapers was astonishing when it burst on the scene in 1952. Today it's no longer an unusual sight because of the many other nontraditional structures that have been erected to imitate it in the intervening years. Subway: E, F to Fifth Ave.

Lexington Hotel 511 Lexington Ave. at 48th St. (212) 755-4400 or (800) 448-4471, fax (212) 751-4091

A moderately expensive hotel near Grand Central Station with comfortable rooms, offering all the usual amenities in establishments geared to business guests. Subway: E, F to Lexington Ave.; 6 to 51st St.

Li-Lac Chocolates 120 Christopher St. btw Bleecker and Hudson Sts. (212) 242-7374

The specialty here since the 1920s has been excellent chocolate and other sweets, all prepared at the store. Subway: 1, 9 to Christopher St.-Sheridan Square. Open daily, hours vary. Major credit cards.

Liberation Book Shop 421 Lenox Ave. at 131st St. (212) 281-4615

A celebrated spot with a very extensive stock of books and periodicals by African-American, Caribbean, and African authors featuring history, poetry, art, and fiction. Subway: 2, 3 to 135th St. Open Tues–Fri 3 p.m.–7 p.m., Sat noon–4 p.m. No credit cards.

Liberty Helicopter Tours (212) 465-8905 www.libertyhelicopters.com

This is the way to see the sights in and around Manhattan from the sky. The itinerary varies based on the flight pattern of the specific tour. Tours depart from two different heliports, last only a few minutes, and are expensive.

Liberty Island

Once known as Bedloe's Island, this is where the celebrated lady bearing the torch resides and is the main tourist feature of this small, oval island. *See also* Statue of Liberty, Statue of Liberty/Ellis Island Museum Ferry.

Liberty Warehouse 43 W 64th St. btw Central Park W and Broadway

On the roof of this former warehouse structure is a 55-foot scale replica of the Statue of Liberty that has been perched here since the end of the nineteenth century. Subway: 1, 9 to 66th St.-Lincoln Center.

Libraries *see* B. Altman Building/New York Public Library Science, Industry and Business Library, Brooklyn Public Library, Kurdish Library and Museum, Lincoln Center Library for the Performing Arts, New York Public Library, New York Society Library, Pierpont Morgan Library, Queens Borough Public Library Main Branch.

Life 158 Bleecker St. btw Sullivan and Thompson Sts. (212) 420-1999

This trendy West Village late-hours dance spot revises its formula each night, drawing different crowds based on themes; getting in is not a certainty. Subway: A, B, C, D, E, F, Q to W 4th St.-Washington Square. Open 10 p.m.–4 a.m. Cover charge varies.

Limousine Tours (212) 765-2114

These tours cover Manhattan's main tourist highlights in a vehicle that accommodates up to eight passengers. There's a morning and afternoon tour, each lasting 4 hours, departing from 325 W 49th St. between Eighth and Ninth Aves. *See also* Boat Tours, Bus Tours, Helicopter Tours, Special Interest Tours, Walking Tours.

Lincoln Center Festival (212) 546-2656

Featuring the finest of the world's performing arts, ranging from ballet, theatre, modern dance, and opera to media-based art and puppetry, this regular annual series is offered in July and runs for several weeks each year. Subway: 1, 9 to 66th St.-Lincoln Center.

Lincoln Center for the Performing Arts Broadway btw 62nd and 66th Sts. www.lincolncenter.org

This vast complex has become one of New York's most vibrant cultural sites for performances of music, theatre, and dance. More than 5 million people a year are drawn here to attend events at the Metropolitan Opera House, Avery Fisher Hall, Alice Tully Hall, the Vivian Beaumont Theatre, the Mitzi E. Newhouse Theatre, and the Juilliard School of Music, as well as the popular events scheduled in the Center's open outdoor spaces. Subway: 1, 9 to 66th St.-Lincoln Center.

Lincoln Center Library for the Performing Arts 40 Lincoln Center Plaza (212) 870-1630 www.nypl.org/research/lpa/lpa.html

This branch of the New York Public Library at Lincoln Center specializes in theatre, music, dance, film, and television and offers not just books but recordings and videos that can be listened to or watched on the site. It is also the setting for readings, talks, and performance programs by well-known artists and writers. Subway: 1, 9 to 66th St.-Lincoln Center.

Lincoln Center Out-of-Doors (212) 875-5108

A series of family-oriented music, dance, puppet, and other special free events offered in the evening in and about Lincoln Center all through the month of August. Subway: 1, 9 to 66th St.-Lincoln Center.

Lincoln Center Theatre (212) 362-7600

Two different auditoriums are contained in this building—the Vivian Beaumont 1,000-seat house and the smaller Mitzi E. Newhouse Theatre. Subway: 1, 9 to 66th St.-Lincoln Center.

Lincoln Center Tours (212) 875-5350

Three tours are offered: the classic tour through three of the main theatres; the art and architecture tour, centered on the buildings and art contained in the center's structures and spaces; and the pianoforte tour, which includes the viewing of a workshop where Old World traditions are used to restore concert pianos. Subway: 1, 9 to 66th St.-Lincoln Center.

Lincoln Plaza Broadway btw 62nd and 63rd Sts. (212) 757-2280

A movie house showing foreign and independent films in its six viewing spaces. Subway: 1, 9 to 66th St.-Lincoln Center.

Lincoln's Birthday Sales *see* Presidents Day Sales.

Literary Walk *see* Central Park Mall.

Little Asia *see* Flushing.

Little Athens *see* Astoria.

Little Church Around the Corner *see* Church of the Transfiguration.

Little India
Though most of New York's Indian population now lives in Queens, the excellent and inexpensive Indian restaurants on 6th St. between First and Second Aves. offer an exotic atmosphere. Another small and shrinking ethnic pocket can be found along Lexington Ave. between 27th and 29th Sts., where food and music stores feature Indian products. Subway: (6th St.) L to Third Ave.; (Lexington Ave.) 6 to 28th St.

Little Italy
What is left of the teeming Italian neighborhood from its immigrant past has its center on Mulberry St., where Italian flags still wave. Still crowded with restaurants, cafés, bakeries, and souvenir shops, the concentration is principally around Grand and Hester Sts. The Italian population has dwindled dramatically, while the boundaries of Chinatown continue to encroach on this traditional Italian enclave. Subway: 6 to Spring St.; J, M to Bowery.

Little Korea
This is a commercial district in Manhattan situated between 23rd and 31st Sts. along Broadway. It is a neighborhood with some 350 wholesale, import, and Korean banking establishments; on 32nd and 33rd Sts. between Fifth Ave. and Broadway, there are some twenty Korean restaurants and bars. Subway: N, R to 23rd St.

Little Lebanon in Bay Ridge
This enclave of Lebanese families has taken root in an old but changing residential neighborhood in Brooklyn located in the far southwestern part of the borough. Subway: R to Bay Ridge Ave.

Little Odessa by the Sea *see* Brighton Beach.

Little Red Lighthouse
This 40-foot historic building began in 1880 in Sandy Hook, N.J., before being moved to its present site in Fort Washington Park. Accessible below the George Washington Bridge by steps at the intersection of W 181st St. and Pinehurst, one can still see this much cherished, restored relic of another time. Subway: A to 181st St.

Little Ukraine
Even though many of the community's earlier immigrant population has dispersed, 7th St. between Second and Third Aves. is still thriving as part of the lively East Village scene. Subway: L to Third Ave.

The Living Room 84 Stanton St. near Allen St. (212) 533-7235
Furnished with soft couches, this pleasant watering hole showcases

emerging folk and rock performing groups. Subway: F to Second Ave. Open nightly from 7 p.m. Cover charge.

Loeb Boathouse *see* Central Park Loeb Boathouse.

Lola 30 W 22nd St. btw Fifth and Sixth Aves. (212) 675-6700

The specialty here is zesty Caribbean dishes, but some Italian and American food is also served. Live blues, jazz, and reggae music adds to this spot's nightly appeal. Prices are fairly expensive. Subway: F to 23rd St. Lunch Mon–Sat, dinner daily. Major credit cards.

Lombardi's 32 Spring St. btw Mott and Mulberry Sts. (212) 941-7994

Since the beginning of the twentieth century, with an interruption of a few years, this family has been serving some of the city's finest coal-fired, brick-oven pizzas at inexpensive prices. In mild weather, the garden out back is an added treat. Subway: 6 to Spring St.; N, R to Prince St. Open 11:30 a.m. to late daily. Cash only.

Londel's 2620 Eighth Ave. btw 139th and 140th Sts. (212) 234-6114

A modest-priced comfortable restaurant offering a variety of Southern-style tasty dishes. Subway: B, C to 135th St. Lunch and dinner Tues–Sun. Major credit cards.

Long Island City

This aging industrial enclave in Queens is directly east of the Queensboro Bridge and just minutes by subway from Manhattan. Though largely given over to windowless factory buildings, the area has had an influx of artists and galleries attracted by the spaces available here at rents only a fraction of those across the river. Subway: N, 7 to Queensboro Plaza.

Lord & Taylor 424 Fifth Ave. btw 38th and 39th Sts. (212) 391-3344 www.lordandtaylor.com

This venerable shopping emporium offers ten floors of elegant and ample stocks of American-style clothing fashions for men and women. Subway: B, D, F, Q to 42nd St.; 7 to Fifth Ave. Open seven days, hours vary. Major credit cards.

Lortel Theatre *see* Lucille Lortel Theatre.

Los Kabayitos Puppet Theatre *see* Los Kabayitos Puppet Theatre under K.

Louis Armstrong Archives Rosenthal Library, Queens College, 6530 Kissena Blvd., Flushing, Queens (718) 997-3670 www.satchmo.net

The papers, letters, photographs, scrapbooks, and recordings of the famous jazz artist are accessible here by appointment by telephoning the library. Subway: 7 to Flushing-Main St., then Bus Q17, Q25, or Q34 to college campus. Mon–Fri 9 a.m.–5 p.m. Sat hours by special appointment.

Louis Armstrong House www.satchmo.net

The Armstrong home, designated on the National Register of Historic Places, is the red brick building at 34-56 107th St. in Corona, Queens, where the celebrated trumpet artist lived from the 1940s until the end of his life in 1971. Subway: 7 to 103rd St.-Corona Plaza.

Louise Nevelson Plaza

Situated in the space between Maiden Lane and Liberty Street can be found a number of striking sculptures on the piece of land named for the well-known American sculptress. Subway: A, C, J, M, Z, 2, 3, 4, 5 to Fulton St.-Broadway Nassau.

Lower East Side

Bounded roughly by E Houston St. on the north, the Bowery on the west, the East River on the east, and Delancey St. on the south, this is one of the least changed Manhattan neighborhoods. This is still a community of immigrants, but the majority of the current residents are now Asian and Hispanic rather than Jewish, as at the beginning of the twentieth century. Today shopping is the lure for bargain hunters drawn to the area, especially on Sundays, for the cheap prices on everything from women's fashions to linens to electronic products to most any other consumer need, especially on Orchard St. and the streets that surround it. Subway: F, J, M, Z to Delancey St.-Essex St.

Lower East Side Business Improvement District Tours (212) 226-0110 or (888) 825-8374 www.lowereastsideny.com

From April through December, free walking tours are sponsored on Sundays at 11 a.m. through this historic neighborhood.

Lower East Side Conservancy Tours (212) 598-1200

Guided tours of neighborhood synagogues and a tasting tour of the Lower East Side are offered from time to time by this organization.

Lower East Side Festival of the Arts Theatre for the New City, 155 First Ave. at 10th St. (212) 254-1109

This outdoor festival occasion on a weekend late in May or early June celebrates the community's contribution to the culture of the arts, with performances and appearances by entertainers and artists all through the three-day weekend event. Subway: 6 to First Ave. or Astor Pl.

Lower East Side Jewish Festival (888) 825-8374

On a Sunday in mid- or late June on Grand St. between Orchard and Clinton Sts., there are Jewish musical performances, activities for children, a festive atmosphere, and stands selling Kosher foods and Judaica. Subway: F, J, M, Z to Delancey St.-Essex St.

Lower East Side Tenement Museum 90 Orchard St. at Broome St. (212) 431-0233

America's first urban, living history museum designated a national historic site consists of a ground floor of temporary exhibits, while the upstairs remains as it was when occupied by its residents until the building was condemned in 1935. Visitors are conducted on an obligatory guided tour through the apartment, bringing the story of immigrant families to life. Subway: F, J, M, Z to Delancey St.-Essex St.; B, D, Q to Grand St. Open daily, hours vary. Admission charge.

Lower East Side Tenement Museum Walking Tours 90 Orchard St. at Broome St. (212) 431-0233 www.tenement.org

In addition to the tours conducted within the museum itself, there is also a walking tour, "The Streets Where We Lived: A Multiethnic Heritage Tour," through this historic New York neighborhood. Subway: F, J, M, Z to Delancey St.-Essex St.; B, D, Q to Grand St.

Lower Manhattan

This is where the city began, clustered below Chambers St. and down to the lowest tip of the island where the Hudson River and East River come together. Now this district is often termed the financial district, with Wall Street as its symbolic center. It's where untold numbers come each working day only to abandon the neighborhood and leave its streets deserted after dark except for the small pockets of structures that have been converted to residential use.

Lubavitch Hasidim *see* Crown Heights, Williamsburg.

Lubavitch Synagogue Eastern Pkwy. at Kingston Ave., Brooklyn

This house of worship serves as a continuous center for prayer, liturgical expression, and meditation, with the men occupying the lower-level benches and the women seated upstairs. Tours are offered by the Chassidic Discovery Center (800) 838-8687; tours include a visit to the synagogue, details of the Lubavitch sect's core religious traditions and history, as well as a visit to a Mikvah (a women's bathhouse where ritual cleansing takes place). Subway: 3 to Kingston Ave.

Lucille Lortel Theatre 121 Christopher St. btw Bedford and Hudson Sts. (212) 239-6200
Long a leading venue for off-Broadway theatrical performances, this Village showplace has staged a number of attention-getting productions. Subway: 1, 9 to Christopher St.-Sheridan Square.

Lucille's Grill *see* BB King Blues Club and Grill.

Lucky Strike 59 Grand St. btw Wooster St. and W Broadway (212) 941-0479
This moderate-priced SoHo bistro attracts a young trendy clientele for its well-prepared basic dishes and homemade bread. Subway: 1, 9, A, C, E, N, R to Canal St. Lunch and dinner daily. Major credit cards.

Luna Lounge 171 Ludlow St. btw Houston and Stanton Sts. (212) 260-2323
All kinds of comic performers take the mike at this less traditional comedy showcase. Subway: F to Second Ave. Open daily 7 p.m.–4 a.m. Admission charge. Proof of age 21.

Lunchtime and Outdoor Concerts
Midday at many building atriums and other public spaces around town, musical free events are offered during the milder seasons. Some favorite spots with performances on particular days are the Winter Garden Atrium at the World Financial Center (212) 945-0505, St. Peter's Lutheran Church, 619 Lexington Ave. in midtown at 64th St. (212) 935-2200, and St. Paul's Chapel at Fulton St. and Broadway in lower Manhattan (212) 602-0874.

Lundy Brothers 1901 Emmons Ave. at Ocean Ave., Sheepshead Bay, Brooklyn (718) 743-0022
A long-time seafood restaurant favorite, closed for a long time, once again attracts large numbers of customers for the moderate-priced popular dishes at this waterfront spot. Subway: D, Q to Sheepshead Bay. Lunch and dinner Mon–Sat, brunch and dinner Sun. Major credit cards.

Lunt-Fontanne Theatre 205 W 46th St. btw Broadway and Eighth Ave. (212) 575-9200
This house was constructed in 1910, remained unused during the 1930s, and later was used as a movie theatre until its restoration and reactivation in 1957, when it was rechristened after the celebrated dramatic couple Alfred Lunt and Lynn Fontanne. Subway: A, C, E to 42nd St.-Port Authority; N, R, S, 1, 2, 3, 7, 9 to Times Square-42nd St.

Lutèce 249 E 50th St. btw Second and Third Aves. (212) 752-2225
www.arkrestaurants.com

Among the very best in New York, this comfortable and elegant dining spot in an old brownstone building offers the very finest classic French cuisine unpretentiously at quite expensive prices with advance reservations necessary. Subway: 6 to 51st St. Lunch Tues–Fri, dinner Mon–Sat. Major credit cards.

Lyceum Theatre 149 W 45th St. btw Sixth and Seventh Aves. (212) 239-6200

The very oldest New York legitimate house, the first to be designated a historic landmark, has been in use since its construction in 1903 and has showcased many successful runs, of which *Born Yesterday* with Judy Holliday holds the record with 1,600 performances. Subway: B, D, F, Q to 42nd St.

M&G Soul Food Diner 383 W 125th St. at Morningside Ave. (212) 864-7326

A popular, inexpensive, casual Harlem spot where the fried chicken tastes exactly like fried chicken should. Subway: A, B, C, D to 125th St. Open 24 hours daily. No credit cards.

M. Knoedler & Co. 19 E 70th St. btw Fifth and Madison Aves. (212) 794-0550

One of New York's oldest and most renowned galleries is the showplace for contemporary abstract and pop art creations by some of the nation's best known artists. Subway: 6 to 68th St. Open Mon–Sat, hours vary.

MacDougal Alley

This colorful alleyway of highly prized picturesque rowhouses and old-time street lamps can be found just north of Washington Square Park off MacDougal St. to the west. Subway: A, B, C, D, E, F, Q to W 4th St.

Macy's 151 W 34th St. btw Broadway and Seventh Ave. (212) 695-4400 www.macys.com

Occupying an entire square city block, the "world's largest store," with its ten floors and more than 2 million square feet of merchandise, carries anything and everything. They even have a visitor's center to assist with any type of shopping requirement, including personal guides to help customers at no cost. Subway: B, D, F, N, Q, R to 34th St.-Herald Square; 1, 2, 3, 9 to 34th St.-Penn Station. Open daily, hours vary. Major credit cards.

Macy's Fireworks Display

The highlight of the city's Independence Day celebration on July Fourth takes place over the East River, when this grand extravaganza can be seen best from along FDR Dr. and Battery Park after sunset. Subway: 1, 9 to South Ferry.

Macy's Flower Show (212) 494-4495

From the week before Easter in April until mid-May, this lush display of plants, trees, and lovely flowers graces the main floor and windows of Macy's department store at Herald Square, W 34th St. and Broadway. Subway: B, D, F, N, Q, R to 34th St.-Herald Square; 1, 2, 3, 9 to 34th St.-Penn Station.

Macy's Thanksgiving Day Parade (212) 494-2922

On the last Thursday in November this parade moves from Central Park W and 77th St. down Central Park W to Columbus Circle, then down Broadway to Herald Square at 34th St. with floats, marching bands, and giant balloons while 2 million spectators watch the procession along the way. The celebration begins the night before, when the balloons are inflated at 79th St. and Central Park W.

Madame Tussaud's New York 234 W 42nd St. btw Seventh and Eighth Aves. (800) 246-8872 www.madame-tussauds.com

A newly established 5-story American branch of the celebrated British wax museum. The almost 200 life-size wax notables included in the display behind the façade of the old Harris Theatre include celebrities from the American sports, entertainment, and political world as well as international personalities. Subway: N, R, S, 1, 2, 3, 7, 9 to 42nd St.-Times Square. Open daily 10 a.m.–8 p.m. Admission charge.

Madison Avenue

All the way from Manhattan's 50s to the 90s, this ritzy street is one long procession of expensive boutiques, chic art galleries, and specialty shops tailored to the consumer needs of the elegant class, which seeks topnotch design and contemporary high-style goods of every type. The blocks from 42nd to 57th Sts. form the neighborhood that has come to make Madison Ave. synonymous with the American advertising industry. Buses M1, M2, M3, M4 all run up Madison Ave.

Madison Lexington Venture Building 135 E 57th St. at Lexington Ave.

A stylishly designed, award-winning structure in which the building curves inward, forming an arc around which columns of green marble form a circle with a fountain. Subway: 4, 5, 6 to 59th St.

Madison Square

Located between 23rd and 26th Sts. and Madison and Fifth Aves. is

Madison Square, which boasts the Saint-Gaudens statue of Admiral Farragut of Civil War fame; a statue of former Secretary of State William Henry Seward, remembered for being instrumental in the purchase of Alaska from Russia; and the eternal light flagpole honoring American dead in France during World War I. Subway: N, R to 23rd St.

Madison Square Garden W 31st to W 33rd Sts. at Seventh Ave. (212) 465-6741 www.thegarden.com

This is the venue for some of the city's major indoor sports events. Major and minor boxing events are scheduled here several times a year. Wrestling is held more regularly and draws enthusiastic crowds to watch the performances. The New York Knicks (basketball) and Rangers (ice hockey) play their home games here. There are occasional pop or rock music concerts, Ringling Brothers and Barnum & Bailey Circus appears here every spring, and other recurring annual events take place here. Subway: 1, 2, 3, 9, A, C, E to 34th St.-Penn Station.

Madison Square Garden Tours (212) 307-7171 or (212) 465-5800

The All Access Tour includes visits to the players' locker rooms, backstage at the Garden Theatre, the inside of a luxury viewing suite, and preparations for garden events. Subway: 1, 2, 3, 9, A, C, E to 34th St.-Penn Station.

Madras Mahal 104 Lexington Ave. btw 27th and 28th Sts. (212) 684-2788

This vegetarian Indian restaurant features a wide range of dishes that are both bountiful and tasty at moderate prices. Subway: 6 to 28th St. Lunch and dinner daily. Major credit cards.

Le Madri 168 W 18th St. btw Sixth and Seventh Aves. (212) 727-8022

An elegant Tuscan dining spot serving a variety of risotto dishes, thin-crust pizzas, excellent grilled vegetables, and more with moderately expensive prices. A garden patio is available during warm weather. Subway: 1, 9 to 18th St. Lunch Mon–Sat, dinner daily. Major credit cards.

Magazines *see* Newspapers and Magazines.

Main Street 446 Columbus Ave. btw 81st and 82nd Sts. (212) 873-5025

A bright, noisy, busy restaurant serving American food selections from meat loaf to roasted chicken at moderate prices, all served family style. Subway: B, C to 81st St.-Museum of Natural History. Dinner daily, lunch Sat and Sun. Major credit cards.

Majestic Apartments 115 Central Park W at 72nd St. (212) 873-6800

For many, many years this Art Deco building with twin towers has been a favorite luxury dwelling, housing famous and infamous celebrities. Subway: B, C to 72nd St.

Majestic Theatre 247 W 44th St. btw Broadway and Eighth Ave. (212) 239-6200

This is the biggest Broadway theatrical house and over many years has been the setting for innumerable musical successes. Subway: A, C, E to 42nd St.-Port Authority; N, R, S, 1, 2, 3, 7, 9 to Times Square-42nd St.

Major New York City Museums *see* American Museum of Natural History, Brooklyn Museum of Art, The Cloisters, Cooper-Hewitt Design Museum, The Frick Collection, Guggenheim Museum, Metropolitan Museum of Art, Museum of Modern Art, National Museum of the American Indian, New Museum for Contemporary Art, Pierpont Morgan Library, Whitney Museum of American Art, Whitney Museum of American Art at Philip Morris Building. *See also* Art and Design Museums, Ethnic and Community Museums, Historical Museums, Media Museums, Military Museums, Museums of Particular Interest to Children and Teens, Science and Technology Museums, Specialized City Museums.

Malaysian Restaurants *see* Asian Restaurants.

Malcolm Shabazz Harlem Market 116th St. btw Fifth and Lenox Aves.

The entrance is through brightly colored, fake minarets beyond which can be found a bazaar of African offerings from masks, to cloth, to jewelry, beads and dolls, and more, which is open daily from early until late. Subway: 2, 3 to 116th St.

Malcolm Shabazz Mosque 102 W 116th St. at Lenox Ave.

Topped by a dome with a star and a crescent, this house of worship is named for civil rights leader Malcolm X, who preached here in the 1960s. Subway: 2, 3 to 116th St.

Malibu Studios Hotel 2688 Broadway at 103rd St., NY 10025 (212) 222-2954 or (800) 647-2227, fax (212) 678-6842 www.malibuhotel nyc.com

Clean, budget accommodations on the Upper West Side with ample neighborhood restaurants and night life and Columbia University not far away. Subway: 1, 9 to 103rd St.

The Mall in Central Park *see* Central Park Mall.

Manganaro's 488 Ninth Ave. btw 37th and 38th Sts. (212) 563-5331

This old-fashioned groceria Italiana dates from the 1890s and offers the sights, flavors, and tantalizing smells of everything you might expect to find in such a first-class emporium. There's a little restaurant in back where you can get hero sandwiches, pastas, and more, to eat there or carry out with you, all at moderate prices. Subway: A, C, E to 34th St.-Penn Station. Mon–Sat, hours vary. Major credit cards.

Manhattan

For many, Manhattan *is* New York. This 12-mile-long, 3-mile-wide, finger-shaped island is surrounded by the Harlem River on the north, the East River on the east, the Hudson River on the west, and to the south lies the Upper New York Bay. By a wide margin, the smallest of the five boroughs in area, it is jammed with the skyscrapers, theatres, museums, hotels, restaurants, and other famous attractions that make it the enormous attraction it is to visitors.

Manhattan Beach

Located on the Atlantic Ocean in Brooklyn and running around one quarter mile from Ocean Ave. to MacKenzie St., the beach is used primarily by locals living in this affluent neighborhood close to Sheepshead Bay. Subway: D, Q to Sheepshead Bay.

Manhattan Bridge

This bridge was constructed in 1905, but over the years, with the gradually increasing volume of heavy auto, truck, and train traffic requiring modifications in its approaches and structure, it has lost its allure and cannot compete with its grander neighbor to the south, the Brooklyn Bridge. Subway: F to E Broadway.

Manhattan Center Hammerstein Ballroom *see* Hammerstein Ballroom at the Manhattan Center.

Manhattan College Manhattan College Pkwy. and W 242nd St., Bronx (718) 862-8000 www.manhattan.edu

This private, 139-year-old liberal arts college across from Van Cortlandt Park started as a high school. Subway: 1, 9 to 242nd St.

Manhattan Mall Sixth Ave. from 33rd to 34th Sts. www.manhattan mallny.com

Located just south of Macy's, this ninety-store retail complex's features include colored lights and glass elevators, while the shops are a reminder of those found in strip malls from coast to coast. Subway: B, D, F, N, Q, R to 34th St.-Herald Square.

Manhattan Park

This luxury apartment development is located on Roosevelt Island in an attractive residential area accessible by public transportation from Manhattan. Subway: Q to Roosevelt Island Tramway from E 60th St. and Second Ave.

Manhattan Plaza Health Club 450 W 43rd St. btw Ninth and Tenth Aves. (212) 594-0554 www.mphc.com

In addition to racquetball courts, this club offers access to hard-surface tennis courts. Subway: A, C, E to 42nd St.-Port Authority. Daily 6 a.m.–midnight. Major credit cards.

Manhattan Street Numbers

Using the following prescriptive formula will locate the cross street of virtually every Manhattan address.

North–South Avenues

Step A: Cancel the last figure of the house number.
Step B: Divide the remainder by two.
Step C: Add the key number, or deduct as indicated.

Example: 1400 Broadway: Cancel the last figure, result 140.
Divide by two = 70.
Deduct 31 = 39th St.

*On streets or address numbers preceded by an asterisk, omit Step B from the computation.
**On streets or address numbers preceded by two asterisks, omit Steps A and B from the computation and divide the house number by 10.

Avenue	Addresses	Key No.	Avenue	Addresses	Key No.
A, B, C, D		3	Tenth		13
First		3	Eleventh		15
Second		3	Amsterdam		59
Third		10	Columbus		59
Fourth		8	Lexington		22
Fifth			Madison		27

1–200	13	Park	34		
201–400	16	West End	59		
401–600	18	**Central Park W	60		
601–775	20	**Riverside Dr.			
*776–1286	Deduct 18			*1–567	73
Ave. of the Americas	Deduct 12			*Above 567	78
Seventh		Broadway			
1–1800	12			1–754 are below 8th St.	
Above 1800	20			754–858	Deduct 29
Eighth	9			858–958	Deduct 25
Ninth	13			Above 1000	Deduct 31

East–West Numbered Streets

Addresses begin at the streets listed below.

East Side		West Side	
Address	**Avenue**	**Address**	**Avenue**
1	Fifth Ave.	1	Fifth Ave.
101	Park Ave.	101	Ave. of the Americas
201	Third Ave.	201	Seventh Ave.
301	Second Ave.	301	Eighth Ave.
401	First Ave.	401	Ninth Ave.
501	York Ave. or Ave. A	501	Tenth Ave.
601	Ave. B	601	Eleventh Ave.

Manhattan Theatre Club 311 W 43rd St. btw Eighth and Ninth Aves. (212) 399-3000

This club stages dramatic and musical productions by promising new playwrights and sponsors the Writers in Performance series, offering readings by prominent authors. Subway: A, C, E to 42nd St.-Port Authority.

Manhattan Theatre Club/Writers in Performance *see* Writers in Performance/Manhattan Theatre Club.

Manhattan Tours (212) 319-2894

This company specializes in unique tours behind the scenes of design and fashion showrooms, artists' lofts, theatres, and restaurants.

Maps of New York City

The New York City Convention and Visitors Bureau at 810 Seventh Ave. at 53rd St. offers a useful map as a pull-out feature of its official NYC guide, as well as a separate official New York City map. These can be ordered by phoning (212) 397-8222 or (800) NYCVISIT. Subway and bus maps are available free at many subway token booths and from the Transit Authority offices at Grand Central and Penn Stations. They are also available at the Metropolitan Transit Authority booth at the Times Square Visitors Center at 1560 Broadway between 46th and 47th Sts.

Le Marais 150 46th St. btw Sixth and Seventh Aves. (212) 869-0900

A kosher, Parisian-style bistro offering typically French dishes in a decidedly Gallic ambiance. They serve well-prepared food at moderately expensive prices. Subway: N, R to 49th St.; B, D, F, Q to 50th St.-Rockefeller Center. Lunch and dinner daily, except for Fri dinner, Sat lunch. Major credit cards.

Marathon *see* New York City Marathon.

Marble Collegiate Reformed Church 1 W 29th St. at Fifth Ave. (212) 686-2770

This Romanesque Revival church built in 1854 was constructed using marble blocks. It was made famous by Dr. Norman Vincent Peale, who was its pastor for 50 years until 1984, and it maintains many socially active programs and services. Subway: 6, N, R to 28th St.

March 405 E 58th St. btw First Ave. and Sutton Pl. (212) 754-6272

A classy, understated, elegant dining spot coupling classic food preparation with innovative creations. Reservations required at this expensive restaurant. Subway: 4, 5, 6 to 59th St., then Bus M57 or M31 east. Dinner daily. Major credit cards.

Marcus Garvey Park 120th to 124th Sts. across Fifth Ave.

This was originally Mount Morris Park before being redesignated in 1973. At the highest point of this hilly, rocky stretch is an octagonal cast-iron watchtower built in 1856 with a spiral staircase and bell. Subway: 2, 3 to 125th St.

Mardi Gras 70-22 Austin St. btw 70th Rd. and Sixty-Ninth Ave., Forest Hills, Queens (718) 261-8555

This moderate-priced small restaurant serves such popular Cajun dining favorites as crawfish. Subway: E, F, G, R to Forest Hills-71st Ave. Mon–Thurs 4 p.m.–midnight. Fri–Sat noon–1 a.m. Sunday brunch and dinner. Major credit cards.

Marichu 342 E 46th St. btw First and Second Aves. (212) 370-1866

Basque cuisine is featured in this pleasant and friendly restaurant where seafood dishes are emphasized at moderately expensive prices. There is a garden for warm weather outdoor dining. Subway: S, 4, 5, 6, 7 to Grand Central-42nd St.; N, R, S, 1, 2, 3, 7, 9 to Times Square-42nd St., then Bus M42 or M104 east. Lunch and dinner Mon–Fri, dinner Sat and Sun. Major credit cards.

Marine Midland Bank Building 140 Broadway btw Liberty and Cedar Sts.

This towering structure designed by Skidmore, Owings & Merrill is best known for the huge Isamu Noguchi red cube sculpture that occupies the plaza in front of the building. Subway: 4 or 5 to Wall St.

Mario's 2342 Arthur Ave. near 186th St., Bronx (718) 584-1188

This Southern Italian family establishment has been luring Manhattan dwellers to the Bronx for decades for the exceedingly good range of well-prepared food choices well beyond pastas and pizzas at moderately expensive prices. No nearby subway; taxi is recommended. Lunch and dinner daily. Major credit cards.

The Mark 25 E 77th St. btw Madison and Fifth Aves. (212) 744-4300 or (800) 843-6275, fax (212) 744-2749 www.markhotel.com

Once a residential building, this well-located Upper East Side hotel is an elegant and charming hostelry that bears all the comfortable hallmarks of a fine and sophisticated European-style establishment with concomitant expensive rates. Subway: 6 to 77th St.

Markets *see* Chelsea Market, Essex Street Market, Fulton Fish Market, Gansevoort Market, Gourmet Garage, Greenmarkets, La Marqueta, Manganaro's, Tower Market, Zabar's. *See also* Flea Markets, Produce.

Marlborough Gallery 40 W 57th St. btw Fifth and Sixth Aves. (212) 541-4900 www.marlboroughgallery.com

This gallery features the paintings, sculptures, and mixed-media artistic works of well-known American and international artists. Subway: N, R to Fifth Ave.; Q to 57th St. Mon–Sat 10 a.m.–5:30 p.m.

Marqueta *see* La Marqueta under L.

Marquis Theatre 211 W 45th St. at Broadway (212) 382-0100

This is a relative newcomer to the lineup of Broadway performance houses; it has been the showplace for a number of musical comedy productions. Subway: N, R, S, 1, 2, 3, 7, 9 to 42nd St.-Times Square.

Martin Beck Theatre 302 W 45th St. btw Eighth and Ninth Aves. (212) 239-6200

Since being built in 1924 this venerable showplace has been the scene of many celebrated new Broadway productions and revivals. Subway: A, C, E to 42nd St.-Port Authority.

Martin Luther King Jr. Day Parade (212) 374-5176

On the third Sunday in May, this celebration of Dr. King's civil rights leadership takes the form of a parade on Fifth Ave. from 44th to 86th Sts. while also offering tribute to African-American U.S. military veterans.

Marvin Gelfand's Walk of the Town (212) 222-5343

Marvin Gelfand presents specially arranged tours by a historian and New York specialist who focuses on the worlds of writing and politics and where they intersect.

Mary Boone Gallery 745 Fifth Ave. btw 57th and 58th Sts., Fourth Floor (212) 752-2929

Transplanted from SoHo this is a topnotch gallery featuring installations and works by talented emerging American and European artists. Subway: N, R to Fifth Ave. Tues–Sat 10 a.m.–6 p.m. Summer closing—showings by appointment only.

Masjid al Farouq 552–554 Atlantic Ave. btw 4th and 5th Sts., Brooklyn

This Art Deco structure houses a mosque attended mostly by Arabs from the neighborhood but also by Pakistani, Afghan, and African-American Muslims. Subway: D, Q, 2, 3, 4, 5 to Atlantic Ave.

Massawa 1239 Amsterdam Ave. at 121st St. (212) 663-0505

This restaurant offers inexpensive, well-prepared meat and vegetarian Ethiopian and Eritrean meals eaten by hand with spongy *injera* bread. Subway: A, B, C, D, 1, 9 to 125th St. Lunch and dinner daily. Major credit cards.

Mavalli Palace 46 E 29th St. btw Park and Madison Aves. (212) 679-5535

This is one of the city's best choices for savory Indian vegetarian cooking at moderate prices. Subway: 6 to 28th St. Lunch and dinner Tues–Sun. Major credit cards.

Mayflower Hotel 15 Central Park W at 61st St., NY 10023 (212) 265-0060 or (800) 223-4464, fax (212) 265-0227 www.mayflower hotel.com

A comfortable, well-worn, mid-range hotel with front rooms facing the park that is quite near to Lincoln Center. Subway: A, B, C, D, 1, 9 to 59th St.-Columbus Circle.

Mayor's Mansion *see* Gracie Mansion.

Mayor's Office for People with Disabilities 100 Gold St., Second Floor btw Frankfort and Spruce Sts., NY 10038 (212) 788-2830

This office publishes a free access guide and offers information about questions pertaining to rights, facilities, etc. Subway: 4, 5, 6 to Brooklyn Bridge; N, R to City Hall.

McBurney YMCA 206 W 24th St. at Seventh Ave., NY 10011 (212) 741-9226, fax (212) 741-8724

This YMCA has a wide range of no-frills rooms with shared bathroom and shower facilities at modest rates for stays up to twenty-five days, with free access to the pool and gym. Advance reservations a good idea during peak travel periods. Subway: C, E to 23rd St.

McGraw Hill Building 330 W 42nd St. btw Eighth and Ninth Aves.

This bluish green Art Deco structure was formerly the operating headquarters of the giant publishing firm and was designed by the same architect who conceived the *Daily News* building at its E 42nd St. location. The building is now known as the Group Health Insurance Building. Subway: A, C, E to 42nd St.-Port Authority.

McNulty's Tea and Coffee 109 Christopher St. btw Bleecker and Hudson Sts. (212) 242-5351 www.mcnultys.com

This house has been selling coffee and tea to shoppers for more than 100 years and offers a complete range of gourmet blends and flavors to satisfy the most discriminating. Subway: 1, 9 to Christopher St.-Sheridan Square. Open daily, hours vary. Major credit cards.

McSorley's Old Ale House 15 E 7th St. btw Second and Third Aves. (212) 473-9148

They serve only two beers here, light and dark, and two mugs at a time. It's been going since 1854 and these days attracts many college types, and only since the early 1970s, women who find the ancient fixtures, the warm ale, or the male crowd appealing. Subway: 6 to Astor Pl.; N, R to 8th St. Daily hours vary. No credit cards.

Meadowlands Race Track East Rutherford, N.J. (201) 935-8500 www.thebigm.com
From January to August, there is harness racing and from September to December the thoroughbred horses run. New Jersey Transit Bus from Port Authority Bus Terminal, 42nd St. and Eighth Ave.

Media Museums *see* American Museum of the Moving Image, Museum of Television and Radio, Newseum/NY. *See also* Art and Design Museums, Ethnic and Community Museums, Historical Museums, Major New York City Museums, Military Museums, Museums of Particular Interest to Children and Teens, Science and Technology Museums, Specialized City Museums.

Medieval Festival (212) 795-1600
Every October in Fort Tryon Park in Manhattan, this celebration is held. Subway: A to 190th St.

Mediterranean Restaurants *see* Middle Eastern and Mediterranean Restaurants.

Meer Lake in Central Park *see* Central Park Meer Lake.

Meet Me in Brooklyn *see* Brooklyn Information and Culture (BRIC).

La Mela 167 Mulberry St. btw Grand and Broome Sts. (212) 431-9493
In the heart of little Italy this friendly restaurant dishes out great portions of all the Italian favorites to neighborhood and tourist customers at reasonable prices. Subway: B, D, Q to Grand St. Daily lunch and dinner. Major credit cards.

Melrose Games *see* Chase Bank Melrose Games.

Meltemi 905 First Ave. at 51st St. (212) 355-4040
Deliciously prepared Greek dishes are featured in this unpretentious, popular restaurant with moderate prices. Subway: 6 to 51st St.; E, F to Lexington Ave. Lunch and dinner daily. Major credit cards.

Merce Cunningham Dance Studio 55 Bethune St., 11th Floor, btw Washington and West Sts. (212) 691-9751 www.merce.org

This studio is in an apartment of the Westbeth complex; performances by emerging modern choreographers vary greatly. Subway: 1, 2, 3, 9 to 14th St.; A, C, E, L to 14th St.

Merchant's House Museum 29 E 4th St. btw Bowery and Lafayette St. (212) 777-1089 www.merchantshouse.com

In this red brick townhouse dating from the 1830s the furnishings and personal effects remain and are on view from the original owners. Subway: 6 to Astor Pl.; N, R to 8th St.; B, D, F, Q to Broadway-Lafayette. Closed Tues and Wed. Admission charge.

Mercury Lounge 217 E Houston St. at Essex St. (212) 260-4700 www. mercuryloungenyc.com

A small, Lower East Side club showcasing a variety of established and non-mainstream national and local rock and pop groups. Subway: F to Second Ave. Bar open nightly at 6 p.m., shows at 8 p.m. Major credit cards.

Merken Concert Hall 129 W 67th St. btw Broadway and Amsterdam Ave. (212) 501-3330

This hall stages various types of musical offerings from conventional chamber to ethnic and contemporary music in a house with excellent acoustics. Subway: 1, 9 to 66th St.-Lincoln Center.

Mermaid Parade *see* Coney Island Mermaid Parade.

Merry-Go-Round in Central Park *see* Central Park Carousel.

Mesa Grill 102 Fifth Ave. btw 15th and 16th Sts. (212) 807-7400

A fashionable, colorful, and noisy spot featuring zesty and inventive Southwestern American grilled dishes at moderately expensive prices. Subway: 4, 5, 6, L, N, R to 14th St.-Union Station. Lunch Mon–Fri, dinner nightly, brunch Sat and Sun. Major credit cards.

Meskerem 468 W 47th St. btw Ninth and Tenth Aves. (212) 664-0520

This restaurant has inauspicious surroundings, but it produces exotic, authentic, flavorful Ethiopian chicken, meat, and vegetable dishes to be scooped up by using *injera,* a form of spongy bread, at inexpensive prices. Subway: C, E to 50th St. Lunch and dinner daily. Major credit cards.

Messiah Sing-In

Staged in mid-December at Avery Fisher Hall in Lincoln Center (212) 875-5030 and sponsored by the National Chorale, which sponsors several concerts each year with information about their offerings at (212) 333-5233. Subway: 1, 9 to 66th St.-Lincoln Center.

The Met *see* Metropolitan Museum of Art, Metropolitan Opera.

Met Life Building 200 Park Ave. just north of Grand Central Station

Known as the Pan Am Building when it was erected in 1963, this giant, 59-story blue structure slices Park Ave. in two above 44th and 45th Sts., adding a dramatic and massive presence to the neighborhood. Subway: 4, 5, 6, S to Grand Central-42nd St.

Metropolitan Club 1 E 60th St. at Fifth Ave. (212) 838-7400

John P. Morgan commissioned Stanford White to design this neoclassical structure in 1894 and to make it bigger and more imposing than any of the other private clubs in the city. Today it numbers many corporate presidents and foreign heads of state among its membership. Subway: N, R to Fifth Ave.; 4, 5, 6 to 59th St.

Metropolitan Life Insurance Building 1 Madison Ave. btw 23rd and 24th Sts.

When the huge, four-sided clock tower was added in 1909 to this 1893 building it was for a while the world's tallest building. When it is lit up at night, this structure is an eye-catching familiar element of the city skyline. Subway: N, R, 6 to 23rd St.

Metropolitan Museum of Art Fifth Ave. btw 80th and 84th Sts. (212) 535-7710 www.metmuseum.org

The most celebrated American museum and one of the world's greatest comprises more than 2 million works and embraces the cultures of virtually every region going back to the classical world and antiquity. Attendance is normally very great, but the abundance on display permits leisurely viewing of any one of the major collections, where countless priceless treasures are to be found. This is a venue deserving far more than one casual visit. There are regular classical music performances, attractive casual and formal dining, and a lovely roof garden open in good weather from May to October. Subway: 4, 5, 6 to 86th St. Closed Mon. Open Tues–Sun, hours vary. Admission charge.

Metropolitan Opera Metropolitan Opera House, Lincoln Center, 65th St. at Columbus Ave. (212) 362-6000 www.metopera.org

On a gigantic stage, the world's greatest singers combine their talents with renowned conductors and outstanding musicians to perform celebrated productions from fall through spring, with ticket prices reaching stratospheric levels even as they are often difficult to find. Subway: 1, 9 to 66th St.-Lincoln Center.

Metropolitan Opera House Lincoln Center, 65th St. at Columbus Ave. (212) 362-6000

This theatre is home to the renowned American Opera Company and the celebrated American Ballet Theatre. This centerpiece building of Lincoln Center was created by Wallace Harrison in 1966 and features an awe-inspiring glass façade. Chagall murals adorn the lobby, and a red-carpeted white marble staircase and crystal chandeliers all add to the opulent splendor. Subway: 1, 9 to 66th St.-Lincoln Center.

Metropolitan Opera House Backstage (212) 769-7020

At the Lincoln Center for the Performing Arts, 65th St. at Columbus Ave., tours take visitors behind the scenes to see where and how things happen from the end of September to around June. Subway: 1, 9 to 66th St.

Metropolitan Opera Parks Concerts (212) 362-6000

Free performances are given in parks throughout the city during July and August each year.

Mexican Restaurants *see* Alamo, Cowgirl Hall of Fame, Gabriela's, Mi Cocina, Rosa Mexicano, Zarela.

Mezzaluna 1295 Third Ave. btw 74th and 75th Sts. (212) 535-9600

Specializing in brick-oven, thin-crust pizza, this crowded spot serves plain fare to assuage hunger pangs. Subway: 6 to 77th St. Lunch and dinner daily. Major credit cards.

Mezzogiorno 195 Spring St. at Sullivan St. (212) 334-2112

Designed as a Florentine trattoria with art abundantly on display, the Italian food served in this moderate-priced, busy, crowded restaurant is first-rate, and the pizzas are truly outstanding. Subway: 1, 9 to Houston St. Lunch and dinner daily. Major credit cards.

Mi Cocina 57 Jane St. at Hudson St. (212) 627-8273

This moderately priced West Village Mexican restaurant is small and crowded, but their dishes are flavorful and lovingly prepared, and everything served is excellent, from appetizers to main courses. Subway: E to 14th St. Dinner daily, brunch Sun. Major credit cards.

The Michelangelo 152 W 51st St. btw Sixth and Seventh Aves., NY 10019 (212) 765-1900 or (800) 237-0990, fax (212) 581-7618 www. michelangelohotel.com

This luxury hotel has European flavor and charm. It features extra-large rooms decorated in different styles, with all the usual amenities of a premier-class hostelry. Subway: B, D, F, Q to 47th-50th Sts.-Rockefeller Center; B, D, E to Seventh Ave.

Mickey Mantle's 42 Central Park S btw Fifth and Sixth Aves. (212) 688-7777 www.mickeymantles.com

Chock-full of baseball memorabilia and video screens, this spot is popular with kids for its hamburgers and light food. More substantial dishes are also served in the dining area. Subway: N, R to Fifth Ave. Lunch and dinner Mon–Fri. Breakfast, lunch, and dinner Sat and Sun. Major credit cards.

Middle Eastern and Mediterranean Restaurants *see* Moroccan Star, Persepolis, Picholine. *See also* Greek Restaurants, Turkish Restaurants.

Midsummer Night Swing (212) 875-5766

Live bands perform different music each night for outdoor dancing from swing to mambo to salsa to country and more at the Fountain Plaza in Lincoln Center at 65th St. and Columbus Ave. from mid-June to mid-July. Subway: 1, 9 to 66th St.-Lincoln Center.

Midtown

Usually considered to be the area from Central Park S to around 42nd St., with Fifth Ave., the premier headquarters for upscale consumerism, as its north–south artery. It embraces the Broadway theatre district and Rockefeller Center and takes in the busy streets running east and west with their museums, galleries, restaurants, towering commercial buildings, the diamond district on 47th St. between Fifth and Sixth Aves. (at each end of this one block, the street lamps are diamond shaped), and stretches over to Seventh Ave. on its western edge, while Seventh Ave. and Broadway share common ground in the Times Square area from 42nd to 47th Sts.

Midtown East

Beginning at around 34th St. and reaching its crest from 42nd St. and running east of Fifth Ave. north to around 59th St., Midtown East is the rough counterpart of Midtown West. Here is the district with the skyscrapers and the grand avenues like Madison, Park, Lexington, and Third running south to north along the way. Pulsing with the dynamism of powerful business in action, sidewalks teeming with office workers, streets jammed with cabs hurtling frenetically forward or stuck in traffic jams, this district is home to countless corporate headquarters in their glass and steel high-rise buildings, expensive boutiques, posh restaurants, and the residential enclaves of many of New York's rich and successful.

Midtown Tennis Club 341 Eighth Ave. at 27th St. (212) 989-8572 www.midtowntennis.com

This place offers eight indoor hard courts and four outdoor courts during the milder seasons. Subway: C, E to 23rd St.; 1, 9 to 28th St. Open daily, hours vary. Major credit cards.

Midtown West

Running roughly from 34th St. to 59th St., this area west of Sixth Ave. is grittier than its counterpart on the east side. It does encompass the area of bright lights, Broadway theatres, innumerable hotels and restaurants, Times Square, neon signs, but farther west there's less to see except older residential buildings, warehouses, and commercial structures leading toward the West Side Highway and the Hudson River docks.

Midwood *see* Aleppo in Flatbush.

Military Museums *see* Intrepid Sea–Air–Space Museum. *See also* Art and Design Museums, Ethnic and Community Museums, Historical Museums, Major New York City Museums, Media Museums, Museums of Particular Interest to Children and Teens, Science and Technology Museums, Specialized City Museums.

Mill Rock Island

Since 1953 this island has been under the control of the city parks department. It takes its name from the water-powered mill that stood here in the eighteenth century before the island was run by the Army Corps of Engineers until the mid-twentieth century. It is located in the East River opposite East 96th St. and comprises some 2 acres of largely undeveloped land. It is the only city parkland accessible only by water.

Millennium Film Workshop 66 E 4th St. btw Second Ave. and the Bowery (212) 673-0090 www.millenniumfilm.org

From October to June this media arts center offers an extensive program of innovative new screen offerings as well as classes and workshops. Subway: 6 to Astor Pl.; N, R to 8th St.

Millennium Hilton 55 Church St. btw Fulton and Day Sts., NY 10007 (212) 693-2001 or (800) 752-0014, fax (212) 571-2316 www.hilton.com

A luxury business-district hotel with commanding views from the upper stories of New York harbor and the Brooklyn Bridge plus a rooftop swimming pool, rooms offering modern high-tech amenities, and a fitness center. Subway: 1, 9 to Cortlandt St.

Millionaires' Row *see* Museum Mile.

Minetta Lane

A pretty, narrow street off MacDougal St. in Greenwich Village whose name derives from Minetta Brook, which once ran through the neighborhood and still flows underground. Minetta Lane leads to Minetta St. which, like Minetta Lane, was a speakeasy alley during Prohibition days. Subway: A, B, C, D, E, F, Q to W 4th St.

Minetta Lane Theatre 18 Minetta Lane btw Minetta Lane and Sixth Ave. (212) 420-8000

This comfortable, small, Village performance space stages new dramas and musical productions. Subway: A, B, C, D, E, F, Q to W 4th St.

Minetta Tavern 113 MacDougal St. at Minetta Lane (212) 475-3850

A very old bar lined with murals and memorabilia from the Village of the 1930s, this tavern also serves good North Italian food in the relaxed restaurant section in the back at moderate prices. Subway: A, B, C, D, E, F, Q to W 4th St. Lunch and dinner daily. Major credit cards.

Mini Marathon

This 10-kilometer road-running race for women takes place in late June each year from Central Park W at W 66th St. to Central Park W at W 67th St.

Miniature Golf *see* Flushing Meadows-Corona Park, Nellie Bly Amusement Park.

Minskoff Theatre 1515 Broadway at 45th St. (212) 869-0550

Opened in 1973, this house is equipped for modern high-tech productions in a 1,621-seat modern performance space where Broadway theatre is staged. Subway: N, R, S, 1, 2, 3, 7, 9 to 42nd St.-Times Square.

Mitzi E. Newhouse Theatre *see* Lincoln Center Theatre.

Model Boat Pond in Central Park *see* Central Park Model Boat Pond.

Molyvos 871 Seventh Ave. btw 55th and 56th Sts. (212) 582-7500 www.molyvos.com

Styled like an upscale taverna, this place serves a complete range of delicious Greek home-cooking selections at fairly moderate prices. Reservations suggested. Subway: B, D, E to Seventh Ave.; N, R to 57th St. Lunch Mon–Fri, dinner daily. Major credit cards.

MoMa *see* Museum of Modern Art.

Montauk Club 25 Eighth Ave. at Lincoln Pl., Brooklyn (718) 638-0800 www.montaukclub.com

Perhaps the most striking building in the Park Slope neighborhood, this mansion built in 1891 in the style of the Gothic Venetian palaces is home to the long-standing men's club that occupies all but the upper floors, which have been transformed into condominium apartments. Subway: F to Seventh Ave.

Montrachet 239 W Broadway btw Walker and White Sts. (212) 219-2777

This is one of the finest expensive restaurants, offering inventive modern French dishes all prepared perfectly and served professionally but unpretentiously. Reservations required. Subway: 1, 9 to Franklin St. Lunch Fri, dinner Mon–Sat. Major credit cards.

Monuments *see* American Merchant Marines Memorial, Castle Clinton, Central Park Cleopatra's Needle, East Coast War Memorial, Fort Greene Park, Grant's Tomb, Soldiers' and Sailors' Monument, Vietnam Veterans Memorial, Worth Monument.

Moondance Diner 80 Sixth Ave. btw Grand and Canal Sts. (212) 226-1191

This genuine old diner car with oval ceiling and counter service offers good, filling meals with lots of atmosphere and cheap prices. Subway: A, C, E to Canal St. Mon–Fri 8:30 a.m.–11 p.m. Weekend 24 hours. Major credit cards.

Mooney House *see* Edward Mooney House.

Moravian Cemetery Richmond Rd. at Todt Hill Rd., Donegan Hills, Staten Island

A serene cemetery that seems more like parkland with its winding paths and grassy hills designed by Frederick Law Olmsted of Central Park fame. Here can be found an elaborately adorned crypt where Commodore Cornelius Vanderbilt, who began the Staten Island Ferry, and other members of his family rest. Subway: 1, 9 to South Ferry; N, R to Whitehall St., then ferry to Staten Island. From Staten Island St. George Ferry Terminal, take Bus S74 or S76. Open daily 8 a.m.–6 p.m.

Morgan Guaranty and Trust Company Building 23 Wall St. btw Broad and William Sts.

Constructed in 1913 by the celebrated financier J. P. Morgan, this building's exterior still bears the marks of a 1920 explosion that killed or wounded more than 400 people and is thought to have been an anarchist attack against Morgan and American capitalism. Subway: 2, 3, 4, 5 to Wall St.

Morgan Library *see* Pierpont Morgan Library.

Morningside Heights

Located between Morningside Park and Riverside Dr. and running from around 110th St. to 125th is this unique neighborhood. It is sprinkled with modest-priced restaurants, bars, and bookstores, is home to residential pockets of undergraduate and graduate students, university faculty, middle-class families, and a cluster of academic and religious institutions, including Columbia University and the Cathedral of St. John the Divine. The net effect is to give the community the distinctive flavor and ambiance of a college town dramatically different from the larger city within which it is imbedded. Subway: 1, 9, B, C to Cathedral Pkwy.-110th St.

Moroccan Star 205 Atlantic Ave. btw Court and Clinton Sts., Brooklyn Heights, Brooklyn (718) 643-0800

Probably the city's best Moroccan restaurant, this modestly priced, friendly, family-run dining spot serves the full range of excellent North African specialties from couscous to chicken stew. Subway: 2, 3, 4, 5 to Borough Hall. Lunch and dinner daily. Major credit cards.

Morris-Jumel Mansion and Museum 65 Jumel Terrace at W 160th St. and Edgecombe Ave. (212) 923-8008

Constructed in 1765 and situated in a small pleasant park, this is Manhattan's sole remaining colonial-period home and since 1903 has displayed in its thirteen rooms different aspects of the furnishings and decorative works from the genteel life of an earlier period. The small herb and rose garden behind the house is another attractive feature. Subway: C to 163rd St. Wed–Sun 10 a.m.–4 p.m. Modest admission charge.

Mosque of the Islamic Cultural Center *see* Islamic Cultural Center and Mosque.

Mosques *see* Islamic Cultural Center and Mosque, Malcolm Shabazz Mosque, Masjid al Farouq.

Mostly Mozart Festival (212) 875-5103 or (212) 546-2656

During July and August, celebrated ensembles and soloists appear at Lincoln Center's Avery Fisher Hall and Alice Tully Hall in a series of impressive classical music performances. Subway: 1, 9 to 66th St.-Lincoln Center.

Mother 432 W 14th St. at Washington St. (212) 366-5680 www.mothernyc.com

This venue stages unusual imaginative events for every type of audience:

gay, straight, and undecided. The themes vary widely from one night to the next and might run to impromptu poetry readings to cross-dressing events to outrageous multimedia extravaganzas, all presented in an upbeat spirit to the enthusiastic audience of club regulars and tourists. Subway: A, C, E to 14th St.; L to Eighth Ave. Hours and admission vary with events.

Mother A.M.E. Zion Church 140 W 137th St. btw Lenox Ave. and Adam Clayton Powell Blvd. http://motherafricanmethodistezchurch. com

Begun downtown in 1796 as the first church in the city organized and run by Black people, the present church building was designed by an African-American architect and is known as the Freedom Church because of its relationship to the Underground Railroad. Subway: 2, 3 to 135th St.

Mott Street

This is the principal commercial street in Chinatown and is a colorful scene of crowds winding in and out of the lively fish and vegetable markets, bakeries, and restaurants that dot the avenue. It runs between E Houston St. and Worth St. Subway: J, M, N, R, Z, 6 to Canal St.

Mount Morris Park *see* Marcus Garvey Park.

Mount Morris Park Historical District

Between 118th and 124th Sts. in the area west of Marcus Garvey Park is a district of once-grand late-nineteenth-century Victorian-style town-houses that have deteriorated with time but still constitute this landmark community. Subway: 2, 3 to 125th St.

Mount Olivet Baptist Church 201 Lenox Ave. at 120th St. (212) 666-6890

This pseudo-Greco-Roman-columned structure was once Temple Israel, one of the most imposing synagogues in New York. Subway: 2, 3 to 116th St.

Mount Vernon Hotel Museum and Garden 421 E 61st St. btw York and First Aves. (212) 838-6878

Formerly known as the Abigail Adams Smith Museum, this Federal-style building constructed in 1799 as the carriage house for President John Adams's daughter was later used as a hotel and home. Colonial Dames of America have operated the property as a museum since 1939 and provide tours of nine restored rooms. A charming eighteenth-century formal garden adjoins the museum. Subway: N, R to Lexington Ave.; 4, 5, 6 to 59th St. Closed Mon. Modest admission charge. No credit cards.

Movie Groups *see* Film Groups.

Movie Organizations *see* Film Groups.

Movies *see* Film Groups, Film Revivals, Foreign and Independent Films.

Mulberry Street *see* Little Italy.

Il Mulino 86 W 3rd St. btw Sullivan and Thompson Sts. (212) 673-3783

This popular Greenwich Village favorite, one of the city's best Italian restaurants, offers large portions, big crowds, high decibel levels, a long wait even with reservations made well in advance, and fairly expensive prices. Subway: A, B, C, D, E, F, Q to W 4th St. Lunch Mon–Fri, dinner Mon–Sat. Major credit cards.

Municipal Art Society 457 Madison Ave. btw 50th and 51st Sts. (212) 935-3960 www.mas.org

This center for urban design offers a gallery and a bookshop and features exhibits on architecture and public projects. It is located in the complex of the historically attractive Villard Houses. Subway: 6 to 51st St.; E, F to Fifth Ave.; B, D, F, Q to 50th St.-Rockefeller Center.

Municipal Art Society Walking Tours (212) 935-3960 or (212) 439-1049

The society sponsors a very wide range of historical and architectural tours of many neighborhoods and unique districts of the city year-round led by well-qualified guides.

Municipal Building 1 Centre and Chambers Sts.

This enormous towering structure built in 1914 is said to be the city's first skyscraper. It houses government offices and a heavily used civil marriage chapel. The building's most notable features are the towers at the top with the copper statue, *Civic Fame,* at the peak and the way the building straddles Chambers St. Subway: 4, 5, 6 to Brooklyn Bridge; N, R to City Hall.

Municipal Pools

Outdoor pools at various locations in the city are free from July to September. One that is particularly well maintained is the Asser Levy Pool at 23rd St. and FDR Dr. (212) 447-2020. Information about the locations of other city pools is available from the city parks department (800) 201-7275. Indoor pools require membership, which must be bought at any recreation center and which then permits the holder to make use of any city pool for one year. Details are available from the city parks department.

Municipal Tennis Courts

There are many well-maintained public tennis courts around the city, but one must have a permit to use them. Information about acquiring a permit for use during the season from April to November and the location of courts is available from the Department of Parks (212) 360-8133 or (800) 201-7275.

Murder Ink 2486 Broadway btw 92nd and 93rd Sts. (212) 362-8905 www.murderink.com

Specializing in mystery, detective, and thriller titles, this bookstore has an exceedingly large inventory of in-print, out-of-print, used, and classic whodunits. Subway: 1, 2, 3, 9 to 96th St. Mon–Sat, hours vary. Major credit cards.

Murray Hill

This residential neighborhood was once home to some of the city's most aristocratic families. The district runs east from Madison Ave. from about 35th St. to 42nd St., and the streets are lined by many of the charming brownstone structures that once housed the elite as well as newer apartment buildings that are little different from those to be found elsewhere in Manhattan. Subway: 6 to 33rd St.

Murray Hill Inn 143 E 30th St. btw Lexington and Third Aves., NY 10016 (212) 683-6900 or (888) 996-6376, fax (212) 545-0103 www.murrayhillinn.com

A small hotel of fifty rooms offering basic, clean accommodations at modest prices on a quiet street in a convenient central location. Some rooms have shared baths. Subway: 6 to 28th St.

El Museo del Barrio 1230 Fifth Ave. at 104th St. (212) 831-7272 www.elmuseo.org

The only museum in the country centered on Puerto Rican, Latin American, and Caribbean art. The permanent exhibition includes pre-Colombian artifacts, handicrafts, religious carvings, and a range of paintings and sculptures. Changing displays regularly show the work of contemporary artists and modern themes. Special lectures, educational events, and film showings are important elements of the museum's program. Subway: 6 to 103rd St. Wed–Sun 11 a.m.–5 p.m. Closed Mon–Tues. Modest admission charge.

Museum for African Art 593 Broadway btw Houston and Prince Sts. (212) 966-1313 www.africanart.org

Changing exhibitions of Africa's tribal and historic culture as well as striking displays of African-American art are featured in this major showcase for modern and traditional art forms, including paintings, sculpture, masks, and much more. Gallery lectures, film screenings, and workshops are also scheduled here. Subway: N, R to Prince St.; 6 to Spring St. Open Tues–Sun, hours vary. Closed Mon. Modest admission charge.

Museum Mile

Once called Millionaires' Row, the stretch of Fifth Ave. roughly from the Frick Collection at E 70th St. up to El Museo del Barrio at E 104th St. is now known as Museum Mile. It is home to some of the city's most prestigious museums with the country's richest collections of artistic artifacts. The neighborhood buildings along the way are probably still the addresses of more millionaires and billionaires than any other street in New York.

Museum Mile Festival (212) 606-2296

During this annual event on the first or second Tuesday evening in June the museums along Fifth Ave., from 82nd to 104th St., remain open until late at night and schedule unusual exhibits while the streets are filled with music and celebrants. Subway: 4, 5, 6 to 86th St.

Museum of American Financial History 28 Broadway at Bowling Green Park (212) 908-4100 www.financialhistory.org

This museum mounts exhibitions of artifacts featuring trading and capital markets, antique stocks and bonds, ticker tape machine displays, and memorabilia from the halcyon and dark days of U.S. financial history. The museum sponsors a walking tour, called "World of Finance," which is a weekly paid event. Subway: 4, 5 to Wall St.; 1, 9, N, R to Rector St. Open Tues–Sat 10 a.m.–4 p.m. Modest admission charge.

Museum of American Folk Art 2 Lincoln Square, Columbus Ave. btw 65th and 66th Sts. (212) 977-7298 www.folkartmuseum.org

Changing exhibitions offer striking arts and crafts from all over the country, ranging from native paintings, to pottery, to trade signs, to Navajo rugs, to carousel horses, to novelty wind-up toys, and more. The Folk Art Institute of the museum sponsors public lectures and workshops. Subway: 1, 9 to 66th St.-Lincoln Center. Open Tues–Sun 11:30 a.m.–7:30 p.m. Admission free.

Museum of American Illustration 128 E 63rd St. btw Park and Lexington Aves. (212) 838-2560

In the building of the Society of Illustrators, this gallery offers rotating exhibits drawn from its large collection on such themes as cartoons, war propaganda, advertising, and children's books. Subway: N, R to Lexington Ave.; 4, 5, 6 to 59th St. Tues–Sat, hours vary. Closed Sun–Mon. Admission free.

Museum of Bronx History 3266 Bainbridge Ave. at 208th St. (718) 881-8900

Administered by the Bronx Historical Society in a landmark 1758 fieldstone farmhouse, the Valentine-Varian House, this museum's exhibits feature artifacts from the history of the city's northernmost borough from the precolonial era to modern times. Subway: D to 205th St.; 4 to Mosholu Pkwy. Open Sat and Sun, hours vary. Modest admission charge.

Museum of Jewish Heritage 18 First Pl. at Battery Park, Battery Park City (212) 908-1800 www.mjhnyc.org

Created as a memorial to Holocaust victims and survivors, this museum serves as a tribute to Jewish life in the United States and around the world. In a building shaped like a Star of David, there are three floors of exhibits using historical and cultural artifacts, photographs, and film clips to demonstrate facets of the Jewish experience. Subway: N, R to Whitehall St.; 1, 9 to South Ferry; 4, 5 to Bowling Green. Open Sun–Thurs, hours vary. Admission charge.

Museum of Modern Art 11 W 53rd St. btw Fifth and Sixth Aves. (212) 708-9480 www.moma.org

Perhaps the world's leading museum devoted to Postimpressionist, late-nineteenth-century, and twentieth-century art ranging from painting and sculptures to silverware and furniture and boasting one of the nation's largest international collections of films. Special events range from regular screenings of foreign, independent, and classic films to lectures, workshops, jazz performances in the garden café, "Conversations with Contemporary Artists," to free summer musical concerts in the sculpture garden. Subway: E, F to Fifth Ave. Open Thurs–Tues, hours vary. Closed Wed. Admission charge. *See also* City Pass.

Museum of Natural History *see* American Museum of Natural History.

Museum of Television and Radio 25 W 52nd St. btw Fifth and Sixth Aves. (212) 621-6800 www.mtr.org

This museum offers ninety-six television and radio consoles that can be used to monitor selections from its archives of some 60,000 TV and radio broadcasts from the 1920s, with more added each year. There's also a small, gallery of exhibits and scheduled theatre screenings of special subjects like TV shows from abroad and unusual commercials. From October through March during the annual Children's TV Festival, some of the finest children's TV programs from around the world are on view. Subway: E, F to Fifth Ave. Tues–Sun, hours vary. Admission charge.

Museum of the Chinese in the Americas 7 Mulberry St. at Bayard St., 2nd Floor (212) 619-4785 www.moca-nyc.org

The only American museum centered on preserving the history of the Chinese in North and South America, this small, interesting place in Chinatown offers a permanent exhibit called "Where Is Home?" Features include individual stories, mementos, photos, personal artifacts, and poetry. Subway: J, M, N, R, Z, 6 to Canal St. Tues–Sat 10:30 a.m.–5 p.m. Modest admission charge.

Museum of the Chinese in the Americas Tours (212) 619-4785

Walking tours are occasionally offered around Chinatown concentrating on the history, culture, and other features of this ethnic neighborhood.

Museum of the City of New York 1220 Fifth Ave. btw 103rd and 104th Sts. (212) 534-1672 www.mcny.org

The focus is on the city's history from Dutch settlement to the modern era. Exhibits are featured on four floors and include paintings, photographs, maps and prints, furniture, clothing, and an extensive display of dolls and dollhouses. Changing exhibits treat matters like ethnic groups in the city and New York's theatrical history. Subway: 6 to 103rd St. Wed–Sun, hours vary. Admission charge.

Museum of the City of New York Cultural Walks (212) 534-1672

From spring to fall historical and architectural walking tours of one to two hours are conducted on Sunday afternoons to various neighborhoods in Manhattan.

Museums *see* Art and Design Museums, Ethnic and Community Museums, Historical Museums, Major New York City Museums, Media Museums, Military Museums, Museums of Particular Interest to Children and Teens, Science and Technology Museums, Specialized City Museums.

Museums of Particular Interest to Children and Teens *see* American Museum of Natural History, American Museum of the Moving Image, Brooklyn Children's Museum, Central Park Charles A. Dana

Discovery Center, Children's Museum of Manhattan, Children's Museum of the Arts, Ellis Island Museum of Immigration, Intrepid Sea–Air–Space Museum, Museum for African Art, Museum of American Folk Art, Museum of the City of New York, National Museum of the American Indian, New York City Fire Museum, New York Hall of Science, New York City Transit Museum, New York Unearthed, Prospect Park Lefferts Homestead Children's Museum, Queens County Farm Museum, Rose Center for Earth and Space, Sony Wonder Technology Lab, South Street Seaport Museum, Staten Island Children's Museum, Statue of Liberty. *See also* Art and Design Museums, Ethnic and Community Museums, Historical Museums, Major New York City Museums, Media Museums, Military Museums, Science and Technology Museums, Specialized City Museums.

Music Box Theatre 239 W 45th St. btw Broadway and Eighth Ave. (212) 239-6200

Built in 1921, this attractive performance venue has been the setting for countless Broadway successes since it was constructed by Sam Harris and Irving Berlin. Subway: N, R, S, 1, 2, 3, 7, 9 to Times Square-42nd St.; A, C, E to 42nd St.-Port Authority.

Musical Entertainment *see* Classical Music; Country Music; Jazz Spots; Lunchtime and Outdoor Concerts; Opera Music; Popular Music; Rock, Alternative, and Ethnic Music.

Myers of Keswick 634 Hudson St. btw Horatio and Jane Sts. (212) 691-4194 www.myersofkeswick.com

The place to go for every type of imported English food specialty one can imagine as well as freshly prepared and baked foods like kidney pie and kippers plus cheeses and chocolates. Subway: E to 14th St. Daily, hours vary. Major credit cards.

Mysterious Bookshop 129 W 56th St. btw Sixth and Seventh Aves. (212) 765-0900 www.mysteriousbookshop.com

Stocked with New York's largest inventory of new, secondhand, and rare hardcover and paperback books of this genre, this is the mecca for lovers of all types of published thrillers. Subway: D, F to Seventh Ave.; N, R to 57th St. Mon–Sat 11 a.m.–7 p.m. Major credit cards.

N

NBC Studios 30 Rockefeller Plaza at 50th St. btw Fifth and Sixth Aves. (212) 664-7174 www.nbcbano.com/nystudios.html

All 6-year-olds and older can take the 1-hour tour of the studios and production facilities, where many popular national programs originate. Subway: B, D, F, K, Q to 47th-50th Sts.-Rockefeller Center. Open Mon–Sat 9:30 a.m.–4:30 p.m. Admission charge.

Narrowest House in New York 75$^{1}/_{2}$ Bedford St. btw Commerce and Morton Sts.

Built in 1893 and just 9$^{1}/_{2}$ feet wide, this building was constructed in a former entryway. The 3-story structure is now unoccupied and boarded up without any marker. Subway: A, B, C, D, E, F, Q to W 4th St.

NASDAQ Market Site 43rd St. and Broadway at Times Square (877) NASDAQ1 www.nasdaq.com

This place offers a high-tech interactive experience demonstrating through video and special effects the global stock market, enabling visitors to play an interactive investment game and to watch live financial broadcasts. Subway: 1, 2, 3, 9, N, R to Times Square-42nd St. Open daily, hours vary. Admission charge.

Nathan's Famous Surf Ave. at Stillwell Ave., Coney Island, Brooklyn (718) 946-2202

No trip to Coney Island is complete without a hot dog from this stand, which has been sizzling them on the grill here since 1916. Subway: B, D, F, N to Coney Island-Stillwell Ave. Open daily 8 a.m.–3 a.m.

National Academy of Design 1083 Fifth Ave. at 89th St. (212) 369-4880 www.nationalacademy.org

This museum, school of fine arts, and association of artists was begun by a group of engravers, sculptors, architects, and artists in 1825. It is housed in one of Fifth Ave.'s opulent nineteenth-century Beaux Arts mansions, and more than 6,000 paintings, drawings, and sculptures are included in its permanent collection. Subway: 4, 5, 6 to 86th St. Open Wed–Sun, hours vary. Closed Mon–Tues. Admission charge.

National Arts Club 15 Gramercy Park S (212) 475-3424

This club was begun in 1898 and has been housed in this impressive large brownstone structure since 1906. Members have included many of the country's leading artists since its inception. It is open to the public several times a year for exhibitions. Subway: 6, N, R to 23rd St.

National Audubon Society 700 Broadway at E 4th St. (212) 979-3000

The Audubon Society organizes bird counts during the year and maintains a special library accessible by appointment. Through regional offices and local chapters, they promote environmental protection and endangered species, national forests, and the Arctic National Wildlife Refuge. Subway: G to Astor Pl.; N, R to 8th St.

National Black Theatre 2033 Fifth Ave. near 125th St. (212) 926-1049

This performing arts center is the showcase for innovative works from a Black perspective of dramatic and musical creations about the Black experience. Subway: 2, 3, 4, 5, 6 to 125th St.

National Boat Show Jacob K. Javits Convention Center, 655 W 34th St. at Twelfth Ave. (212) 922-1212 www.boatshows.com

This annual ten-day event takes place in January; the latest in pleasure craft and marine equipment is on display. Subway: A, C, E to 34th St.-Penn Station.

National Design Museum *see* Cooper-Hewitt Design Museum.

National Horse Show Madison Square Garden, Seventh Ave. at 33rd St. (212) 465-6741

For a week in November every year, this event draws equine enthusiasts from every point on the compass. Subway: 1, 2, 3, 9, A, C, E to 34th St.-Penn Station.

National Institute of Arts and Letters *see* American Academy of Arts and Letters.

National Museum of the American Indian 1 Bowling Green btw State and Whitehall Sts. (212) 668-6624 www.nmai.si.edu/heye/index.html

A branch of the Smithsonian Institution, this museum is housed in the striking Beaux Arts Alexander Hamilton U.S. Custom House and offers the largest collection of North, South, and Central American indigenous cultures; it is staffed primarily by Native American Indians. The collection holds more than a million artifacts, and the sights and sounds of the artful exhibits are offered in very accessible and attractive forms. Subway: 4, 5 to Bowling Green; N, R to Whitehall St.; 1, 9 to South Ferry. Open daily 10 a.m.–5 p.m., Thurs until 8 p.m. Admission free.

Nederlander Theatre 208 W 41st St. btw Seventh and Eighth Aves. (212) 921-8000

Formerly the National Theatre, this house opened in 1921 and has been the venue for innumerable dramatic and musical productions throughout its history. Subway: A, C, E to 42nd St.-Port Authority; N, R, S, 1, 2, 3, 7, 9 to Times Square-42nd St.

Negril 362 W 23rd St. btw Eighth and Ninth Aves. (212) 807-6411

Jamaican fare featuring dishes like jerk chicken, goat, and island stews at very modest prices are served in this restaurant boasting a giant aquarium as part of its picturesque ambiance. Subway: C, E to 23rd St. Lunch and dinner daily. Major credit cards.

Neighborhoods *see* Ethnic Neighborhoods.

Neil Simon Theatre 250 W 52nd St. btw Broadway and Eighth Ave. (212) 757-8646

Built in 1927 as the Alvin Theatre, this house seats 1,400 and showcases various types of Broadway theatrical productions. Subway: 1, 9, E to 50th St.; N, R to 49th St.

Nell's 246 W 14th St. btw Seventh and Eighth Aves. (212) 675-1567

A lounge as well as a dance club featuring live jazz, blues, and reggae music upstairs with dancing to disc jockey sounds in the basement. Subway: 1, 2, 3, 9, A, C, E to 14th St.; 1 to Eighth Ave. Open nightly from 10 p.m. Cover charge. Major credit cards.

Nellie Bly Amusement Park 1824 Shore Pkwy., Brooklyn (718) 996-4002

A small, old-fashioned center designed for little kids on up with bumper cars and other standards, such as airplanes and motorcycles that go in circles as well as a go-cart raceway, a petting zoo, and miniature golf. Subway: N to Bay Pkwy., then Bus B6 to the park. Open daily, hours vary.

Nelson Rockefeller Park Hudson River at Chambers St. (212) 267-9700

An ideal place for children to enjoy the playground activities and sports, games, and art programs available as well as view the boats on the river. Subway: 1, 9, N, R to Cortlandt St.

Neue Galerie 1048 Fifth Ave. at 86th St. (212) 628-6200 www. neuegalerie.org

This new museum opened in late fall 2001 in a Fifth Ave. mansion and is dedicated to showing German and Austrian fine and decorative arts. Two special exhibits are planned to be shown each year along with rotating displays of works from its own collection and from private collections. Subway: 4, 5, 6 to 86th St. Open Fri–Mon 11 a.m.–7 p.m. Admission charge.

Nevelson Plaza *see* Louise Nevelson Plaza.

New Amsterdam Theatre 216 W 42nd St. btw Broadway and Eighth Ave. (212) 307-4747

This venerable house built in 1903, which was once the setting for the Ziegfeld Follies, has been transformed and restored to its earlier opulence by the Disney Company and since 1997 has been home to the stage production of *The Lion King,* which promises to run for years to come. Subway: N, R, S, 1, 2, 3, 7, 9 to Times Square-42nd St.; A, C, E to 42nd St.-Port Authority.

New Directors, New Films (212) 875-5610

During late March and early April this series showcases works by emerging American film makers under sponsorship of the Film Society of Lincoln Center and the Museum of Modern Art, where the films are shown. Subway: E, F to Fifth Ave.

New Museum of Contemporary Art 583 Broadway btw Prince and Houston Sts. (212) 219-1222 www.newmuseum.org

This museum offers changing exhibits and avant-garde workshops of living American and international artists; the exhibits are innovative, socially committed, and frequently radically unorthodox, often using interactive devices and video elements. Subway: N, R to Prince St.; B, D, F, Q to Broadway-Lafayette St. Closed Mon–Tues. Other days hours vary. Modest admission charge.

New School University 66 W 12th St. btw Fifth and Sixth Aves. (212) 229-5488 or (800) 319-4321 www.newschool.edu

Beyond its eclectic formal course offerings, the New School organizes numerous lecture and music series. The Academy of American Poets schedules occasional readings here, and the New School also sponsors regular culinary tours in ethnic neighborhoods all around the city. Information at (212) 229-5690. Subway: B, D, F, Q to 14th St.

New Victory Theatre 209 W 42nd St. btw Broadway and Eighth Ave. (212) 382-4020 www.newvictory.org

Originally built in 1890, this is the oldest city performance center, still alive after the renovations that transformed it into a lovely refurbished venue exclusively committed to imaginative productions for children. It bills itself as "New York's Theatre for Kids and Families." Subway: 1, 2, 3, 7, 9, N, R, S to Times Square-42nd St.; A, C, E to 42nd St.-Port Authority.

New World Bed and Breakfast 150 Fifth Ave., Suite 711, NY 10011 (212) 675-5600 or (800) 443-3800, fax (212) 675-6366

This bed-and-breakfast offers various types of accommodations from hostel apartments to studios to large apartments for stays of varying lengths in many Manhattan neighborhoods. Subway: 6, F, N, R to 23rd St.

New World Grill 329 W 49th St. btw Eighth and Ninth Aves. (212) 957-4745

This popular restaurant features tasty and nutritious well-prepared American-style dishes at moderate prices that attract pre-theatre diners. It specializes in vegetarian food. Subway: C, E to 50th St. Lunch Mon–Fri, dinner daily, brunch on weekends. Major credit cards.

New Year's Eve Celebrations

This holiday is traditionally celebrated in Manhattan by large crowds in Times Square, where the Big Apple ball drops during the last moments of the year (212) 768-1560. First Night is the family-oriented, alcohol-free festival around the city at different locations (212) 922-9393. A 4-mile midnight run in Central Park is sponsored by the New York Road Runners Club (212) 860-4455. There are also fireworks at South Street Seaport and in Prospect Park in Brooklyn.

New York Apple Tours *see* City Sightseeing.

New York Aquarium in Coney Island *see* Aquarium for Wildlife Conservation.

New York Botanical Garden 200th St. at Southern Blvd. (Kasimir-off Blvd.), Bronx (718) 817-8777 www.nybg.org

This is one of the city's foremost treasures and the country's premier public garden. It offers 250 acres of gloriously cared-for trees, flowers, shrubs, and pristine parkland trails. There are innumerable specialty gardens, a fern forest, and the Enid Haupt Conservatory, a glass house that boasts a rain forest of medicinal herb plants and a 12-acre children's discovery center replete with hands-on activities. Subway: D to Bedford Park Blvd. Open Tues–Sun 10 a.m.–6 p.m. Modest admission charge.

New York Buddhist Church Riverside Dr. btw 105th and 106th Sts. (212) 678-0305

The imposing bronze statue of the Buddha in front of the building identifies this otherwise unremarkable-appearing house of worship of members of this religious sect. Subway: 1, 9 to 103rd St.

New York Ceramics Fair *see* Winter Antiques Show.

New York City Ballet (212) 870-5500 www.nycballet.com

During the winter season from mid-November through February and the spring from late April through June, this world-celebrated company of more than ninety dancers offers a wide repertoire of classic performances to the accompaniment of traditional and modern music at the New York State Theatre at Lincoln Center, 65th St. and Columbus Ave. Subway: 1, 9 to 66th St.-Lincoln Center.

New York City Ballet Spring Season

This season takes place from April to June each year with performances at the New York State Theatre, Lincoln Center, 65th St. and Columbus Ave. (212) 870-5570, and at the Metropolitan Opera House also at Lincoln Center (212) 362-6000. Subway: 1, 9 to 66th St.-Lincoln Center.

New York City Cultural Walking Tours (212) 979-2388

These tours concentrate on history, architecture, unique neighborhoods, landmark sites, and other memorable Manhattan views during regularly scheduled public tours as well as specialized, privately arranged tours.

New York City Fire Museum 278 Spring St. btw Hudson and Varick Sts. (212) 691-1303 www.nycfiremuseum.org

In a renovated turn-of-the-century firehouse this museum on three levels staffed by some actual firefighters features the history of fire prevention and fire fighting with exhibitions of attractive old engines and pumps, hose nozzles, ladders, axes, fire alarms, helmets, buckets, and badges, all sure to delight children of all ages. Subway: E to Spring St. Open Tues–Sun 10 a.m.–4 p.m. Modest admission charge.

New York City Marathon (212) 860-4455 www.nyrrc.org

On the first Sunday in November more than 20,000 runners from all over the world gather at the Staten Island side of the Verrazano Narrows bridge and begin the 26.2-mile race through all five boroughs before finishing the course at the Tavern on the Green in Central Park while more than 1 million spectators cheer them on along the way.

New York City Marble Cemetery *see* New York Marble Cemetery.

New York City on Stage (212) 768-1818 www.tdf.org

Information is available here on theatre, dance, and musical performances throughout the city.

New York City Opera New York State Theatre, Lincoln Center, 65th St. and Columbus Ave. (212) 870-5570 www.nycopera.com

A smaller theatre than the Metropolitan Opera House, with tickets normally more accessible at lower prices featuring classic and innovative productions of style and vivacity. Subway: 1, 9 to 66th St.-Lincoln Center.

New York City Opera Season

Now operating on a season split between September–November and February–April, the City Opera appears at the New York State Theatre, Lincoln Center, 65th St. and Columbus Ave. (212) 870-5570. Subway: 1, 9 to 66th St.-Lincoln Center.

New York City Pass *see* City Pass.

New York City Police Academy Museum *see* Police Museum.

New York City Police Headquarters Building 240 Centre St. btw Broome and Grand Sts.

Constructed in 1909, this lavish Renaissance Revival building with Corinthian columns and striking dome served as headquarters until 1973. In 1988 it was transformed into luxury condominiums and is now known by its street address: 240 Centre St. Subway: J, M, N, R, Z to Canal St.

New York City Police Museum *see* Police Museum.

New York City Transit Museum Boerum Pl. and Schermerhorn St., Brooklyn (718) 243-3060 www.mta.nyc.ny.us/museum

Actually housed in an abandoned subway station of the 1930s, here one can find memorabilia and history, 100 years of transit artifacts, and photos and wander through more than twenty restored subway cars and buses from the past. A small New York City Transit Museum Gallery and Store can be found at Grand Central Terminal; it features changing exhibits about public transit. Subway: (main location) 2, 3, 4, 5, A, C, F to Borough

Hall; (Grand Central) 4, 5, 6 to Grand Central-42nd St. Open Tues–Sun, hours vary. Modest admission charge.

New York Comedy Club 241 E 24th St. btw Second and Third Aves. (212) 696-5233 www.newyorkcomedyclub.com

An intimate club showcasing leading comics at modest cover charges. Subway: 6 to 23rd St. Open nightly, hours vary. Cover charge. Minimum drinks charge. Major credit cards.

New York Convention and Visitors Bureau 810 Seventh Ave. btw 52nd and 53rd Sts. (212) 484-1200 or (212) 484-1222 or (800) 669-7810 www.nycvisit.com

An invaluable source of information for brochures about entertainment, museums, hotels, and interesting sights and experiences in the city as well as free tickets to live TV shows. Travel counselors are also prepared to respond to specific questions in person or by telephone about any aspect of tourism about the city. Subway: N, R to 49th St.; 1, 9 to 50th St.

New York County Courthouse 60 Centre St. in Foley Square

This building was constructed in 1926, and the Corinthian portico at the top of the wide staircase is the main feature. Six wings radiate from the central rotunda, each housing a single court. Thousands of marriages take place here each year. Subway: 4, 5, 6 to Brooklyn Bridge; N, R to City Hall.

New York Design Center 200 Lexington Ave. at 32nd St. (212) 679-9500 www.nydc.com

This 16-story building contains showrooms for every type of home decoration and furniture. Some areas may not be open to the public. Subway: 6 to 33rd St.

New York Film Festival (212) 875-5610

Since beginning in 1963, this three-week event beginning in mid-September has been showing premier performances of more than twenty-five important cinematic offerings. The showings take place at Lincoln Center's Alice Tully and Avery Fisher Halls, and tickets are typically quickly sold out well in advance. Subway: 1, 9 to 66th St.-Lincoln Center.

New York Flower Show (212) 465-6000

At Madison Square Garden every year during March or April this colorful event takes place. Subway: 1, 2, 3, 9, A, C, E to 34th St.-Penn Station.

New York Fringe Festival (212) 307-0229

For ten days in late August hundreds of theatrical, musical, dance, comedy, and other forms of entertainment art are performed in small venues around the Lower East Side at all hours. Subway: F, J, M, Z to Delancey St.

New York Giants Giants Stadium, East Rutherford, N.J. (201) 935-8222 www.giants.com

From August to December the team plays in the National Football League, but most tickets are typically sold out to season ticket holders or bought a year or two in advance. Subway: A, C, E to 42nd St.-Port Authority, then take bus from Port Authority Bus Terminal to Meadowlands Sports Center.

New York Hall of Science 47-01 111th St., Flushing Meadows, Corona Park, Queens (718) 699-0005 www.nyhallsci.org

This is a hands-on museum of science and technology, offering more than 200 exhibits and an outdoor science playground. Children from preschool age upward learn about sound, light, motion, microscopic organisms, and other science concepts while being entertainingly and interactively involved. Subway: 7 to 111th St. Open daily, hours vary. Admission charge.

New York Historical Society 2 W 77th St. at Central Park W (212) 873-3400 www.nyhistory.org

The oldest museum in New York holds a wide collection of paintings and decorative arts going back to the seventeenth century as well as fine furniture and silver. The library boasts 650,000 volumes, more than 2 million manuscripts, and rich documentary holdings as well as maps and atlases. It schedules changing exhibitions drawn from its treasures. Subway: 1, 2, 3, 9 to 79th St.; B, C to 81st St. Open Tues–Sun 11 a.m.–5 p.m. Admission charge.

New York Is Book Country (212) 207-7242

More than 150 publishers and booksellers have stalls or stands on Fifth Ave. between 48th and 57th Sts. and from Madison to Sixth Ave. on 52nd and 53rd Sts., usually on the third Sunday in September, displaying their wares, with a good number of authors on site to sign copies of their books for customers. Subway: E, F, N, R to Fifth Ave.

New York Islanders (516) 935-2213 or (800) NYISLES www.new yorkislanders.com

This hockey team plays at the Nassau Memorial Coliseum, Hempstead Turnpike, Uniondale, Long Island, and tickets are normally available for those willing to make the trip from town to watch them. Subway: 1, 2, 3, 9 to 34th St.-Penn Station; then Long Island Railroad to Hempstead Station, then walk one block to Hempstead Bus Terminal and take Bus N70, N71, or N72.

New York Jazz Festival (212) 219-3006

Jazz performances featuring the full range of jazz styles take place at many city venues for a two-week period in early June under the sponsorship of a corporation whose name is used to identify that year's festival.

New York Jets www.newyorkjets.com

The Jets play at New Jersey's Meadowlands as part of the American Football Conference of the National Football League. For ticket information call (516) 560-8200. Subway: A, C, E to 42nd St.-Port Authority, then take bus from Port Authority Bus Terminal to Meadowlands Sports Center.

New York Jewish Film Festival (212) 875-5600 or (212) 875-5600

This film series takes place every January at the Walter Reade Theatre at Lincoln Center Plaza. Subway: 1, 9 to 66th St.-Lincoln Center.

New York Knicks www.nba.com/knicks

The Knicks (short for Knickerbockers) play home basketball games at Madison Square Garden (212) 465-6741, but tickets are hard to come by unless ordered well in advance. Subway: 1, 2, 3, 9, A, C, E to 34th St.-Penn Station.

New York Kom Tang Soot Bul House 32 W 32nd St. btw Fifth and Sixth Aves. (212) 947-8482

One of the better Korean restaurants in the city, this one specializes in barbecuing and offers the traditional side dishes like kimchi to go with beef or chicken at inexpensive prices. Subway: B, D, F, N, Q, R to 34th St.-Herald Square. Open Mon–Sat 24 hours. Major credit cards.

New York Life Insurance Building 51 Madison Ave. btw 26th and 27th Sts.

Designed in 1928 by Cass Gilbert, this elaborate building covers an entire block and is crowned by a gold pyramid top that is stunningly lighted up at night. The towering lobby is adorned with giant hanging lamps and handsome bronze doors. Subway: 6, N, R to 28th St.

New York Like a Native (718) 393-7537 www.nylikeanative.com

This company features a 4-hour walking tour in Brooklyn from Park Slope to Brooklyn Heights focused on architecture, history, and public spaces.

New York Magazine www.newyorkmag.com

This glossy weekly provides extensive listings of the arts, dining, entertainment, and culture with good reviews, features, and columnists on life style, fashion, and other facets of the lively city scene.

New York Marathon *see* New York City Marathon.

New York Marble Cemetery off Second Ave. at E 2nd St.

Down a short alley in the East Village behind two iron gates is the city's first nonsectarian cemetery. Founded in 1830, it includes 156 underground marble vaults with no gravestones but only plates set into the walls. The New York City Marble Cemetery, located a block away on 2nd St. between First and Second Aves., was established a bit later and can more easily be seen from the sidewalk. The purpose for using the vaults is thought to have been to reduce the risks of contagion. These places are the final resting places for many whose names can still be found in city street signs like Varick, Hoyt, and Mott. Subway: F to Second Ave.

New York Mercantile Exchange 1 North End Ave., World Financial Center (212) 299-2499 www.nymex.com

This is the counterpart of the New York Stock Exchange, except here the floor trading is in physical commodities like oil, gold, silver, and natural gas rather than stock. There's a visitor's gallery from which to view the trading excitement as well as a museum that shows how futures trading developed and how it's used to buy and sell global commodities. Subway: N, R, 1, 9 to Cortlandt St. Open Mon–Fri 9 a.m.–5 p.m. Admission free.

New York Mets Shea Stadium, 123-01 Roosevelt Ave. at 126th St., Flushing, Queens (718) 507-8499 www.mets.com

The Mets play their home baseball games in the National League during the season from April through October, and tickets are generally easy to get. Subway: 7 to Willets Pt.-Shea Stadium.

New York Newspapers and Magazines *see* Newspapers and Magazines.

New York Noodletown 28$^{1}/_{2}$ Bowery at Bayard St. (212) 349-0923

Some of New York's best Chinese food is served in an exceedingly modest room, which provides not just noodles but a wide range of seafood and meat dishes at inexpensive prices. Subway: N, R, 6 to Canal St. Open daily 9 a.m.–4 a.m. No credit cards.

New York Observer www.observer.com

This weekly pink newspaper concentrates on the sophisticated political, business, finance, and media scene with irony and wit. It is sold around town for $1 a copy.

New York Palace Hotel 451-455 Madison Ave. btw 49th and 50th Sts. (212) 888-7000 www.newyorkpalace.com

The opulent New York Palace Hotel has incorporated six Italianate Renaissance-style brownstones constructed in the 1870s by McKim, Mead & White as a large palazzo, formerly owned by the Roman Catholic diocese. Afternoon tea is now served in the refurbished grand rooms beneath a vaulted ceiling designed by Stanford White. The Urban Center occupies the north wing, with a bookshop reported to be the best place for architectural books in the city. Subway: E, F to Fifth Ave.; 6 to 51st St.

New York Philharmonic Avery Fisher Hall, Lincoln Center, Broadway at 64th St. (212) 875-5030 or (212) 721-6500 www.nyphil harmon.org

The season begins in September and runs through early June, offering world-celebrated performances featuring talented guest artists and the works of European and American composers. Occasional workday morning rehearsals are open to the public at bargain prices. Subway: 1, 9 to 66th St.-Lincoln Center.

New York Philharmonic Parks Concerts (212) 875-5709 www. nyphilharmon.org/parks/

During July the Philharmonic offers many free outdoor concerts at public sites all around the boroughs, including Central Park.

New York Post

Longest running of the city's daily newspapers (founded in 1801), the *Post* offers strongly conservative and sensationalistic news coverage with good reviews of cultural activities and popular columnists.

New York Press

A free weekly Manhattan newspaper rival to the *Village Voice*, the *Press* features reviews and listings for eating, drinking, and entertainment events in town plus lively critiques of culture and politics.

New York Public Library Fifth Ave. btw 40th and 42nd Sts. (212) 869-8089 www.nypl.org

The central branch of the New York Library contains some 8 million volumes available only for reference use. The building itself inside and out is a celebrated Beaux Arts architectural treasure. Free 1-hour tours of the exhibitions and the library itself are offered. Subway: 7 to Fifth Ave.; B, D, F, Q to 42nd St. Open Mon–Sat, hours vary. Admission free.

New York Public Library Celeste Bartos Forum Fifth Ave. btw 40th and 42nd Sts. (212) 930-0855

This forum sponsors several series, featuring distinguished writers and other intellectual and cultural figures who discuss topics of current humanistic, scientific, artistic, and literary concern. Subway: 7 to Fifth Ave.; B, D, F, Q to 42nd St.

New York Public Library for the Performing Arts *see* Lincoln Center Library for the Performing Arts.

New York Public Library Science, Industry, and Business Library *see* B. Altman Building/New York Public Library Science, Industry, and Business Library.

New York Radio Stations *see* Radio Stations.

New York Rangers (212) 465-6741 www.thegarden.com

From late fall to late spring, Madison Square Garden hosts the home games of the city's team in the National Hockey League. Subway: 1, 2, 3, 9, A, C, E to 34th St.-Penn Station.

New York Road Runners Club 9 E 89th St. btw Fifth and Madison Aves. (212) 860-4455 www.nyrrc.org

This club organizes a schedule of runs and races year-round that are open to the public. One of the more popular events is the Runner's World Midnight Run in Central Park on New Year's Eve. The best known event is the New York City Marathon. Subway: 4, 5, 6 to 86th St.

New York Skyride Empire State Building, 350 Fifth Ave. at 34th St., 2nd Floor (212) 279-9777 or (888) 759-7433 www.skyride.com

A flight-simulated speedy aerial big-screen tour of the city and its skyline viewed from tilted seats with enveloping sound. Subway: B, D, F, N, Q, R to 34th St.-Herald Square. Open daily 10 a.m.–10 p.m. Admission charge.

New York Society Library 53 E 79th St. btw Madison and Park Aves. (212) 288-6900 www.nysoclib.org

A 12-floor private membership library dating to 1754 in which only the reading and reference room on the ground floor are open to the public. This is a lovely, quiet place, with membership open to those for whom the strong collections in literature, history, art history, and New York City make the annual charge a worthwhile expenditure. Subway: 6 to 77th St.

New York Society of Ethical Culture 2 W 64th St. btw Central Park W and Broadway (212) 874-5210 www.nysec.org

This organization has helped a number of other groups get started, such as the American Civil Liberties Union. It runs a well-regarded private school, which enrolls many offspring of its adherents and sponsors frequent lectures, recitals, and readings open to the public. Subway: A, B, C, D, 1, 9 to 59th St.-Columbus Circle.

New York Sports Clubs 888 Seventh Ave. (212) 246-6700 www. nysc.com

The headquarters of this chain has branches at many locations in the city. Here can be found the largest number of squash courts in town plus clinics and coaching opportunities, as well as tournaments of the best and worst players. Call for information about locations and phone numbers or consult the Manhattan phone directory for a listing with locations and phone numbers.

New York State Theatre 65th St. at Columbus Ave. (212) 870-5570

This theatre is home to the celebrated New York City Ballet and the New York City Opera. Operatic and dance performances are presented at popular prices in a house designed by Philip Johnson in 1964 that has been called a "little jewel box" because of the rhinestone lights and chandeliers inside and outside. Subway: 1, 9 to 66th St.-Lincoln Center.

New York Stock Exchange 20 Broad St. btw Wall and Exchange Sts. (212) 656-5165 www.nyse.com

The stocks of more than 2,000 companies are traded in this building, which looks like a Roman temple. Tickets are distributed at the entrance for admission to the visitor's gallery overlooking the trading floor. The interactive education center has a self-guided tour, video displays, a film on the history of the exchange, and staff members to help visitors make sense of the chaotic activity on the floor. Subway: 2, 3, 4, 5 to Wall St. Open Mon–Fri 9 a.m.–4 p.m. Admission free.

New York Theatre Workshop 79 E 4th St. btw Bowery and Second Ave. (212) 460-5475

This company produces works by promising American and foreign playwrights using yet-unheralded directors to stage the productions. Subway: 6 to Astor Pl.; N, R to 8th St.

The New York Times

This is New York's most distinguished daily, and it offers excellent entertainment and arts coverage particularly in its Friday Weekend and Sunday Arts and Leisure sections. Thorough treatment of theatre, music, dance, jazz, film, the arts, and other cultural events are featured.

New York Transit Museum *see* New York City Transit Museum.

New York Underground Film Festival (212) 925-3440
Every mid-March, this interesting, off-beat movie series takes place at varying city locations.

New York Unearthed 17 State St. at Battery Park btw Pearl and Whitehall Sts. (212) 748-8628
Run by the South Street Seaport, this small but fascinating collection of artifacts was retrieved during construction in the downtown area and includes pottery bits, Indian items, coins, and jewelry from different periods of the city's history. The "Systems Elevator" offers a simulated ride to a dig site, and in the basement is a glass-enclosed laboratory where archeologists can be seen at work. Subway: 1, 9 to South Ferry; N, R to Whitehall St. Open Mon–Fri noon–6 p.m. Admission free.

New York University Washington Square www.nyu.edu
This is the nation's largest private university and one of the city's biggest property owners. It now occupies most of the buildings around Washington Square Park, having taken over many of the old historic townhouses, and it extends well beyond for blocks around. Subway: A, B, C, D, E, F, Q to W 4th St.

New York University Grey Art Gallery and Study Center *see* Grey Art Gallery and Study Center at New York University.

New York Video Festival (212) 875-5638
Sponsored by the Film Society of Lincoln Center, this event takes place late in July or early August each year. Subway: 1, 9 to 66th St.-Lincoln Center.

New York Waterway (800) 533-3779 www.nywaterway.com
This company offers various cruises of the New York harbor departing from Pier 78 at W 38th St. at Twelfth Ave., with free bus pickup from a number of Manhattan locations. It also features daylong Hudson River cruises from May to November, sailing historic sightseeing itineraries along the Hudson River Valley including land visits to celebrated sites. Hudson River cruises usually require reservations well in advance during peak tourist travel periods.

New York Yankees Yankee Stadium, River Ave. at 161st St., Bronx (718) 293-4300; ticket office (212) 293-6000 www.yankees.com
From April through October the team plays its home games here. Tick-

ets can usually be bought the day of the game, but it's a good idea to check first. Subway: 4, B, D to 161st St.-Yankee Stadium.

The New Yorker

The city's sophisticated literary magazine features highbrow film, theatre, music, and dance reviews in addition to its popular cartoons, poems, and fiction. It also carries extensive listings of offerings at museums, theatres, galleries, readings, and entertainment spots.

Newark International Airport

This airport is in New Jersey. The quickest means of travel, but the most expensive, is by taxi. Sharing the ride with two or three others is more economical. Other means of traveling to Newark Airport are the following:

Across from Grand Central Station—Park Ave. and 41st St.
Olympia Trails Airport Express Bus—$11, every 20–30 minutes
5 a.m.–11 p.m. (212) 964-6233

Port Authority Bus Terminal—42nd St. and Eighth Ave.
Olympia Trails Airport Express Bus—$11, every 15–30 minutes
24 hours a day (212) 964-6233

Hotels—Shared Van
SuperShuttle Manhattan Service (midtown hotels) $15 (212) 258-3826
Express Shuttle U.S.A.—service from certain midtown Manhattan hotels, $19
(212) 315-3006

PATH Rapid Transit
Stops at 33rd St., 23rd St., 14th St., 9th St., Christopher St.
Service to Newark's Penn Station for connection with Airlink Bus No. 302
PATH $1; Airlink Bus No. 302 $4, 6:26 a.m.–1:27 a.m.
PATH (800) 234-PATH; Airlink Bus No. 302 (973) 762-5100

Penn Station—33rd St. and Eighth Ave.
NJ Transit or Amtrak trains to Newark's Penn Station: Connect to Airlink
Bus No. 302
NJ Transit train $2.50, Amtrak $7, Airlink Bus No. 302 $16–$24
NJ Transit and Airlink (973) 762-5100
Amtrak (800) USA-RAIL

Olympia Trails Airport Express Bus—34th St. and Eighth Ave.
$11, every 20–30 minutes
5:10 a.m.–11:10 p.m. (212) 964-6233

Fares were in effect in fall 2001 and may have changed since then. For more details on getting to or from Newark Airport call (800) AIRRIDE.

Newhouse Center for Contemporary Art Snug Harbor Cultural Center, 1000 Richmond Terrace, Tyson St. at Snug Harbor Rd., Staten Island (718) 448-2500

This center offers the artistic creations of unknown, emerging, and established artists working across the range of different art forms. Subway: 1, 9 to South Ferry; N, R to Whitehall St., then ferry to Staten Island. From Staten Island St. George Ferry Terminal, take Bus S40 to Snug Harbor Cultural Center. Open daily, hours vary. Admission free.

News Building *see* Daily News Building.

Newseum/NY 580 Madison Ave. btw 56th and 57th Sts. (212) 317-4760

This branch of the Freedom Forum Foundation's Arlington, Virginia, museum centers on enhancing understanding of journalism through its programs of photography exhibits, films, lectures, and panel discussions, all designed to encourage public discussion of First Amendment concerns in a small space but with well-thought-out, stimulating displays. Tours are offered as well. For recorded event information, call (212) 317-7596. Subway: E, F to Fifth Ave.; 4, 5, 6 to Lexington Ave. Open Mon–Sat 10 a.m.–5:30 p.m. Admission free.

Newspaper Row *see* Park Row.

Newspapers and Magazines *see Big Apple Parents' Paper, Daily News,* Hotaling's News Agency, *New York* Magazine, *New York Observer, New York Post, New York Press, The New York Times, The New Yorker, Paper, Poetry Calendar, Time Out New York, Village Voice, Wall Street Journal.*

Next Wave Festival (718) 636-4111

This important series of cultural events from September to December each year is staged at the Brooklyn Academy of Music. Included are experimental and avant-garde performances of dance, music, and theatre by famous and emerging American and international artists. Subway: D, Q, 2, 3, 4, 5 to Atlantic Ave.

Nha Trang 87 Baxter St. btw Bayard and Canal Sts. (212) 233-5948

A simple, unpretentious Vietnamese restaurant with a helpful staff serving genuine Southeast Asian dishes at modest prices. Subway: J, M, N, R, Z, 6 to Canal St. Lunch and dinner daily. No credit cards.

Nicholas Roerich Museum 319 W 107th St. btw Broadway and Riverside Dr. (212) 864-7752 www.roerich.org

In a charming townhouse on a quiet street is a small, unusual collection of personal possessions and the artistic works of Roerich, a Russian émigré, artist, and explorer. The most notable art displayed are the landscapes of the Himalayas. Poetry readings and concerts are also offered here in Roerich's one-time home. Subway: 1, 9 to Cathedral Pkwy.-110th St. Open Tues–Sun 2 p.m.–5 p.m. Admission free.

Il Nido 251 E 53rd St. btw Second and Third Aves. (212) 753-8450

The decor suggests a farmhouse in Tuscany, while the food in this fashionable, upscale, expensive Italian restaurant is prepared masterfully. Reservations required. Subway: E, F to Lexington Ave.; 6 to 51st St. Lunch and dinner Mon–Sat. Major credit cards.

Night Clubs *see* Baktun, Bar Code/Galactic Circus, Brandy's Piano Bar, Chicago City Limits, Copacabana, Cotton Club, Duplex Cabaret, Hard Rock Café, Harley-Davidson Café, Latin Quarter, Life, Mother, Rainbow Grill, Roxy, Webster Hall. *See also* Comedy Clubs, Jazz Spots.

Night Court Criminal Courts Building, Room 218, 100 Centre St. btw White and Leonard Sts. (212) 374-5880

The criminal courts are open to the public, but the place that holds the most fascination during the late hours when it holds forth is here, where the arraignment of suspects takes place. Subway: 4, 5, 6 to Brooklyn Bridge-City Hall; J, M, N, R, Z, 6 to Canal St.; 1, 9 to Franklin St.

92nd Street Y 1395 Lexington Ave. btw 91st and 92nd Sts. (212) 996-1100 www.92ndsty.org

This uncommon institution is famous for the innumerable cultural events it sponsors. There are walking and bus tours covering all the boroughs and many aspects of life in the city. The Unterberg Poetry Center has been offering live readings of literature and poetry for more than half a century, and there are frequent concerts, discussion panels, and public lectures, as well as the normal gymnasium and physical activities available here. Subway: 6 to 96th St.

Ninth Avenue Street Festival (212) 581-7217

Along Ninth Ave. from 37th to 57th Sts. on a weekend in mid-May there is a feast of foods, music, dance, and other colorful entertainment. The food is the main drawing card; thousands flock here to sample the abundance of tantalizing ethnic specialties prepared in barbecues, grills, and woks on the streets along the way. Subway: A, C, E to 42nd St.-Port Authority; C, E to 50th St.

Ninth Street Community Garden and Park 144 Ave. C at 9th St.

For more than 20 years this award-winning community effort of area adults and children has demonstrated how people can brighten a neighborhood with things that grow. Still lack of permanent status makes the future of gardens like this uncertain because of the possibility of sale or development by the city, resulting in neighborhood controversy. Subway: 6 to Astor Pl.

Nobu 105 Hudson St. at Franklin St. (212) 219-0500

Home to some of the finest Japanese food in New York, this TriBeCa favorite offers charming decor to go with its exceptional dishes. It's quite expensive, and reservations are a must. There's also Next Door Nobu at the same address (212) 234-4445, somewhat more casual and with a similar menu but following a no-reservations policy. Subway: 1, 9 to Franklin St. Nobu: Lunch Mon–Fri, dinner daily. Next Door Nobu: Dinner daily. Major credit cards.

Noguchi Museum 32-37 Vernon Blvd. at 33rd Pl., Long Island City, Queens (718) 204-7088 www.noguchi.org

In an industrial section of Queens can be found this extraordinary museum, which includes twelve galleries and a traditional serene Japanese fountain garden featuring more than 300 creative works of the celebrated Japanese sculptor Isamu Noguchi. A guided tour is offered daily (718) 721-1932. Subway: N to Broadway, then down Broadway toward the East River, turn left on Vernon Blvd. Open April–October, Wed–Sun, hours vary. Modest admission charge.

NoHo

An abbreviation for North of Houston, this neighborhood covers the area around Broadway from Astor Pl. running south to Houston St. Like its neighbor to the south, SoHo, it continues to develop into a thriving consumer community of trendy shops, dining and night spots, and high-priced antique boutiques. Subway: 6 to Astor Pl.; N, R to 8th St.

North Brother Island

An abandoned island with the strange history of having been used to house, until her death in the early twentieth century, the quarantined cook "Typhoid Mary" who was an unaffected carrier and transmitter of typhoid. Today it's inaccessible except to unusual bird species. It is located in the eastern arm of the East River at the entrance to Long Island Sound.

North Meadow Recreation Center *see* Central Park Conservancy, Central Park North Meadow Recreation Center.

North River Park btw the World Financial Center and Chambers St. along the Hudson River

A recent addition to the city's park system, this long, narrow stretch is replete with basketball and handball courts, a soccer field, and good running and skating paths beside the river. Subway: E to World Trade Center; 1, 9, N, R to Cortlandt St.

Norwegian Day Parade (718) 851-4678

In Bay Ridge, Brooklyn, this patriotic celebration of Norwegian independence takes place every year on the Sunday nearest May 17. The procession includes floats, colorful ethnic costumes, and marching sons of Norway moving down Brooklyn's Fifth Ave. from 90th St. to Leif Ericson Park at 66th St. Subway: R to 95th St.

Numismatic Society *see* American Numismatic Society.

Nuyorican Poets Café 236 E 3rd St. btw Aves. B and C (212) 505-8183

This long-standing space hosts poetry contests, theatre and film scenario readings, workshops, and other sparkling, innovative, new literary and musical offerings for critical young audiences, justly celebrated for the liveliness and high interest level of the activities. Subway: F to Second Ave. Dates, times and admission details vary.

NYU *see* New York University.

O'bon Festival (212) 678-0305

On a weekend in early July each year, Bryant Park (behind the New York Public Library) is the place where kimono-garbed Japanese dancers perform to the beat of drums in this colorful and historic rite. Subway: B, D, F, Q to 42nd St.; 7 to Fifth Ave.

Oceana 55 E 54th St. btw Madison and Park Aves. (212) 759-5941

Ranks with the very best of Manhattan's deluxe and expensive fish restaurants for the excellent seafood dishes, the attentive service, and the fine wine choices. Reservations suggested. Subway: E, F to Fifth Ave. Lunch Mon–Fri, dinner Mon–Sat. Major credit cards.

Ocularis (718) 388-8713

This group arranges the showing of a wide range of movies weekly at various venues around town. Details of showing dates, locations, and prices are provided on a taped message.

Odeon 145 W Broadway btw Duane and Thomas Sts. (212) 233-0507

A spacious, trendy Art Deco style TriBeCa favorite with tasty food, moderate prices, and chic clientele. Subway: 1, 9 to Chambers St. Lunch Mon–Fri, dinner daily, brunch Sat and Sun. Major credit cards.

Odessa 1113 Brighton Beach Ave. btw 13th and 14th Sts., Brighton Beach, Brooklyn (718) 332-3223

Dancing and music on weekend nights go with the wide range of delicious, moderately priced Russian food specialties. Subway: D, Q to Brighton Beach. Open 7 p.m.–3 a.m. Fri–Sun. Major credit cards.

Odessa by the Sea *see* Brighton Beach.

Off-Broadway and Off-Off-Broadway Theatre *see* American Place Theatre, Astor Place Theatre, Atlantic Theatre Company, Bouwerie Lane Theatre, Brooklyn Academy of Music, Cherry Lane Theatre, Circle in the Square Theatre, Douglas Fairbanks Theatre, 47th Street Theatre, Hudson Guild Theatre, Irish Arts Center, Irish Repertory Theatre, Jane Street Theatre, John Houseman Theatre, Joseph L. Papp Public Theatre, The Kitchen, La MaMa e.t.c., Lamb's Theatre, Lincoln Center Theatre, Lucille Lortel Theatre, Manhattan Theatre Club, Minetta Lane Theatre, New York Theatre Workshop, Orpheum Theatre, P.S. 122, Performing Garage, Players Theatre, Playwrights Horizons, Primary Stages, Promenade Theatre, St. Luke's Church, Second Stage Theatre, Signature Theatre Company, SoHo Repertory Theatre, Sullivan Street Playhouse, Theatre for the New City, Theatre Four, Union Square Theatre, Variety Arts Theatre, Vineyard Theatre, WPA Theatre, Westside Theatre. *See also New York* Magazine, *The New Yorker, Time Out New York, Village Voice.*

Ohm 16 W 22nd St. btw Fifth and Sixth Aves. (212) 229-2000

Spread out over 10,000 square feet, this multi-level place is a combined dining, lounge, and nightspot. Busy and upscale, it attracts an eclectic crowd drawn for any of its features and attractions. Subway: F, N, R to 23rd St. Open Thurs–Sat 8 p.m.–4 a.m. Admission charge. Major credit cards.

The Old Homestead 56 Ninth Ave. btw 14th and 15th Sts. (212) 242-9040

The city's longest surviving steakhouse dates from 1868; the expensive but tender, mammoth beef portions are still prepared lovingly and served graciously in a handsome dining room with fine wood panel walls. Subway: A, C, E to 14th St.; L to Eighth Ave. Lunch and dinner daily. Major credit cards.

Old Merchant's House 29 E 4th St. btw Lafayette St. and the Bowery (212) 777-1089

This museum contains the house's original Victorian, Federal, and American Empire furnishings, as well as the kitchen utensils and ornaments of its occupants from the nineteenth century. It remains today a good representation of the living style of a well-to-do New York family of this period. Subway: N, R to 8th St.; 6 to Astor Pl. Open Thurs–Mon 1 p.m.–5 p.m. Modest admission charge.

Old New York City Police Headquarters 240 Centre St.
Situated on the corner of Centre and Broome Sts., this imposing green-domed, lavishly ornamented palatial structure has been transformed into a high-priced condominium. Subway: J, M, N, R, Z, 6 to Canal St.

Old New York County Courthouse *see* Tweed Courthouse.

Old St. Patrick's Cathedral 263 Mulberry St. btw Prince and Houston Sts. (212) 226-8075
Here is the predecessor to the famous Fifth Ave. cathedral. After a fire destroyed the original structure in the 1860s and the archdiocese moved the cathedral uptown in 1879, it became a parish church, which it remains to this day. Subway: N, R to Prince St.; B, D, F, Q to Broadway-Lafayette.

Old Town 45 E 18th St. btw Broadway and Park Ave. S (212) 529-6732
A truly old-fashioned bar (vintage 1892) with all the trappings—high ceiling, tile floor, huge bar, and flavor of the classic watering hole. Subway: N, R, 6 to 23rd St.

Ollie's Noodle Shop 190 W 44th St. btw Broadway and Eighth Ave. (212) 921-5988
Cheap, filling, and tasty noodles, soups, vegetables, and meat dishes draw the noisy crowd to this always-busy Chinese eatery. There are three other locations: 1991 Broadway between W 67th and W 68th Sts. (212) 595-8181, 2315 Broadway at W 84th St. (212) 362-3111, and 2957 Broadway at W 111th St. (212) 932-3300. Subway: (W 44th St.) A, C, E to 42nd St.-Port Authority; N, R, S, 1, 2, 3, 7, 9 to Times Square-42nd St.; (1991 Broadway) 1, 9 to 66th St.-Lexington Center; (2315 Broadway) 1, 9 to 86th St.; (2957 Broadway) B, C to Cathedral Pkwy.-110th St. Lunch and dinner daily. Major credit cards.

On-Line Sources on New York *see* Web Sites About New York.

Onassis Reservoir *see* Central Park Jacqueline Kennedy Onassis Reservoir.

One Fifth Avenue
This charming Art Deco building is located on the southwest corner of Fifth Ave. and 8th St., which was once the meeting place for an early New York women's political club of the 1920s. Subway: A, B, C, D, E, F, Q to W 4th St.; N, R to 8th St.-NYU.

125th Street
This is the heart of Harlem, the celebrated main drag, where the flavor

and beat are reflected in the sounds and sights that make it the uptown capital. From the Apollo Theatre to the throngs of shoppers, to the street hustlers and evangelists, to the music blaring from the record stores, it's all here. The neighborhood has been experiencing a renaissance and is once again a popular tourist destination. Subway: (western end) A, B, C, D to 125th St. (Frederick Douglass Blvd.); (eastern end) 2, 3 to 125th St. (Lenox Ave.).

One World Festival (212) 686-0710

Sponsored by New York's Armenian community, 35th St. between First and Second Aves. is closed off to celebrate this multi-ethnic street bazaar and block party every year on Saturday and Sunday of the second weekend of September. Food stands selling the specialties of several world cultures as well as regional crafts and arts, with lively musical and folk dance companies performing during the afternoon in nearby St. Vartan Park, are all part of the colorful festivities. Subway: 6 to 33rd St.

Ontological Theatre *see* St. Mark's-in-the-Bowery Church.

Opera in the Parks *see* Metropolitan Opera Parks Concerts.

Opera Music *see* Amato Opera Theatre, Brooklyn Academy of Music, Hunter College, Juilliard School of Music, Metropolitan Opera, New York City Opera Season, New York State Theatre, St. Peter's Lutheran Church.

Orchard Beach

This beach was created by the city parks department in 1936 by carting in the white sand from the Rockaways. It is part of Pelham Bay Park and is located in northeast Bronx on Long Island Sound. It is in sadly neglected condition and is best enjoyed out of the summer season for quiet strolling along its broad walkway. Subway: 6 to Pelham Bay Park, then bus to beach.

Orchard Street

New York's perennial street of bargains is the Lower East Side's most celebrated destination for discount shopping. Jammed with stores, street racks, and stalls from Houston St. south to Canal St., it still bears the flavor of its Jewish immigrant past. Peak time is Sunday morning. There are even free tours of the neighborhood offered on Sundays in all but the winter season by the Lower East Side Business Improvement District (212) 226-9010, where one can learn about the history of the district and where to find the greatest buys. Subway: F, J, M, Z to Delancey St.-Essex St.

Oriental Garden 14 Elizabeth St. near Canal St. (212) 619-0085

Not much for decor and style, but what is offered here is some of

Chinatown's best seafood dishes at modest prices. Subway: J, M, N, R, Z, 6 to Canal St. Open seven days 8:30 a.m.–midnight. American Express or cash.

Orpheum Theatre 126 Second Ave. at St. Marks Pl. (212) 477-2477

This East Village house seats many more than most off-Broadway venues and hosts new American plays by well-known and emerging playwrights. Subway: 6 to Astor Pl.; N, R to 8th St.-NYU.

Orso 322 W 46th St. btw Eighth and Ninth Aves. (212) 489-7212

At this well-frequented spot for pre- or post-theatre Italian meals, the food is good and moderately priced, and the cheerful ambiance sometimes includes a familiar face or two from the Broadway stage. Subway: A, C, E to 42nd St.-Port Authority. Lunch and dinner daily. MasterCard and Visa only.

Out-of-Doors Festival (212) 875-5108

Held annually at Lincoln Center from mid-August to September is this series of free dance and music performances. Subway: 1, 9 to 66th St.-Lincoln Center.

Out of the Darkness (212) 580-7668

Each year on December 1, this candlelit procession marches to City Hall to commemorate World AIDS Day in conjunction with the reading of the names vigil. It is carried out under the sponsorship of AREA (American Run for the End of AIDS), and precise details are available by calling the office.

Outdoor Concerts *see* Lunchtime and Outside Concerts.

Outdoor Dining *see* Barbetta, Caffé Bianco, Caffé Reggio, Lombardi's, Le Madri, Marichu, Museum of Modern Art, Stanhope Hotel, Uncle Nick's.

Outsider Art Fair (212) 274-8900

Held at the Puck Building in SoHo, 295 Lafayette St. at Houston St., usually the last weekend in January, this is a showing by thirty-some American and European exhibitors of works in a very wide range of media forms. Subway: 6 to Bleecker St.; B, D, F, Q to Broadway-Lafayette. Admission charge.

Oxbridge 1623 Third Ave., NY 10128 (212) 348-8100 or (800) 550-7071, fax (212) 348-8362 www.oxbridgeny.com

This agency arranges the rental of furnished apartments around town by the week or by the month.

Oyster Bar at Grand Central Grand Central Terminal, Lower Level, 42nd St. and Vanderbilt Ave. (212) 490-6650

This popular subterranean eatery under cavernous tiled ceilings serves twenty to thirty types of fresh oysters and the same number of seafood dishes; this favorite New York experience includes a high decibel level and fairly expensive prices. Subway: S, 4, 5, 6, 7 to Grand Central-42nd St. Lunch and dinner Mon–Sat. Major credit cards.

P.S. 1 The Institute for Contemporary Art 22-25 Jackson Ave. at Forty-Sixth Ave., Long Island City, Queens (718) 784-2084 www.ps1.org

A renovated public school building serves as the largest American center for changing exhibitions of a wide range of modern, avant-garde art forms from this country and abroad. It recently joined forces with Manhattan's Museum of Modern Art. Subway: E, F to 23rd St.-Ely Ave.; 7 to 45th Rd.-Courthouse Square. Wed–Sun noon–6. Modest admission charge.

P.S. 44 *see* Columbus Avenue Flea Market.

P.S. 122 150 First Ave. at 9th St. (212) 477-5288 www.ps122.org

This small, popular East Village performance center offers cutting-edge experimental short-run productions of dance, music, single-person performances, film, and videos. Subway: F to Second Ave.; N, R to 8th St.; 6 to Astor Pl.

P.S. 183 Flea Market 419 E 67th St. btw York and First Aves.

Every Saturday this location is the site of bargain seekers flocking to examine the bargains to be found. Subway: 6 to 68th St.-Hunter College.

Pace Wildenstein Gallery 32 E 57th St. btw Fifth and Madison Aves. (212) 421-3292

This celebrated showplace has long shown the works of leading American and European artists and also displays African art. Subway: 4, 5, 6 to 59th St.; N, R, to Fifth Ave. Open Mon–Fri 10 a.m.–5:30 p.m.

Palace Theatre 1564 Broadway at 47th St. (212) 730-8200

This venerable, spacious auditorium was the stage for early-twentieth-century greats like Sarah Bernhardt, later becoming the leading vaudeville performance center, then a movie house and since the mid-1960s it's been the venue for big Broadway musicals. Subway: N, R, to 49th St.

Paley Park

Located on what was once the site of the celebrated Stork Club, this small open space on the north side of E 53rd St. between Madison and Fifth Aves. is a tiny park named for the founder of CBS, William Paley, with a small waterfall squeezed into an area between two towering buildings. Subway: E, F to Fifth Ave.

Palio 151 W 51st St. btw Sixth and Seventh Aves. (212) 245-4850

This elaborately appointed, tranquil room features luxurious Italian dining at beautifully set, well-separated tables; the fare and the service are outstanding, and the dinner tab is very high. Reservations required. Subway: B, D, F, Q to 47th–50th Sts.-Rockefeller Center. Lunch Mon–Fri, dinner Mon–Sat. Major credit cards.

Palm 837 Second Ave. btw 44th and 45th Sts. (212) 687-2953

A favorite beef house since its start as a speakeasy in 1926, celebrated for its steaks, chops, and lobsters, with a down-to-earth flavor but expensive prices. Its twin, Palm Too, is right across the street at 840 Second Ave. (212) 697-5198. Subway: S, 4, 5, 6, 7 to Grand Central-42nd St. Lunch and dinner Mon–Fri, dinner only Sat. Major credit cards.

Pamir 1437 Second Ave. btw 74th and 75th Sts. (212) 734-3791

Filling Afghan food is served at this moderately priced dining spot, where the various lamb and vegetarian dishes come pleasantly seasoned and flavored and the bread is especially tasty. A second location is at 1065 First Ave. at 58th St. (212) 644-9258. Subway: (Second Ave.) 6 to 77th St.; (First Ave.) 4, 5, 6 to 59th St. Lunch Sat and Sun. Dinner nightly. Visa and MasterCard.

Pan Asian Repertory Theatre www.panasianrep.org

This, the largest American company of its type, performs the works of Asian and Asian-American artists at Playhouse 46 in St. Clement's Church, 423 W 46th St. between Ninth and Tenth Aves. (212) 246-7277. Subway: A, C, E to 42nd St.-Port Authority.

Papaya King 255 W 43rd St. btw Broadway and Eighth Ave. (212) 940-4590 www.papayaking.com

A popular stopping-off point for youngsters is this heavily frequented place where the specialties are all-beef hot dogs and hamburgers. A second location is at 121 W 125th St. between Lenox and Seventh Aves. (212) 665-

5732. Subway: (W 43rd St.) N, R, S, 1, 2, 3, 7, 9 to Times Square-42nd St.; A, C, E to 42nd St.-Port Authority; (W 125th St.) 2, 3 to 125th St. Lunch and dinner daily. No credit cards.

Paper

This monthly is particularly strong for the current slant on what's going on at the night spots, bars, and fashion shops of the downtown scene.

Paper Bag Players (212) 362-0431 or (212) 772-4448 www.paper bagplayers.org

Performing during the winter season for an audience of under-10-year-olds, this company stages its joyful productions using settings of boxes and bags at the Sylvia and Danny Kaye Playhouse of Hunter College on E 68th St. between Park and Lexington Aves. Subway: 6 to 68th St.-Hunter College.

Papp Public Theatre *see* Joseph L. Papp Public Theatre.

Parades *see* African-American Day Parade, Columbus Day Parade, Coney Island Mermaid Parade, Easter Parade, Greek Independence Day Parade, Halloween Parade in Greenwich Village, Hispanic Day Parade, India Day Parade, International Cultures Parade, Lesbian and Gay Pride Parade, Macy's Thanksgiving Day Parade, Martin Luther King Jr. Day Parade, Norwegian Day Parade, Philippine Independence Day Parade, Puerto Rican Day Parade, Pulaski Day Parade, St. Patrick's Day Parade, Salute to Israel Parade, Veterans Day Parade, Von Steuben Day Parade.

Paramount Building 1501 Broadway btw 43rd and 44th Sts.

The celebrated movie theatre of the 1930s and '40s, where performance headliners drew long lines of teenagers, is long gone, but this massive 1927 structure with its setback levels rising to the Art Deco tower, clock, and globe remains as a reminder of its earlier days of glory. Subway: N, R, S, 1, 2, 3, 7, 9 to Times Square-42nd St.

The Park 109 E 56th St. btw Park and Lexington Aves. (212) 750-5656

Some of the best dining in the city takes place in this strikingly attractive restaurant with plush seating, spectacular chandeliers, and elegant service, all at fairly expensive prices. Subway: 4, 5, 6 to 59th St.; E, F to Lexington Ave. Breakfast and lunch Mon–Fri, dinner Tues–Sat. Major credit cards.

Park Avenue

Divided by a well-maintained green center strip, this celebrated wide boulevard running from 33rd to 96th Sts. is lined on each side by solemn-looking national corporate headquarters buildings and high-rise apartment dwellings that house some of the city's most affluent. The outward appearance of this awesome canyon reflects the solemnity of the serious wealth contained within the interiors of the imposing structures. Subway: (south end) 6 to 33rd St.; (north end) 4, 5, 6 to 86th St.

Park Row

Along the southeast border of City Hall Park lies the celebrated street once designated Newspaper Row that was home from the 1850s until the 1920s of most of New York's newspapers, including Joseph Pulitzer's *New York World,* Horace Greeley's *New York Tribune,* and the *New York Times.* The *Times's* regional site at 41 Park Row is now the building housing Pace University. Subway: 4, 5, 6 to Brooklyn Bridge-City Hall; N, R to City Hall.

Park Slope

Along the western edge of Prospect Park and south of Grand Army Plaza in Brooklyn is an attractive residential neighborhood of beautiful, well-maintained brownstone townhouses that date from the last part of the nineteenth century. The district boasts tree-lined streets and a wide variety of striking architectural styles and rivals Brooklyn Heights in popularity for the desirability of its much sought-after apartments. Subway: F to Seventh Ave.; 2, 3 to Grand Army Plaza.

Parks and Playgrounds *see* Admiral George Dewey Promenade, Alley Pond Environmental Center, Asser Levy Playground, Astor Place, Battery Park, Bryant Park, Carl Schurz Park, Central Park, Central Park Heckscher Playground, City Hall Park, Columbus Park, Cunningham Park, Dyckman Fields, East River Park, Flushing Meadows-Corona Park, Forest Park, Fort Greene Park, Fort Tryon Park, Gateway National Recreation Area, Gramercy Park, The Greenbelt, High Rock Park Conservation Center, Hudson River Park, Inwood Hill Park, International Wildlife Conservation Park, Jackie Robinson Park, Jacob Riis Park, Jamaica Bay Wildlife Refuge, Kazimiroff Nature Trail, Marcus Garvey Park, Mill Rock Island, Nelson Rockefeller Park, New York Botanical Garden, Ninth Street Community Garden and Park, North River Park, Orchard Beach, Paley Park, Pelham Bay Park, Playspace, The Promenade, Prospect Park, Riverbank State Park, Riverside Park, Robert F. Wagner, Jr. Park, The Rockaways, Sara Delano Roosevelt Park, Snug Harbor Cultural Center, Socrates Sculpture Park, Tompkins Square Park,

Van Cortlandt Park, Washington Market Park, Washington Square Park.

Parsons School of Design 2 W 13th St. btw Fifth and Sixth Aves. (212) 229-8987 www.parsons.edu

At the exhibition center, this educational institution offering coursework in interior, product, textile, and theatre design, holds free exhibitions, often of student and faculty works, including photography, graphic arts, sculpture, and computer-produced creations. Subway: F to 14th St.; L to Sixth Ave.

Participatory Sports Activity *see* Bicycling, Boating, Bowling, Climbing, Golf, Handball, Horseback Riding, Ice Skating, In-Line Skating, Miniature Golf, New York Marathon, Pool, Racquetball, Roller Skating, Running, Sailing, Squash, Swimming, Tennis, Yoga.

Patchin Place

A tiny courtyard off W 10th St. between Greenwich St. and Sixth Ave., this delightful cul-de-sac with a row of ailanthus trees contains a group of ten small residences built in the mid-nineteenth century that in the 1920s and 1930s housed a number of literary and cultural celebrities of the period. Subway: A, B, C, D, E, F, Q to W 4th St.

Patria 250 Park Ave. S at 20th St. (212) 777-6211 www.patria nyc.com

Imaginative Latin and South American specialties are prepared beautifully at this popular, lively, fairly expensive Caribbean dining establishment where reservations are advisable. Subway: 6 to 23rd St. Lunch Mon–Fri, dinner daily. Major credit cards.

Patsy's 19 Old Fulton St. btw Front and Water Sts., Brooklyn Heights, Brooklyn (718) 858-4300

Aficionados rate the pizza here the very best in the city. The atmosphere is simple: red-checkered tablecloths cover the tables, photos of Sinatra deck the walls, jukebox music swells, and prices are inexpensive. Subway: A, C to High St.; 2, 3 to Clark St. Lunch and dinner daily. No credit cards.

Paul Taylor Dance Company (212) 431-5562 www.ptdc.org

This company stages its performances around the city and country year-round, usually including a short run annually at the City Center.

Paula Cooper Gallery 534 W 21st St. btw Tenth and Eleventh Aves. (212) 255-1105

This is one of the more prestigious Manhattan galleries, featuring the works of some of the brightest contemporary luminaries of the art scene. Subway: C, E to 23rd St. Open Mon–Fri, 10 a.m.–5 p.m.

Payard Patisserie and Bistro 1032 Lexington Ave. btw 73rd and 74th Sts. (212) 717-5252 www.payard.com

A genuinely Parisian standard is met at this spot, which offers all the finest French pastries, lunch and dinner, and afternoon tea service. Subway: 6 to 77th St. Open Mon–Sat 7 a.m.–11 p.m. Major credit cards.

Peacock Alley Waldorf Astoria Hotel, 301 Park Ave. at 50th St. (212) 872-4895

Luxurious ambiance as well as professional service, ample space, comfortable seating, and superlative French cuisine are features of this attractive and expensive restaurant, where reservations are necessary. Subway: E, F to Lexington Ave.; 6 to 51st St. Mon–Fri breakfast, Tues–Sat dinner, Sun brunch. Major credit cards.

Pearl Oyster Bar 18 Cornelia St. btw Bleecker and W 4th Sts. (212) 691-8211

This is clearly the place for oysters as well as other excellently prepared seafood specialties, all at only moderately expensive prices. Subway: A, B, C, D, E, F, Q to W 4th St. Lunch Mon–Fri, dinner Mon–Sat. MasterCard and Visa.

Pearl Paint 308 Canal St. btw Church St. and Broadway (212) 431-7923 or (800) 221-6845

This is a discount supermarket of artists' materials with an enormous selection of every type of graphic and artistic supplies for virtually every need, staffed by a very large team of knowledgeable and helpful clerks. Subway: J, M, R, Z, 6 to Canal St. Open daily, hours vary. Major credit cards.

Pearl Theatre 80 St. Marks Pl. btw Second and Third Aves. (212) 598-9802

This theatre is home to a resident repertory company that revives classic theatrical works by such timeless dramatists as Molière and Shakespeare for modest admission prices. Subway: 6 to Astor Pl.; N, R to 8th St.-NYU.

The Peking (212) 748-8600

Located at Pier 16 in the South Street Seaport complex, this ship, constructed in 1911, is the second largest sailing vessel ever built. You can climb aboard to see the living quarters, watch a film about the ship's passage around Cape Horn, and participate in a 1-hour tour, which is included in the price of admission. Subway: 2, 3, 4, 5, A, C, J, M, Z to Fulton St.-Broadway Nassau. Open daily 10 a.m.–6 p.m. Admission charge.

Pelham Bay Golf Course (718) 885-1258 www.americangolf.com

Reputed to be the most challenging of the city's public golf courses is Split Rock, with its more than 6,200 yards at this Bronx location. Subway: 6 to Pelham Bay Park, then Bus Bx45.

Pelham Bay Park Bronx

With its more than 2,100 acres of salt marshes, wooded areas, lagoons, seashore, playing fields, tennis courts, golf courses, and picnic grounds, this is New York City's largest park, located where the Bronx meets Long Island Sound. Some of the parkland is scenically extraordinary, and history and nature walks are offered by park rangers, with schedule information at (718) 430-1890. Subway: 6 to Pelham Bay Park.

Pell Street

Running through Chinatown, this street is celebrated for having so many beauty and barber shops that it is often called Haircut Street, with many of the shops having the vanishing flavor and features of old-time establishments. Pell St. runs from Mott St. to the Bowery. Subway: J, M, N, R, Z, 6 to Canal St.

Pen and Brush Club 16 E 10th St. at Fifth Ave. (212) 475-3669 www.penandbrush.org

Founded in 1893, this organization for professional women has the longest history of any of its kind in the country. It contains a gallery, which is open daily 1 p.m.–6 p.m. Subway: N, R to 8th St.-NYU; 6 to Astor Pl.

Penang 109 Spring St. btw Greene and Mercer Sts. (212) 274-8883 www.penang.com

Featuring a jungle setting complete with waterfall and palm trees, the whimsical decor does not detract from the wonderfully authentic and delicious, moderately priced Malaysian culinary concoctions. Other locations have similarly distinctive physical arrangements and equally zesty dishes at 240 Columbus Ave. at 71st St. (212) 769-3988, 1596 Second Ave. between 82nd and 83rd Sts. (212) 585-3838, and 38-04 Prince St. at Main St., Flushing, Queens (718) 321-2078. Subway: (Spring St.) N, R to Prince St.; (Columbus Ave.) 1, 2, 3, 9 to 72nd St.; (Second Ave.) 4, 5, 6 to 86th St.; (Flushing) 7 to Main St. Lunch and dinner daily. Major credit cards.

Pennsylvania Hotel *see* Hotel Pennsylvania.

Pennsylvania Station

Running between Seventh and Eighth Aves. and from 31st to 33rd Sts., the present station was renovated in 1963 and sits beneath Madison Square Garden. The station enjoyed far greater architectural splendor during its past, and for history buffs the 34th Street Partnership offers a free monthly tour, which describes the earlier times; information about the tour is available at (212) 868-0521. Subway: 1, 2, 3 7, 9, A, C, E to 34th St.-Penn Station.

Penny Whistle Toys 1283 Madison Ave. at 91st St. (212) 369-3868

Less grandiose than F.A.O. Schwarz, this shop features unusual and old-time toy favorites disdaining those promoting martial activity by kids. There's a second store at 448 Columbus Ave. at 81st St. (212) 873-9090. Subway: (Madison Ave.) 4, 5, 6 to 86th St.; (Columbus Ave.) 1, 9 to 79th St.; B, C to 81st St. Open daily, hours vary. Major credit cards.

La Pequeña Colombia 83-27 Roosevelt Ave. at 84th St., Jackson Heights, Queens (718) 478-6528 www.lapequenacolombia.com

Little Colombia dishes out huge portions of its fine Latin specialties at inexpensive prices at this spacious and popular spot. Subway: 7 to 82nd St. Open seven days from 8 or 10 a.m.–midnight. No credit cards.

Performance Art *see* Exit Art, The Kitchen, The Knitting Factory, La MaMa e.t.c., Mother, Nuyorican Poets Café, P.S. 122, Performing Garage, Surf Reality, Symphony Space, Tunnel.

Performance Space 122 *see* P.S. 122.

Performance Theatre *see* Performance Art.

Performing Arts Research Center *see* Lincoln Center Library for the Performing Arts.

Performing Garage 33 Wooster St. btw Grand and Broome Sts. (212) 996-3651 www.thewoostergroup.org

This is the home of the experimental, avant-garde Wooster Group; it also showcases dance performances, regular reading programs, and visiting artists. Subway: C, E to Spring St.

Le Périgord 405 E 52nd St. btw First Ave. and FDR Dr. (212) 755-6244

An Old World, luxurious French restaurant with well-separated tables, quiet ambiance, excellent gourmet dining fare, and the very expensive prices that are the natural accompaniment. Reservations suggested. Subway: E, F to Lexington Ave.; 6 to 51st St. Open Mon–Fri for lunch, dinner daily. Major credit cards.

Periyali 35 W 20th St. btw Fifth and Sixth Aves. (212) 463-7890

The decor of white stucco walls suggests the flavor of a Greek taverna, the food is first rate, and the service is amiable at this moderately expensive spot. Subway: F, N, R to 23rd St. Lunch Mon–Fri, dinner Mon–Sat. Major credit cards.

Persepolis 1423 Second Ave. btw 74th and 75th Sts. (212) 535-1100

This Persian restaurant features Middle Eastern fare, which has become very popular. Here the well-known appetizers are excellent, as are the skewered kebabs, while the prices are in the moderate range. Subway: 6 to 77th St. Lunch and dinner daily. Major credit cards.

Persian Restaurants *see* Middle Eastern and Mediterranean Restaurants.

Peruvian Restaurants *see* Coco Roco. *See also* Latin American Restaurants.

Pete's Tavern 129 E 18th St. at Irving Pl. (212) 473-7676

This bar has been operating since 1864, lending some credence to its claim to be New York City's oldest. Food is served, but it's the ambiance and the drink at this aged watering hole that attracts people. Subway: L, N, R, 4, 5, 6 to 14th St.-Union Square. Open daily 11 a.m.–midnight and later on weekends.

Peter Cooper Village

Running from 20th to 23rd Sts. and from First Ave. to East River Dr., like its neighbor to the south, Stuyvesant Town, this private community of residential apartment buildings is a peaceful middle-class neighborhood owned by Metropolitan Life Company. Walking paths surrounded by trees give this urban community a quiet, rustic flavor. Subway: 6 to 23rd St., then Bus M23 east to First Ave.

Peter Luger 178 Broadway btw Driggs and Bedford Aves., Williamsburg, Brooklyn (718) 387-7400

Meat is the drawing card at this 100-year-old institution that serves enormous, well-charred cuts of prime beef. Expensive, but not much on decor, this is a prime destination for the many who class this lively place the best steakhouse in the five boroughs. Reservations advisable. Subway: J, M, Z to Marcy Ave. Lunch and dinner daily. No credit cards.

Petrossian 182 W 58th St. at Seventh Ave. (212) 245-2214

At the ultimate in luxurious Russian/continental dining, the caviar of your choice is served to begin the event. The Art Deco interior, abundance of marble, the fur trimming on the banquettes, and the seriously attentive service enhance the elegance of this expensive dining experience. Reservations suggested. Subway: N, R to 57th St. Lunch Mon–Fri, dinner daily, weekend brunch. Major credit cards.

Philip Morris Building 120 Park Ave. at 42nd St.

The interesting features of this building just across from Grand Central Station are the striking glass atrium with its sculpture; it is also home to a branch of the Whitney Museum of American Art. Subway: S, 4, 5, 6, 7 to Grand Central-42nd St.

Philip Randolph Square *see* Randolph Square.

Philippine Independence Day Parade (212) 683-2990

This procession is held on a Sunday in early June, running along Madison Ave. from 40th St. down to 23rd St., where a street fair and celebration continues the birthday party.

Pho Bang 157 Mott St. near Hester St. (212) 966-3797

This very inexpensive restaurant serves a wide range of succulent Vietnamese dishes. Subway: J, M, N, R, Z, 6 to Canal St. Open daily 10 a.m.–10 p.m. No credit cards.

Piano Bars *see* Duplex Cabaret.

La Piccola Cucina 2770 Broadway btw 106th and 107th Sts. (212) 222-2381

This appetizing gourmet grocery shop offers a variety of specially prepared foods as well as a good selection of tempting Italian baked products and pastries. Subway: 1, 9 to 103rd St. Daily 11:30 a.m.–8:30 p.m. MasterCard and Visa.

Picholine 35 W 64th St. btw Broadway and Central Park W (212) 724-8585

For Mediterranean food, this attractive restaurant, stylishly arranged like a French country inn, features delicious menu choices running from seafood to meat dishes, with everything prepared imaginatively. A popular, fairly expensive spot with reservations advisable. Subway: 1, 9 to 66th St.-Lincoln Center. Lunch Tues–Sat, dinner daily. Major credit cards.

Pickwick Arms 230 E 51st St. btw Second and Third Aves., NY 10022 (212) 355-0300, fax (212) 755-5029 www.pickwickarms.com

Located in a relatively quiet East Side district near many popular midtown destinations, this low-budget hotel offers small, clean rooms, some with bath, some with shared bath, and a rooftop café with fine views. Subway: 6 to 51st St.

Pier 17 South Street Seaport

This area at Fulton and South Sts. along the East River has been transformed into a three-level, glass-enclosed shopping center crammed with upscale retail shops and restaurants. The surroundings of docks and ships and the striking views of the East River and Brooklyn Bridge are a treat for the eyes. Subway: 2, 3, 4, 5, A, C, J, M, Z to Fulton St.-Broadway Nassau.

Pierpont Morgan Library 29 E 36th St. btw Madison and Park Aves. (212) 685-0610 www.morganlibrary.org

This small, perfect museum in an Italian Renaissance-style mansion offers world-class treasures of illuminated medieval and Renaissance manuscripts, rare books, drawings, and prints, and there are frequently changing exhibitions of works from the collections. The light-filled atrium with its indoor trees and plants is a lovely spot for lunch or tea. Guided tours are available, with information at (212) 685-0008, ext. 2716. Subway: 6 to 33rd St. Open Tues–Sun, hours vary. Admission charge.

Pierre Hotel 2 E 61st St. at Fifth Ave., NY 10021 (212) 838-8000 or (800) PIERRE4, fax (212) 826-0319

Elegant, famous, and luxurious, this hotel is a favorite with heads of state and celebrities. Service is discreet, and rooms and suites look out over Central Park with rates that are extremely expensive. The afternoon tea service in the magnificently frescoed rotunda is a special treat. Subway: N, R to Fifth Ave.

Pierrepont Street

Located in the heart of Brooklyn Heights and running along this historic street is a helter-skelter mélange of big, old private residences that have been for the most part transformed into apartment buildings. These buildings house the principally professional families seeking easy commutes from just over the Brooklyn Bridge into Manhattan. Pierrepont St. runs from Cadman Plaza W to Columbia Heights. Subway: 2, 3 to Clark St.; M, N, R to Court St.

Pig Heaven 1540 Second Ave. btw E 80th and E 81st Sts. (212) 744-4333

This popular favorite for zesty Cantonese and Szechwan dishes emphasizes pork and a varied selection of dumplings. It offers efficient and helpful service as well as modest prices. Subway: 6 to 77th St. Open daily 11:30 a.m.–midnight. Major credit cards.

Pizzerias *see* Arturo's, John's Pizzeria, Lombardi's, Mezzaluna, Mezzogiorno, Patsy's, Sofia Fabulous Pizza, Totonno's.

Places That Appeal to Children and Teens *see* All Star Café, Amato Opera Theatre, Aquarium for Wildlife Conservation, ARTime, Astroland, *Big Apple Parents' Paper,* Big City Kites, Books of Wonder, Brooklyn Bridge, Brooklyn Children's Museum, Castle Clinton, Central Park Belvedere Castle, Central Park Carousel, Central Park Delacorte Clock, Central Park Model Boat Pond, Central Park Tisch Children's Zoo, Central Park Wildlife Conservation Center, Chelsea Piers, Chinatown, Circle Line Cruises, Coney Island, Deno's Wonderwheel Park, Empire State Building, Enchanted Forest, F.A.O. Schwarz, Hard Rock Café, Harley-Davidson Café, Horse-Drawn Carriage Rides, International Wildlife Conservation Park, Los Kabayitos Puppet Theatre, Madison Square Garden Tours, Mickey Mantle's, NBC Studios, Nellie Bly Amusement Park, New Victory Theatre, New York Botanical Garden, New York City Fire Museum, New York City Transit Museum, New York Hall of Science, New York Skyride, Papaya King, Paper Bag Players, Penny Whistle Toys, Planet Hollywood, Playspace, Police Museum, Popover Café, Prospect Park, Prospect Park Wildlife Center, Puppet Playhouse, Puppetworks, Radio City Music Hall, Rockefeller Center, Rose Center for Earth and Space, Snug Harbor Cultural Center, Socrates Sculpture Park, Sony Wonder Technology Lab, South Street Seaport Museum, Staten Island Ferry, Staten Island Zoo, Tanner's Magic Studio, Times Square, The Unisphere, Urban Park Rangers, Van Cortlandt Park, Virgin Megastore, Wave Hill, XS Virtual Game Arena. *See also* Amusement Parks, Carousels, Museums of Particular Interest to Children and Teens, Parks and Playgrounds, Puppet Theatres, Zoos.

PlanEat Thailand 184 Bedford St. btw N 6th and 7th Sts., Williamsburg, Brooklyn (718) 599-5758

Fine ingredients and old-fashioned Thai cooking produce some delicious Southeast Asian dishes at this modest restaurant with reasonable prices across the Williamsburg Bridge in Brooklyn. Subway: L to Bedford Ave. Open daily 11:30 a.m.–1:00 a.m. No credit cards.

Planet Hollywood 140 W 57th St. btw Sixth and Seventh Aves. (212) 333-7827 www.planethollywood.com

Jammed with movie memorabilia and the highest noise level in town, this gaudy, child-friendly tourist destination serves moderately expensive Southwest dishes and hamburgers. Subway: N, R to 57th St. Open daily 11 a.m.–midnight, later on weekends. Major credit cards.

Players Club 16 Gramercy Park S btw Park Ave. S and Irving Pl. (212) 475-6116

Edwin Booth bought this building in 1888 and engaged Stanford White to remodel the 1845 structure, transforming the handsome columned building into what has become a famous membership organization intended primarily for actors but accepting a select number of celebrities like Winston Churchill. It maintains an excellent special library devoted to the theatre, which is accessible to scholars (212) 228-7610. Subway: 6 to 23rd St.

Players Theatre 115 MacDougal St. btw Bleecker and W 3rd Sts. (212) 254-5076

This theatre performs productions running from serious dramatic works to musicals. Subway: A, B, C, D, E, F, Q to W 4th St.

Playgrounds *see* Parks and Playgrounds.

Playspace 2473 Broadway at 92nd St. (212) 769-2300

An indoor play center designed for kids from 1 to 8 where there is a giant sandbox, a maze, a slide, a 2-story firehouse, toys, games, and ample room to run around. Subway: 1, 2, 3, 9 to 96th St. Daily 7 a.m.–5:30 p.m. Admission charge.

Playwrights Horizons 416 W 42nd St. btw Ninth and Tenth Aves. (212) 564-1235 www.playwrightshorizons.org

This prize company is committed to staging the works of new playwrights and composers and over the years has showcased more than 300 dramas and musicals, including several award-winning productions. Subway: A, C, E to 42nd St.-Port Authority.

Plaza Hotel 768 Fifth Ave. at Central Park S (212) 759-3000

One of New York's loveliest hotels, this 1907 structure is the only one to have been designated a national historic landmark. The Palm Court off the lobby has small tea tables, flowers galore, and a Tiffany ceiling, while the Oak Bar at its back features panels of heavy wood. The exceedingly expensive prices seem not to deter the many who come to experience the flavor of this elegant New York setting. It's all very much worth a peek both inside and outside the building. Subway: N, R to Fifth Ave.

Plaza Hotel Palm Court 768 Fifth Ave. at Central Park S (212) 546-5350

Afternoon tea becomes a celebratory event at New York's legendary hotel's Palm Court, where the tea service includes finger sandwiches, cream cakes, and hot buttered scones. Subway: N, R to Fifth Ave. Open Mon–Sat 3:45 p.m.–6:00 p.m., Sun 4 p.m.–6 p.m. Major credit cards.

Plymouth Church of the Pilgrims Orange St. btw Henry and Hicks Sts., Brooklyn Heights, Brooklyn (718) 624-4743 www.plymouth church.org

This simple red brick building was built in 1850 and has stained-glass windows designed by Tiffany. Its fame stems from being the pulpit for Henry Ward Beecher's sermons against slavery and as a way station and refuge on the Underground Railroad for escaping slaves. Subway: A, C to High St.

Plymouth Theatre 236 W 45th St. btw Broadway and Eighth Ave. (212) 239-6200

One of Broadway's venerable performance houses, the Plymouth was built to seat 1,000 in 1917 and has been the showcase for innumerable American and British productions. Subway: A, C, E to 42nd St.-Port Authority; N, R, S, 1, 2, 3, 7, 9 to Times Square-42nd St.

Pó 31 Cornelia St. btw Bleecker and W 4th Sts. (212) 645-2189

A small, exceedingly popular Village restaurant that offers some of the city's heartiest, tastiest, and most memorable Italian fare at moderate prices where reserving well in advance is essential. Subway: A, B, C, D, E, F, Q to W 4th St. Open Tues for dinner, Wed–Sun for lunch and dinner. American Express only.

Poe Cottage *see* Edgar Allan Poe Cottage.

Poetry Calendar 611 Broadway, Suite 905, NY 10012 (212) 260-7097

A monthly subscription publication, also distributed free at a number of bookstores, that provides thorough details of upcoming literary and prose reading events. Other sources of comparable information can be found in the *New Yorker, Time Out New York,* and the *Village Voice.*

Poetry Project *see* St. Mark's Poetry Project.

Poetry Readings *see* Book and Poetry Readings.

Poetry Society of America 15 Gramercy Park S (equivalent to 20th St.) btw Park Ave. S and Irving Pl., NY 10003 (212) 254-9628 www. poetrysociety.org

The society sponsors free and paid programs at different venues around the city, including bookstores, museums, theatres, and concert halls where poets read from their own works or in sessions that feature the reading of selections from celebrated poets of the past. A calendar of events is available upon request from the society. Subway: 6 to 23rd St.

Poets' House 72 Spring St. btw Broadway and Lafayette Sts. (212) 431-7920 www.poetshouse.org

A comfortable, quiet, free library and reading room with a comprehensive collection of poetry books and current issues of many small poetry and literary magazines. Information is also available about the program of live poetry readings. Subway: C, E, 6 to Spring St.

Polanka 22 Warren St. near Church St. (212) 385-9987

This small, lower Manhattan spot serves delicious Polish cooking, provides attentive service, shows original art on its walls, features different types of music on different nights, and most significantly, its prices are inexpensive. Subway: A, C, E to Chambers St. Lunch and dinner Mon–Sat. Major credit cards.

Police Headquarters *see* New York City Police Headquarters Buildings.

Police Museum 25 Broadway (212) 301-4440 www.nycpolice museum.org

This museum houses the largest collection of law enforcement memorabilia imaginable. There are all sorts of firearms, uniforms, New York police badges going back to 1845, counterfeit money, fingerprint equipment, photos of criminals, and much more. The museum was scheduled to move early in 2002 to its new location at 100 Old Slip between South Street Seaport and Battery Park with substantially increased exhibition space in a building that was headquarters of the department's first precinct from 1909 to 1973. Subway: 4, 5 to Bowling Green. Tues–Sat 10 a.m.–6 p.m. Admission free.

Polish in New York *see* Greenpoint.

Polish Restaurants *see* Polanka, Primorski, Teresa's, Veselka. *See also* Russian Restaurants.

El Pollo 1746 First Ave. btw 90th and 91st Sts. (212) 966-7810

The portions are huge, and the roasted chicken and other menu choices are deliciously prepared while the prices are very cheap, which explains why this spot is such a great favorite. Subway: 4, 5, 6 to 86th St. Lunch and dinner daily. Major credit cards.

Pomander Walk

Modeled after the stage set of a Broadway theatrical hit of 1911, this tiny, quaintly picturesque street of Tudor townhouses between Broadway and West End Ave. on 94th St., with turn-of-the-century lampposts and flowered walks, looks precisely like the London mews from which it takes its name. Subway: 1, 2, 3, 9 to 96th St.

Pongsri Thai 244 W 48th St. btw Broadway and Eighth Ave. (212) 582-3392

Well-prepared, succulent dishes attract diners to this theatre district spot, which offers an extensive selection of spicy or less-so choices, pleasing service, and moderate prices. A second location is 311 Second Ave. at 18th St. (212) 477-4100. Subway: (W 48th St.) 1, 9, C, E to 50th St.; (Second Ave.) L, N, R, 4, 5, 6 to 14th St.-Union Square; L to Third Ave. Lunch and dinner daily. Major credit cards.

Pool see Amsterdam Billiard Club, Billiard Club, Chelsea Billiards, Corner Billiards, East Side Billiard Club.

Popover Café 551 Amsterdam Ave. btw 86th and 87th Sts. (212) 595-8555

Dining at this comfortable, kid-friendly restaurant with its stuffed teddy bears is a pleasant experience, and the excellent popovers make a splendid accompaniment to the homemade soups and other American-style dishes offered at this spacious and inviting mid-priced favorite. Subway: 1, 9 to 86th St. Breakfast, lunch, and dinner daily. Major credit cards.

Popular Music see The Apollo Theater, Beacon Theatre, Carnegie Hall, Radio City Music Hall, Shea Stadium, Town Hall.

Port Authority Bus Terminal

Considerably spruced up in recent years, this hub of the northeast bus network, between 40th and 42nd Sts. and Eight and Ninth Aves., is an efficiently operated, huge bus station with more than 6,000 coaches arriving and departing daily. At the rear of the terminal's second floor is Leisure Time Bowling (212) 268-6909, one of the few bowling alleys to be found in Manhattan. Subway: A, C, E to 42nd St.-Port Authority.

Portland Square Hotel 132 W 47th St. btw Sixth and Seventh Aves. (212) 382-0600 or (800) 388-8988, fax (212) 382-0684 www.port landsquarehotel.com

This budget hotel, with some of the lowest rates in town, lies smack in the heart of the Broadway theatre district. Heavy bookings, particularly by foreign visitors and cost-conscious Americans, make early advance reservations a must. Subway: N, R to 49th St.; B, D, F, Q to 47th–50th Sts.-Rockefeller Center.

Poseidon Bakery 629 Ninth Ave. btw 44th and 45th Sts. (212) 757-6173

This timeless Greek pastry shop was first opened in the neighborhood in the early 1920s and is the only bakery where the phyllo dough is still made by hand, without additives. All the delicious specialties like baklava, cheese pie, and spinach pie are available here at very inexpensive prices. Subway: A, C, E to 42nd St.-Port Authority. Tues–Sat 9 a.m.–7 p.m. No credit cards.

Post Office *see* General Post Office.

Present Company Theatorium 196-198 Stanton St. btw Attorney and Ridge Sts. (212) 420-8877 www.presentcompany.org

This is one of the biggest and most comfortable downtown performance venues. It also runs the New York International Fringe Festival, a nonstop orgy of events from Shakespeare parody to weird nude clowns running loose, held every August at many sites in the city. Subway: F, J, M, Z to Delancey St.-Essex St.

Presidents Day Sales

During the February days around Lincoln and Washington's birth dates, like many retail establishments across the country, many department and specialty stores in New York feature mammoth sales events.

Primary Stages 354 W 45th St. btw Eighth and Ninth Aves. (212) 333-4052

This nonprofit theatre showcases work by emerging American playwrights. Subway: A, C, E to 42nd St.-Port Authority.

Primorski Restaurant 282 Brighton Beach Ave. btw 2nd and 3rd Sts., Brighton Beach, Brooklyn (718) 891-3111

Tasty authentic Russian dishes make this a very popular restaurant, where the extensive menu includes the dishes one could expect, from borscht to stuffed cabbage, at inexpensive prices with live music until late at night. Subway: D, Q to Brighton Beach. Open daily 11 a.m.–2 a.m. No credit cards.

Printing House Racquet and Fitness Club 421 Hudson St. btw Leroy and Clarkson Sts. (212) 243-7600

With its courts open at any time to non-members, this is a prime penthouse facility with sweeping views for racquetball aficionados. Subway: 1, 9 to Houston St. Open Mon–Fri 6 a.m.–11 p.m., Sat–Sun 8 a.m.–8 p.m. Admission charge.

Prison Ship Martyrs Monument *see* Fort Greene Park.

Produce *see* Antique Flea and Farmers Market, Balducci's, Chelsea Market, Essex Street Market, Gourmet Garage, Greenmarkets, Guss's Pickles, La Marqueta, La Piccola Cucina, Sahadi Importing Company.

Professional Wrestling *see* Wrestling.

The Promenade
This half-mile-long waterfront walkway in Brooklyn Heights runs from Remsen St. at the south to Orange St. at the north end. Directly above the Brooklyn-Queens Expressway traffic, this popular esplanade affords surprising views of downtown Manhattan, the colorful Staten Island ferry making its regular run, the Statue of Liberty, and the Brooklyn Bridge. It's hard to imagine a better situated place for sitting on a bench and taking in one of New York's most stunning vistas. Subway: 2, 3 to Clark St.; M, N, R to Court St.; A, C to High St.

Promenade Art Show (718) 625-0080
During October each year the historic Brooklyn Heights broadwalk features this showing in a place where the views of downtown Manhattan are strong competition for the works on display. Subway: 2, 3 to Clark St.; M, N, R to Court St.; A, C to High St.

Promenade Theatre 2162 Broadway at 76th St. (212) 580-1313
Located well north of the midtown Broadway theatre district, this venue stages productions by established as well as emergent playwrights. Subway: 1, 9 to 79th St.

Prospect Park Brooklyn (718) 965-8999 www.prospectpark.org
The same designers who first conceived Central Park, Olmstead and Vaux, were responsible for this 526-acre pastoral setting; its long meadow of lawn is the longest stretch of green space in New York. The park includes a number of attractions particularly suited to kids. A free trolley bus (718) 965-8967 on weekends carries passengers around to the favorite spots. At the boathouse there are information and maps on park activities (718) 855-7882. Calling (718) 965-8999 yields a programmed detailing of multiple aspects of park activities. Subway: 2, 3 to Grand Army Plaza; D to Seventh Ave.

Prospect Park Lefferts Homestead Children's Museum Park entrance at Flatbush Ave. and Empire Blvd., Brooklyn (718) 789-2322

This Dutch colonial farmhouse was constructed around 1780 and was moved to its park location in 1918. The exhibits and displays feature life in the early nineteenth century, and there are several rooms where children can play with period reproduction furniture. The 2-story, eight-room building also includes two rooms furnished with antiques used by the family that owned it at the time it was first built. Subway; D, Q to Prospect Park. Open Thurs–Sun, hours vary. Admission free.

Prospect Park Litchfield Villa Prospect Park W and 3rd St., Brooklyn

Located on the western side of the park, this mansion was constructed in 1857 and designed by a leading architect of the period. Since 1883 it has been the site of the park's administration offices, and visitors may view the impressive interior of the domed rotunda. Subway: F to Seventh Ave.

Prospect Park Wildlife Center 450 Flatbush Ave. at Prospect Park, Brooklyn (718) 399-7339

This zoo combines indoor and outdoor components and is home to a number of unusual and endangered species. The setting in Prospect Park showcases the animals in a fairly realistic wildlife habitat. Subway: D to Prospect Park. Open daily March–November, hours vary. Modest admission charge.

Prospect Park Wollman Rink *see* Wollman Memorial Rink in Prospect Park.

Provence 38 MacDougal St. btw Houston and Prince Sts. (212) 475-7500

Featuring a menu of excellent Provençal dishes, this moderately expensive SoHo spot, with a garden in back for mild weather dining, offers an ambiance of the south of France that transcends its fine cooking. Subway: C, E to Spring St.; N, R to Prince St. Lunch and dinner daily. Major credit cards.

Public Lectures *see* Brecht Forum, Brooklyn Public Library, New School University, 92nd Street Y, New York Public Library Celeste Bartos Forum, New York Society of Ethical Cultures, Newseum/NY, Queens Historical Society in Kingsland Homestead, Shady Ground, Staten Island Institute of Arts and Sciences, Studio Museum in Harlem. *See also* Book and Poetry Readings.

Public Theatre *see* Joseph L. Papp Public Theatre.

Public Toilets *see* Rest Rooms.

Publications *see* Newspapers and Magazines.

Puck Building 295 Lafayette St. at Houston St. (212) 274-8900
This 1886 construction housed the satirical magazine *Puck,* then something of an American version of *Punch.* Today the first floor is the staging area for many stylish galas and art shows, while the rest has become apartments and offices. A statue of the grinning Puck still remains on the northeast corner of this unusual red brick building. Subway: B, D, F, Q to Broadway-Lafayette St.

Puerto Rican Day Parade (718) 401-0404
This big celebration takes place on the first Sunday in June, when dozens of rhythmic bands, colorful floats, and festively attired celebrants pass in an endless rousing procession from 44th to 86th Sts. along Fifth Ave. to the delight of huge crowds along the way.

Puerto Ricans in New York *see* El Barrio.

Pulaski Day Parade (212) 374-5176
On the Sunday afternoon closest to October 5 each year, Fifth Ave. between 31st and 52nd Sts. is the place where General Pulaski, a hero of the American Revolutionary War, receives tribute from some forty or fifty floats and as many different marching bands. Decked out in festive costumes, they parade by to the delight of New York's Polish community and the hundreds of others who line the streets along the route.

Pulse Theatre *see* Kramer's Reality Tour.

Puppet Playhouse 555 E 90th St. at York Ave., inside Asphalt Green (212) 369-8890
Weekend marionette performances are staged from October to May each year, lasting a little under an hour and appealing most to children from 3 to 6 or so. Subway: 4, 5, 6 to 86th St., then Bus M86 east to East End and 90th St.

Puppet Theatres *see* Los Kabayitos Puppet Theatre, Puppet Playhouse, Puppetworks.

Puppetworks 338 Sixth Ave. at 49th St., Brooklyn (718) 965-3391
www.puppetworks.org

This company performs attractively staged productions of beloved children's stories like Cinderella. Each season two different plays are shown on alternate weeks with classical musical accompaniments to the antics of the marionettes. Subway: F to Seventh Ave.; N, R to 9th St. Performances on Sat and Sun. Admission charge.

Quad Cinema 34 W 13th St. btw Fifth and Sixth Aves. (212) 255-8800 www.quadcinema.com

With only four small screens, this movie house offers selections that are not often seen elsewhere ranging from first-run art and foreign movies to the work of independent producers and documentaries. Subway: F to 14th St.; L, N, R, 4, 5, 6 to 14th St.-Union Square.

Queens

Although home to New York's two major airports, JFK and LaGuardia, this big sprawling borough, the site of a rich variety of attractions and dozens of colorful ethnic enclaves, is perhaps the most unappreciated and least visited by outsiders. Many of its resources are little more than a subway ride away from mid-Manhattan. The Queens Tourism Council is trying to change this by offering a 24-hour calendar of cultural events at (718) 291-ARTS or (800) 454-1329, and by distributing the free *Discover Queens,* an informative brochure with details of the borough's history, neighborhoods, and tourist attractions.

Queens Borough Public Library Main Branch 89-11 Merrick Blvd. btw 89th and 90th Sts., Queens (718) 990-0767 or (718) 990-0768 www.queenslibrary.org

This is the central library of the Queens system and in addition to its collections offers a small art gallery and a wide range of community-oriented programs. Subway: E, J, Z to Sutphin Blvd.-Archer Ave. Open Mon–Sat, hours vary. Admission free.

Queens Botanical Garden 43-50 Main St., Flushing, Queens (718) 886-3800 www.queensbotanical.org

This 39-acre site in the middle of Queens offers an herb garden, a 5,000-bush rose garden, and a number of theme gardens, like the Victorian-style wedding garden. Subway: 7 to Flushing-Main St. Open Tues–Sun, hours vary by season. Admission free.

Queens College *see* Colden Center for the Performing Arts at Queens College.

Queens County Farm Museum 73-50 Little Neck Pkwy., Floral Park, Queens (718) 347-3276 www.queensfarm.org

This is a true working farm spread out on 47 acres at the border of Nassau County, with sheep, cows, geese, ducks, and other animals as well as a big orchard. There's also a pretty farmhouse with wooden beam ceilings. Many special events are scheduled throughout the year, and weekend hayrides delight kids of all ages. Subway: E, F to Kew Gardens-Union Turnpike, then Bus Q46 to Littleneck Pkwy. Open Mon–Fri 9 a.m.–5 p.m., Sat–Sun 10 a.m.–5 p.m. Admission free except for special events and $2 hayride.

Queens Ethnic Folk Festival Czech Hall, 29-19 Twenty-Fourth Ave., Queens (718) 274-4925

Each year around the second week in September this celebration of ethnic newcomers features nine or ten dance groups from different regions of the world performing in native costume during the day. The party moves outdoors for folk dancing and ethnic eating, with everyone participating until midnight. Subway: N to Astoria Blvd.-Hoyt Ave.

Queens Historical Society in Kingsland Homestead 143-35 Thirty-Seventh Ave., Flushing, Queens (718) 939-0647 www.preserve.org/queens/kingsland.htm

The society is a museum and research library that collects and preserves Queens history. It also plans, researches, and mounts history-related exhibitions. It conducts house tours, slide and lecture presentations, and walking tours. It is located in the 1774 historic landmark Kingsland Homestead. Subway: 7 to Flushing-Main St. Open Mon–Fri 9:30 a.m.–5 p.m. Tours offered Tues, Thurs, and Sat afternoons.

Queens Museum of Art New York City Building, Flushing Meadows-Corona Park, Queens (718) 592-4700 www.queensmuse.org

This was the setting for the 1964 World's Fair, but its chief claim to fame beyond its temporary art exhibits and permanent collection is the Panorama of the City of New York, a more-than-9,000-square-foot model of all the buildings, bridges, highways, and landmarks, featuring some 900,000 structures, with everything built on a scale of 1 inch per 100 feet.

Night falls every few minutes, and lights illuminate the miniature city in all its striking splendor. Subway: 7 to Willets Pt.-Shea Stadium. Wed–Fri 10 a.m.–5 p.m., Sun 2 p.m.–5 p.m. Modest admission charge.

Queens Theatre in the Park Flushing Meadows-Corona Park, Queens (718) 760-0664 www.queenstheatre.org

Located in the former New York State Pavilion of the 1964 World's Fair, this theatre presents drama, comedy, dance, children's entertainment, a film series at its Main Stage Theatre, and its small cabaret and Studio Theatre. Subway: 7 to Willets Pt.-Shea Stadium.

Queens Wildlife Center 53-51 111th St., Flushing Meadows-Corona Park, Queens (718) 271-1500 www.wcs.org/zoos/wildlifecenters/queens

This zoo was renovated in 1992 and features American wildlife, including mountain lions, bison, bobcats, coyotes, and elk in something resembling their natural habitat. Few barriers separate spectators from the animals. Subway: 7 to 111th St. Open Mon–Fri 10 a.m.–5 p.m., Sat–Sun 10 a.m.–5:30 p.m., hours vary slightly in summer. Modest admission charge.

Queensboro Bridge

This cantilevered structure from Manhattan to Queens was constructed in 1909 and has also been popularly termed the 59th Street Bridge. The bridge was the first major one in New York City to depart from the suspension form, and the third of eight bridges built across the East River. It has a total length of 7,450 feet and a height above water of 135 feet.

Quikbook 381 Park Ave. S, NY 10016 (212) 779-ROOM or (800) 789-9887, fax (212) 779-6120 www.quikbook.com

This reliable service offers reduced hotel rates at moderate to expensive New York hotels. It operates 9 a.m.–7 p.m. Mon–Fri.

Quintessential New York (212) 501-0827

Specialized tours feature behind-the-scenes looks at difficult-to-penetrate private worlds. They might include visits to such places as an artist's SoHo studio or an artisan's workshop.

R

RCA Building *see* Rockefeller Center.

Racquetball *see* Manhattan Plaza Racquet Club, Printing House Racquet and Fitness Club.

Radical Walking Tours (718) 492-0069

More than a dozen subjects are treated in these 2- to 3-hour walking tours to different sections of the city. Each tour treats its theme from a left-wing and underground perspective. Topics and neighborhoods such as Harlem and its political, entertainment, and cultural history; Greenwich Village, with its riots, revolutionaries, art, and theatre past; and the Lower East Side and its radical movements, are part of the repertoire.

Radio City Music Hall 1260 Sixth Ave. at 50th St. (212) 247-4777 www.radiocity.com

This Art Deco national landmark treasure created by Roxy, a 1930s impresario, with its more than 6,000 seats, 144-foot stage, palatial staircase, giant chandeliers, and mighty organ, stages rock concerts, award ceremonies, major celebrities, and special events. Its two-month-long Christmas extravaganza showcases the fabled Rockettes chorus line. Subway: B, D, F, Q to 47th-50th Sts.-Rockefeller Center.

Radio City Music Hall Christmas Spectacular *see* Christmas Spectacular at Radio City Music Hall.

Radio City Stage Door Tour (212) 247-4777

This 1-hour walking tour includes the Art Deco interior, behind-the-scenes secrets of the giant stage, and a chance to meet one of the celebrated Rockettes. Subway: B, D, F, Q to 47th-50th Sts.-Rockefeller Center. Mon–Sat 10 a.m.–5 p.m., Sun 11 a.m.–5 p.m. Tours begin about every half hour. Admission charge.

Radio Stations
FM Radio Stations

88.3 (WBGO) Jazz (National Public Radio)

89.9 (WKCR) Columbia University, fine jazz

90.7 (WFUV) Contemporary folk/Celtic/international (National Public Radio)

91.5 (WNYE) Educational/community/children

92.3 (WXRK) "K Rock" Classic rock/Howard Stern

92.7 (WLIR) "Modern" rock (alternative/80s new wave)

93.1 (WPAT) Spanish

93.9 (WNYC) Classical (National Public Radio)

95.5 (WPLJ) Top 40

96.3 (WQXR) Classical

97.1 (WBLS) "Hot 97" Hip-hop, R&B

97.5 (WALK) Adult contemporary

97.9 (WSKQ) Spanish

98.7 (WRKS) "Kiss" Urban contemporary

99.5 (WBAI) Varied/ethnic

99.9 (WEZN) Adult contemporary

100.3 (WHTZ) "Z100" Top 40

101.1 (WCBS) Oldies

101.9 (WQCD) Smooth jazz

102.7 (WNEW) Rock

103.5 (WKTU) Pop/disco

104.3 (WAXQ) Classic rock

105.1 (WMXV) Adult contemporary

105.9 (WNWK) Multi-ethnic

106.7 (WLTW) Light rock

107.5 (WBLS) Urban contemporary

AM Radio Stations

570 (WMCA) Christian/talk

620 (WJWR) Sports

660 (WFAN) Sports/Imus in the Morning

710 (WWOR) News/talk

770 (WABC) Talk/news/Rush Limbaugh

820 (WNYC) News/talk (National Public Radio)

880 (WCBS) News

930 (WPAT) Contemporary

970 (WWDJ) Christian music

1010 (WINS) News around the clock

1050 (WEVD) News/talk

1130 (WBBR) News

1190 (WLIB) Afro-Caribbean news/talk

1280 (WADO) Spanish

1380 (WKDM) Multi-ethnic

1560 (WQEW) Children's programming

1600 (WWRL) Gospel/soul/talk

Rainbow Grill 30 Rockefeller Center btw 49th and 50th Sts. (212) 632-5100

The old Promenade Bar 65 floors up is now gone and with it much of the elegance and romance of this famous, glamorous ambiance. Tables are

lined up in double rows, and only window-seat diners enjoy the spectacular view. The bar has shrunken dramatically. The food is simple Italian fare,
and the prices are stratospheric. There's still dining and dancing on Friday
and Saturday nights, but now the place is often booked for private functions,
so reservations ahead are essential, as are jacket and tie. Subway: B, D, F,
Q to 47th-50th Sts.-Rockefeller Center. Open nightly 5:30 p.m.–midnight.
Major credit cards.

The Ramble in Central Park *see* Central Park Ramble.

Randall's Island

Originally a separate island, Randall's Island is now joined to Ward's
Island by a landfill, and the Triborough Bridge crosses overhead. Downing
Stadium located here was undergoing renovations in 2001 with usual
events normally scheduled unable to take place.

Randolph Square

Named for A. Philip Randolph, the organizer of the Brotherhood of
Sleeping Car Porters and the moving spirit behind the Roosevelt administration's creation of the Fair Employment Practice Commission, which led
to Blacks gaining World War II defense work, this square can be found at
the intersection of Adam Clayton Powell Blvd., St. Nicholas Ave., and
117th St. Subway: 2, 3, B, C to 116th St.

Rao's 455 E 114th St. btw First and Pleasant Aves. (212) 722-6709

This homey, low-key, ten-table family restaurant has been around a
very long time and serves excellent southern Italian food at inexpensive
prices. Reservations need to be made well in advance, and getting to this
Spanish Harlem place is best negotiated by taxi. Subway: 6 to 116th St.
Dinner daily. No credit cards.

Raoul's 180 Prince St. btw Sullivan and Thompson Sts. (212) 966-
3518

This seemingly Parisian transplanted bistro is a popular and trendy
SoHo dinner spot, with the flavor of a neighborhood hangout from the
bar scene to the dimly lit romantic dining room. It offers fairly expensive,
excellent French specialty dishes and attentive service; advance reservations
are a good idea. Subway: C, E to Spring St. Dinner daily. Major credit
cards.

Rasputin 2670 Coney Island Ave., Brighton Beach, Brooklyn (718)
332-8333

This is a favorite spot in Brooklyn's own Russian enclave. The mostly
Eastern European clientele comes for dancing, dining, and drinking, with

bountiful meals and lots of vodka. A live, lavish floor show on weekend nights heightens the level of festivities. Subway: F to Ave. X; D to Neck Rd. Open Mon–Thurs 11 a.m.–9 p.m., Fri–Sat 11 a.m.–3 a.m. Major credit cards.

Ratner's Dairy Restaurant and Bakery 138 Delancey St. btw Norfolk and Suffolk Sts. (212) 677-5588

Since 1905 this has been the favorite Lower East Side place for non-meat Jewish dishes. It is a huge, busy, colorful place serving authentic foods like blintzes, gefilte fish, smoked salmon, whitefish, and lots more. Breads and pastries are sold to go. The restaurant is also home to the Lansky Lounge (212) 677-9489, named for a Jewish mobster celebrity. This club, accessible through the restaurant, is a night spot located upstairs, where there was once a famous speakeasy. It can also be entered through 104 Norfolk St. between Rivington and Delancey Sts. Subway: F, J, M, Z to Delancey St.-Essex St. Restaurant and bakery open Sun–Thurs 8 a.m.–7 p.m.; Fri 8 a.m.–4 p.m. Lansky Lounge open daily 6 p.m.–2 a.m. Major credit cards.

Red Hook

This Brooklyn neighborhood near the waterfront has been reduced to an isolated community left behind by time. Many of the remaining residents live in what's left of the cheap housing or the Red Hook housing projects. While there are renewal plans under discussion, the district is not recommended as a location for tourists to explore.

Le Refuge 166 E 82nd St. btw Third and Lexington Aves. (212) 861-4505

This charming French country restaurant is an altogether unpretentious, quiet, and intimate place with a garden open in mild weather where the food is excellent, the service professional, and the dining is highly pleasurable and moderately expensive. Subway: 4, 5, 6 to 86th St. Lunch and dinner daily, brunch Sat and Sun. Major credit cards.

Le Régence Hôtel Plaza Athénée, 37 E 64th St. btw Park and Madison Aves. (212) 606-4647

Haute cuisine is served with style in this elegant and expensive French restaurant, where dining is a memorable experience. Subway: N, R to Fifth Ave. Lunch and dinner daily. Major credit cards.

Reggae Music *see* Rock, Alternative, and Ethnic Music.

Regis and Kelly (212) 456-3537

For tickets to this popular family show, there's a wait of more than a year. To request up to four tickets, send a postcard with name, address, and phone number to Live Tickets, P.O. Box 23077 Ansonia Station, New York, NY 10023. For standby tickets the line forms early in the morning at ABC Studios, 7 Lincoln Square (Columbus Ave. and W 67th St.). One standby ticket per person is distributed based on first-come, first-served arrivals, but no one under 10 is admitted.

Remi 145 W 53rd St. btw Sixth and Seventh Aves. (212) 581-4242

Northern Italian food is the specialty at this lively, noisy, and strikingly attractive spot with a skylighted atrium garden and a 120-foot mural of Venice. Dishes are beautifully and attentively presented and go well beyond the typical fare at this moderately expensive dining spot, where reservations are advisable. Subway: B, D, E to Seventh Ave. Lunch and dinner daily. Major credit cards.

Repertorio Español Gramercy Arts Theatre, 138 E 27th St. btw Third and Lexington Aves. (212) 889-2850

Spanish productions, frequently featuring the tempestuous classic performer Pilar Rioja, are staged by this repertory company. Subway: 6 to 28th St.

Rest Rooms

Public facilities in New York can be difficult to find. Best bets are department stores, hotels, museums, public libraries, and bookstores.

Restaurant Week www.restaurantweek.com

Since it started in 1992, many of the city's most celebrated restaurants have been offering a prix fixe lunch during one week in late June. Each year the price goes up one cent, so in 2002 the price is $20.02. Participating restaurants vary each year but include some of the finest, providing an inexpensive way to taste the best of New York's dining spots. Full page *New York Times* ads identify the participating restaurants, but to learn early call the New York Convention and Visitor's Bureau (212) 484-1222. A few of the restaurants extend the offer until Labor Day, and there's been a move of late to offer the same inducement in late January or early February.

Restaurants *see* Afghan Restaurants, American Restaurants, Asian Restaurants, Barbecue and Ribs Restaurants, Brazilian Restaurants, Cafés, Cajun Restaurants, Caribbean Restaurants, Chinese Restaurants, Coffee and Cakes, Contemporary Restaurants, Continental Restaurants, Delicatessens, Diners, Ethiopian Restaurants, French Restaurants, German Restaurants, Greek Restaurants, Hamburgers, Indian Restaurants, Italian Restaurants, Japanese Restaurants, Jewish Restaurants, Korean Restaurants, Kosher Restaurants, Latin American Restaurants, Mexican Restaurants, Middle Eastern and Mediterranean Restaurants, Peruvian Restaurants, Pizzerias, Polish Restaurants, Romanian Restaurants, Russian Restaurants, Seafood and Fish Restaurants, Soul Food Restaurants, Southern Restaurants, Southwestern Restaurants, Spanish Restaurants, Steak Restaurants, Tea Rooms, Thai Restaurants, Turkish Restaurants, Vegetarian Restaurants, Vietnamese Restaurants.

Ribs *see* Barbecue and Ribs Restaurants.

Richard Rodgers Theatre 220 W 46th St. btw Broadway and Eighth Ave. (212) 221-1211

This is one of Broadway's classic houses, where many shows have held the stage for popular runs, including *Guys and Dolls,* beginning in 1950 for 1,194 performances. Subway: 1, 9, C, E to 50th St.

Richmond *see* Staten Island.

Richmond County Fair (718) 351-1611

On the grounds of Historic Richmond Town in Staten Island, the city's only authentic county fair takes place annually on the first weekend in September. Subway: 1, 9 to South Ferry; N, R to Whitehall St., then ferry to Staten Island. From Staten Island St. George Ferry Terminal, take Bus S74 to Historic Richmond Town.

Richmond Town *see* Historic Richmond Town.

Ricki Lake Show (212) 352-3322

For tickets send postcards to Ricki Lake, 226 W 26th St., NY 10001, at least a month in advance. Standby tickets are available beginning two hours before taping (Mon–Thurs 3 p.m. and 5 p.m., Fri noon and 3 p.m.). Only those 18 or older with photo identification are admitted. Subway: 1, 9 to 28th St.

Riis Park *see* Jacob Riis Park.

Riker's Island

This is the island in the East River where the city maintains a number of penal institutions, of which the biggest and best known is the Men's House of Detention where some 5,000 are incarcerated.

Ringling Brothers and Barnum & Bailey Circus (212) 465-6741 www.ringling.com

Every spring in late March or early April the circus comes to Manhattan for its annual Madison Square Garden performances. Late the night before, or very early on the day the show is to begin, the performing animals, including the bears and elephants, walk from the train through the streets to the Garden in colorful parade. Subway: 1, 2, 3, 9, A, C, E to 34th St.-Penn Station.

River Café 1 Water St. at the East River, Brooklyn Heights (718) 522-5200

Romantic views of Manhattan are unsurpassed at this spectacularly situated restaurant tucked under the Brooklyn Bridge. The excellent American cuisine, featuring steak and seafood dishes and unusually imaginative dessert concoctions, is attractively prepared, fresh, and delicious at this glamorous dining spot. Naturally, prices are steep, reservations well ahead are essential, and jackets are required. Subway: A, C to High St.; 2, 3 to Clark St. Lunch and dinner daily. Major credit cards.

River Flicks at Chelsea Piers Pier 62 at W 23rd St. on the Hudson River (212) 336-6600

During summer months, there are free Wednesday night showings of movies in which water is a distinguishing feature, e.g., *Jaws*. Subway: C, E to 23rd St., then Bus M23 east to Twelfth Ave.

River to River Downtown Walking Tour (212) 321-2823

A New York native and retired teacher leads 2-hour walking tours for individuals and groups around lower Manhattan, flavoring the details of the views with insights into history and legend.

Riverbank State Park (212) 694-3600

Situated on the Hudson River between 137th and 145th Sts., this is one of the best equipped and most popular parks in the city, offering year-round ice skating, indoor and outdoor pools, tennis courts, running tracks, roller skating rinks, basketball and handball courts, baseball diamonds, playgrounds, bike paths, a cultural center, and picnic grounds. Concerts take place in the park's amphitheatre in summer. Subway: 1, 9 to 145th St.

Riverdale

Stretching from the eastern edge of Van Cortlandt Park to the Hudson River, this hilly and remote section of the Bronx, home to winding roads, beautiful foliage, and residential mansions, is one of the most desirable and little known corners of the city. It is the region in which Wave Hill and Fonthill Castle are to be found. To explore this area without an automobile is very difficult.

Riverside Church 490 Riverside Dr. btw 120th and 122nd Sts. (212) 870-6700 www.theriversidechurchny.org

Inspired by the Chartres cathedral and with many elaborately decorative stone carvings on its exterior, this imposing 22-story interdenominational, interracial, and international church can seat 2,500, and its tower holds a 74-bell carillon, the world's largest. From the observation deck reached by elevator, the views of the Hudson River and upper Manhattan are awe-inspiring. In addition to its Sunday services, there is an active political and community program as well as music, theatre, and dance performances. Subway: 1, 9 to 116th St.-Columbia University. Open Mon–Sat 9 a.m.–5 p.m., Sun noon–4 p.m. following 10:45 a.m. services. Tower visit Tues–Sat 11 a.m.–4 p.m., Sun noon–6 p.m. Modest charge for tower visit.

Riverside Drive

Considered one of the city's most handsome residential streets, this exclusive, wide, shaded avenue is tree-lined with a blend of palatial townhouses, residential mansions, and newer apartment buildings. Along its route between about 72nd and 106th Sts. a number of historic landmarked districts are to be found in the 70s, 80s, and lower 100s. Subway: (south end) 1, 2, 3, 9 to 72nd St.; (north end) 1, 9 to 103rd St.

Riverside Park

Between Riverside Dr. and the Hudson River, this long, narrow, sloping, grassy area with paths for walking, jogging, and bicycling runs from 72nd to 159th Sts. and has been designated one of the city's handful of scenic landmarks. The statue of Eleanor Roosevelt rising at the entrance at 72nd St., the 79th Street Boat Basin at the water's edge, the Civil War Soldiers' and Sailors' Monument with 96-foot-high marble columns at 89th St., and Grant's Tomb at 122nd St. are much-frequented sites along the way.

Riverside Towers Hotel 80 Riverside Dr. at 80th St., NY 10024 (212) 877-5200 or (800) 724-3136, fax (212) 873-1400

With a choice West Side location opposite beautiful parklands and with views of the Hudson River, this budget-priced hotel offers simple, furnished, basic sleeping accommodations with small kitchenettes in each room. Reserve well in advance. Subway: 1, 9 to 79th St.

Riverview Terrace

This unusual private street near Sutton Place at 58th St. boasts the Secretary General of the United Nation's official residence at the south end of Sutton Terrace Square. Subway: 4, 5, 6 to 59th St., then Bus M57 east on 57th St.

Rizzoli 31 W 57th St. btw Fifth and Sixth Aves. (212) 759-2424

This elegant bookstore offers browsers a private clublike ambiance in which to examine new titles with strong emphasis on art, architecture, photography, music and dance, foreign language, and coffee-table books. Two more locations are in SoHo at 454 W Broadway between Houston and Prince Sts. (212) 674-1616 and at 3 Vesey St. at the World Financial Center (212) 385-1400. Subway: (57th St.) N, R to 57th St.; (W Broadway) N, R to Prince St.; (World Financial Center) 1, 9 to Cortlandt St. Open daily, hours vary. Major credit cards.

Robert F. Wagner, Jr. Park btw Battery Pl. and the Hudson River

Paths, lawns, and attractively landscaped gardens lead down to the river with many benches available and two brick deck-topped structures from which to take in the panoramic views of the New York harbor and the Statue of Liberty. Subway: (north side) 1, 9 to Rector St.; (south side) 1, 9 to South Ferry.

Rock, Alternative, and Ethnic Music *see* Arlene Grocery, Baktun, Bitter End, The Bottom Line, Bowery Ballroom, Brownie's, CBGB & OMFUG, Chicago B.L.U.E.S., Hammerstein Ballroom at the Manhattan Center, Irving Plaza, Knitting Factory, The Living Room, Lola, Mercury Lounge, Nell's, Ohm, S.O.B.'s, Town Hall, Tunnel, Village Underground, Webster Hall.

The Rockaways

A public open space on the Atlantic along the southernmost strip of Queens, this, the largest municipal beach in the United States, extends more than 7 miles from Beach 1st St. in Far Rockaway to Beach 149th St. The boardwalk runs from Beach 3rd St. all the way to Beach 126th St. This is the only place in New York where it's possible to surf. Subway: (eastern side) A to Far Rockaway-Mott Ave.; (western side) A, S to Rockaway Park-Beach 116th St.

Rockefeller Center www.rockefellercenter.com

Nothing speaks more eloquently for Manhattan than this massive nineteen-building complex occupying New York's choicest real estate between 48th and 51st Sts. and Fifth and Sixth Aves. It's the world capital of the communications industry, major publishing firms, attractively used public spaces, plazas and concourses, restaurants, shops, boutiques, and interconnecting tunnel passageways. It bridges between business- and Art-Deco-designed architectural treasures. It's home to Radio City Music Hall, the ice skating rink, NBC Studios, the *Today Show*'s studios, and the sparkling and enormous decorative Christmas tree every December. It attracts large numbers of tourists in all seasons. Subway: B, D, F, Q to 47th-50th Sts.-Rockefeller Center.

Rockefeller Center Christmas Tree-Lighting Ceremony *see* Tree-Lighting Ceremony.

Rockefeller Center Ice Rink
Located on the lower plaza, down the steps from the Channel Gardens, which run from Fifth Ave. between 49th and 50th Sts., is a winter ice rink that attracts hordes of skaters in season, some graceful and others inept, but all attracting the attention of countless tourists and passers-by. In summer months the space holds a fashionable outdoor dining area. Subway: B, D, F, Q to 47th-50th Sts.-Rockefeller Center.

Rockefeller Park *see* Nelson Rockefeller Park.

Rockettes *see* Christmas Spectacular at Radio City Music Hall, Radio City Music Hall.

Rodgers Theatre *see* Richard Rodgers Theatre.

Roerich Museum *see* Nicholas Roerich Museum.

Roger Smith 501 Lexington Ave. at 47th St., NY 10017 (212) 755-1400 or (800) 445-0277, fax (212) 319-9130
This is among the best of the midtown East Side hotels, with attractively decorated rooms, a fine restaurant, and excellent sculpture and art adorning the lobby. It's a popular place with bands and guests, who enjoy the artistic ambiance. The staff is very helpful, and breakfast is included in the price at this moderately expensive hostelry. Subway: E, F to Lexington Ave.; 6 to 51st St.

Roller Skating *see* Battery Park, Central Park Wollman Memorial Rink, Chelsea Piers Roller Rinks, Hudson River Park, North River Park, Riverbank State Park, Roxy, West Street. *See also* In-Line Skating.

Romanian Restaurants *see* Sammy's Famous Romanian Restaurant.

Roosevelt Birthplace *see* Theodore Roosevelt Birthplace.

Roosevelt Island
Roosevelt Island is connected to Manhattan by an aerial tramway that takes visitors over the East River in four minutes in an enclosed car rising 250 feet above the water. The tram can be boarded at the tram station at 59th St. and Second Ave. and costs $3 for a round trip. To explore the island there's a minibus from the tramway plaza to Octagon Park at the northern tip. There is a residential community on the island, which is only

2 miles long and some 800 feet wide. The walk along the East River on the west side offers clear views of Manhattan's Upper East Side.

Roosevelt Museum *see* Theodore Roosevelt Birthplace.

Rosa Mexicana 1063 First Ave. at 58th St. (212) 753-7407

This restaurant features classic Mexican regional fare, such as guacamole, ceviche, molés, grilled shrimp, crepas, and more, all prepared to make tasty and flavorsome dishes at mid-range prices. Subway: 4, 5, 6 to 59th St.; N, R to Lexington Ave. Dinner daily. Major credit cards.

Rose Center for Earth and Space American Museum of Natural History, Central Park W at 79th St. (212) 769-5100

This spectacular new 6-story structure incorporates the Hall of Planet Earth, a multi-level demonstration of how the Earth functions; the Dynamic Earth Globe, where one can see the planet rotate; and the Hall of the Universe. It's all a far cry beyond the old Hayden Planetarium and sure to delight young and old viewers with its interactive displays and innumerable fascinating exhibitions. Subway: 1, 9 to 79th St.; C to 81st St. Open daily with evening hours on Fri and Sat. Admission charge.

Rose Museum *see* Carnegie Hall.

Roseland 239 W 52nd St. btw Broadway and Eighth Ave. (212) 247-0200

This historic dance and music center dates to 1919. It is experiencing a renaissance with its transformation into a venue for various types of popular music several times a month. Concert program details are available at (212) 777-1234. Subway: B, D, E to Seventh Ave.; C, 1, 9 to 50th St. Ticket prices vary based on the performers.

Rosen's Delicatessen 23 E 51st St. btw Fifth and Madison Aves. (212) 541-8320

This huge restaurant is best known for its corned beef and pastrami sandwiches, but it attracts a considerable breakfast clientele as well. Subway: 6 to 51st St.; E, F to Fifth Ave.

Rosie O'Donnell Show

The waiting list for this very popular family program is one year. Address requests to *Rosie O'Donnell Show,* NBC, 30 Rockefeller Plaza, NY 10112. No children under 5 are admitted. Tapings are Mon.–Thurs. at 10 a.m. Standby tickets, which do not guarantee admission, are available at 8 a.m., but the line at the 49th St. entrance starts hours earlier. More information is available at (212) 664-4000.

Roundabout Theatre Company 231 W 39th St. btw Seventh and Eighth Aves. (212) 719-1300
Shows are performed featuring name stars in classic dramas, comedies, and musicals. Subway: N, R, S, 1, 2, 3, 7, 9 to Times Square-42nd St.; A, C, E to 42nd St.-Port Authority.

Rowboats *see* Boating.

Roxy 515 W 18th St. btw Tenth and Eleventh Aves. (212) 645-5156 or (212) 627-0404 www.roxynyc.com
A huge dance space with some nights given over to roller disco draws the eclectic New York crowd here from everywhere and every persuasion, to the accompaniment of loud sound, lights, and movement. Subway: A, C, E to 14th St. Hours vary with events.

Royal Princess and Excalibur (718) 934-1014
These boats offer dinner, lunch, and brunch cruises around the city to the accompaniment of live music, departing from Battery Park City Marina (opposite Winter Garden–1 Financial Center Tower). Subway: 1, 9 to Cortlandt St. Major credit cards.

Royale Theatre 242 W 45th St. btw Broadway and Eighth Ave. (212) 239-6200
This long-standing, spacious house in the heart of the Broadway theatre district often showcases musical productions. Subway: N, R to 49th St.; C, E to 50th St.

Running *see* Battery Park, Central Park Jacqueline Kennedy Onassis Reservoir, Cunningham Park, East River Esplanade, New York Road Runners Club, North River Park, The Promenade, Prospect Park, Riverbank State Park, Riverside Park.

Russ & Daughters 179 E Houston St. btw Houston and Allen Sts. (212) 475-4880 www.russanddaughters.com
This long-standing Lower East Side family establishment specializes in smoked fish, pickled herring, lox, chocolate, and various types of caviar at bargain prices at the store or through mail order shipments (800) RUSS229. Subway: F to Delancey St. Open Mon–Sat 9 a.m.–7 p.m., Sun 8 a.m.–5:30 p.m. MasterCard and Visa.

Russian Orthodox Cathedral of St. Nicholas *see* St. Nicholas Russian Orthodox Church.

Russian Orthodox Cathedral of Transfiguration 228 N 12th St. at Driggs St., Brooklyn (718) 387-1064

Splendid copper-covered domes on the exterior and a wooden screen with painted icons are the distinguishing characteristics of this church. Subway: L to Bedford Ave.; G to Nassau Ave. Open Sunday mornings only.

Russian Restaurants *see* Firebird, Gypsy Tea Kettle, Odessa, Petrossian, Primorski Restaurant, Rasputin, Russian Samovar, Russian Tea Room. *See also* Polish Restaurants.

Russian Samovar 256 W 52nd St. btw Broadway and Eighth Ave. (212) 757-0168

The specialty, of course, is Russian fare in this moderately expensive West Side eatery, which attracts many theatre people, Russian and otherwise. Subway: C, E to 50th St. Lunch Tues–Sat, dinner Mon–Sat. Major credit cards.

Russian Tea Room 150 W 57th St. btw Sixth and Seventh Aves. (212) 974-2111 www.russiantearoom.com

Following renovation, this classic café features signature dishes like blinis, borscht, and chicken Kiev. Frequented by business and entertainment luminaries as well as the literati, this expensive lunch and dinner favorite offers fantastic, colorful, decorative motifs complete with a 15-foot revolving bear-shaped aquarium. Subway: N, R to 57th St. Lunch and dinner daily. Major credit cards.

Russians in New York *see* Brighton Beach.

S

S.O.B.'s 204 Varick St. near Houston St. (212) 243-4940 www.sobs music.com

A stylish multi-ethnic venue for more than just the sounds of Brazil, this is a prime spot for hearing musicians from Latin America playing music from everywhere, as well as jazz. It offers good Caribbean food as well as drink and, of course, there's a dance floor. Subway: 1, 9 to Houston St. Mon–Sat from 7 p.m. on. Cover charge. Major credit cards.

Sahadi Importing Company 187 Atlantic Ave. btw Court and Clinton Sts., Brooklyn (718) 624-4550 www.sahadis.com

A popular destination for selecting from a tremendous inventory of Middle Eastern appetizing foods, exotic groceries, and delicious prepared dishes. Subway: 2, 3, 4, 5 to Borough Hall. Open Mon–Sat 9 a.m.–7 p.m. MasterCard, Visa.

St. Ann and the Holy Trinity Church 157 Montague St. at Clinton St., Brooklyn (718) 875-6960

A national historic landmark, this Episcopal church is home to sixty stained-glass windows that were among the earliest made in the United States. The Center for Restoration and the Arts is engaged in restoring them. Cultural activities are sponsored by the church. Information about these programs is available at (718) 858-2424. Subway: M, N, R to Court St.

St. Bartholomew's Church Park Ave. btw 50th and 51st Sts. (212) 751-1616 www.stbarts.org

A dramatic Byzantine structure of limestone and brick with a mosaic dome, this Episcopal church was completed in 1919 and is dwarfed by the towering skyscrapers in its vicinity. The church sponsors musical events throughout the year featuring sacred music, choral works, organ recitals, and concerts of early music. Subway: 6 to 51st St.

St. Charles Borromeo Roman Catholic Church 211 W 141st St. btw Adam Clayton Powell and Frederick Douglass Blvds. (212) 281-2100 www.st-charlesbor.org

This is the church of New York's first Black bishop and one of the largest African-American worship centers in the United States. Subway: B, C to 135th St.

St. Frances X. Cabrini Shrine 701 Fort Washington Ave. at 190th St. (212) 923-3536

This site is dedicated to the patron saint of immigrants and the first American saint. On display are personal objects and clothes belonging to her. Subway: A to 190th St. Open 9 a.m.–4:30 p.m. daily.

St. George

This town adjacent to the ferry terminal in Staten Island has not realized its potential; empty storefronts are ubiquitous, even though many of the streets on hills hereabouts afford splendid views over the water. The neighborhood is home, however, to a small historic district featuring a collection of residential buildings of various architectural styles.

St. George Hotel Clark and Henry Sts., Brooklyn Heights, Brooklyn (718) 624-5000

This giant Brooklyn landmark building constructed in 1885 was once the city's largest hotel, with more than 2,600 rooms and a renowned swimming pool. After years of disuse from 1970 on, the hotel has recently been transformed into a student hostel, and only those with student identification are eligible to be guests at very modest rates. Subway: 2, 3 to Clark St.

St. George's Episcopal Church 209 E 16th St. btw Second Ave. and Rutherford Pl. (212) 475-0830

This striking Romanesque Revival building is noted for being the worship site for the plutocrat J. P. Morgan. Subway: L, N, R, 4, 5, 6 to 14th St.-Union Square.

St. George's Episcopal Church 135-32 Thirty-Eighth Ave., Flushing, Queens (718) 359-1171

This church has been at this site since 1853, when it was constructed to replace the original house of worship. It is open for prayer Mon–Fri noon–1:30 p.m. Subway: 7 to Main St.-Flushing.

St. George's Ukrainian Catholic Church 30 E 7th St. btw Second and Third Aves. (212) 674-1615

While a Roman Catholic church, this worship center has handsome icons such as those found in Greek Orthodox churches, a huge dome, and sixteen splendid stained-glass windows. The church hosts many events for the local Ukrainian population, notably the folk festival held here each spring. Subway: N, R to 8th St.-NYU.

St. James Church 865 Madison Ave. btw 71st and 72nd Sts. (212) 774-4200

This imposingly dignified Episcopal worship site is best known for the sweeping lines of its attractive Byzantine-style altar. Subway: 6 to 68th St.

St. James Theatre 246 W 44th St. btw Broadway and Eighth Ave. (212) 239-6200

This splendid large Georgian performance center can hold 2,600 theatregoers and has been home to many famous Broadway hits from the time it opened in 1927 to the present. Subway: A, C, E to 42nd St.-Port Authority; N, R, S, 1, 2, 3, 7, 9 to Times Square-42nd St.

St. John the Baptist Church 210 W 31st St. btw Seventh and Eighth Aves. (212) 564-9070

A small Roman Catholic church located in the city's busy fur district, this religious site began in 1840 and has an impressive interior of white marble Gothic arches with painted religious scenes on the walls and handsome stained-glass windows. Subway: A, C, E, 1, 2, 3, 9 to 34th St.-Penn Station. Open daily 8 a.m.–6 p.m., Wed until 8 p.m.

St. John's Episcopal Church 9818 Fort Hamilton Pkwy., Bay Ridge, Brooklyn (718) 745-2377

This long-standing church was founded in 1834 and had a number of illustrious southern Civil War military officers as members of the congregation while they served at Fort Hamilton before that war. Subway: R to Bay Ridge-95th St. Open Mon–Fri 9 a.m.–3 p.m., Sat 11 a.m.–2 p.m., Sun after 8 a.m. and 10 a.m. services.

St. John's University Red Storm Madison Square Garden, Seventh Ave. at 32nd St. (212) 465-6741

The popular local basketball team plays its home games here from November to March.

St. Luke in the Fields Church *see* Church of St. Luke in the Fields.

St. Luke's Church 308 W 46th St. btw Eighth and Ninth Aves. (212) 239-6200

This is the setting for the long-playing participation theatre, the popular comedy *Tony 'n' Tina's Wedding*. The exuberantly played Italian-American ceremony takes place here before adjourning to the Edison Hotel down the street for the dinner party, which the audience takes part in as part of the production. Subway: A, C, E to 42nd St.-Port Authority; C, E to 50th St.

St. Luke's Garden behind the Church of St. Luke in the Fields, 487 Hudson St. at Barrow St.

This grassy area of garden and benches offers a haven for quiet relaxation in a protected space that is open during the day and can be entered through a gate between the church and the school. Subway: 1, 9 to Christopher St.

St. Luke's Place btw Hudson St. and Seventh Ave. S

This quiet West Village block is home to a handsome tree-shaded row of fifteen Italianate brick and brownstone townhouses constructed in the 1850s that line the north side of the street. Subway: 1, 9 to Houston St.

St. Marks Bookshop 31 Third Ave. btw St. Marks Pl. and 9th St. (212) 260-7853

This store is headquarters for alternative literature, as well as serious coverage of feminism, cultural critiques, small and university press books, mainstream materials, and several hundred journals covering a wide range of subject interests. Subway: 6 to Astor Pl. Open Mon–Sat 10 a.m.– midnight, Sun 11 a.m.–midnight. Major credit cards.

St. Mark's-in-the-Bowery Church 131 E 10th St. at Second Ave. (212) 674-6377

This Episcopal church was built in 1799 and restored and later repaired after a fire only in the recent past. It is celebrated as a community and cultural center and meeting hall, and is the performance site for the Danspace Project (212) 674-8112, the St. Mark's Poetry Project (212) 674-0910, and the Ontological Theatre (212) 533-4650. It is one of the city's oldest continually used church buildings. Subway: 6 to Astor Pl.

St. Mark's Poetry Project St. Mark's-in-the-Bowery Church, 131 E 10th St. at Second Ave. (212) 674-0910 www.poetryproject.com

Since 1966 this program has sponsored performances and reading activities several times a week featuring both established and budding poets. Subway: N, R to 8th St.; 6 to Astor Pl. Modest admission charge.

St. Martin's Episcopal Church 230 Lexington Ave. at W 122nd St. (212) 534-4531

Originally the Holy Trinity Episcopal Church, this prominent Harlem church is generally considered the finest Romanesque Revival religious building complex in the city. Subway: 2, 3 to 125th St.

St. Nicholas Historic District *see* Striver's Row.

St. Nicholas Russian Orthodox Church 15 E 97th St. btw Fifth and Madison Aves. (212) 289-1915

Constructed in 1902, this Baroque structure with five domes topped with crosses conducts services in Russian. Its interior has marble columns, and the altar is enclosed by elaborate wooden gold-trimmed screens. Subway: 6 to 96th St. Open for services Sat 6 p.m., Sun 10 a.m., or by appointment.

St. Patrick's Cathedral Fifth Ave. btw 50th and 51st Sts. (212) 753-2261

This Gothic structure is the largest Roman Catholic church in the United States and can seat as many as 2,500 people. When it opened in 1879, it was north of where the city then ended on 42nd St. The exterior is constructed of white marble with bronze doors, and it boasts an inspiring interior with striking stained-glass windows, giving this famous New York landmark the grandeur of the great European cathedrals. Subway: E, F to Fifth Ave. Open daily 7 a.m.–8 p.m.

St. Patrick's Day Parade

In one of New York's most colorful spectacles, on March 17 every year thousands parade up Fifth Ave. from 44th to 86th Sts., while many more thousands of spectators begin to line the streets long before the start at 11 a.m. or so to watch virtually every Irish band and organization in the United States and Ireland and every politician of every creed (clad in green) prance proudly up the avenue. Daily newspapers and local media broadcast the precise parade route and time on March 17.

St. Patrick's Old Cathedral *see* Old St. Patrick's Cathedral.

St. Paul's Chapel Broadway btw Church and Fulton Sts. (212) 602-0872

Across from the World Trade Center site and built in 1766, with a spire and clock tower added in 1794, this Georgian-style national landmark is New York's oldest public building still in use. George Washington's pew (marked by a plaque) is still where he used it to worship on Inauguration Day in 1789. Classical concerts are held here at lunchtime on some days most of the year, with other musical events offered at other times. Subway: 4, 5 to Fulton St.

St. Paul's Chapel (Columbia University) *see* Columbia University St. Paul's Chapel.

St. Peter's Episcopal Church 344 W 20th St. btw Eighth and Ninth Aves. (212) 929-2390

This fieldstone mid-nineteenth-century structure is an early New York example of Gothic Revival architecture. The rectory to its right in Greek Revival style was built before it in 1832 but was replaced by the larger structure. The parish hall to the left of the church at 336 W 20th St. (212) 645-8015, is home to the Atlantic Theatre Company, begun by playwright David Mamet. Subway: C, E to 23rd St.

St. Peter's Lutheran Church 619 Lexington Ave. btw 53rd and 54th Sts. (212) 935-2200

A contemporary small worship center incorporating nothing of traditional church trappings, this granite structure is called the "Jazz Church" because of the many funerals of musicians that have taken place here. The church sponsors an extensive range of jazz, opera, theatre, and social group activities in addition to the worship services. Subway: E, F to Lexington Ave.

St. Thomas Church 1 W 53rd St. at Fifth Ave. (212) 757-7013

This Episcopal church built in the early twentieth century, with striking French Gothic features, ornate stonework exterior carvings, stained glass, numerous impressive interior statues, and a handsome bell tower, offers concerts and special programs. Its celebrated choir may be heard Sunday mornings and at evensong daily. Guided 30-minute tours are offered following the service on Sunday at 12:30 p.m. Information about the concert series is available at (212) 264-9360. Subway: E, F to Fifth Ave.

Saks Fifth Avenue 611 Fifth Ave. btw 49th and 50th Sts. (212) 753-4000 www.saksfifthavenue.com

The celebrated flagship store of the national chain synonymous with designer fashion, style, and high-quality brands, this store is the epitome of the New York department store shopping experience. The 8th-floor café serves light fare with striking views over St. Patrick's Cathedral and Fifth Ave. Subway: B, D, F, Q to 47th-50th Sts.-Rockefeller Center; E, F to Fifth Ave. Open daily, hours vary. Major credit cards.

Sakura Matsuri Festival *see* Cherry Blossom Festival.

La Saline

This is the neighborhood in Brooklyn where Haitians have settled in the Crown Heights area on the south side of Eastern Parkway to Flatbush. Subway: 3 to Sutton Ave.-Rutland Rd.

Sally Jessy Raphael www.sallyjr.com

This popular TV show tapes its broadcasts Mon–Wed from 1 p.m. to 3 p.m. Admission reservations can be made up to the day before by calling (800) 411-7941. Standby admission tickets are available on the day of the taping by standing in line at the Hotel Pennsylvania at 33rd St. between Seventh Ave. and Broadway beginning at 9 a.m. Subway: 1, 2, 3, 9 to 34th St.-Penn Station.

Salmagundi Club 47 Fifth Ave. near 11th St. (212) 255-7740 www.salmagundi.org

Home to the oldest artists' club in the nation (founded in 1871), this last remaining lower Fifth Ave. brownstone mansion retains the elegance of the former private residence, which it has occupied at this site since 1917. The ground floor of the building, where exhibitions open to the public are offered occasionally, retains much of its nineteenth-century charm. Subway: L, N, R, 4, 5, 6 to 14th St.-Union Square.

Salute to Israel Parade (212) 245-8200

To celebrate the independence of the Jewish state, usually on the first Sunday in June each year, a phalanx of Jewish Zionist organizations, Jewish religious schools, Jewish war veterans, and bands from various public high schools and other supportive groups march up Fifth Ave. from 57th to 86th Sts., with hundreds of joyous celebrants and numerous floats taking part in the procession.

Sammy's Famous Romanian Restaurant 157 Chrystie St. btw Rivington and Delancey Sts. (212) 673-0330

Famous for all the dishes that wreak havoc with the arteries, this shabby place with loud, live Yiddish music offers huge portions of steak, chopped liver mixed with schmaltz (chicken fat), fried Jewish dumplings (kreplach), sour pickles, and seltzer water to wash down all the heavy and spicy food. Inexpensive and colorful but recommended only for those with healthy digestive systems. Subway: B, D, Q to Grand St.; F, J, M, Z to Delancey St.-Essex St. Mon–Thurs 4 p.m.–10 p.m., Sat–Sun until midnight. Major credit cards.

San Domenico 240 Central Park S btw Broadway and Seventh Ave. (212) 265-5959

This choice dining spot offers excellent Northern Italian specialties and pastas; reservations are a must, and prices are fairly expensive. Subway: N,

R to 57th St.; A, B, C, D, 1, 9 to 59th St.-Columbus Circle. Lunch and dinner daily. Major credit cards.

San Gennaro Feast *see* Feast of San Gennaro.

San Remo Apartments 145-146 Central Park W btw 74th and 75th Sts. (212) 877-0300

Also known as Twin Towers of Central Park W, this familiar New York skyline landmark was completed in 1931. With its elaborate towers and their columned pseudo-temples at the peaks, this mammoth apartment dwelling has been and remains home to many celebrities, while some have been rejected by the screening board of this exclusive and exceedingly expensive luxury enclave. Subway: B, C to 72nd St.

Sandobe Sushi 330 E 11th St. btw First and Second Aves. (212) 780-0328

Some of the best sushi in the city can be found at this restaurant, which offers delicious, generous portions at very inexpensive prices. Subway: L to First Ave.; 6 to Astor Pl. Open 5:30 p.m.–1 a.m. daily. No credit cards.

Sara Delano Roosevelt Memorial House 45-47 E 65th St. btw Madison and Park Aves.

This pair of identical structures was designed by Charles Platt in 1908 for use by the Roosevelt family, and FDR lived here after being stricken by polio. Here he rekindled the fires of ambition to relaunch his political life as an elected official. The buildings are not open to the public. Subway: N, R to Fifth Ave.; B, Q to Lexington Ave.

Sara Delano Roosevelt Park btw Houston and Canal Sts. and Chrystie and Forsyth Sts.

Named for FDR's mother, this 8-block-long and 1-block-wide park's most colorful feature through much of the year is the morning ritual of the old Chinese men who bring their caged birds to a grassy area at the north end of the park, where they remove the cloths from the cages so that the birds can greet the day's sunshine with a symphony of song. It is a ceremony still practiced as well in mainland China. Subway: F to Delancey St.

Sarabeth's Kitchen 423 Amsterdam Ave. btw 80th and 81st Sts. (212) 496-6280 www.sarabeth.com

Homestyle food, marmalade, and baked goods are some of what attracts such a loyal following, particularly for breakfast and weekend brunch, at this cheerful and bright moderate-priced restaurant. There are two other locations on the East Side as well: 1295 Madison Ave. between 92nd and 93rd Sts. (212) 410-7335, and at the Whitney Museum of Art, 945 Madison Ave. between 74th and 75th Sts. (212) 570-3670. Subway: (Amsterdam Ave.) 1, 9 to 79th St.; (Madison Ave.) 6 to 96th St. At Amsterdam Ave. and 1295 Madison Ave., breakfast, lunch, and dinner daily. At Whitney Museum, lunch is served Tues–Fri, brunch Sat and Sun. Major credit cards.

Sardi's 234 W 44th St. btw Broadway and Eighth Ave. (212) 221-8440 www.sardis.com

The celebrity caricatures on the walls are viewed more by tourists than thespians these days in this restaurant throwback to the theatre's golden age of the 1940s and '50s. It remains popular with theatregoers more for the nostalgia than the cuisine. Subway: A, C, E to 42nd St.-Port Authority; N, R, S, 1, 2, 3, 7, 9 to Times Square-42nd St. Lunch and dinner Tues–Sun. Major credit cards.

Saturday Night Live www.nbc.com/snl/

An annual ticket lottery drawn from postcards mailed to arrive early in August sent to Tickets, *Saturday Night Live,* 30 Rockefeller Plaza, NY 10112, is used to select who gets two tickets to either the dress rehearsal or the actual show. The winners are notified a week or two before the date of the show's taping. A few standby tickets are distributed one to a person at 9:15 a.m. only to those 16 or older for same-night tapings on Saturdays when there's a show at 11:30 p.m. the same night. Call ahead (212) 664-4000 to make sure there will be a show because some Saturdays reruns are broadcast. The line forms very early at the 49th St. side of the GE Building at Rockefeller Plaza, but understand that having a standby ticket doesn't guarantee admission.

Savanna 414 Amsterdam Ave. btw 79th and 80th Sts. (212) 580-0202

This fine small restaurant offers some of the best French food in town at modest prices in an unassuming brick dining room. Subway: 1, 9 to 79th St. Dinner Mon–Fri, lunch and dinner Sat–Sun. Major credit cards.

Sax & Company (212) 832-0350

This company offers tours of museums, artists' studios, private collections, and other types of art venues.

Scandinavia House: The Nordic Center in America 58 Park Ave. btw 37th and 38th Sts. (212) 879-9779 www.amscan.org

This center offers Nordic culture in visual arts, design, literature, exhibitions, film screenings, performances, and readings. Subway: 4, 5, 6, 7 to Grand Central-42nd St.

Scandinavians in New York *see* Bay Ridge.

Schapiro Wine Company 126 Rivington St. (212) 674-4404

Since 1899 this family has been bottling kosher wines on the Lower East Side and enjoys virtual landmark status. Free wine tastings are available on Sunday at 1 p.m. and 2 p.m. They also offer paid tours of the Lower East Side at varying times. Subway: F, J, M, Z to Delancey St.-Essex St. Open Sun–Thurs 10 a.m.–5 p.m., Fri 10 a.m.–3 p.m.

Schermerhorn Row Fulton and South Sts.

Restored as part of the South St. development, this unique and charming block of Georgian-Federal warehouses constructed in 1811 on what was then a wharf along the shoreline, now houses a number of popular dining spots, including the North Star Pub at 93 South St. Subway: 4, 5 to Fulton St.

Schomburg Center for Research in Black Culture 515 Lenox Ave. at 135th St. (212) 491-2200 www.nypl.org/research/sc/

This is a branch of the New York Public Library, home to its Division of Negro History, and the world's premier collection on Black and African culture. It serves also as a media center containing major holdings of prints and photos, oral history, personal papers, and art works. Included in its offerings are the Langston Hughes Theatre for special programs and performances and two art galleries with changing exhibitions of the work of African and African-American artists. Tours can be arranged by appointment (212) 491-2265. Subway: 2, 3 to 135th St. Mon–Wed noon–8 p.m., Thurs–Sat 10 a.m.–6 p.m.

Schurz Park *see* Carl Schurz Park.

Schwarz Toy Store *see* F.A.O. Schwarz.

Science and Technology Museums *see* American Museum of Natural History, American Museum of the Moving Image, Intrepid Sea–Air–Space Museum, New York Hall of Science, New York Unearthed, Rose Center for Earth and Space, Sony Wonder Technology Lab. *See also* Art and Design Museums, Ethnic and Community Museums, Historical Museums, Major New York City Museums, Media Museums, Museums of Particular Interest to Children and Teens, Specialized City Museums.

Sculpture *see* Acquavella, Admiral George Dewey Promenade, American Merchant Marines Memorial, The Art Show, Central Park Bethesda Fountain and Terrace, Hall of Fame for Great Americans, Henry Street Settlement Abrons Art Center, Louise Nevelson Plaza, Marine Midland Bank Building, Museum of Modern Art, Noguchi Museum, Parsons School of Design, Snug Harbor Cultural Center, Socrates Sculpture Park, Studio Museum in Harlem, Tree of Hope Sculpture, Trinity Church, Ukrainian Institute of America, United Nations.

Seafest *see* Tugboat Challenge.

Seafood and Fish Restaurants see Aqua Grill, Le Bernardin, Blue Water Grill, Estiatorio Milos Restaurant, Gage & Tollner, Lundy Brothers, Marichu, Oceana, Oriental Garden, Oyster Bar at Grand Central, Pearl Oyster Bar, River Café, Water Club, Water's Edge.

Seagram Building 375 Park Ave. btw 52nd and 53rd Sts.

Considered by many the best of 1950s Modernist New York constructions, this building was designed by Mies van der Rohe and Philip Johnson and consists of two rectangles of bronze and glass and an innovation for that period, an open forecourt plaza as a public space. Inside the building can be found the famed Four Seasons Restaurant with an interior that has been classed as a historic landmark. Subway: E, F to Lexington Ave.; 6 to 51st St.

Seamen's Church Institute 241 Water St. btw Beekman St. and Peck Slip (212) 349-9090 www.seamenschurch.org

The top floor of this red brick structure looks very much like a steamship's hull; the organization continues its service as a philanthropic agency. The gallery shows rotating exhibits, some on maritime themes. Subway: 2, 3 to Fulton St. Open Mon–Fri 8:30 a.m.–4:30 p.m. Admission free.

Seaport Museum *see* South Street Seaport Museum.

Seasonal Celebrations *see* Events in New York by Month.

Seasonal Events in New York *see* Events in New York by Month.

Second Stage Theatre 307 W 43rd St. at Eighth Ave. (212) 246-4422 www.secondstagetheatre.com

Begun as a company committed to presenting deserving plays whose reception the first time around was unfavorable, this group now also showcases works of promising new American playwrights. Subway: A, C, E to 42nd St.-Port Authority.

Selwyn Theater *see* American Airlines Theatre.

Services for Disabled *see* Disabled Services.

Shabazz Mosque *see* Malcolm Shabazz Mosque.

Shady Ground

In the southwestern corner of Staten Island several buildings still stand from the period during the Civil War when one of the nation's oldest free Black communities was established here by oyster fishermen. The Sandy Grove Historical Society at 1538 Woodrow Rd. (718) 317-5796 preserves the record of these settlers. It also schedules exhibits, shows films, offers lectures, and maintains a research library. It arranges an annual celebration on June 30 to which all are welcome. Subway: 1, 9 to South Ferry; N, R to Whitehall St., then ferry to Staten Island. From Staten Island St. George Ferry Terminal, take Bus S74 to Sandy Grove. Open Mon–Thurs by appointment, Sun 1 p.m.–5 p.m. Closed Fri–Sat.

Shakespeare & Company 716 Broadway at Washington Pl. (212) 529-1330 www.shakeandco.com

There is no connection to Sylvia Beach's Paris bookstore except perhaps in the intelligent, eclectic quality of the book stock and the informed service from the literate staff. There are three other branches: 939 Lexington Ave. between 68th and 69th Sts. (212) 570-0201; 137 E 23rd St. between Lexington and Third Aves. (212) 505-2021; and 1 Whitehall St. at Broadway (212) 742-7025. Subway: (Broadway) N, R to 8th St.; (Lexington Ave.) 6 to 68th St.-Hunter College; (E 23rd St.) 6 to 23rd St.; (Whitehall St.) 4, 5 to Bowling Green. All but the Whitehall St. store open daily, hours vary. Whitehall St. Mon–Fri 8 a.m.–7 p.m., closed on weekends. Major credit cards.

Shakespeare in the Park (212) 539-8750 or (212) 539-8500

Beginning in late June and running through August each year the Joseph L. Papp Public Theatre presents two plays at the Delacorte Theatre in Central Park. The series attracts stage and screen stars as performers for these first-rate productions. A limit of two tickets is available free to those in line first at the Central Park Delacorte Theatre and at the Public Theatre at 425 Lafayette St. downtown, both of which begin distribution at 1 p.m. for the 8 p.m. performances. Subway: (Delacorte Theatre) B, C to 81st St.; (Papp Theatre) N, R to Astor Pl.

Shea Stadium

Located east of Jackson Heights in Queens, this 55,000-seat ball park is home to the New York Mets. It also hosts the occasional popular music concert, as it did when the Beatles appeared here in 1965. Subway: 7 to Willets Pt.-Shea Stadium.

Shearith Israel Spanish and Portuguese Synagogue 8 W 70th St. near Central Park W (212) 873-0300

This is the home of the oldest Jewish congregation in the United States, founded in 1654. The present building was constructed in 1897 and is noted for its Tiffany glass windows. The "Little Synagogue" adjoining is a replica of this orthodox group's first synagogue, built on the Lower East Side in 1730. Subway: B, C to 72nd St.

Sheep Meadow in Central Park *see* Central Park Sheep Meadow.

Sheepshead Bay

Only a 20-minute walk from Brighton Beach, Emmons Ave. runs right along the colorful dock lined with fishing boats. The neighborhood is a picturesque slice of New York, where fresh-caught fish is sold on the piers by the fisher folk every evening and where one can arrange to rent a fishing boat or go out on one of the boats that take out visitors. The easier way to get at the fish is to dine at Lundy's, a celebrated seafood restaurant at 1901 Emmons Ave. (718) 743-0022. Subway: D, Q to Sheepshead Bay.

Sheridan Square

Bordered by W 4th St. and Washington Pl., Barrow and Grove Sts., this is little more than a jumbled intersection where traffic buzzes by, but it is the very heart of Greenwich Village. The square is often confused with Christopher Park, a green space located adjacent to it. General Philip Sheridan's statue (the Civil War soldier and Lincoln's nemesis) perplexingly is found in the park rather than the square. The area is home to many off-Broadway theatres and night spots and is near where the 1969 Stonewall Inn riots took place, later seen as a landmark triumph for the then-emergent gay rights movement. Subway: 1, 9 to Christopher St.-Sheridan Square.

Shopping Malls *see* Manhattan Mall, Pier 17, Trump Tower, World Financial Center. *See also* Department Stores.

Showman's Café 375 W 125th St. btw St. Nicholas and Morningside Aves. (212) 864-8941

This top Harlem jazz spot features the finest musical artists. Subway: A, B, C, D to 125th St. Shows Mon–Thurs 8:30 p.m.; Fri–Sat 10:30 p.m. No cover, two-drink minimum. Major credit cards.

Shrine of St. Mother Elizabeth Ann Seton 7 State St. and Broadway (212) 269-6865

Located across from Battery Park, the rectory of the shrine is a Federal-style, red brick townhouse typical of the eighteenth-century mansions that once lined this street. Mother Seton founded America's first order of nuns in 1809 and in 1975 became the first native-born American to be canonized. The shrine is small, quiet, and decorated with religious scenes of the saint's life. Masses are held here daily. Subway: N, R to Whitehall St.; 1, 9 to South Ferry. Weekdays 6:30 a.m.–5:30 p.m., weekends by appointment.

Shubert Alley btw W 44th and 45th Sts., one block west of Broadway

This private pedestrian street is rich in theatrical lore. Unemployed actors once lined up for casting calls, and many present-day theatregoers wait near the stage doors after performances hoping to get their playbills autographed. Subway: N, R, S, 1, 2, 3, 7, 9 to 42nd St.-Times Square; A, C, E to 42nd St.-Port Authority.

Shubert Theatre 225 W 44th St. btw Broadway and Eighth Ave. (212) 239-6200

Built in 1913 by the Shubert family, long associated with the Broadway stage, this old-time performance site over the years has been home to many of New York's most memorable theatrical productions. Subway: A, C, E to 42nd St.-Port Authority; N, R, S, 1, 2, 3, 7, 9 to 42nd St.-Times Square.

Shun Lee Palace 155 E 55th St. btw Lexington and Third Aves. (212) 371-8844

This spacious and elegant setting befits the grand Cantonese and Szechwan dining offered in this fairly expensive, chic, and long-standing East Side establishment. Subway: 4, 5, 6 to 59th St.; N, R to Lexington Ave. Lunch and dinner daily. Major credit cards.

Siam Inn Too 954 Eighth Ave. btw 51st and 52nd Sts. (212) 757-3520

This is a very modest, small place, but the food is excellent and plentiful. All the Thai specialties are pleasantly served at very inexpensive prices. Subway: C, E to 50th St. Lunch Mon–Fri, dinner daily. Major credit cards.

Sideshows by the Seashore *see* Coney Island Museum.

Sights and Entertainment for Children *see* Amusement Parks, Carousels, Museums of Particular Interest to Children and Teens, Parks and Playgrounds, Places That Appeal to Children and Teens.

Sightseeing Tours *see* Boat Tours, Bus Tours, Helicopter Tours, Limousine Tours, Special Interest Tours, Walking Tours.

Signature Theatre Company 555 W 42nd St. btw Tenth and Eleventh Aves. (212) 244-7529

The fare performed by this unusual, prize-winning company is the work of one resident playwright during the entire theatre season. Subway: A, C, E to 42nd St.-Port Authority.

Silver Lake Golf Course 915 Victory Blvd. at Clove Rd., Staten Island (718) 447-5686 www.americangolf.com

An attractive country setting is the venue for this difficult-to-negotiate course. Subway: 1, 9 to South Ferry; N, R to Whitehall St., then ferry to Staten Island. From Staten Island St. George Ferry Terminal, take Bus S67. Open daily from dawn to dusk. Major credit cards.

Simon Theatre *see* Neil Simon Theatre.

Singer Building 561-563 Broadway

A handsomely ornate 12-story structure built in 1904 by celebrated architect Ernest Flagg, this building features balconies of wrought iron, handsome green arches, red terra-cotta panels, and large windows. Subway: 6 to Bleecker St.; N, R to Prince St.

Sixth Avenue *see* Avenue of the Americas.

Skating *see* Ice Skating, In-Line Skating, Roller Skating.

Skyscraper Museum 710 Maiden Lane btw Water and Pearl Sts. (212) 968-1961 www.skyscraper.org

An itinerant since beginning in 1997, the museum anticipates opening in its permanent location in 2002 at the base of the Ritz-Carlton Downtown Hotel in a 5,800-square-foot specially designed space. It exhibits the history of the high-rise multistory colossus that came to epitomize the New York skyline, showing how they are constructed and why the world's tallest buildings so reflect the essence of the .city. Subway: 2, 3, 4, 5, A, C, J, M, Z to Fulton St.-Broadway Nassau. Open Tues–Sat noon–6 p.m. Modest admission charge.

Small Press Book Fair (212) 764-7021

Every March some 150 small and independent presses converge in the General Society of Mechanics and Tradesmen building at 20 W 44th St. between Fifth and Sixth Aves. in Manhattan for a several-day program of readings, book-making and printing demonstrations, and workshops on a range of publishing topics. Subway: B, D, F, Q to 42nd St.; S, 4, 5, 6, 7 to Grand Central-42nd St.

Small's 183 W 10th St. at Seventh Ave. S (212) 929-7565

This place is the jazz bargain of the West Village, where the price of admission offers scheduled performances from 10 p.m. until 2 a.m. followed by jam sessions until daybreak. No alcohol is served, but there are juice and soft drinks, and you can bring your own bottle. Subway: 1, 9 to Christopher St. Nightly 10 p.m.–8 a.m. Admission charge. No credit cards.

Smith & Wollensky 797 Third Ave. at 49th St. (212) 753-1530 www.smithandwollensky.com

This classic New York steakhouse features enormous prime cuts of beef served by waiters who've been here since this style of eating was all the rage. The succulent meat is perfectly prepared, and the expensive prices reflect it. Reservations essential. Subway: E, F to Lexington Ave.; 6 to 51st St. Lunch Mon–Fri, dinner daily. Major credit cards.

Smith Museum *see* Mount Vernon Hotel Museum and Garden.

Smith Street Brooklyn

The stretch of only nine blocks, bounded by Carroll and Baltic Sts., has attracted a growing number of high-priced restaurants that are very much sought after, attested to by the lines of anxious diners waiting for tables, particularly on weekends. Subway: F, G to Smith St.-9th St.

Sniffen Court Historic District 150-158 E 36th St. btw Park and Lexington Aves.

Ten brick Romanesque Revival carriage houses form a charming and picturesque row. They were erected in the mid-nineteenth century by John Sniffen and remain beautifully preserved just off a very busy Manhattan street. Subway: 6 to 33rd St.

Snug Harbor Cultural Center 1000 Richmond Terrace, Staten Island (718) 448-2500 www.snug-harbor.org

About 2 miles west of the ferry terminal in New Brighton is a complex of twenty-eight buildings built between 1831 and 1880, once a retired sailors' home, now restored as a national historical landmark. It offers Greek

Revival, Italianate, and Beaux Arts architectural styles spread across a great estate. Features include visual and performing arts, parklands, botanical gardens, and a children's museum. There are galleries and studios for emerging artists, an annual outdoor sculpture festival, and concert performances in its Veterans Memorial Hall. The Newhouse Center for Contemporary Art schedules indoor and outdoor exhibitions. Tours are offered on weekends. Subway: 1, 9 to South Ferry; N, R to Whitehall St., then ferry to Staten Island. From Staten Island St. George Ferry Terminal, take Bus S40 to Snug Harbor. Open daily 8 a.m.–dusk. Admission to grounds free.

Soccer

This is a popular spectator sport on summer weekends around Manhattan and the outer boroughs at the parks in Latin American, Italian, and Polish neighborhoods. The sport is not played professionally in New York City; to watch it one would need to travel to the Giants Stadium in New Jersey to see the New York/New Jersey MetroStars play.

Society of Illustrators *see* Museum of American Illustration.

Socrates Sculpture Park Broadway at Vernon Blvd., Long Island City, Queens (718) 956-1819

This 4¹/₂-acre waterfront is both a working site for sculptors and an exhibit area. Unlike most art on exhibition, here the constructions are hands-on and climb-on pieces, ideally suited for kids' explorations. This is part of the New York park system, and one by-product of a visit is the splendid view of Manhattan's skyline and the East River. Subway: N to Broadway. Daily 10 a.m. to sunset (weekends only in winter). Admission free.

Sofia Fabulous Pizza 1022 Madison Ave. near 79th St. (212) 734-2676

This Italian café features some of the best pizza and focaccia in Manhattan. It is popular with fashionable locals for its food and its moderate prices. Subway: 6 to 77th St. Daily 11 a.m.–midnight. Major credit cards.

SoHo

This acronym stems from the area's location, South of Houston (pronounced *How-ston*) St. It is bordered by Canal St. to the south, Lafayette St. to the east, and Sixth Ave. to the west. It is no longer primarily the district for members of the budding artistic community it was in the 1960s. Now it is better known for its boutiques, designer stores, museums, galleries, and dining spots. Its handsome nineteenth-century cast-iron buildings, cobblestone streets, and trendy cafés and bars all contribute to the continental flavor of this popular city destination, but the neighborhood's gentrification has led to the exodus of a number of creative galleries and artists seeking lower rent quarters elsewhere. Subway: B, D, F, Q to Broadway-Lafayette; C, E to Spring St.; N, R to Prince St.

SoHo Cast-Iron Historic District

More cast-iron constructed buildings still stand in the area between W Houston and Canal Sts. than anywhere else in the United States. It survives because local artists started moving into area lofts in the 1960s and conservationists succeeded in keeping the old factory structures from being destroyed through achieving historic landmark status for the neighborhood. The district's core is to be found on five cobblestoned blocks on Greene St., where some fifty structures constructed in the last half of the nineteenth century remain standing. Subway: 6 to Bleecker St.

SoHo Repertory Theatre 46 Walker St. btw Broadway and Church St. (212) 941-8632 www.sohorep.org

This small house produces innovative modern works by American playwrights. Subway: A, C, E, N, R to Canal St.

SoHo Sanctuary 119 Mercer St. btw Spring and Prince Sts. (212) 334-5550 www.sohosanctuary.com

Treatments at this yoga studio and fitness center are limited to female clients. Subway: N, R to Prince St.; C, E to Spring St. Open Tues–Sun, hours vary. Major credit cards.

Soldiers' and Sailors' Monument Riverside Dr. at 89th St.

This marble memorial to those who died in the Civil War was erected in 1902. It stands 100 feet tall in the center of an esplanade 100 feet wide lined with cannons. It was declared a city landmark in 1976. Subway: 1, 9 to 86th St.

Solomon R. Guggenheim Museum *see* Guggenheim Museum, Guggenheim Museum SoHo.

Sony Building 550 Madison Ave. btw 55th and 56th Sts.

This post-modern building was originally built for AT&T and designed by Philip Johnson in 1984. Its unusual roof contributes to making the building a landmark skyscraper, but its primary claim to fame is due to it being home to the Sony Wonder Technology Lab. Subway: E, F, N, R to Fifth Ave.; 4, 5, 6 to 59th St.

Sony IMAX Theatre *see* Sony Lincoln Square.

Sony Lincoln Square 1998 Broadway at 68th St. (212) 336-5000

This shopping mall of movie theatres contains twelve screens for viewing conventional box office features plus an 8-story, 600-seat IMAX theatre designed for viewing not only large-scale formatted films but also three-dimensional imagery, including a short film jaunt through New York City's history. With its glitzy escalators, giant murals, and gift shop selling movie memorabilia, the place tries to recapture the feeling of yesterday's great cinema palaces. Subway: 1, 9 to 66th St.-Lincoln Center.

Sony Wonder Technology Lab 550 Madison Ave. at 56th St. (212) 833-8100 www.sonywondertechlab.com

This is a highly popular spot, particularly for kids and teenagers. It offers an interactive four-level wonderland of hands-on experience with futuristic communications technology. Visitors log on before proceeding through a series of exhibits and laboratories allowing a host of different participatory activities, including producing and editing video music and games. Subway: E, F, N, R to Fifth Ave.; 4, 5, 6 to 59th St. Open Tues–Sun, hours vary. Admission free.

Sotheby's 1334 York Ave. at 72nd St. (212) 606-7000 www.sothebys. com

Sotheby's conducts several hundred auctions a year, but admission for some of them requires an admission ticket. What's going on the block is available for advance public viewing, and the goods run the gamut of rare and expensive art and artifacts to the personal effects of the wealthy and celebrated. Subway: N, R to 57th St., then crosstown Bus M31 east to York Ave. and 72nd St.

Soul Food Restaurants *see* Copeland's, Londel's, M&G Soul Food Diner, Sylvia's. *See also* Southern Restaurants.

South Bronx

The area south of Fordham Rd. has been infamous since the 1960s as the scene of great piles of rubble spread out among downtrodden and burned-out tenements, with frequent incidents of crime. The renaissance began in the late 1990s with the redevelopment of Charlotte St. with its suburban-looking Charlotte Gardens, the renovation of numerous buildings, the spawning of housing cooperatives, and the influx of long-absent retail businesses. The resurgence, the so-called "Bronx Miracle," however, is still a work in progress with much of the region still in decrepit state. Subway: (west side) stops along B, C, D; (east side) stops along 2, 5, 6.

South Bronx Island

This 7-acre wooded island at the eastern arm of the East River near La-Guardia Airport is part of Queens. Owned by the city, it is now abandoned and can be visited only by the birds who frequent it.

South Street Seaport East River at the foot of Fulton St. (212) SEA-PORT www.southstreetseaport.com
This marketplace features more than 100 restaurants, shops, and cafés. Frequent public entertainment and special events take place here, and sightseeing cruises originate at the water's edge. Subway: A, C, J, M, Z, 2, 3, 4, 5 to Fulton St.-Broadway Nassau.

South Street Seaport Museum 207 Front St. at Fulton St. on the East River (212) 748-8600 www.southstseaport.org
Spread among buildings from the eighteenth and nineteenth century, there are three galleries, a children's center, a maritime craft center, and a library, with a fleet of historic ships docked at the adjacent harbor. On display are old shipping records, maps, model ships, photographs, and various collected pieces from the Fulton Fish Market. Subway: A, C, J, M, Z, 2, 3, 4, 5 to Fulton St.-Broadway Nassau. Open 10 a.m.–6 p.m. daily. Admission charge. Major credit cards.

South Street Seaport Museum Tours (212) 748-8590
This company offers walking tours of the waterfront and its historic ships as well as very early morning explorations of the lively Fulton Fish Market during its busiest period on the first and third Wednesdays of the month at 6 a.m. Subway: A, C, J, M, Z, 2, 3, 4, 5 to Fulton St.-Broadway Nassau.

Southern Restaurants *see* Charles' Southern Style Kitchen, The Hog Pit, Justin's, Londel's, Sylvia's. *See also* Soul Food Restaurants.

Southwestern Restaurants *see* Cowgirl Hall of Fame, Mesa Grill.

Spa at Equinox 140 E 63rd St. btw Park and Third Aves. (212) 750-4671 and 205 E 85th St. btw Second and Third Aves. (212) 396-9611
The mind–body orientation is reflected in the gym and unique facial and body treatments that are provided after the fitness workout at this spot, which is said to be a popular haunt of theatrical celebrities. Subway: (E 63rd St.) N, R to Lexington Ave.; 4, 5, 6 to 59th St.; (E 85th St.) 4, 5, 6 to 86th St. Open 10 a.m.–8 p.m. daily. Major credit cards.

Spanish and Portuguese Synagogue *see* Shearith Israel Spanish and Portuguese Synagogue.

Spanish Harlem *see* El Barrio.

Spanish Restaurants *see* El Faro, El Quijote, Helena's, Marichu, Tapas Lounge.

Sparks Steakhouse 210 E 46th St. btw Second and Third Aves. (212) 687-4855

Sparks is still home to huge, high-quality, juicy cuts of beef and the unrepentant carnivores who consume them, dining and drinking in a boisterous, swanky setting with brisk attention from the waiters, an extensive wine list, and the moderately expensive prices to go with it. Subway: S, 4, 5, 6, 7 to Grand Central-42nd St. Dinner Mon–Sat. Major credit cards.

Spas *see* Fitness Centers.

Special Events in New York *see* Events in New York.

Special Interest Tours *see* Art Tours of Manhattan, ARTime, Big Apple Greeter, Brooklyn Attitude Tours, Brooklyn Center for the Urban Environment Tours, Central Park Bicycle Tours, Central Park Conservancy, Discovery Tour, Gracie Mansion Conservancy Tour, Grand Central Partnership Business Improvement District, Grand Central Station Tours, Greenwich Village Literary Pub Crawl, Harlem Spirituals, Harlem Your Way!, Jack Eichenbaum Tours, Joyce Gold Tours, Kramer's Reality Tour, Lincoln Center Tours, Lower East Side Business Improvement District Tours, Lower East Side Conservancy Tours, Lower East Side Tenement Museum Walking Tours, Madison Square Garden Tours, Manhattan Tours, Marvin Gelfand's Walk of the Town, Metropolitan Opera House Backstage, Municipal Art Society Walking Tours, Museum of American Financial History, Museum of the Chinese in the Americas Tours, Museum of the City of New York Cultural Walks, NBC Studios, New York City Cultural Walking Tours, New York Like a Native, New York Public Library, New York Skyride, New School University, Queens Historical Society in Kingsland Homestead, Quintessential New York, Radical Walking Tours, Radio City Stage Door Tour, Sax & Company, South Street Seaport Museum Tours, Stadium Tours, Street Smarts New York, Wall Street Walking Tour, World of Finance Tours. *See also* Boat Tours, Bus Tours, Helicopter Tours, Limousine Tours, Walking Tours.

Specialized City Museums *see* Coney Island Museum, Consolidated Edison Building, Federal Hall National Museum, General Post Office, Museum of the City of New York, New York City Fire Museum, New York City Transit Museum, New York Mercantile Exchange, Police Museum, Queens County Farm Museum, Skyscraper Museum, South Street Seaport Museum, Waterfront Museum. *See also* Art and Design Museums, Ethnic and Community Museums, Historical Museums, Major New York City Museums, Media Museums, Military Museums, Museums of Particular Interest to Children and Teens, Science and Technology Museums.

Specialty Food Stores and Bakeries *see* Balducci's, Barney Greengrass, Bouley Bakery, Bubby's Restaurant Bar and Bakery, Dean & DeLuca, DiPalo's, Economy Candy, Gourmet Garage, Guss's Pickles, H&H Bagels, Hungarian Pastry Shop, Kitchen Market, Kossar's Bialystoker Kuchen Bakery, Li-Lac Chocolates, Manganaro's, McNulty's Tea and Coffee, Myers of Keswick, Payard Patisserie and Bistro, La Piccola Cucina, Poseidon Bakery, Ratner's Dairy Restaurant and Bakery, Russ & Daughters, Sahadi Importing Company, Sarabeth's Kitchen, Schapiro Wine Company, Teuscher Chocolatier, Yonah Schimmel Knishes Bakery, Zabar's, Zito and Sons Bakery.

Spectator Sports *see* Baseball, Basketball (spectator sport), Boxing, Chase Bank Melrose Games (track and field), Football, Horse Racing, Ice Hockey, New York City Marathon, Soccer, Tennis (spectator sport), Wrestling.

Spirit of New York Cruises Pier 61 at Chelsea Piers, W 23rd St. at the Hudson River (212) 727-2789 www.spiritcruises.com
Luxury year-round lunch and dinner cruises of 2 to 3 hours around New York harbor sites feature excellent viewing, climate-controlled dining, dancing, and entertainment aboard a sleek, handsome yacht. Subway: C, E, F, 1, 9 to 23rd St., then crosstown Bus M23 west to Twelfth Ave. Lunch and dinner cruises May–November. Days and hours vary. Major credit cards.

Spoken Word *see* Book and Poetry Readings, Public Lectures.

Sports *see* Chelsea Piers Sports Center, Fitness Centers, Participatory Sports Activity, Spectator Sports.

Squash *see* New York Sports Clubs, Printing House Racquet and Fitness Club.

Stadium Tours (718) 579-4531
Approximately 1 hour long, this Yankee Stadium tour includes the dugout area, press box, clubhouse, monument park, scoreboard operation,

and accounts of the legends and heroes of Yankee baseball history. Subway: 4, B, D, to 161st St.-Yankee Stadium. Mon–Sat at noon. Admission charge.

Stadiums *see* Shea Stadium, Stadium Tours, Yankee Stadium.

Stage Delicatessen 834 Seventh Ave. btw 53rd and 54th Sts. (212) 245-7850

Noisy, crowded, and celebrated as much for its rude wait staff as for the gargantuan size of its top-grade corned beef and pastrami sandwiches and cheesecake slices, Stage combines authentic New York flavor with the puzzled faces of tourists trying to determine what to make of it all. Subway: N, R to 57th St.; E, D to Seventh Ave. Open daily 6 a.m.–2 a.m. Major credit cards.

Stand-Up New York 236 W 78th St. at Broadway (212) 595-0850 www.standupny.com

This is the platform for bright, aspiring comic entertainers as well as celebrities of national and television fame, who pop in at this night club from time to time. Subway: 1, 9 to 79th St. Nightly, hours vary. Cover charge, drink minimum. Major credit cards.

Stanhope Hotel 995 Fifth Ave. at 81st St. (212) 650-4700

This lavish, luxury hotel has period French furnishings and fine crystal chandeliers. Its Melrose Restaurant opens into an expensive sidewalk café during mild weather. Subway: 6 to 77th St.

Staten Island

Often labeled the forgotten borough, Staten Island, or Richmond, connected more with the city once the Verrazano-Narrows Bridge opened in 1964, linking it with Brooklyn. Residents still feel ignored and perennially talk of secession. Still, beyond the ferry terminal the borough offers hills, greenery, lakes, open spaces, and fine views of the harbor. The city's second smallest and least known borough is spread out, and cars, buses, and bicycles (in that order) are the best ways to negotiate the island to see the neighborhoods and cultural attractions.

Staten Island Botanical Garden Snug Harbor Cultural Center, 1000 Richmond Terrace, Building H, Staten Island (718) 273-8200 www. sibg.org

This garden features an expansive acreage of garden collections and a variety of instructional exhibits, sculptures, fountains, and the New York Chinese Scholar's Garden, an authentic 1-acre walled garden of Ming design on a terraced hillside overlooking a pond in a Chinese park landscape of trees and bamboo. Subway: 1, 9 to South Ferry; N, R to Whitehall St., then ferry to Staten Island. From Staten Island St. George Ferry Terminal, take Bus S40 to Snug Harbor. Open April–November, Tues–Sat 10 a.m.–5 p.m. Admission charge.

Staten Island Chamber of Commerce 130 Bay St., Staten Island (718) 727-1900 www.sichamber.com

The chamber is a useful source of tourist information in the form of brochures and bus maps as well as assistance with particular questions about the borough. Close to Staten Island St. George Ferry Terminal. Open Mon–Fri 9 a.m.–5 p.m.

Staten Island Children's Museum Snug Harbor Cultural Center, 1000 Richmond Terrace, Staten Island (718) 273-2060

The museum features interactive hands-on exhibits permitting kids to examine bugs close up, play with puppets and toys, try on costumes, and construct their own works of art. During busy summer months, admission to some of the special exhibits and events may require reservations. Subway: 1, 9 to South Ferry; N, R to Whitehall St., then ferry to Staten Island. From Staten Island St. George Ferry Terminal, take Bus S40 to Snug Harbor. Open Tues–Sun noon–5 p.m. Modest admission charge.

Staten Island Ferry (718) 390-5253

Staten Island's greatest attraction is the 20- to 30-minute free ferry ride that operates 24 hours a day, seven days a week from its own terminal at lower Manhattan's Battery Park. The views are extraordinary, and many passengers simply stay on for the return ride without disembarking. Subway: 1, 9 to South Ferry; N, R to Whitehall St., then ferry to Staten Island.

Staten Island Ferry Collection St. George Ferry Terminal, Staten Island (718) 727-1135

In the Staten Island Ferry waiting room right off the lobby of the terminal, this exhibition displays a wide range of ship wheels and whistles, drawings, old photos, and scale models of historical ferries. Admission free.

Staten Island Historical Society Museum Historic Richmond Town, 441 Clarke Ave., Staten Island (718) 351-1611

This museum contains a collection of photographs of the borough's history, as well as furniture, kitchenware, and tools. It hosts a series of special seasonal events during the year, such as the fall celebration of craftspeople giving demonstrations of their techniques. It is located in Historic Richmond Town. Subway: 1, 9 to South Ferry; N, R to Whitehall St., then ferry to Staten Island. From Staten Island St. George Ferry Terminal, take Bus

S74 to Historic Richmond Town. Open Wed–Sun, hours vary. Modest admission charge.

Staten Island Institute of Arts and Sciences 75 Stuyvesant Pl. (718) 727-1135 www.siias.org

Located two blocks from the ferry terminal, this is one of New York City's oldest museums, founded in 1881. It offers rotating exhibits of the arts, natural sciences, and the borough's history and culture, and sponsors occasional lectures and walking tours. Open Mon–Sat 9 a.m.–5 p.m., Sun 1 p.m.–5 p.m. Modest admission charge.

Staten Island Nature Preserve *see* The Greenbelt.

Staten Island Zoo 614 Broadway in Barrett Park (718) 442-3100 www.statenislandzoo.org

This small zoo of excellent quality has a well-known collection of reptiles and also features an African savannah tropical rain forest and an aquarium as well as a separate children's zoo. Subway: 1, 9 to South Ferry; N, R to Whitehall St., then ferry to Staten Island. From Staten Island St. George Ferry Terminal, take Bus S48. Open daily 10 a.m.–4:45 p.m. Modest admission charge.

Statue of Liberty on Liberty Island (212) 363-3200 www.nps.gov/stli/

This symbol of America has a height of 305 feet from the ground to the torch and dominates New York harbor. A gift from France in 1884, restored in 1986, it includes an exhibit in the base on how the world's largest statue was built. One can climb the 354-step unair-conditioned stairway to the top with the crowds or take the elevator. At the base of the statue's pedestal are the famous words of Emma Lazarus on a bronze tablet: "Give me your tired, your poor, your huddled masses yearning to breathe free." Open daily. *See also* Liberty Warehouse.

Statue of Liberty/Ellis Island Museum Ferry (212) 269-5755

Ferry service runs from near the Castle Clinton National Monument in Battery Park in lower Manhattan every half hour from 9:30 a.m. until 3:30 p.m. (be prepared for long waiting lines). One can disembark first at Liberty Island and then go on to visit Ellis Island, using the same ticket, which also provides for return to Manhattan. Subway: 1, 9 to South Ferry; N, R to Whitehall St.; 4, 5 to Bowery Green.

Steak Restaurants *see* Ben Benson's Steak House, Gallagher's, Keen's Steak House, The Old Homestead, Palm, Peter Luger, River Café, Smith & Wollensky, Sparks Steakhouse.

Steinway

Just east of Astoria in Queens is this neighborhood, which takes its name from the Steinway Piano Factory at 1 Steinway Pl., near the William Steinway House at 18-33 41st St. in Long Island City. The company has been manufacturing pianos since 1872. The plant, which produces more than 90 percent of the grand pianos used across the United States at public performances, can be visited. Call (718) 721-2600 to arrange it. Subway: N to Astoria-Ditmars Blvd.

Stonewall Inn *see* Christopher Street, Waverly Place.

Strand Book Store 828 Broadway at 12th St. (212) 473-1452 www. strandbooks.com

This is the world mecca for used-book lovers, with its 8 miles of shelving holding some 2 million volumes of secondhand, out-of-print, and rare books at discount prices. The subject categories are almost infinite, making this store a true browser's paradise. The Strand Book Annex, located at 95 Fulton St. between William and Gold Sts. (212) 732-6070, is another treat. Subway: (Broadway) 4, 5, 6, L, N, R to 14th St.-Union Square; (Fulton St.) A, C, E to Fulton St.-Broadway Nassau; 2, 3 to Fulton St. Daily, hours vary. Major credit cards.

Strawberry Fields in Central Park *see* Central Park Strawberry Fields.

Street Markets *see* Flea Markets, Markets.

Street Smarts New York (212) 969-8262

Weekend walking tours on various topics treat such themes as famous crimes, speakeasies, or Broadway ghosts. Tours run about two hours, rain or shine, at a modest price.

Strictly Roots 2058 Adam Clayton Powell Blvd. at 123rd St. (212) 864-8699

This bookstore in Harlem sponsors a spoken word series, occasionally with musical accompaniment, in its Word Thursdays events on the second and last Thursday each month at 8 p.m. Subway: A, B, C, D, 2, 3 to 125th St. Contribution suggested.

Striver's Row

Along 138th to 139th Sts. between Adam Clayton Powell and Frederick Douglass Blvds. is the St. Nicholas Historic District, commonly referred to by the envious appellation Striver's Row. These are a group of elegant nineteenth-century brownstones designed by three prominent architectural firms in the 1890s. The residences became home to successful and prominent Black entertainers and professionals from the time they were first attracted to these tree-lined, serene streets in the 1920s and 1930s. Subway: B, C to 135th St.

Student Services

Students carrying proof of student status are often accorded discounts in admission at museums and theatres. Columbia University's Information and Visitors Service (212) 854-4902 issues a weekly calendar of its events. Hunter College (212) 772-4000 and New York University (212) 998-4900 offer much the same kinds of information. At NYU at the Loeb Student Center, 3-5 Washington Pl., 6th Floor (212) 998-4900, there's a lounge and material available on student activities.

Studio 54 254 W 54th St. btw Broadway and Eighth Ave. (212) 239-6200

This is where the discotheque craze reached its height. It has been used as a Broadway theatrical venue in more recent years. Subway: 1, 9 to 50th St.; C, E to 50th St.

Studio Museum in Harlem 144 W 125th St. btw Lenox and Seventh Aves. (212) 864-4500 www.studiomuseuminharlem.org

This institution began as a studio for working artists and has evolved into the principal showcase in the nation for contemporary African-American painting, sculpture, and photography. There are galleries on two levels for changing exhibitions of African-American, African, and Caribbean artists and three galleries given over to the permanent collection of works by major Black artists. A lively lecture series and performance and concert events are offered throughout the year. Subway: A, B, C, D, 2, 3, 4, 5, 6 to 125th St. Wed–Sun, hours vary. Closed Mon–Tues. Modest admission charge.

Sturgeon King *see* Barney Greengrass.

Stuyvesant Town

Close by the Gramercy Park area is the large, tree-lined, Metropolitan Life Company–owned housing apartment complex Stuyvesant Town. Like Peter Cooper Village situated directly north of it, this settlement, which begins at 14th St. and runs to 20th St. and from East River Dr. to First Ave., exudes an air of spic-and-span, middle-class orderliness and carefree tranquillity. Subway: L, N, R, 4, 5, 6 to 14th St.-Union Square.

Subway

It may be noisy, confusing at first, and chronically maligned, but New

York City's subway system is the fastest and most efficient way to get about. It's inexpensive and generally quite safe during busy day and evening hours. It operates 24 hours a day, seven days a week. Subway fare is $1.50 (half price for seniors and disabled), and up to three children under 44 inches tall ride free with one adult. Subway tokens are sold at booths in the stations. The MetroCard is used by most riders because it allows free transfers for up to 2 hours between subway and bus lines. MetroCards are sold in several forms for $3 to $80. For $15, one buys eleven rides for the price of ten. Thirty dollars buys twenty-two rides for the cost of twenty. Unlimited-ride cards permit unlimited travel on subway and bus lines for specific periods. A seven-day pass costs $17. For $63, one can buy a thirty-day pass. Many hotels sell the daily Fun Pass for $14, permitting unlimited rides for 24 hours, but unfortunately they are not sold at subway token booths as are the other MetroCards. Call (212) 638-7622 to learn the closest location to purchase a Fun Pass. A free copy of the subway system map and help in planning the best route are available at any subway token booth.

> Because of the damage to the lower Manhattan subway system after September 11, 2001, the most certain way to ascertain which subway stations are open and which lines are operating is to refer to the Metropolitan Transit Authority's Web site, which is being continuously updated: www.mta.nyc.ny.us.

Subway Maps *see* Maps of New York City.

Sugar Hill

Running from 143rd to 156th Sts. between St. Nicholas and Edgecombe Aves., this enclave on a steep incline above Harlem received its nickname because of the sweet life that the affluent and successful Harlem elite enjoyed here from the 1920s to the 1960s. The attractive stone rowhouses of three and four stories remain in excellent condition. Subway: A, B, C, D to 145th St.; C to 155th St.

Suite 303 Chelsea Hotel, Third Floor, 222 W 23rd St. btw Seventh and Eighth Aves. (212) 633-1011

Run like a hard-to-get-into night club, this salon caters to many in the music and fashion industries, carries its own hair products, and treats its male and female clients in an uncrowded and comforting ambiance. Subway: C, E, 1, 9 to 23rd St. Open Tues–Sat, hours vary. MasterCard and Visa.

Sullivan Street Playhouse 181 Sullivan St. btw Houston and Bleecker Sts. (212) 674-3838

This theatre has been home since 1960 to *The Fantasticks,* the longest running show in American history. Upstairs a small gallery shows off memorabilia about the show from everywhere in the world. Subway: A, B, C, D, E, F, Q to W 4th St.

Summer Festival at Snug Harbor Cultural Center (718) 448-2500

During July and August on Staten Island, music and art are features of the regular annual program at this cultural center. Subway: 1, 9 to South Ferry; N, R to Whitehall St., then ferry to Staten Island. From Staten Island St. George Ferry Terminal, take Bus S40 to Snug Harbor.

Summer Garden Concerts (121) 708-9400

In the sculpture garden of the Museum of Modern Art on W 54th St. between Fifth and Sixth Aves., from early July to mid-August, free musical programs are offered on non-rainy Fridays and Saturdays at 8:30 p.m. featuring performances of classical music by Juilliard students and graduates. Subway: E, F to Fifth Ave.; B, D, F, Q to 47th-50th Sts.-Rockefeller Center.

SummerStage (212) 360-2770

At the Ramsey Playfield at 72nd St. in mid-Central Park, the City Parks Foundation sponsors a constantly broadening program of outdoor concerts featuring renowned and newer artists ranging from jazz performers to the New York Grand Opera, poetry readings, and other entertainment forums free or at low cost on weekday evenings and weekend afternoons starting in June. Subway: B, C to 72nd St.

Sunnyside Queens

This area began in the 1920s as the setting for Sunnyside Gardens, the first planned garden city in the United States, but lost most of its homeowners during the Depression when they defaulted on their mortgages. It is located around Queens Blvd. in the streets numbered in the 40s. It's best known as a neighborhood of predominantly Irish immigrants of different generations and as an example of early model-community, middle-income housing development. Subway: 7 to 40th or 46th Sts.

Supper Club 240 W 47th St. btw Broadway and Eighth Ave. (212) 921-1940 www.thesupperclub.com

Every Friday and Saturday night this plush pre-World War II dance hall and supper club hosts a sixteen-piece big band dance orchestra with continuous music for dining and dancing for an older dinner crowd from 8 p.m. to midnight, and a two-act cabaret review at 9:30 p.m. and 10:30 p.m. From 11 p.m. to 4 a.m., the sounds shift to mambo and hot swing jump.

The food is new American with Mediterranean influences; jackets and ties are obligatory. Subway: 1, 9, C, E to 50th St. Open Fri and Sat at 5 p.m. Music and dancing 8 p.m.–4 a.m. Cover charge. Major credit cards.

Surf Reality 172 Allen St. btw Stanton and Rivington Sts. (212) 673-4182 www.surfreality.org

A small theatre and dance space that celebrates off-beat performance art and comedy with an innovative, experimental, or alternative slant. Subway: F to Second Ave.

Surrogate's Court and Hall of Records 31 Chambers St. at Centre St.

Located at the north end of City Hall Park, this ornate structure dating from 1911 reflects traditional Beaux Arts style, with sculpture and ornament embellishing the columned facade. The central hall features marble stairways and a painted mosaic ceiling. The Hall of Records maintains public records back to 1664, and there is a permanent exhibition on display featuring historical papers and photos illustrating New York's history from the early seventeenth century forward. Subway: N, R to City Hall; 4, 5, 6 to Brooklyn Bridge-City Hall.

Sushi *see* Japanese Restaurants.

Sushisay 38 E 51st St. btw Madison and Park Aves. (212) 755-1780 www.sushisay.com

With a tranquil setting below the street, the finest selections at this Japanese restaurant are the moderately expensive sushi and sashimi choices. Subway: E, F to Fifth Ave.; 6 to 51st St. Lunch Mon–Fri, dinner Mon–Sat. Major credit cards.

Sutton Place

Running parallel to the East River from E 54th St. north for five blocks, this neighborhood is the epitome of New York luxury, with its elegant townhouses and low-rise apartment buildings and its absence of heavy street traffic. Excellent views of the river and the Queensboro Bridge may be seen from small parks at the end of 55th St. and coming out of 57th St. Subway: N, Q, R to 57th St., then crosstown Bus M57 east to Sutton Pl.

Swann Galleries 104 E 25th St. btw Park and Lexington Aves. (212) 254-4710 www.swanngalleries.com/index.cgi

This auction house specializes in American rare books, maps, atlases, autographs, photographs, and art on paper. Auctions are held throughout the year on Thurs evenings, with viewing of the objects on the preceding Sat and Mon–Wed. Subway: 6 to 23rd St.

Sweet Basil 88 Seventh Ave. S btw Bleecker and Grove Sts. (212) 242-1785

This is one of the West Village's most popular spots for straight-ahead and traditional jazz, featuring top-drawer performers. Jazz brunch is offered on Saturdays and Sundays. Subway: 1, 9 to Christopher St.-Sheridan Square. Shows nightly from 9 p.m. Cover charge and drink minimum. Major credit cards.

Swimming *see* Asphalt Green, Barbizon Hotel, Chelsea Piers Sports Center, Harlem YMCA, Municipal Pools, Riverbank State Park, St. George Hotel, U.N. Plaza Park Hyatt, Van Cortlandt Park, Vanderbilt YMCA, West Side YMCA, YMCA/YWCAs, YWCA of the City of New York. *See also* Beaches.

Swinburne Island *see* Hoffman and Swinburne Islands.

Sylvan Terrace 160th St. west of St. Nicholas Ave.

Located west of the Morris-Jumel Mansion and Museum, this short block with a row of historic buildings along the cobblestone street is considered to be one of New York's most charming scenes. Subway: C to 163rd St.-Amsterdam Ave.

Sylvia and Danny Kaye Playhouse *see* Hunter College.

Sylvia's 328 Lenox Ave. btw 126th and 127th Sts. (212) 996-0660

Harlem's legendary soul food dining spot features such favorites as barbecued ribs, collard greens, black-eyed peas, candied yams, Southern fried chicken, and other down-home dishes. The food is filling, tasty, and cordially served at inexpensive prices. On Sunday there's a joyful gospel brunch. Subway: 2, 3 to 125th St. Open Mon–Sat 7:30 a.m.–10:30 p.m., Sun 12:30 p.m.–7 p.m. Major credit cards.

Symphony Space 2537 Broadway btw 94th and 95th Sts. (212) 864-1414 www.symphonyspace.org

First a skating rink, this has become one of New York's principal performing centers, with an eclectic range of offerings from the classical to the eccentric. Best known perhaps for its sponsorship of Selected Shorts, readings by celebrated actors and actresses of well-known short stories, and the Foreign Film Festival every July. Subway: 1, 2, 3, 9 to 96th St.

Synagogues *see* Beth Hamedrash Hagodol Synagogue, Bialystoker Synagogue, Central Synagogue, Congregation Shearith Israel, Eldridge Street Synagogue, Lubavitch Synagogue, Shearith Israel Spanish and Portuguese Synagogue, Temple Emanu-El.

Synod of Bishops of the Russian Orthodox Church Outside Russia 75 E 93rd St. at Park Ave. (212) 534-1601

This lovely Georgian mansion contains substantially the same interior design arrangement from its 1917 origins except for the early ballroom, which was transformed into a cathedral. Subway: 6 to 96th St.

Syrians in New York *see* Aleppo in Flatbush.

TKTS www.tdf.org/programs/tkts/

Unsold tickets for Broadway and off-Broadway shows are sold for half or three-quarter price on the day of performance at the TKTS booth at Duffy Square at 47th St. and Broadway. Ticket purchase hours are 3 p.m.–8 p.m. for Mon–Sat evening tickets, 10 a.m.–3 p.m. for Wed and Sat matinee performances, and noon–7 p.m. for Sun matinee and evening tickets. A surcharge is added to the price of each ticket, and payment must be made with either cash or traveler's checks. The Duffy Square booth generally has a wide selection of plays. Subway: N, R to 49th St; 1, 9 to 50th St.

Tabla 11 Madison Ave. at 25th St. (212) 889-0667

This restaurant offers an attractive ambiance in which to enjoy excellent Indian food designed to satisfy the tastes of the most discriminating diners. Prices are moderately high, but the choices are wide ranging and deliciously prepared. Subway: 6, N, R to 28th St. Mon–Fri lunch and dinner, Sat dinner. Major credit cards.

Tai Hong Lau 70 Mott St. btw Bayard and Canal Sts. (212) 219-1431

Excellent Cantonese food is offered at moderate prices in this somewhat less pedestrian looking than most Chinatown restaurants. Subway: J, M, N, R, Z, 6 to Canal St. Daily 10:30 a.m.–11 p.m. American Express.

Takahachi 85 Ave. A btw E 5th and E 6th Sts. (212) 505-6524

This unpretentious, small Japanese restaurant has excellent food and outstanding sushi offered at modest prices, but they accept no reservations. Subway: 6 to Bleecker St. Dinner daily. Major credit cards.

Takashimaya 693 Fifth Ave. btw 54th and 55th Sts. (212) 350-0100

This aesthetically pleasing branch of a Japanese department store chain features a garden atrium, four levels of men's and women's clothing, charming household items, assorted other items elegantly displayed, and wrapped gifts and accessories. The lower-level café, the Tea Box, offers attractive sweets and light fare with tea, and on the same level assorted colorful and beautifully designed teapots and loose tea can be found. Subway: E, F to Fifth Ave. Open Mon–Sat 10 a.m.–7 p.m. Major credit cards.

Tammany Hall

All that remains of the fabled Democratic political machine headquarters of yesteryear is the red brick building at 100 E 17th St. Today it houses the New York Film Academy, where the next generation of movie makers is groomed. Subway: L, N, R, 4, 5, 6 to Union Square.

Tang Pavilion 65 W 55th St. btw Fifth and Sixth Aves. (212) 956-6888

This Chinese restaurant is a classic version of the downtown Chinatown restaurants with a large menu of exotic Shanghai and Soo Chow dishes. Prices are moderate to high, and reservations are advisable. Subway: B, D, F, Q to 47th-50th Sts.-Rockefeller Center. Daily 11:45 a.m.–10:30 p.m. Major credit cards.

Tanner's Magic Studio 24 W 25th St. btw Broadway and Sixth Ave. (212) 929-4500

This store, established in 1934, is the world's largest for magic with a staff of magician salespeople performing free throughout the day. There are some 8,000 magic sets, tricks, show kits, and other foolery for sale. Subway: F to 23rd St. Open Mon–Fri 10 a.m.–5:30 p.m., Sat 10 a.m.–4 p.m. Major credit cards.

Tap City Festival (646) 230-9564 www.nyctapfestival.com

This annual dance event held in July each year consists of performances, seminars, classes, and films at various venues around Manhattan. Some performances are free, but most are priced.

Tapas *see* Spanish Restaurants.

Tapas Lounge 1078 First Ave. btw 58th and 59th Sts. (212) 421-8282

The specialty is Spanish tidbits, but there's also music, paella, soft lights, and a lively ambiance, and the prices are modest. Subway: 4, 5, 6 to 59th St.; N, R to Lexington Ave. Open nightly from 5 p.m. Major credit cards.

Tavern on the Green in the Park at Central Park W and W 67th St. (212) 873-3200 www.tavernonthegreen.com

An enormous fantasyland of glittering glass, mirrors, chandeliers, and thousands of lights, this landmark fairy-tale castle provides a festive atmosphere and better romantic park views than the pricey American/continental meals served. Reservations are advisable. A Crystal Room table offers the most brilliant setting. Subway: 1, 9 to 66th St.-Lincoln Center. Lunch and dinner daily. Major credit cards.

Taxis

To avoid the bother of public transportation, the alternative is the New York taxicab, which can be hailed on any street. In midtown at midday walking may be far swifter. Late at night they work most efficiently and conveniently. An illuminated sign on the roof indicates its availability, unless "Off Duty" is lit. Up to four people can ride in any official city yellow cab for the same fare. There is a base rate in entering the cab with a surcharge after 8 p.m., and the meter registers the fare by adding the cost for each one-fifth mile covered or per minute in stopped or very slow-moving traffic. On reaching the destination, 15 to 20 percent is customarily added to the metered cost as a tip to the driver.

Tea and Sympathy 108 Greenwich Ave. btw 12th and 13th Sts. (212) 807-8329

Traditional British high tea is served with all the accompaniments in this tearoom, which also offers other English staples, such as shepherd's pie and fish cakes. Subway: A, C, E, 1, 2, 3, 9 to 14th St. Daily 11:30 a.m.–10:30 or 11 p.m. No credit cards.

Tea Rooms *see* Algonquin Hotel, Café Gitane, Café on Five, Carlyle Hotel, Pierre Hotel, Plaza Hotel Palm Court, Russian Tea Room, Takashimaya, Tea and Sympathy, Waldorf-Astoria, Yaffa's Tea Room. *See also* Cafés, Coffee and Cakes.

Teachers College 525 W 120th St. east of Broadway (212) 678-3000

Founded in 1887, this celebrated graduate educational institution is housed in red brick Victorian buildings located north of Columbia University's main campus. Subway: 1, 9 to 125th St.

The Tearoom *see* Gypsy Tea Kettle.

Teens in New York *see* Amusement Parks, Museums of Particular Interest to Children and Teens, Places That Appeal to Children and Teens.

Television Shows in New York *see Late Night with Conan O'Brien, Late Show with David Letterman, Regis and Kelly, Ricki Lake Show, Rosie O'Donnell Show, Sally Jessy Raphael, Saturday Night Live, Today Show.*

Temple Emanu-El 1 E 65th St. at Fifth Ave. (212) 744-1400

Built of limestone in 1929, this Moorish and Romanesque institution is one of the largest synagogues in the world and numbers in its congregation many of the city's most prominent Reform Jewish families. It can hold as many as 2,500 worshippers and is open daily. Guided group tours are arranged by appointment. Subway: 6 to 68th St.-Hunter College.

Tennis (participatory sport) *see* Bowlmor Lanes, Central Park North Meadow Recreation Center, Cunningham Park, Forest Park, Fort Washington Park, Manhattan Plaza Racquet Club, Midtown Tennis Club, Municipal Tennis Courts, Pelham Bay Park, Riverbank State Park, Van Cortlandt Park.

Tennis (spectator sport) *see* Chase Championships, U.S. Open Tennis Championships.

Tepper Gallery 110 E 25th St. btw Park Ave. S and Lexington Ave. (212) 677-5300

This relaxed and informal New York City version of Christie's auctions large lots of varying quality china, silver, and furniture. Sale items are on view the day before the sales event. Auctions at 10 a.m. Sat, viewing on Fri. Subway: N, R, 6 to 23rd St.

Teresa's 103 First Ave. btw 6th and 7th Sts. (212) 228-0604

All the Polish specialties like *bigos* and *pierogi* are available in healthy portions at this inexpensive and modest luncheonette-style East Village eatery. Subway: N, R to 8th St.; 6 to Astor Pl. Daily 7 a.m.–11 p.m. Major credit cards.

Terra Blues Bar, Restaurant and Music 149 Bleecker St. btw Thompson St. and LaGuardia Pl. (212) 777-7776

This small club showcases local musicians, but on occasion it also features better-known performers of blues, jazz, and modern music forms. Subway: A, B, C, D, E, F, Q to W 4th St. Open nightly 7 p.m.–2:30 a.m., 3:30 a.m. on weekends. Small cover charge. Major credit cards.

Teuscher Chocolatier 620 Fifth Ave. at Rockefeller Center (212) 246-4416

This shop on the promenade at Rockefeller Center is home to perhaps the finest and most expensive chocolates in Manhattan. Subway: E, F to Fifth Ave.; B, D, F, Q to 47th-50th Sts.-Rockfeller Center. Mon–Sat 10 a.m.–6 p.m., Sun 11 a.m.–5 p.m. Major credit cards.

Tex-Mex Restaurants *see* Mexican Restaurants.

Thai Restaurants *see* Jai-Ya Thai, PlanEat Thailand, Pongsri Thai, Siam Inn Too, Thailand.

Thailand 106 Bayard St. at Baxter St. (212) 349-3132
Some of the city's best Thai cookery is offered here at modest prices and consumed at long communal tables. Subway: 6, J, M, N, R, Z to Canal St. Daily 11:30 a.m.–11:30 p.m. American Express only.

Thalia Spanish Theatre 4117 Greenpoint Ave., Sunnyside, Queens (718) 729-3880
This center for emerging and established playwrights, directors, and actors presents three productions a year plus ongoing music and dance programs. It is widely known also as a performance venue for zarzuela, or Spanish operetta. Subway: 7 to 40th St.-Lowery, then walk east on Queens Blvd. to 41st St., turn right and walk two blocks to Greenpoint Ave.

Thanksgiving Day Parade *see* Macy's Thanksgiving Day Parade.

Theatre *see* Broadway Theatres, Off-Broadway and Off-Off-Broadway Theatre, Performance Art, Theatre Companies, Theatre Development Fund, Theatre Tickets, Theatres.

Theatre Companies *see* Atlantic Theatre Company, Classic Stage Company Repertory, Ensemble Studio Theatre, Irish Repertory Theatre, Jean Cocteau Repertory, Jewish Repertory Theatre, Manhattan Theatre Club, New York Theatre Workshop, Pan Asian Repertory Theatre, Pearl Theatre, Primary Stages, Repertorio Español, Roundabout Theatre Company, Second Stage Theatre, Signature Theatre Company, Vineyard Theatre, WPA Theatre.

Theatre Development Fund 1501 Broadway, 21st Floor, NY 10036 btw 43rd and 44th Sts. (212) 221-0013 www.tdf.org
This nonprofit service organization for the performing arts fosters works of artistic merit and extends the audience for new productions through discount ticket programs. A book of four vouchers for $28 may be bought, entitling the holder to one admission per voucher to more than 100 theatre, music, and dance performances throughout the city. Informa-

tion by phone 24 hours a day is offered at (212) 768-1818 and daytime at (212) 221-0885 on live performance events all over town. Subway: N, R, S, 1, 2, 3, 7, 9 to Times Square-42nd St.

Theatre District

While some few theatres are located on Broadway, most of them can be found on the side streets surrounding Times Square. The district is generally said to run from 42nd to 57th Sts. along Broadway and on the cross streets from Seventh to Ninth Aves. In all, there are some forty legitimate theatre houses in this neighborhood, of which twenty-two have been designated city landmarks. West 44th and 45th Sts. between Seventh and Eighth Aves. have many celebrated houses alongside each other, and with the resuscitation of W 42nd St. between Broadway and Eighth Ave., some of the long-decrepit old grand theatres have undergone a transformation into such twenty-first-century entertainment palaces as the New Victory Theatre (209 W 42nd St.) and the Ford Center for the Performing Arts (213-215 W 42nd St.). Subway: (south end) N, R, S, 1, 2, 3, 7, 9 to Times Square-42nd St.; (north end) N, R to 49th St.

Theatre for the New City 155 First Ave. btw 9th and 10th Sts. (212) 254-1109

This cultural complex is best known for presenting innovative and experimental productions by new playwrights, often bringing together music and dance with drama. Free outdoor performances are offered during summer months at various locations. Subway: L to First Ave.

Theatre Four 424 W 55th St. btw Ninth and Tenth Aves. (212) 757-3900

A small theatrical playhouse located far west of Broadway. Subway: C, E to 50th St.

Theatre Row

Forty-Second St. between Ninth and Tenth Aves. is the street popularly called Theatre Row, where a group of small low-budget or experimental performance venues is located, among which can be found the Harold Clurman Theatre at 412 W 42nd St. and Playwrights Horizons at 416 W 42nd St. Subway: A, C, E to 42nd St.-Port Authority.

Theatre Ticket Bargains *see* TKTS.

Theatre Tickets

Broadway and off-Broadway show tickets are sold at the Broadway Ticket Center at the Times Square Visitors Center at 1560 Broadway between 46th and 47th Sts. (*see* Tourist Information); unsold tickets can frequently be purchased at the box office an hour before curtain time. Numerous ticket brokers selling expensive seats can be reached through hotel desks. For discounted seats for same-day performances, the TKTS booth in Times Square is the best bet (*see* TKTS).

Theatres *see* Alice Tully Hall, Alvin Ailey American Dance Theater, Amato Opera Theatre, Ambassador Theatre, American Airlines Theatre, American Ballet Theatre, American Place Theatre, The Apollo Theater, Astor Place Theatre, Atlantic Theatre Company, Avery Fisher Hall, Beacon Theatre, Belasco Theatre, Booth Theatre, Broadway Theatre, Brooklyn Academy of Music, Brooklyn Center for the Performing Arts, Brooks Atkinson Theatre, Carnegie Hall, Cherry Lane Theatre, City Center of Music and Drama, Colden Center for the Performing Arts at Queens College, Douglas Fairbanks Theatre, Ensemble Studio Theatre, Ethel Barrymore Theatre, Eugene O'Neill Theatre, Ford Center for the Performing Arts, 47th Street Theatre, Gershwin Theatre, Golden Theatre, Helen Hayes Performing Arts Center, Henry Street Settlement Abrons Art Center, Hudson Guild Theatre, Hunter College, Imperial Theatre, Irish Arts Center, Irish Repertory Theatre, Jamaica Center for Arts and Learning, Jan Hus Presbyterian Church, Jane Street Theatre, Jean Cocteau Repertory, Jewish Repertory Theatre, John Houseman Theatre, Joseph L. Papp Public Theatre, Joyce Theatre, Judson Memorial Church, Los Kabayitos Puppet Theatre, Knitting Factory, La MaMa e.t.c., Lamb's Theatre, Lincoln Center for the Performing Arts, Lincoln Center Theatre, Lucille Lortel Theatre, Lunt-Fontanne Theatre, Lyceum Theatre, Majestic Theatre, Manhattan Theatre Club, Marquis Theatre, Martin Beck Theatre, Metropolitan Opera House, Minetta Lane Theatre, Minskoff Theatre, Music Box Theatre, National Black Theatre, Nederlander Theatre, Neil Simon Theatre, New Amsterdam Theatre, New Victory Theatre, New York State Theatre, New York Theatre Workshop, Orpheum Theatre, Palace Theatre, Pan Asian Repertory Theatre, Paper Bag Players, Pearl Theatre, Players Theatre, Plymouth Theatre, Present Company Theatorium, Primary Stages, Promenade Theatre, Puppet Playhouse, Puppetworks, Queens Theatre in the Park, Repertorio Español, Richard Rodgers Theatre, Royale Theatre, St. James Theatre, St. Luke's Church, St. Mark's-in-the-Bowery Church, St. Peter's Lutheran Church, Shubert Theatre, SoHo Repertory Theatre, Studio 54, Sullivan Street Playhouse, Thalia Spanish Theatre, Theatre for the New City, Theatre Four, Town Hall, Union Square Theatre, Variety Arts Theatre, Virginia Theatre, WPA Theatre, Walter Kerr Theatre, Westside Theatre, Winter Garden Theatre.

Theodore Roosevelt Birthplace 28 E 20th St. btw Broadway and Park Ave. S (212) 260-1616 www.nps.gov/thrb/

Rebuilt by members of Roosevelt's family in 1923 to accurately represent his boyhood home, this national historic site is a brownstone building containing five elegant Victorian-period rooms with many original furnishings. There is an obligatory tour led on the hour by a National Park Service guide through the 2nd- and 3rd-floor living quarters. Chamber music concerts are offered here on Saturday afternoons during much of the year. Subway: 6, N, R to 23rd St. Wed–Sun 9 a.m.–5 p.m. Admission charge.

Theresa Hotel 2090 Adam Clayton Powell Jr. Blvd. at 125th St.

Now an office building, this tall, narrow structure is where African-American celebrities stayed from the 1930s through the 1950s, when most downtown establishments were inhospitable to Blacks. During a 1960 United Nations visit, Fidel Castro and his entire Cuban entourage moved here from a midtown hotel, complaining of poor treatment and punctuating his political statement by a well-publicized meeting at the Theresa with Nikita Krushchev. Subway: A, B, C, D, 2, 3 to 125th St.

Three Lives and Company 154 W 10th St. at Waverly Pl. (212) 741-2069 www.threelives.com

Customers flock back regularly to this well-stocked bookstore in clear response to the interested and helpful service and assistance. Subway: A, B, C, D, E, F, Q to W 4th St. Sun–Tues 1 p.m.–8 p.m., Wed–Sat 1:30 p.m.–8:30 p.m. Major credit cards.

Tibetan Museum *see* Jacques Marchais Museum of Tibetan Art.

Tickets for the Theatre *see* High 5 Tickets to the Arts, Theatre Tickets.

Tiffany and Company 727 Fifth Ave. at 57th St. (212) 755-8000 www.tiffany.com

The pinnacle of elegance, this world-famous jewelry establishment occupies one corner of the city's most colorful intersection. Window displays can be highly artful, and the diamond rings, watches, and pearls sold here are stylish and awe inspiring. Subway: N, R to Fifth Ave.; B, Q to 57th St. Daily except Sun, 10 a.m.–6 p.m., until 7 p.m. on Thurs. Major credit cards.

Time Café *see* Fez.

Time Out New York

Begun in 1995, this popular weekly available on newsstands on Thursdays offers comprehensive, well-arranged coverage of what's going on in New York City from theatre to music to dance to book events and children's activities, plus feature and news stories on life style, shopping events, and entertainment subjects.

Times Square

Taking its name from the venerable *New York Times,* which used to be at Times Tower (now designated 1 Times Square) at the triangle intersection of 42nd St., Broadway, and Seventh Ave., this district is Manhattan's energy center. Encompassing the area from 42nd to 47th Sts. and running up Broadway and Seventh Ave., the neighborhood extends both east and west to embrace the side streets, where many of the more than 300 theatres can be found. High-voltage neon signs, constant hordes of gawking tourists, movie palace marquees, and countless shops and restaurants add up to make this the most celebrated world capital of glitz. With the major cleanup and revitalization of recent years and shorn of the sleazy sex shops and street hustlers, the new fresh-scrubbed look of these streets reinforces Times Square's perennial popularity and extends its appeal to family visitors from everywhere in the world. Subway: N, R, S, 1, 2, 3, 7, 9 to Times Square-42nd St.

Times Square Visitors Center 1560 Broadway btw 46th and 47th Sts.

Sponsored by the Times Square Business Improvement District, this information bureau located in the heart of Times Square offers citywide information from tourism counselors; sells Broadway theatre tickets and MetroCards for public transportation; books boat, bus, and walking tours; and provides helpful brochures about the city's popular visitor destinations. It is open seven days a week 8 a.m.–8 p.m. Subway: N, R, S, 1, 2, 3, 7, 9 to Times Square-42nd St.

Tipping

The standard 15 to 20 percent is customary for waiters and taxicab drivers. Bellhops normally receive fifty cents a bag, with $1 minimum, hotel doormen $1 for flagging a cab, restroom attendants fifty cents, and hotel maids fifty cents or $1 per day upon checkout.

Tisch Children's Zoo *see* Central Park Tisch Children's Zoo.

Today Show

The place to be and to be seen by those who are fans of this TV favorite is outside the windows of the broadcast studio on the sidewalk of 49th St. at Rockefeller Plaza between Fifth and Sixth Aves. before 7 a.m. on weekdays, where the faithful congregate whatever the weather. Subway: B, D, F, Q to 47th-50th Sts.-Rockefeller Center.

Todt Hill

This upscale residential area of Staten Island is replete with tree-surrounded luxury homes off Richmond Rd. and south of the Staten Island Expressway. It is fairly inaccessible except by automobile.

Tom's Restaurant 2880 Broadway at 112th St. (212) 864-6137

This neighborhood favorite in Morningside Heights offers standard diner fare at low prices. It is best known for its milkshakes, hamburgers, and fries and the frequent views of it, which were seen on the popular TV show *Seinfeld.* Subway: 1, 9 to Cathedral Pkwy.-110th St. Open Sun–Wed 6 a.m.–1:30 a.m., Thurs–Sat 24 hours. No credit cards.

The Tombs 100 Centre St.

This is the Criminal Courts Building made famous in TV shows like *NYPD Blue, Law and Order,* and *100 Centre St.* This 1939 building combines Art Deco with Babylonian temple styles. Here is where the night courts hold sway weekdays from 5 p.m. to 1 a.m. and where the lobby calendar identifies what's on the docket for those who would like to observe the proceedings. The tower connects by skywalk to the prisoner detention center, which gives the structure its mournful nickname. Subway: 6, J, M, N, R, Z to Canal St. Building open Mon–Fri 9 a.m.–5 p.m. Night court Mon–Fri 5 p.m.–1 a.m.

Tompkins Square Books and Records 111 E 7th St. btw Ave. A and First Ave. (212) 979-8958

This welcoming used book and record store has low prices and fine old records that can be listened to before purchasing. Subway: 6 to Astor Pl.; F to Second Ave. Open Mon–Fri 5 p.m.–midnight, Sat–Sun noon–midnight. No credit cards.

Tompkins Square Park 7th to 10th Sts. and Aves. A and B

This is the East Village's lively and interesting neighborhood park, with its mélange of guitar-playing hippies, tourists, oddballs, yuppies, homeless, and animals all coming together on the grass under giant old trees. On any weekend, one might happen upon a free concert or craft fair or simply witness spontaneous performances of every kind. Subway: 6 to Astor Pl.

Totonno's 1524 Neptune Ave. btw W 15th and W 16th Sts., Coney Island, Brooklyn (718) 372-8606

Connoisseurs insist that this is where to find New York's most delicious coal-burning, brick-oven baked pizza. The Brooklyn location opened in 1924, but there's a second location now in Manhattan at 1544 Second Ave. between 80th and 81st Sts. (212) 327-2800. Subway: (Brooklyn) B, D, F, N to Stillwell Ave.-Coney Island; (Manhattan) 4, 5 to 86th St. Brooklyn: open noon–8:30 p.m. Wed–Sun. No credit cards. Manhattan: Open noon–midnight daily. Major credit cards.

Tourist Information

The New York Convention and Visitors Bureau (810 Seventh Ave. btw 52nd and 53rd Sts. (212) 484-1200 or www.nycvisit.com) fields a knowledgeable staff and provides brochures, maps, and information about special hotel packages and discount admission programs for many attractions. They distribute a free *Official New York City Guide* listing hotels, restaurants, tours, and more. For answers to specific questions, speak to a travel counselor at (212) 484-1222 during business hours. For printed literature call (800) NYCVISIT or (212) 484-1222. Subway: B, D, E to Seventh Ave.; N, R to 49th St.

The Times Square Visitors Center (1560 Broadway btw 46th and 47th Sts. (212) 768-1560 or www.timessquarebid.org), managed by the Times Square Business Improvement District, is a convenient location for finding all kinds of information on citywide activities. It includes a tour desk selling tickets for bus and boat tours; a Metropolitan Transit Authority desk, which sells MetroCards, provides public transit maps, and answers questions on the transportation system; a Broadway Ticket Center, providing information on shows and selling tickets (not to be confused with the TKTS booth across the street, where discount theatre tickets are sold); and ATM and currency exchange machines. The center is open daily 8 a.m.–8 p.m. It also sponsors an informative weekly actor-led walking tour of the Broadway theatre district, which focuses on the history, architecture, and current directions of the New York stage. Subway: N, R to 49th St.; 1, 9 to 50th St. *See also* Web Sites About New York.

Tours *see* Boat Tours, Bus Tours, Helicopter Tours, Limousine Tours, Special Interest Tours, Walking Tours.

Tower Books, Records and Video 383 Lafayette St. at 4th St. (212) 228-5100 www.towerrecords.com

Here is a place to browse for books on travel, literature, photography, and paperbacks as well as a wide variety of American and foreign magazines of all types. A number of other branch stores around the city specialize in records and video sales and rental. See the Manhattan phone book for listings. Subway: B, D, F, Q to Broadway-Lafayette St.; 6 to Bleecker St. Daily 9 a.m.–midnight. Major credit cards.

Tower Market Broadway btw W 4th and W 3rd Sts.

This is a weekend open-air street market where shoppers seek bargains in Latin American fabrics, clothing, jewelry, and assorted other merchandise. Subway: 6 to Astor Pl.

Town Hall 123 W 43rd St. btw Sixth and Seventh Aves. (212) 840-2824

This has been a landmark venue since 1921, where excellent acoustics and unblocked viewing make it ideal for cultural and theatrical events, as well as performances of dance and popular, chamber, choral, jazz, and world music. Subway: 1, 2, 3, 7, 9, N, R, S to Times Square-42nd St.; B, D, F, Q to 42nd St.

Track and Field *see* Chase Bank Melrose Games.

Le Train Bleu at Bloomingdale's, 1000 Third Ave. btw 59th and 60th Sts. (212) 705-2100

This restaurant, popular with department store shoppers, is a copy of an Orient Express train dining car with a splendid view of the Queensboro (59th St.) Bridge. Tea service has been discontinued. Subway: N, R to Lexington Ave.; 4, 5, 6 to 59th St. Mon–Sat 10:30 a.m.–5 p.m. Major credit cards.

Transportation in New York *see* Buses, John F. Kennedy International Airport, LaGuardia Airport, Newark International Airport, Subway, Taxis.

Trattoria dell'Arte 900 Seventh Ave. btw 56th and 57th Sts. (212) 245-9800

The bountiful antipasto bar and the art renditions of body parts, such as the giant nose near the bar, are two of the attractions of this pleasant contemporary Italian restaurant set in an attractive airy interior and offering fine service and good food at only moderately high prices. Reservations are advisable. Subway: N, R to 57th St.; B, D, E to Seventh Ave. Lunch Mon–Fri, dinner Mon–Sat, brunch Sat–Sun. Major credit cards.

Tree-Lighting Ceremony (212) 632-3975

Thousands of lights on miles of wire are used to illuminate a giant Norway spruce tree in early December at Rockefeller Center just below the golden Prometheus statue. The celebration is accompanied by an ice skating show, singing, and entertainment while thousands of festive onlookers take in the spectacle. Subway: B, D, F, Q to 47th-50th Sts.-Rockefeller Center.

Tree of Hope Sculpture Adam Clayton Powell Jr. Blvd. at 131st St.

This steel sculpture of purple, black, and green stands rusting on the spot where the Tree of Hope once grew. A nearby plaque commemorates the site with an inscription by Bill "Bojangles" Robinson. Subway: 2, 3 to 135th St.

TriBeCa

Beginning in the late 1970s, residents of SoHo on the lookout for cheaper rents began their migration to the TRIangle BElow CAnal (bounded by Chambers St., Broadway, Canal St., and the West Side Hwy.). Since then the neighborhood of cast-iron nineteenth-century factories and warehouses has been transformed into a trendy community of loft apartments and studios, restaurants, bars, galleries, and boutiques. It combines the flavor of an urban frontier with the residue of the grimy shabbiness of its earlier industrial ambiance. Subway: (north) 1, 9 to Canal St.; (south) 1, 9 to Franklin St.

TriBeCa Film Center 375 Greenwich St. at Franklin St. www.tribe cafilm.com

Located above the ground floor TriBeCa Grill in the 1905 Martinson Coffee Factory landmark building, film makers have been maintaining offices, screening and editing films, and conducting business since it was developed by Robert De Niro in 1989. Subway: 1, 9 to Franklin St.

TriBeCa Grill 375 Greenwich St. at Franklin St. (212) 941-3900 www.myriadrestaurantgroup.com

This brick-walled, spacious bistro is centered by a Tiffany bar transplanted from a former uptown watering hole, Maxwell's Plum. Fine American fare influenced by Italian and Asian cooking is served. This fairly expensive restaurant is a trendy spot where reservations are necessary; diners are attracted as much in hope of a glimpse of celebrity co-owner Robert De Niro as for the wholesome tasty food. Subway: 1, 9 to Franklin St. Lunch Mon–Fri, dinner Mon–Sat, Sun brunch. Major credit cards.

Trinity Cemetery W 153rd to 155th Sts. at Riverside Dr. and Amsterdam Ave.

On the site of what was once a farm of the famous ornithologist John

James Audubon, whose gravestone is adorned with birds and animals, this is the final resting place of many prominent nineteenth-century families. Subway: 1, 9 to 157th St. Open 9 a.m.–4:30 p.m. daily.

Trinity Church Broadway and Wall St. (212) 602-0872 or (212) 602-0800

This Episcopal church was completed in 1846 and is the third building at this site since it was founded in 1698. The Gothic 280-foot spire, sculpted brass doors, pretty cemetery with tombstones of early American notables, and the small museum behind the altar with exhibits on the church and its place in New York history, draw many visitors to this serene setting. In addition to daily services, summertime midday concerts, changing sculpture exhibits in its courtyards, and guided tours are also offered. Subway: 4, 5 to Wall St.; N, R to Rector St. Church open weekdays 7 a.m.– 6 p.m., Sat 8 a.m.–4 p.m. Services Sun 11:15 a.m. Museum open Mon–Fri 9 a.m.–11:15 a.m. and 1 p.m.–3:45 p.m., Sat 10 a.m.–3:45 p.m., Sun 1 p.m.– 3 p.m. Museum closed during concerts. Donations suggested.

Triple Pier Expo (212) 255-0020

For two consecutive weekends in mid-March and again in mid-November Manhattan's largest antiques and collectibles exhibition draws more than 600 dealers, who show their wares along Piers 88, 90, and 92 between 48th and 50th Sts. along the Hudson River. Subway: N, R to 49th St., then take Bus M50 crosstown on 49th St. to Twelfth Ave. Admission charge.

Tropica Met Life Building, 200 Park Ave. btw Lexington and Vanderbilt Aves. (212) 867-6767 www.restaurantassociates.com

The flavor of the tropics is evoked with the wicker chairs, airy upper levels, and palm trees in this fairly expensive dining spot with its well-prepared and appetizing Caribbean fare. Subway: S, 4, 5, 6, 7 to Grand Central-42nd St. Open Mon–Fri for lunch and dinner. Major credit cards.

Trump International Hotel and Tower 1 Central Park W at 60th St. (212) 299-1000 www.trumpintl.com

This luxury hotel and residential condominium casts its long shadow over Central Park's southwest corner and offers every feature that would appeal to high-end travelers, from swimming pool, fitness center, and marble bathrooms to one of the city's most fashionable and expensive restaurants, Jean Georges. Subway: A, B, C, D, 1, 9 to 59th St.-Columbus Circle.

Trump Tower 725 Fifth Ave. btw 56th and 57th Sts.

A 68-story building with apartments for the super rich on the 30th floor and above, this structure features a flamboyant 6-story pink marble atrium offering galleries, boutiques, restaurants, and gardens all in a setting around the dramatic 5-story cascading waterfall to appeal to the taste for opulence that attracts visiting crowds daily 8 a.m.–10 p.m. Subway: E, F to Fifth Ave.; 4, 5, 6 to 59th St.

Tse Yang 34 E 51st St. btw Madison and Park Aves. (212) 688-5447

This elegant and dramatically furnished establishment features excellent Chinese dishes prepared beautifully and served with style in this fairly expensive, unusual Chinese restaurant, where reservations are essential. Subway: E, F to Fifth Ave.; 6 to 51st St. Lunch and dinner daily. Major credit cards.

Tudor City

Up the stone staircases on both sides of E 42nd St. near First Ave. is a little tree-filled park leading to this self-contained historic district of twelve brick buildings with Gothic touches, containing some 3,000 apartments, stores, and restaurants built in the 1920s as a middle-class city within the city. Subway: S, 4, 5, 6, 7 to Grand Central-42nd St., then take Bus M42 crosstown east to First Ave.

Tugboat Challenge (212) 245-0072

On the Sunday before Labor Day a race of the tugboats that work the city's waters and harbors takes place. It ends at Pier 86 as the high point of Seafest, an annual event when ships visit and pier activities take place at the Intrepid Sea–Air–Space Museum. Subway: N, R to 49th St.; 1, 9 to 50th St., then take Bus M50 on 49th St. going west to Twelfth Ave.

Tully Hall *see* Alice Tully Hall.

Tunnel 220 Twelfth Ave. at 27th St. (212) 695-4682

This cavernous former warehouse with three floors and mezzanine near the Holland Tunnel entrance offers a smorgasbord of rooms featuring diverse musical styles, lounges, dance floors, and live acts. The decibel level is high, and enthusiastic partygoers are plentiful. Subway: C, E to 23rd St., then Bus M23 crosstown west to Twelfth Ave. Open Fri–Sun nights, but call to check. Cover charge. No credit cards.

Turkish Kitchen 386 Third Ave. btw 27th and 28th Sts. (212) 679-1810

This is reputed to be the best Turkish restaurant in town for service and moderate prices. Zestful Middle Eastern specialties are served in an attractive, multi-level setting of brightly painted walls with kilims adorning the floors and walls. Subway: 6 to 28th St. Lunch Mon–Fri, dinner daily. Major credit cards.

Turkish Restaurants *see* Turkish Kitchen, Uskudar. *See also* Middle Eastern Restaurants.

Turtle Bay

This classy neighborhood runs to the East River from the upper 40s and boasts a historic district between 48th and 49th Sts. and Second to Third Aves., where elegant brownstones dating from the nineteenth century share the common Turtle Bay Gardens, which are not open to the public. Subway: E, F to Lexington Ave., 6 to 51st St.

TV Show Tickets *see* Television Shows in New York.

Tweed Courthouse 52 Chambers St.

Now housing municipal offices, this building, once the New York County Courthouse, is an imposing columned structure on its outside with a 7-story rotunda inside. Its popular name derives from Tammany Hall's infamous Boss Tweed, said to have swindled the city out of millions, who was eventually tried and sentenced to prison in the very building that is now known by his name. Subway: N, R to City Hall; 4, 5, 6 to Brooklyn Bridge-City Hall. Open Mon–Fri 9 a.m.–5 p.m.

20 Mott Street btw Pell St. and the Bowery (212) 964-0380

Among the most popular Chinatown dim sum restaurants, this 3-story place features a continuous flow of carts bearing appetizing and savory dumplings filled with a wide range of fillings to choose from by pointing. It all makes for exotic dining at quite modest prices. Subway: J, M, N, R, Z, 6 to Canal St. Open daily 10 a.m.–midnight. American Express.

The "21" Club 21 W 52nd St. btw Fifth and Sixth Aves. (212) 582-7200 www.21club.com

Opened on December 31, 1929, this former speakeasy has evolved into a modern celebrity and capitalist bastion with almost landmark status. Food is vastly overpriced, but this is the place for those who want to see or be seen. Reservations are de rigueur, as are jacket and tie. Subway: B, D, F, Q to 47th-50th Sts.-Rockefeller Center. Lunch Mon–Fri, dinner Mon–Sat. Major credit cards.

Twin Peaks 102 Bedford St. btw Grove and Christopher Sts.

What started out as a conventional house in 1835 was capriciously re-modeled and rebuilt in 1926 with stucco, timbers, and a pair of steeply peaked roofs as a haven for artists and theatre people. Subway: A, B, C, D, E, F, Q to W 4th St.; 1, 9 to Christopher St.-Sheridan Square.

Twin Towers of Central Park West *see* San Remo Apartments.

U.N. Plaza Park Hyatt 44th St. at First Ave. (212) 758-1234

This hotel offers non-guest swimming in an attractive pool on the 27th floor for a daily fee. Subway: S, 4, 5, 6, 7 to Grand Central-42nd St.

U.S. Courthouse 40 Centre St. at Foley Square

Designed by the same architect who built the Woolworth Building, Cass Gilbert, this 31-story structure completed in 1936 is set on a classical columned temple base rising to a gilded pyramid tower. It has been the setting for innumerable memorable cases. Subway: 4, 5, 6 to Brooklyn Bridge-City Hall. Open Mon–Fri 9 a.m.–5 p.m.

U.S. Custom House *see* Custom House.

U.S. Open Tennis Championships (718) 760-6200 or (888) 673-6849 www.usopen.org

Played at the Louis Armstrong Memorial Stadium in Flushing Meadows-Corona Park, Queens, in late August and early September, this premier annual sporting event is the grand slam tennis tournament with the finals held on Labor Day weekend. Tickets for earlier rounds can usually be purchased well in advance, but semifinals and finals tickets are exceedingly difficult to come by (888) 673-6849. Subway: 7 to Willets Pt.-Shea Stadium.

U.S. Post Office *see* General Post Office.

U Thant Island *see* Islands in and around New York.

Ukraine *see* Little Ukraine.

Ukrainian East Village Restaurant 140 Second Ave. btw 8th and 9th Sts. (212) 529-5024

Genuine Ukrainian dishes (kielbasa, pierogi, kasha, stuffed cabbage) are pleasingly served in this unassuming place offering bountiful portions at very cheap prices. Subway: 6 to Astor Pl. Daily noon–11 p.m. No credit cards.

Ukrainian Institute of America 2 E 79th St. btw Fifth and Park Aves. (212) 288-8660 www.ukrainianinstitute.org

In an impressive Gothic mansion, this organization, founded in 1948, sponsors concerts and symposia, offers a gallery of Ukrainian paintings and sculptures, and displays various types of ethnic and religious objects. Its days and hours of exhibit openings vary from one exhibition to another, thus it is advisable to call ahead about the scheduled events and programs. Subway: 6 to 79th St.

Ukrainian Museum 203 Second Ave. btw 12th and 13th Sts. (212) 228-0110 www.brama.com/ukrainian_museum/

Located in small galleries on the top floors of an East Village townhouse, this collection offers a display of early-twentieth-century embroidered folk costumes and garments, ceramics, jewelry, and decorative metal and wooden objects. There is a particularly unusual large showing of painted eggs around Easter, as well as an occasional changing exhibit of ethnic art, illuminated manuscripts, and icons. Subway: 6 to Astor Pl.; L to Third Ave. Wed–Sun 1 p.m.–5 p.m. Modest admission charge.

Ukrainian Restaurants *see* Ukrainian East Village Restaurant, Veselka.

Ukrainians in New York *see* Little Ukraine.

Uncle Nick's 747 Ninth Ave. btw 50th and 51st Sts. (212) 245-7992

This Greek restaurant features an exposed kitchen, appetizing displays of fish, a quiet outdoor back garden open in mild weather, and tasty inexpensive meals centered upon fresh fish. Subway: C, E to 50th St. Lunch and dinner daily. Major credit cards.

UNICEF House 3 United Nations Plaza at 44th St. btw First and Second Aves. (212) 391-8558 www.unicef.org

At the Danny Kaye Visitors Center, exhibits and multimedia presentations deal with this international children's advocacy organization's programs to foster global development and world peace. Subway: S, 4, 5, 6, 7 to Grand Central-42nd St. Open Mon–Fri 10 a.m.–5 p.m. Admission free.

Union Square

Located and named for the coming together of Broadway and Fourth Ave. and running from 14th to 17th Sts., this center was famous for radicals and demonstrations in the 1920s and '30s and in the 1980s for its drug culture. This park area is now the setting for New York's largest greenmarket, where farmers and food purveyors from all over the northeast offer their products on Monday, Wednesday, Friday, and Saturday. An outdoor café is open in warm weather in the nearby plaza. There's also a splendid equestrian statue of George Washington from 1856, a statue of Abraham Lincoln, and another of Lafayette. A free walking tour weekly on Saturday afternoons sponsored by the Union Square Business Improvement District focuses upon this area and its colorful history. Details (718) 783-3260. Subway: L, N, R, 4, 5, 6 to 14th St.-Union Square.

Union Square Café 21 E 16th St. btw Fifth Ave. and Union Square W (212) 243-4020

Universally rated a favorite for its classy and zesty American-style cuisine, friendly service, and good acoustics, this fairly expensive place definitely requires reserving ahead to assure a table for dinner. Subway: L, N, R, 4, 5, 6 to 14th St.-Union Square. Lunch and dinner Mon–Sat, dinner Sun. Major credit cards.

Union Square Theatre 100 E 17th St. at Park Ave. S (212) 475-8908

A venue for productions of dramatic and musical theatrical fare. Subway: L, N, R, 4, 5, 6 to 14th St.-Union Square.

Union Theological Seminary W 120th to W 122nd Sts. btw Broadway and Claremont Ave. (212) 662-7100 www.uts.columbia.edu

Since 1910 this gray Gothic quadrangle has been home to the religious study center that was founded in 1836 and contains one of the world's great libraries of theology. Subway: 1, 9 to 125th St.

The Unisphere

Constructed for the World's Fair in 1964 and remaining as its leftover, this 380-ton, 140-foot-tall stainless steel globe has been classed a city landmark and is brightly illuminated after dark. It is located outside the Tennis Center in Flushing Meadows-Corona Park in Queens. Subway: 7 to Willets Pt.-Shea Stadium.

United Nations www.un.org

Past the main entrance between 45th and 46th Sts. at First Ave., buildings that occupy the site include the domed General Assembly Building, the 39-story glass and marble Secretariat Building, and the interconnected Conference Building. It was constructed by the early 1960s on land purchased and donated by John D. Rockefeller Jr. Informative guided tours daily every half hour are conducted in English and other languages (212)

963-8687. The grounds boast the beautiful multicultural UN Rose Garden and modern sculpture park, offering striking views of the East River. Subway: S, 4, 5, 6, 7 to Grand Central-42nd St. Open 9:15 a.m.–4:45 p.m.

United Nations Plaza

Running from 42nd to 48th Sts. and from First Ave. to FDR Dr., the Plaza is where the flags of more than 180 member nations flap in the wind, flying over the part of New York City that is officially an international zone with its own security force, fire department, postage stamps, and post office. Subway: S, 4, 5, 6, 7 to Grand Central-42nd St.

Universities and Colleges *see* Barnard College, Baruch College of the City University of New York, Brooklyn Manhattan Community College, City College of the City University of New York, Columbia University, Cooper Union, Fordham University, General Theological Seminary, John Jay College of Criminal Justice, Manhattan College, New School University, New York University, Teachers College, Union Theological Seminary, Yeshiva University.

University Club 1 W 54th St. at Fifth Ave. (212) 247-2100

This imposing granite structure designed by McKim, Mead & White in 1899, one of the earliest midtown clubs exclusively for college-educated males, admitted women to membership for the first time in 1987. A number of individual universities built their own clubs early in the twentieth century at various Manhattan locations. Subway: E, F to Fifth Ave.; 6 to 51st St.

Unoppressive Bargain Books 24 Carmine St. btw Bleecker and Houston Sts. (212) 229-0079

This tiny shop specializes in selling new titles priced at 50 percent or more off the cover price, offering a very wide range from serious literature to coffee-table books. Subway: A, B, C, D, E, F, Q to W 4th St.; 1, 9 to Houston St. Mon–Fri 11 a.m.–10 p.m., Sat until midnight, Sun noon–10 p.m. Major credit cards.

Upper East Side

This area, stretching from 60th to 96th Sts. and Fifth Ave. to Lexington Ave., covers some 2 square miles and is replete with historic nineteenth-century mansions, museums, exclusive brownstone domiciles, and chic apartment buildings. It bears the hallmarks of its residents' wealth, from uniformed doormen to nannies wheeling elaborate baby carriages, to sleek limousines and kids attired in private school uniforms. The tony shops run north–south along Madison Ave., with its upscale boutiques and cafés catering to residents of this elegant enclave of the privileged.

Upper West Side

Bordered by Central Park to the east, the Hudson River to the west, Columbus Circle to the south, and 110th St. to the north, this large area is a mélange of nineteenth-century landmarks, smart brownstones, and pre–World War II high-rise apartment buildings, some ornate and others seedy. Broadway and Columbus and Amsterdam Aves. are the main north–south arteries for shopping, entertainment, and busy street life. The residential side streets provide housing for a rich mixture of ethnic strains, from Old World Jewish European to Caribbean and Latino, young and old, families and singles, intellectuals to high-tech sophisticates and professionals. This area has a leisurely and friendly ambiance, with a distinctive flavor unlike any other Manhattan neighborhood.

Uptown Hostel 239 Lenox Ave. at 122nd St., NY 10026 (212) 666-0559

This hostel is a small, clean place to stay just above Central Park and near everything going on in Harlem. It offers very cheap rates. It fills early, so reservations need to be made well in advance during busy periods. Subway: 2, 3 to 125th St.

Urban Park Rangers

The Department of Parks and Recreation established this group to patrol the city's parks, to provide helpful information, and to lead free educational walking tours that focus on nature, the environment, bird life, and wild areas all through the year in all the boroughs. For a schedule of walks and details of other park events, many designed for children and families, dial (888) NYPARKS or visit www.nyparks.org.

Urban Ventures 38 W 32nd St., Suite 1412, NY 10024 (212) 594-5650 www.urbanventures.com

This large registry for furnished rooms and apartments and bed-and-breakfasts around town offers a wide price range but is subject to minimum stays of at least three nights.

Uskudar 1405 Second Ave. btw 73rd and 74th Sts. (212) 988-2641

The cuisine here is genuine Turkish food served in a plain venue and providing delicious meals at rock-bottom prices. Subway: 6 to 77th St. Lunch and dinner daily. Major credit cards.

Val Ginter Walking Tours (212) 496-6859

While conducting tours around town on various topics, the specialty here is the who, what, and where of jazz history in Manhattan. It also features a 4-hour motor coach itinerary of jazz venues and an authoritative explanation of the past and current scene.

Valentine Varian House *see* Bronx County Historical Society Museum.

Valentine's Day Marriage Marathon (212) 736-3100

On the Empire State Building's observation deck every February 14, many couples are competitively selected to be married based on short essays explaining why they wish to be married there. Subway: B, D, F, N, Q, R to 34th St.-Herald Square.

Van Cortlandt House (718) 543-3344

This national landmark is a restored stone structure in the Bronx built in 1748 by the Van Cortlandt family and is situated in the park in the northernmost part of the Bronx. Its features include antique furniture and a number of interesting paintings, including a portrait of John Jacob Astor by Gilbert Stuart. It is also home to the oldest dollhouse in the country, as well as a colonial garden and sundial. Subway: 1, 9 to Van Cortlandt Park-242nd St. Open Tues–Fri 10 a.m.–3 p.m., Sat–Sun 11 a.m.–4 p.m. Modest admission charge.

Van Cortlandt Park (718) 430-1890

The third most spacious green stretch in New York covers 1,146 acres running east of Riverdale from W 240th St. to W 263rd St. in the northwest Bronx. The park boasts two golf courses, playing fields, tennis courts, children's areas, and a big swimming pool. The Van Cortlandt Lake and marsh are home to various birds and wildlife, and the nature trail lays claim to being the most untamed wooded area in the city. Walking tours are offered by the Urban Park Rangers (718) 548-7070. Subway: 1, 9 to Van Cortlandt Park-242nd St.

Van Cortlandt Park Golf Course 7 Van Cortlandt Park S at Bailey Ave., Bronx (718) 543-4595 www.americangolf.com

One of some thirteen public courses in the city but distinctive as the oldest public course in the United States, this course is hilly, short, tree-lined, and challenging. Subway: 1, 9 to Van Cortlandt Park-242nd St. Open 30 minutes before sunrise to 30 minutes after sunset. Major credit cards.

Vander Ende-Onderdonk House 1820 Flushing Ave., Ridgewood, Queens (718) 456-1776

Built around 1709, this is a fine example of a Dutch-American farmhouse. It is operated as a museum under the auspices of the Greater Ridgewood Historical Society. Guided house tours are available. Subway: L to Jefferson St. Open Wed and Sat noon–4 p.m. Modest admission charge.

Vanderbilt Avenue

This short street runs along the west side of Grand Central Station from 42nd to 47th Sts. It was named to honor Commodore Cornelius Vanderbilt, who built the station. Subway: S, 4, 5, 6, 7 to Grand Central-42nd St.

Vanderbilt YMCA 224 E 47th St. btw Second and Third Aves. (212) 756-9600, fax (212) 752-0210

There are almost 400 small, air-conditioned rooms, nonsmoking singles and doubles, a few with sinks and baths, at modest prices. Residents have access to two swimming pools, running track, sauna, gym facilities, and a restaurant/café. Reservations are necessary well in advance. Subway: S, 4, 5, 6, 7 to Grand Central-42nd St. Major credit cards.

Variety Arts Theatre 110 Third Ave. btw 13th and 14th Sts. (212) 239-6200

This theatre is home to musical and dramatic productions of pop culture celebrating high and low camp. Subway: L, N, R, 4, 5, 6 to 14th St.-Union Square.

Vegetarian Restaurants *see* Angelica Kitchen, Dojo Restaurant, Hangawi, Josie's, Kate's Joint, Madras Mahal, Mavalli Palace, New World Grill, Zen Palate. *See also* Afghan Restaurants, Indian Restaurants.

Verbena 54 Irving Pl. btw 17th and 18th Sts. (212) 260-5456 www.
verbenarestaurant.com

This small, stylish restaurant has flowers pressed under glass adorning
the walls and a peaceful backyard garden. The menu features moderately
expensive dishes prepared imaginatively to take advantage of the many
home-grown herbs. Subway: L, N, R, 4, 5, 6 to 14th St.-Union Square. Dinner daily, lunch Sat–Sun. American Express.

Verdi Square at the intersection of Broadway and 72nd St.

Located opposite an original subway kiosk built in 1904 and surrounded by constant traffic, this green triangle is home to a statue of the
composer Giuseppe Verdi constructed in 1906. Subway: 1, 9 to 72nd St.

Verrazano-Narrows Bridge

This graceful 4,260-foot-long suspension bridge, the second longest on
the planet, was built in 1964 to span the gap between Brooklyn and Staten
Island and to open the way to hundreds of cars crossing daily in both directions. Subway: R to Bay Ridge-95th St.

Veselka 144 Second Ave. at 9th St. (212) 228-9682

A coffeehouse-flavored East Village Bohemian diner hangout open 24
hours a day and featuring Polish and Ukrainian specialties from borscht to
pierogis to kasha and kielbasa at rock-bottom prices. Subway: N, R to 8th
St.; 6 to Astor Pl. Major credit cards.

Veterans Day Parade (212) 693-1475

Every year on November 11 this parade, sponsored by the United War
Veterans Council of New York County, marches colorfully down Fifth Ave.
from 39th to 23rd Sts.

Victor's Café 236 W 52nd St. btw Broadway and Eighth Ave. (212)
586-7714

For more than 30 years, this has been a theatre district favorite for spicy
and tasty Cuban food and drinks at reasonable prices. Subway: C, E, 1, 9
to 50th St. Lunch and dinner daily. Major credit cards.

Vietnam Veterans Memorial 55 Water St. near South St.

This 14-foot-tall, 70-foot-long wall of translucent blocks of glass is engraved with speeches, news accounts, and touching letters written home by
servicemen and servicewomen. Since construction in 1985, the elements
have weathered the writings, making them difficult to read and making this
monument disappointing compared to the Vietnam Veterans Memorial in
Washington, D.C. The surrounding windswept brick plaza is particularly

bleak and desolate on weekends. Subway: 1, 9 to South Ferry; N, R to Whitehall St.

Vietnamese Restaurants *see* Bo Ky, Le Colonial, Indochine, Nha Trang, Pho Bang.

The Village *see* Greenwich Village.

Village Underground 130 W 3rd St. east of Sixth Ave. (212) 777-7745 www.thevillageunderground.com

This new club features live jazz in a no-smoking basement venue with limited space and large ambitions. Subway: A, B, C, D, E, F, Q to W 4th St. Times vary; call for details.

Village Voice

The city's oldest and largest alternative weekly newspaper is available late Tuesday downtown and early Wednesday elsewhere around town, for free. It carries left-wing politics and investigative reporting, thorough cultural coverage, comprehensive arts and entertainment listings, and classified personal and real estate ads. Competitive weeklies—*New York Press* and *New York Observer*—find strong appeal and readership for their breezy readable style and engaging features.

Villard Houses–Helmesley Palace Hotel *see* New York Palace Hotel.

Vineyard Theatre 108 E 15th St. btw Park Ave. S and Irving Pl. (212) 353-3874 www.vineyard.org

This consistently first-rate theatre company features innovative dramas and musicals by emerging new voices as well as established playwrights. Subway: L, N, R, 4, 5, 6 to 14th St.-Union Square.

Virgil's Real BBQ 152 W 44th St. btw Sixth and Seventh Aves. (212) 921-9494

This spacious, always busy, 2-story establishment takes its barbecue seriously, offering a great range of tasty BBQ styles from North Carolina to Texas. Hefty portions and big selection of drinks, beers, and wines are all at reasonable prices. It makes for messy eating, but hot towels for cleaning up delight customers of all ages. Subway: 1, 2, 3, 7, 9, N, R, S to Times Square-42nd St. Lunch and dinner daily. Major credit cards.

Virgin Megastore 1540 Broadway btw 45th and 46th Sts. (212) 921-1020 www.virginmegastore.com

Situated smack in the center of Times Square, this is said to be the world's biggest music store with its 75,000-square-foot space. It stocks videos and books and features occasional in-store performances. A second location is at 52 E 14th St. at Broadway (212) 598-4666. Subway: (Times Square) N, R, S, 1, 2, 3, 7, 9 to Times Square-42nd St.; (E 14th St.) L, N, R, 4, 5, 6 to 14th St.-Union Square. Open Mon–Sat 9 a.m.–1 a.m., Sun 10 a.m.–11 p.m. Major credit cards.

Virginia Slims Championships

Madison Square Garden (212) 465-6741 is the site for this annual contest, which features the world's women tennis stars in mid-November. Subway: 1, 2, 3, 9, A, C, E to 34th St.-Penn Station.

Virginia Theatre 245 W 52nd St. btw Broadway and Eighth Ave. (212) 239-6200

First opened in 1925, this venerable house has over the years offered conventional Broadway theatrical fare as well as experimental productions and classic revivals. Subway: C, E, 1, 9 to 50th St.

Vivian Beaumont Theatre *see* Lincoln Center Theatre.

Volleyball *see* Chelsea Piers Sports Center.

Von Steuben Day Parade (516) 239-0741

Celebrating on a Saturday or Sunday in the third weekend of September, the metropolitan area German community dons picturesque costumes, brings out the German Drum and Bugle Corps, and parades with dancers, colorful floats, and brewery wagons pulled by draft horses along upper Fifth Ave. from 63rd to 86th Sts. to honor the Prussian general who fought in the American Revolution.

W Hotel *see* Away Spa and Gym at W Hotel.

WPA Theatre 519 W 23rd St. btw Tenth and Eleventh Aves. (212) 206-0523

This is a showcase for new works, classics, and realistic dramas by celebrated as well as lesser-known American playwrights. Subway: C, E to 23rd St.

WWF New York Broadway at 43rd St. (212) 398-2563 www.wwf newyork.com

This is an entertainment complex, a restaurant, and a store marketing World Wrestling Federation collectibles. All kinds of things go on, from video showings of wrestlers to live stage showings of bouts for a charge. The food is reasonably good. Subway: N, R, S, 1, 2, 3, 7, 9 to Times Square-42nd St. Open daily 11 a.m.–11 p.m. Admission is free, but entertainment complex features are priced.

Wagner Park *see* Robert F. Wagner Jr. Park.

Waldorf-Astoria 301 Park Ave. btw 49th and 50th Sts. (212) 355-3000 or (800) 924-3673, fax (212) 872-7272 www.waldorfastoria. com

The pinnacle of Park Ave. addresses, an Art Deco classic, has been restored to its lofty pedestal by the Hilton chain. The refurbished lobby with its grand mosaic tile floor, glorious carpets, and mahogany wall panels recaptures its early grandeur, and the guest room spaces have been enlarged. The Peacock Alley restaurant draws rave reviews and the former coffee shop, Oscar's of the Waldorf, is now a classy American brasserie. There's even a famous hotel within the hotel, the Towers, with its own entrance and more deluxe accommodations for the dignitaries and celebrities who are guests and permanent residents. The Waldorf is a very expensive place to stay, but great to visit for tea with Devonshire cream. Tours of the Waldorf are conducted from time to time. Information about Waldorf tours at (212) 750-5944. Subway: E, F to Lexington Ave.; 6 to 51st St.

Walker's 169 N Moore St. near Vanick St. (212) 941-0142

This comfortable restaurant/tavern still offers up drinks and food as it has since starting up in 1890 in the understated familiar style that makes it such a perennially popular choice with TriBeCa types, financial district wizards, and occasionally famous names. Subway: 1, 9 to Franklin St. Lunch Mon–Fri, dinner daily, brunch Sat and Sun.

Walking Tours *see* Adventure on a Shoestring, Alfred Pommer, Art Tours of Manhattan, Big Onion Walking Tours, Central Park Conservancy Walking Tours of Central Park, Discover New York City Walking Tours, Harlem Your Way!, Jack Eichenbaum Tours, Joyce Gold Tours, Lower East Side Business Improvement District Tours, Lower East Side Tenement Museum Walking Tours, Marvin Gelfand's Walk of the Town, Municipal Art Society Walking Tours, Museum of the Chinese in the Americas Tours, Museum of the City of New York Cultural Walks, New York City Cultural Walking Tours, New York Like a Native, 92nd Street Y, Radical Walking Tours, Radio City Stage Door Tour, River to River Downtown Walking Tour, South Street Seaport Museum Tours, Staten Island Institute of Arts and Sciences, Street Smarts New York, Urban Park Rangers, Val Ginter Walking Tours, Wall Street Walking Tour, World of Finance Tours. *See also* Boat Tours, Bus Tours, Helicopter Tours, Limousine Tours, Special Interest Tours.

Wall Street

Less than a half-mile long and taking its name from a wooden defense wall erected in 1653 by the Dutch, "The Street" is shorthand for New York and capitalism's powerful financial community, even though it is a strikingly narrow and dark canyon running between towering office buildings constructed by great banks and giant corporations. For those interested in the world of high finance, the recommended means to explore the neighborhood is with a tour. Subway: 2, 3 to Wall St. *See also* Wall Street Walking Tour, World of Finance Tours.

Wall Street Journal

This national New York-based financial daily offers coverage of events of investment and corporate concern, serving as a conservative source of news and features primarily appealing to an economically oriented readership.

Wall Street Walking Tour (212) 606-4064

Sponsored by the Downtown Alliance and Delta Airlines, this is a free 90-minute guided tour of the financial district. It begins twice a week starting at noon on Thursday and Saturday, convening on the steps of the U.S. Custom House at 1 Bowling Green between State and Whitehall Sts. Subway: 1, 9 to South Ferry; N, R to Whitehall St.; 4, 5 to Bowling Green.

Walter Kerr Theatre 225 W 48th St. btw Broadway and Eighth Ave. (212) 239-6200

This theatre was constructed in 1921, renovated and reopened in 1983, and renamed only recently for the acclaimed drama critic. In the 1930s it served as the performance center for the Federal Theatre Project of the WPA. Subway: 1, 9, C, E to 50th St.

Walter Reade Theatre Lincoln Center, 70 Lincoln Center Plaza, Broadway at 65th St. (212) 875-5600

This comfortable movie house has excellent viewing from every side for seeing acclaimed independent films and international series of individual nations, serious subjects, and foreign directors. Tickets can be purchased well in advance. Subway: 1, 9 to 66th St.-Lincoln Center.

Ward's Island

The British army used this island as a base during the Revolutionary War, but these days it is where the Manhattan Psychiatric Center (212) 369-0500 and the Firefighters' Training Center are located. It is connected by landfill to Randall's Island. Take Bus M35 to Ward's Island from 125th St. and Lenox Ave.

The Warwick 65 W 54th St. at Sixth Ave., NY 10019 (212) 247-2700 or (800) 223-4099, fax (212) 957-8915 www.warwickhotels.com

The Warwick was once an apartment building, and the rooms here are spacious with roomy closets. No longer the favorite of entertainment celebrities it was in the 1950s and '60s, this fairly expensive hotel offers an elegant lobby and the full range of luxury features. Subway: Q to 57th St.; E, F to Fifth Ave.

Washington Arch

Marking the north entrance to Washington Square Park and the south end of Fifth Ave., the majestic marble memorial was constructed to commemorate the centennial of George Washington's inauguration. Designed by the celebrated architect Stanford White, the sculptor was A. Stirling Calder, father of the mobile artist Alexander Calder. The two statues on either side represent the nation's first president in poses of peace and war. Subway: A, B, C, D, E, F, Q to W 4th St.

Washington Heights

This neighborhood at Manhattan's northern tip has become a predominantly Latino community with Dominicans in the majority, although ethnic flavors of Greek, African, and Jewish still remain in the shops and among the residents. Yeshiva University, Columbia-Presbyterian Medical Center, the Washington Heights Museum Group-American Academy of Arts and Letters, the American Numismatic Society, and Hispanic Society of America are located here. Fort Tryon Park and the Cloisters also draw visitors, but most of the tenement buildings that make up the neighborhood have grown decrepit. Subway: A, C, 1, 9 to 168th St.-Washington Heights.

Washington Heights Museum Group *see* American Academy of Arts and Letters, American Numismatic Society, Hispanic Society of America.

Washington Market Park btw Greenwich and West Sts. and Chambers and Duane Sts.

This well-designed, small TriBeCa park offers a pretty lawn of grassy space and trees, as well as a fine children's playground and gazebo, all on the site of the famous food market of yesteryear. Subway: 1, 2, 3, 9 to Chambers St.

Washington Mews Washington Square N at E 8th St.

This picturesque cobblestone private alleyway directly behind Washington Square's "Row" is lined with stucco structures originally built as horse stables and turned into fashionable townhouses. Subway: A, B, C, D, E, F, Q to W 4th St.

Washington Square at W 4th St.-University Pl.

This is the $9^1/_2$-acre spiritual center of Greenwich Village. On the north rim there is the "Row," a group of Federal-style red brick townhouses celebrated in Henry James's novels and earlier home to many prominent New York families. Now like virtually all the old and newer structures around the square, the buildings are owned, occupied, or leased out by NYU. The square is dominated by the imposing 77-foot-high magnificent marble Washington Memorial Arch, constructed by Stanford White in 1892, beyond which to the north is the start of Manhattan's famous Fifth Ave. Subway: A, B, C, D, E, F, Q to W 4th St.

Washington Square Hotel 103 Waverly Pl., NY 10011 (212) 777-9515 or (800) 222-0418, fax (212) 979-8373 www.wshotel.com

For a prime location in Greenwich Village, this is the place. Rooms are modest and halls narrow, but rates are very reasonable and include continental breakfast and use of the fitness facility. Reserve well ahead for summer bookings. Subway: A, B, C, D, E, F, Q to W 4th St.

Washington Square Music Festival (212) 431-1088

Every Tuesday evening in July there are free outdoor concerts featuring classical music, jazz, and big band sounds. Subway: A, B, C, D, E, F, Q to W 4th St.

Washington Square Outdoor Art Exhibit W 4th St. and University Pl. (212) 982-6255

For well over half a century a Greenwich Village tradition, the works of some 250 artists and craftspeople are on display on twenty blocks in and around Washington Square Park. The exhibition is free and is held on two consecutive weekends at the end of May and early June and then again for two weekends in early September. Subway: A, B, C, D, E, F, Q to W 4th St.

Washington Square Park btw Washington Pl. and W 4th St. and MacDougal St. and Washington Square E

The popular public center of Greenwich Village, the park is a lively setting for serious chess players in its southwest corner, informal street and comic theatre around the fountain in the middle, children romping in its shaded playground, and NYU students and area residents occupying the benches. This is a first-rate place to observe the panorama of colorful and distinctive Village denizens during daylight hours. After nightfall it is often frequented by less savory types. Subway: A, B, C, D, E, F, Q to W 4th St.

Washington Square Row *see* Washington Square.

Washington Square Village Apartments 4 and 2 Washington Square Village

Directly behind the Elmer Bobst Library of New York University is Washington Square Village. This large, well-located apartment complex was designed by I. M. Pei. Subway: A, B, C, D, E, F, Q to W 4th St.

Washington's Birthday Sales *see* Presidents Day Sales.

Water Club 500 E 30th St. at the East River (212) 683-3333 www.thewaterclub.com

The dramatic setting of this glass-enclosed barge permits sweeping water views as the accompaniment for the moderately expensive contemporary American cuisine. Tasty fish and seafood specialties are presented in imaginative forms, and a wide range of tempting, sinful dessert choices is offered. Subway: B, D, F, N, Q, R to 34th St.-Herald Square, then Bus M16 crosstown east on 34th St. to Waterside. Lunch and dinner daily, Sun brunch. Major credit cards.

Water Street

This historic waterfront street was widened during the 1960s by eliminating the warehouses and old brownstones that marked the neighborhood. The southernmost stretch was transformed into a group of towering office buildings. Many of these sleek concrete and glass structures have since become high-priced condominiums. Subway: 2, 3 to Wall St.; A, C, J, M, Z, 2, 3, 4, 5 to Fulton St.-Broadway Nassau.

Water's Edge East River at 44th Dr., Long Island City, Queens (718) 482-0033

Every table at this classy and expensive restaurant offers a superb view of midtown Manhattan. The fare runs to imaginative American cuisine, featuring many seafood specialties. Reservations recommended. Diners can board a free water shuttle that ferries guests every half hour from 6 p.m. on from Manhattan (34th St. and the East River, at the heliport). Subway: E, F to 23rd St.-Ely Ave. Lunch and dinner Mon–Sat. Major credit cards.

Waterfront Museum 290 Conover St., Red Hook Garden Pier, Red Hook, Brooklyn (718) 624-4719 www.waterfrontmuseum.org

The Garden Pier is open 24 hours a day, but the barge (where Bargemusic takes place) is accessible only for special events like its concerts in the summer. Call ahead about programs and activities. Subway: M, N, R to Court St.; A, C, F to Jay St.-Borough Hall, then take Bus B61 from either Jay or Willoughby Sts., or Atlantic Ave. and Court St. to Beard St. stop.

Wave Hill W 249th St. and Independence Ave. (718) 549-3200 www.wavehill.org

This 28-acre public garden and cultural center located in the Riverdale section of the Bronx overlooks the Hudson River and the New Jersey Palisades and is frequently termed the most beautiful place in New York. Boasting acres of woodland, more than 3,000 types of plants, and pastoral trails, the park features guided nature walks, gardening workshops, concerts, and summer dance programs. It adjoins the less-frequented Riverdale Park, with its pathway through stately trees along the river. Subway: 1, 9 to 231st St., then Bus BX7 or 10 northbound to 252nd St. across Parkway Bridge. Turn left, walk to 249th St., turn right and walk to Wave Hill gate. Open year-round Tues–Sun. November 15–March 15, admission free. Modest admission charge for special events.

Waverly Place

Just past the curved row of Federal houses where Waverly Place intersects with Christopher and Grove Sts. is a three-sided building known as the Northern Dispensary. Built at what was then the city's northernmost point, it is one of New York's oldest public buildings and served as a public health clinic until recently. A few doors away at the Stonewall Inn at 51 Christopher St. the gay rights movement was launched with the celebrated first forceful homosexual defiance against police arrests. Subway: 1, 9 to Christopher St.-Sheridan Square.

Wax Museum *see* Madam Tussaud's New York.

Web Sites About New York

Countless Web sites on the Internet will yield useful intelligence on New York but, alas, they come and go unpredictably. What follows is a listing of very informative sites.

- www.nyc.visit.com

  The official Web site of the New York City Convention and Visitors Bureau offers great current information, from planning trips to places kids will enjoy.

- www.nycparks.org

  The New York City Parks Department's official site offers details on what's going on in all the parks in town.

- www.nynetwork.com

  This is a selective helpful roster of New York Web sites.

- www.newyork.citysearch.com

  This site offers reviews and exhaustive listings for entertainment and arts events plus restaurants and shopping. It is prepared in collaboration with the *New York Daily News* and *Time Out New York* magazine.

- www.papermag.com

  This daily updated guide to the range of cultural and street events in town is centered mostly on downtown Manhattan. It has an avant-garde orientation popular with *Paper* magazine readers.

- www.totalny.com

  This site tells you where to go and what to do, written from a street-smart New York angle, with links to discount travel sites.

- www.panix.com/clay/nyc
Termed the New York City Reference, this is a very complete, handy hyperlink index of New York related sites, regularly updated with some 2,000 links to subject areas you might want.

- www.timeout.com
This guide to New York has classified ads as well as listings and features about the city.

- www.newyork.digitalcity.com
This site features local resources and visitors' guide information sponsored by *Newsday*.

- www.villagevoice.com
Essays by well-known writers plus the feature "Choices" offer crisp critiques of current pleasure options.

- www.datalounge.com
This is the gay visitor's guide to city events and the social scene.

- www.newyorktoday.com
This site is the *New York Times*'s excellent offering of information about cultural events and what's happening where in the five boroughs, plus restaurant reviews.

- www.brooklynx.org
Details are here on history, culture, parks, shopping, and events in Brooklyn prepared by the Brooklyn Tourism Council (718) 855-7882.

- www.bronxmall.com
This site covers events in the Bronx and numerous links to the borough's cultural institutions and business community.

- www.si-web.com
General information on Staten Island includes links to borough information and services.

- www.queens.nyc.ny.us
Cultural attractions of Queens include political and economic information.

- www.dizzycity.com
Panoramas permit viewers to look in every direction on a city block as if they were actually there. Viewers look for specific names, categories, or addresses. Select 43rd St. and Broadway, and Times Square appears. For

Manhattan there are 2,500 interactive panoramas, with more than 20,000 close-up pictures of points of interest.

Webster Apartments 419 W 34th St. btw Ninth and Tenth Aves., NY 10001 (212) 967-9000 or (800) 242-7909, fax (212) 268-8569

Primarily designed for short-term stays by working females rather than as a tourist destination, the 390 single rooms with shared bathrooms on each floor are basic, but the facility features lounges, library, dining room, roof terrace with striking views, and a private garden. Weekly rates are based upon salary or student status and include two meals and maid service. Subway: A, C, E to 34th St.-Penn Station.

Webster Hall 125 E 11th St. btw Third and Fourth Aves. (212) 353-1600 www.websterhall.com

Four floors, countless rooms, and an eclectic blend of different music zones featuring acid jazz, reggae, hip-hop, pop, rock, and more to dance to, live bands and DJs on certain nights, and sometimes even trapeze artists and snake charmers liven the scene. Bizarre decor is spread over 40,000 square feet. The crowd is a mélange from college dorms, Wall Street, suburbs, and in town, with a liberal sprinkling of flamboyant attention seekers. Subway: L, N, R, 4, 5, 6 to 14th St.-Union Square. Open different nights. Call for details. Cover charge. Major credit cards.

Weeksville 1698-1708 Bergen St. btw Buffalo and Rochester Sts., Brooklyn (718) 756-5250

This group of four wooden frame houses is what remains of a community of free Blacks dating from the 1840s in Brooklyn's Bedford-Stuyvesant district. Long forgotten until a historian rediscovered the group of buildings by helicopter in 1968, the restored Weeksville Houses can be viewed with photos, maps, and video on display to describe their past. The project is administered by the Weeksville Society, which is working to maintain the sites. Telephone during business hours to arrange a visit when someone from the society will greet you and show you around the properties. Subway: A, C to Utica Ave.; 3, 4 to Crown Heights-Utica Ave.

Welcome Back to Brooklyn Festival (718) 855-7882

During the second week of June this celebration takes place at the newly energized Brooklyn waterfront beneath the Brooklyn Bridge. It is one of Brooklyn's biggest annual festivities and has been running for 20 years. It features some of the finest talents that Brooklyn has produced. Subway: A, C to High St.

West Bank Café 407 W 42nd St. at Ninth Ave. (212) 695-6909

This café serves French and American fare well prepared and modestly priced. It is very popular with people working in as well as attending the theatre, both before and after performances. Reservations required. Subway: A, C, E to 42nd St.-Port Authority. Lunch and dinner daily. Major credit cards.

West End Collegiate Church and School 370 West End Ave. at 77th St. (212) 787-1566

The original structure dates to the early seventeenth century, but the building was reconstructed in 1893 by Robert Gibson employing extra long bricks and Dutch-style gables. It serves as home to one of the city's elite prep schools for young males headed for the Ivy League and beyond. Subway: 1, 9 to 79th St.

West 42nd Street

For many decades the district west of Times Square on 42nd St. was home to sleazy characters, porno movie and entertainment dens, and worse. For some months now, however, sweeping changes have been dramatically transforming 42nd St. between Seventh and Eighth Aves. and beyond into a grand boulevard of family entertainment theatres and gradually but fundamentally changing the character of this popular neighborhood. Subway: A, C, E to 42nd St.-Port Authority; N, R, S, 1, 2, 3, 7, 9 to Times Square-42nd St.

West Indian Carnival (718) 625-1515

On Labor Day weekend each year this annual event takes place on Eastern Pkwy. in Crown Heights, Brooklyn, along a route from Utica Ave. to Grand Army Plaza. On Saturday there's a children's parade, while Sunday is the day for the city's greatest celebration with giant floats, colorful costumes, strutting reggae, calypso, and steel bands, Caribbean food, and one of the city's largest turnouts of onlookers and colorful participants. Subway: 3, 4 to Crown Heights-Utica Ave.; 2, 3 to Eastern Pkwy.-Brooklyn Museum.

West Indians in New York *see* Crown Heights, Flatbush, Jamaica.

West Side YMCA/Writer's Voice *see* Writer's Voice/West Side YMCA.

West Side YMCA 5 W 63rd St. btw Central Park W and Broadway, NY 10023 (212) 787-1301, fax (212) 875-1334

This YMCA offers clean, simple, air-conditioned singles and doubles, some with baths, near Lincoln Center and Central Park. Two pools, saunas, fitness, and sports facilities are free. Booking well ahead is advisable. Subway: A, B, C, D, 1, 9 to 59th St.-Columbus Circle.

West Street

Around ten blocks here have been blocked off from Christopher to Horatio Sts., where skaters can indulge themselves with a good view of the Hudson River. Subway: A, C, E to 14th St.; 1, 9 to Christopher St.-Sheridan Square.

West Village

This area west of Sixth Ave. (Avenue of the Americas) is made into an attractive and picturesque neighborhood by its peculiar mix of winding streets between major avenues. Subway: 1, 9 to Christopher St.-Sheridan Square.

Western Union Building 60 Hudson St. btw Thomas and Worth Sts.

This structure, built in 1930, looms 24 stories above its neighborhood and is built of many different shades of brick. Inside the lobby, the beautiful brickwork and Art Deco letter boxes are particularly striking. Subway: 1, 2, 3, 9, A, C to Chambers St.

Westminster Kennel Club Dog Show at Madison Square Garden btw 31st and 33rd Sts. and Seventh and Eighth Aves. (800) 455-3647 www.westminsterkennelclub.org

Mid-February each year some 3,000 purebred dogs and their proud owners converge upon the Garden to compete for the best-in-show trophies before an audience of thousands of canine aficionados. Subway: 1, 2, 3, 9, A, C, E to 34th St.-Penn Station.

Westside Theatre 407 W 43rd St. btw Ninth and Tenth Aves. (212) 315-2244

This small basement theatre hosts a wide range of current dramas, comedies, and musicals as well as classical theatrical productions from playwrights such as Wilde, Shaw, and Pirandello. Subway: A, C, E to 42nd St.-Port Authority.

White Columns 320 W 13th St. at Horatio St. (212) 924-4212 www.whitecolumns.org

New York's oldest alternative gallery space presents a continuing program of culturally diverse exhibitions with a focus on new and emerging artists. Subway: A, C, E to 14th St.

Whitney Museum of American Art 945 Madison Ave. at 75th St. (212) 570-3676 www.whitney.org

This uniquely designed Marcel Breuer structure, recently renovated, is home to more than 12,000 works of sculpture, photography, and paintings by some 2,000 American artists. Splendid gallery spaces on different levels display temporary exhibitions of American artists, while the 5th floor features selections from among the best of the permanent collection. The Whitney Biennial Exhibition, mounted throughout the museum in even-numbered years, is an always controversial but hugely popular showcase for recent works of contemporary Americans. Free guided tours are offered daily. The museum is also the venue for showing of experimental and independent films. A branch of Sarabeth's Kitchen on the lower level offers excellent but pricey food. Subway: 6 to 77th St. Open Wed–Sun, hours vary. Admission charge.

Whitney Museum of American Art at Philip Morris Building 120 Park Ave. at 42nd St. (212) 878-2550

This midtown branch located in the 42-foot-high lobby and adjacent gallery centers on the work of contemporary artists. The lobby court features large sculptures, and in the gallery there are some five different shows a year displaying modern American works. There's also a convenient seating area and espresso bar. Subway: S, 4, 5, 6, 7 to Grand Central-42nd St. Gallery open Mon–Fri 11 a.m.–6 p.m. Sculpture court open Mon–Sat 7:30 a.m.–9:30 p.m.; Sun 11 a.m.–7 p.m. Admission free.

Wigstock

Annually over the Labor Day weekend this East Village takeoff on Woodstock features celebrated drag queens performing on stage; the antics and costumes of many in the audience are equally fantastic. For details of where and when it all takes place, phone (212) 620-7310.

William Doyle 175 E 87th St. btw Lexington and Third Aves. (212) 427-2730 www.doylenewyork.com

This firm holds several auctions every month and special auctions featuring specific types of collectibles, such as fashion clothing and Lalique, arranged once yearly. Next to the main auction showroom one can find "treasure auctions," offering selections at more modest prices. Auctions usually take place on Wed with viewing on Sat, Mon, and Tues before the auctions. Subway: 4, 5, 6 to 86th St.

Williamsburg

Often termed the new SoHo, in recent years artists and musicians have migrated in droves to occupy low-rent lofts and apartments in this run-down neighborhood just across the bridge from Manhattan. On weekends they have transformed the flavor of the area with the blossoming of well-attended galleries, performance spaces, cafés, and chic dining spots. The newcomers are in sharp contrast to the Latinos who arrived earlier and the other large community, the 40,000 or so members of the Jewish Satmar Hasidic sect. In their long black coats, wide-brimmed hats, full beards, and sideburns, with wives in long skirts and sleeves with wigs or scarves, they lend to the neighborhood the picturesque flavor of an Eastern European shtetl. Subway: J, M, Z to March Ave.

Williamsburg Bridge entrance from Manhattan at Delancey St.

This is the second bridge to be built across the East River to Brooklyn, but in no way does this dreary-looking structure rival the famed Brooklyn Bridge. Subway: F to Delancey St.; J, M, Z to Essex St.

Williamsburg Savings Bank 1 Hanson Pl. at Flatbush Ave.

Standing 512 feet high, this building completed in 1929 is Brooklyn's tallest. The fine interior features pillars, arches, marble floors, tiled ceiling, and a giant painting of the borough glowing under the sun. Subway: 2, 3, 4, D, Q to Atlantic Ave.; B, M, N, R to Pacific St.

Winter Antiques Show Seventh Regiment Armory, 67th and 68th Sts. btw Park and Lexington Aves. (718) 292-7392

New York's most celebrated, prestigious, and expensive antiques event is held every January. During the show's first weekend more affordably priced collectors' items are for sale at the 26th St. Armory farther downtown at Lexington Ave. (212) 255-0020. That same weekend, the annual New York Ceramics Fair is held at the National Academy of Design at Fifth Ave. and 89th St. (212) 289-0496. Subway: 6 to 68th St.-Hunter College.

Winter Garden Theatre 1634 Broadway btw 50th and 51st Sts. (212) 239-6200

This Broadway fixture, since opening in 1911, has hosted celebrated musical and theatrical productions ranging from Al Jolson to *Cats.* Subway: 1, 9 to 50th St.; N, R to 49th St.

Wolcott Hotel 4 W 31st St. btw Broadway and Fifth Ave., NY 10001 (212) 268-2900, fax (212) 563-0096 www.salesatwolcott.com

This hotel offers small, inexpensive rooms in a comfortable garment-district hotel with an unusual, ornate lobby. Subway: 6 to 33rd St.; B, D, F, N, Q, R to 34th St.-Herald Square.

Wollman Memorial Rink in Prospect Park (718) 282-7789

Like its namesake Central Park entertainment venue, this very popular pleasure destination offers skating in winter and rental of pedal boats for use on weekends and holidays from spring into fall. Subway: D to Parkside.

Skating November–March. Boat rentals weekends from April until Memorial Day, during summer months Thurs–Mon.

Wollman Rink in Central Park *see* Central Park Wollman Memorial Rink.

Women's Healthline (212) 230-1111

This service offers a wide range of information for women on health matters, including abortion, birth control, and venereal disease and is prepared to refer inquirers to licensed clinics and hospitals.

Women's Services in New York *see* Lesbian and Gay Community Services Center, Women's Healthline.

Wonder Wheel *see* Coney Island Wonder Wheel.

Woodlawn Cemetery Jerome and Bainbridge Aves. (718) 920-0500

This North Bronx version of Paris's Père Lachaise, with its rolling hills, streams, shady trees, and ornate mausoleums, is the final resting place of some 300,000 New Yorkers, many among the city's most celebrated of the nineteenth and twentieth centuries in business, public life, the arts, and entertainment. The place has been weirdly popular since opening in 1863, with a handy guide available at the entrance office to help locate the cemetery's residents. Subway: 4 to Woodlawn. Open daily 9 a.m.–4:30 p.m.

Woodside

This is an old Queens working-class neighborhood that from the 1920s on was predominantly Irish. The community changed in the 1970s and '80s with the influx of Orientals and Latin Americans, but a new wave of Irish immigrants later on has revived this aging enclave of the Irish. Subway: (west side) 7 to 46th St.; (east side) 7 to Woodside-61st St.

Woodstock Spa and Wellness Center Benjamin Hotel, 125 E 50th St. at Lexington Ave. (212) 813-0100

This is a branch of a Long Island spa of long standing, with its concentration on yoga, personal fitness training, and health concerns as well as spa treatments, located in the hotel's fitness center. Subway: 6 to 51st St.; E, F to Lexington Ave. Mon–Fri 8 a.m.–9 p.m., Sat–Sun 9 a.m.–6 p.m. Major credit cards.

Woolworth Building 233 Broadway btw Barclay St. and Park Pl.

Designed by Cass Gilbert and completed in 1913, once known as the "Cathedral of Commerce," this 800-foot-high structure was New York's tallest building until 1930. The soaring ornate exterior design features grim-looking animal gargoyles and is topped by a pyramid roof. The lobby is replete with Gothic arches, and the vaulted mosaic-covered ceiling is adorned with whimsical sculptured caricatures, even one of F. W. Woolworth himself counting out change. Subway: N, R to City Hall.

World Financial Center Battery Park City btw Vesey and Albany Sts. at the Hudson River www.worldfinancialcenter.com

This is a pleasing complex of four office buildings that range from 34 to 40 stories high. Each building has a differently shaped, geometrically formed tower at the top. The chief visual attraction is the dazzling Winter Garden atrium. A sweeping pink marble staircase leads down to the lower level, which boasts sixteen giant palm trees flanked by forty-some upscale shops and cafés. Just behind the Winter Garden, the plaza looks out on a small yacht marina on the river and affords handsome views of the Statue of Liberty. Subway: 1, 9, N, R to Cortlandt St.

World Financial Center Arts and Events Battery Park City btw Vesey and Albany Sts. (212) 945-0505 www.worldfinancialcenter. com

Scheduled from June through August, free dancing to many different kinds of music is available as are poetry readings, family events, and concerts. The venue is the Winter Garden atrium in the center. For information on dates, times, and activities featured, call (212) 945-0505. Subway: 1, 9, N, R to Cortlandt St.

World of Finance Tours (212) 908-4100

This weekly walking tour is sponsored by the Museum of American Financial History and includes the financial district and the New York Stock Exchange in its itinerary.

World Wide Web Sites About New York *see* Web Sites About New York.

World Yacht Cruises Pier 81 at W 41st St. and Twelfth Ave. (212) 630-8100 or (800) 498-4270 www.worldyacht.com

This is elegant, dressy, romantic cruising to the accompaniment of live music and dancing, offering spectacular views. Dinner and buffet brunch cruises feature sumptuous prix fixe meals. Jackets are obligatory for men in the evening. Days of operation vary by season, and advance reservations are required. Subway: N, R, S, 1, 2, 3, 7, 9 to Times Square-42nd St.; then Bus M42 west to Twelfth Ave. and 41st St.

Worth Monument Fifth Ave. and 26th St.

A quaint cast-iron fence of swords stuck in the ground around an obelisk sits on a triangle in the northwest corner of Madison Square Park to mark the resting place of General William J. Worth, a hero of the mid-nineteenth-century Mexican wars. Subway: N, R, 6 to 23rd St.

Wrestling

Whether this is categorized as theatre or sport, wrestling happens in and around New York, and many people find it greatly entertaining. It happens in a few places: Madison Square Garden (212) 465-6741; Nassau Memorial Coliseum, Uniondale, Long Island (516) 794-9303; and Continental Airlines Arena, East Rutherford, N.J. (201) 935-3900.

Writer's Voice/West Side YMCA 5 W 63rd St. btw Central Park W and Columbus Ave. (212) 875-4120

Novelists, playwrights, and poets read from their works at well-attended events here. Workshops are held for writers here as well. Subway: 1, 9, A, B, C, D to 59th St.-Columbus Circle.

Writers in Performance/Manhattan Theatre Club 311 W 43rd St. btw Eighth and Ninth Aves. (212) 399-3000

This lively series offers readings and discussion panels featuring American and foreign playwrights, poets, and novelists. Subway: A, C, E to 42nd St.-Port Authority.

Wyndham Hotel 42 W 58th St. btw Fifth and Sixth Aves., NY 10019 (212) 753-3500 or (800) 257-1111

This hotel with the flavor of an apartment building is much favored by show business types. It has a well-placed midtown location, spacious well-worn rooms, charm galore, perennial popularity, and it's moderately priced, so reserve far ahead. Subway: N, R to Fifth Ave.; B, Q to 57th St.

XS Virtual Game Arena 1457 Broadway btw 41st and 42nd Sts. (212) 398-5467

This is a 3-story noisy and dark world of innumerable games that run from educational to wildly futuristic, virtually guaranteed to appeal to children of all ages (starting at about 10 or 11). It includes a number of computers for access to the Internet. Subway: N, R, S, 1, 2, 3, 7, 9 to 42nd St.-Times Square. Sun–Thurs 10 a.m.–midnight, Fri–Sat 10 a.m.–2 a.m.

YMCA McBurney *see* McBurney YMCA.

YMCA Vanderbilt *see* Vanderbilt YMCA.

YMCA West Side *see* West Side YMCA.

YMCA/YWCAs *see* de Hirsch Residence at the 92nd Street Y, McBurney YMCA, Vanderbilt YMCA, West Side YMCA, YWCA of the City of New York.

YWCA of the City of New York 610 Lexington Ave. at 53rd St. (212) 755-4500

The 75-foot-long pool is available for use by members of any YWCA as well as non-members. The admission price varies between daytime and evening hours. Subway: E, F to Lexington Ave.; 6 to 51st St.

Yaffa's Tea Room 353 Greenwich St. at Harrison St. (212) 274-9403

In a quaint, cozy setting of unusual eclectic furnishings, this is one TriBeCa venue that serves a complete high tea (upon reservation). It is attached to the Yaffa Bar, a less subdued ambiance with a separate menu. Subway: 1, 2, 3, 9 to Chambers St. Tea service: Mon–Fri 2 p.m.–5 p.m. Major credit cards.

Yankee Stadium E 161st St. at River Ave., Bronx (718) 293-6000

This 56,000-seat stadium in southernmost Bronx has been home to the New York Yankees since 1923. Here's where Babe Ruth, Joe DiMaggio, Lou Gehrig, Mickey Mantle, and other celebrated players won all those world baseball championships. It is also the site where Joe Louis knocked out Germany's Max Schmeling in 1938. You can tour the stadium, including the press box, the dugout, the clubhouse, and the field. Call (718) 579-4531 for tour schedules and price information. Subway: B, D, 4 to 161st St.-Yankee Stadium.

Yeshiva University Amsterdam Ave. btw 183rd and 191st Sts. www.yu.edu

This institution was begun in 1886 and has an enrollment of more than 7,000 students, making it the oldest and largest Jewish university in America. The architecture of the main building is in the Moorish style. The museum formerly on the campus is now housed in the Center for Jewish History at 17 W 16th St. between Fifth and Sixth Aves. (212) 294-8301. Subway: 1, 9 to 181st St.

Yeshiva University Museum *see* Center for Jewish History.

Yivo Institute for Jewish Research 17 W 16th St. btw Fifth and Sixth Aves. (212) 246-6080 www.yivoinstitute.org

Begun in 1925 in Vilna, Lithuania, the institute was moved to New York during World War II to safeguard its collections from the German invaders. The library numbers among its collections not only rare manuscripts and books but countless photographs, documents, and letters. It is now housed in the Center for Jewish History as one component of this recently combined complex of historic organizations. Subway: N, R, 4, 5, 6 to 14th St.-Union Square. Open Mon–Thurs 9:30 a.m.–5 p.m. *See also* Center for Jewish History.

Yoga *see* SoHo Sanctuary, Woodstock Spa and Wellness Center.

Yonah Schimmel Knishes Bakery 137 E Houston St. btw Forsyth and Eldridge Sts. (212) 477-2858

Since 1910, this establishment has been churning out this favorite Jewish kosher treat. A knish has a thin, flaky crust, and its content can be potato, spinach, buckwheat, or any one of five or six other hot, tastefully seasoned, moist fillings. Delicious bagels are also baked here. Subway: F to Second Ave. Daily 9 a.m.–6 p.m. Major credit cards.

Yonkers Raceway Central Ave., Yonkers (914) 968-1200

While outside the city proper, the nearby location hardly deters harness racing enthusiasts from flocking here to place their bets. Subway: 4 to Woodlawn, then no. 20 Bee Line bus to the track.

Yorkville east of Lexington Ave. btw 77th and 96th Sts.

Once home to a large population of Germans and Hungarians, the old Yorkville is gone but not forgotten. Now it's an eclectic mix of tawdry shops and luxury apartment buildings. While most of the landmarks have vanished, a few cafés and bierkellers and a dwindling number of elderly Germans remain. The Von Steuben Day Parade is still held here every September. Subway: (south end) 6 to 77th St.; (north end) 6 to 96th St.

Youth Hostels *see* Hostels.

Z

Zabar's 2254 Broadway at 80th St. (212) 787-2000

People are drawn to this New York gourmet institution for its quality products, bargain prices, and extraordinary selection. Zabar's sells everything from smoked fish to breads to more than 400 kinds of cheese and more than twenty types of coffee. Cooking and kitchen gadgets are found on the 2nd floor. Visit for a view of the crowd of colorful customers and the savory smells of food. The adjoining café serves fine coffee and pastries. Subway: 1, 9 to 79th St. Mon–Fri 8 a.m.–7:30 p.m., Sat 8 a.m.–8 p.m., Sun 9 a.m.–6 p.m. Major credit cards.

Zarela 953 Second Ave. btw 50th and 51st Sts. (212) 644-6740 www.zarela.com

For more than a decade this has been one of the very best places for authentic, moderately priced regional Mexican home cooking served in a festive atmosphere. Subway: 6 to 51st St. Lunch Mon–Fri, dinner daily. Major credit cards.

Zen Palate 34 Union Square E at 16th St. (212) 614-9291 www. zenpalate.com

Zen Palate offers inspired, health-conscious, vegetarian dining. Entrées are imaginatively named, creative and traditional Asian dishes, reflecting the culinary flavor of Japan, Indonesia, and China. Other locations: 663 Ninth Ave. at 46th St. (212) 582-1669 and 2170 Broadway between 76th and 77th Sts. (212) 501-7768. Subway: L, N, R, 4, 5, 6 to 14th St.-Union Square. Lunch and dinner daily. Major credit cards.

Ziegfeld Theatre 141 W 54th St. btw Sixth and Seventh Aves. (212) 765-7600

This grand old picture palace has a giant screen, ornate red decor, and a great sound system. It often features big new Hollywood releases and premier showings. Tickets are sold in advance through reservations. Subway: B, D, E to Seventh Ave. Major credit cards.

Zinc Bar 90 Houston St. btw LaGuardia Pl. and Thompson St. (212) 477-8337

Jazz and drink are served up in this often-crowded cellar venue. Promising new and established jazz and Latin performers are featured. Reservations are not needed. Subway: A, B, C, D, E, F, Q to W 4th St.; 6 to Bleecker St. Open nightly 6 p.m.–2:30 a.m. Cover and drink minimum.

Zion St. Mark's Evangelical Lutheran Church 339 E 8th St. btw First and Second Aves. (212) 650-1648

Services are conducted in German every Sunday at 11 a.m. This church was built in 1888; it is listed on the National Register of Historic Places, with its unusual Munich-style stained-glass windows. Subway: 4, 5, 6 to 86th St.

Zito and Sons Bakery 259 Bleecker St. at Seventh Ave. (212) 929-6139

This bakery is reputed to serve the tastiest Italian bread in Greenwich Village, with a long list of past and present celebrity customers and a wide selection of types of Italian bread. Subway: A, B, C, D, E, F, Q to W 4th St. Mon–Sat 6 a.m.–7 p.m., Sun 6 a.m.–3 p.m. No credit cards.

Zoë 90 Prince St. btw Broadway and Mercer St. (212) 966-6722

This trendy, lively setting in SoHo features contemporary American cuisine and an exceptional choice of U.S. wines. The decibel level is usually high. Weekend brunch is popular at this moderately expensive restaurant. Subway: N, R to Prince St. Lunch Tues–Fri, dinner daily, brunch Sat and Sun. Major credit cards.

Zoos *see* Alley Pond Environmental Center, Aquarium for Wildlife Conservation, Central Park Wildlife Conservation Center, International Wildlife Conservation Park, Prospect Park Wildlife Center, Queens Wildlife Center, Staten Island Zoo.

Zum Stammtisch 69-46 Myrtle Ave., Queens (718) 386-3014 www.zumstammtisch.com

This restaurant of many years standing has an authentic European flavor and look, with German food, German beer, and German management. Wiener schnitzel is the most popular dish in this moderately priced restaurant. Subway: E, F, G, R to Forest Hills-71st Ave., then short taxi ride. Lunch and dinner daily. Major credit cards.